FAIRY TAIL

14

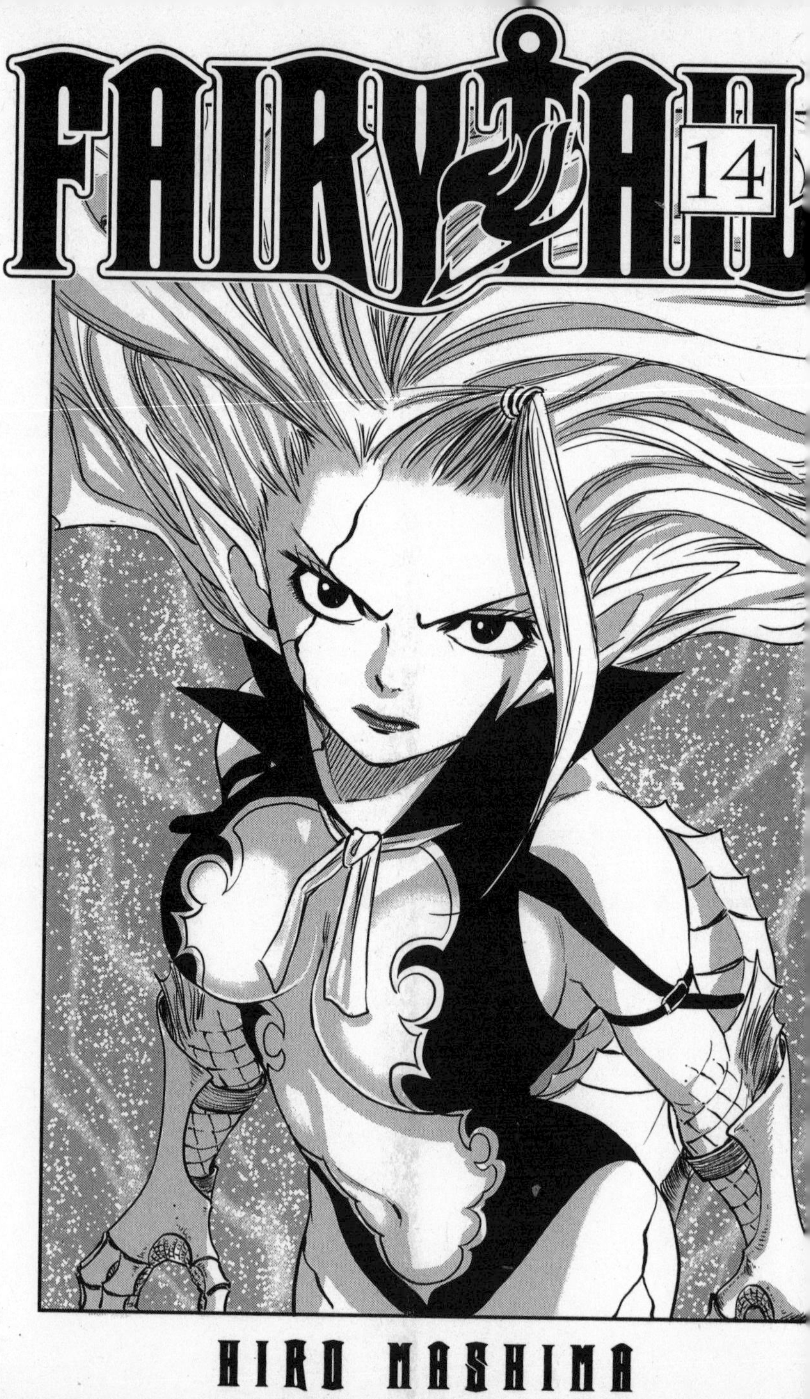

HIRO MASHIMA

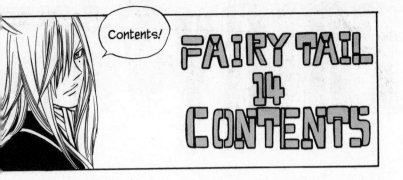

Contents!

FAIRY TAIL 14 CONTENTS

FAIRY TAIL

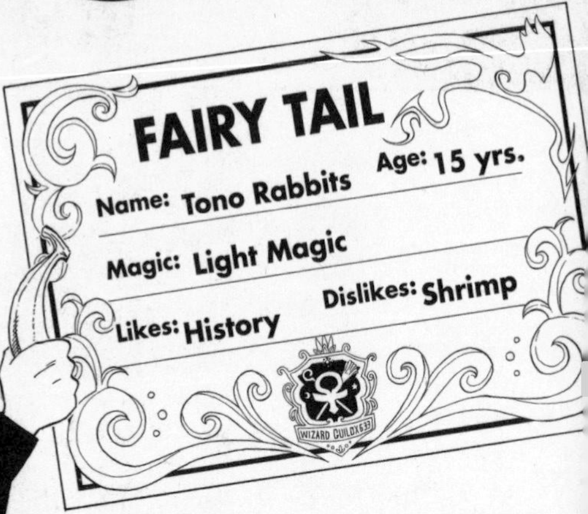
FAIRY TAIL
Name: Tono Rabbits
Age: 15 yrs.
Magic: Light Magic
Likes: History
Dislikes: Shrimp
WIZARD GUILD

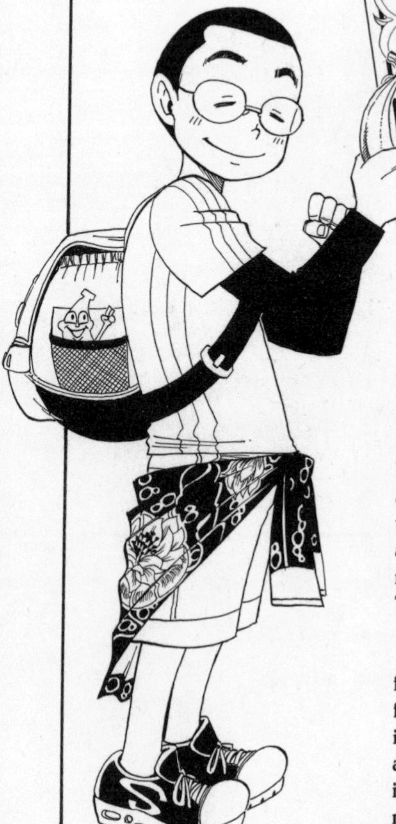

Remarks

He's considered young compared to present-day Fairy Tail members, and everyone has great expectations for his future as a wizard.

His Light Magic stems from the fact that his body radiates light energy like a corona, and his attacks have an area of effect, so they hit multiple targets. Normally he's very reserved, but there are so many rumors surrounding him that the pet name everyone's adopted for him is, "That's our Tono!"

Here's an example:

He lives some three hours by post carriage from the guild, but one day he bought some fast food from a restaurant near the guild and brought it home. It was cold by that time, but he ate it anyway. Nobody knows why, but when everyone in the guild heard the story, they all opened their mouths as one and said, "That's our Tono!"

Chapter 110: Resign

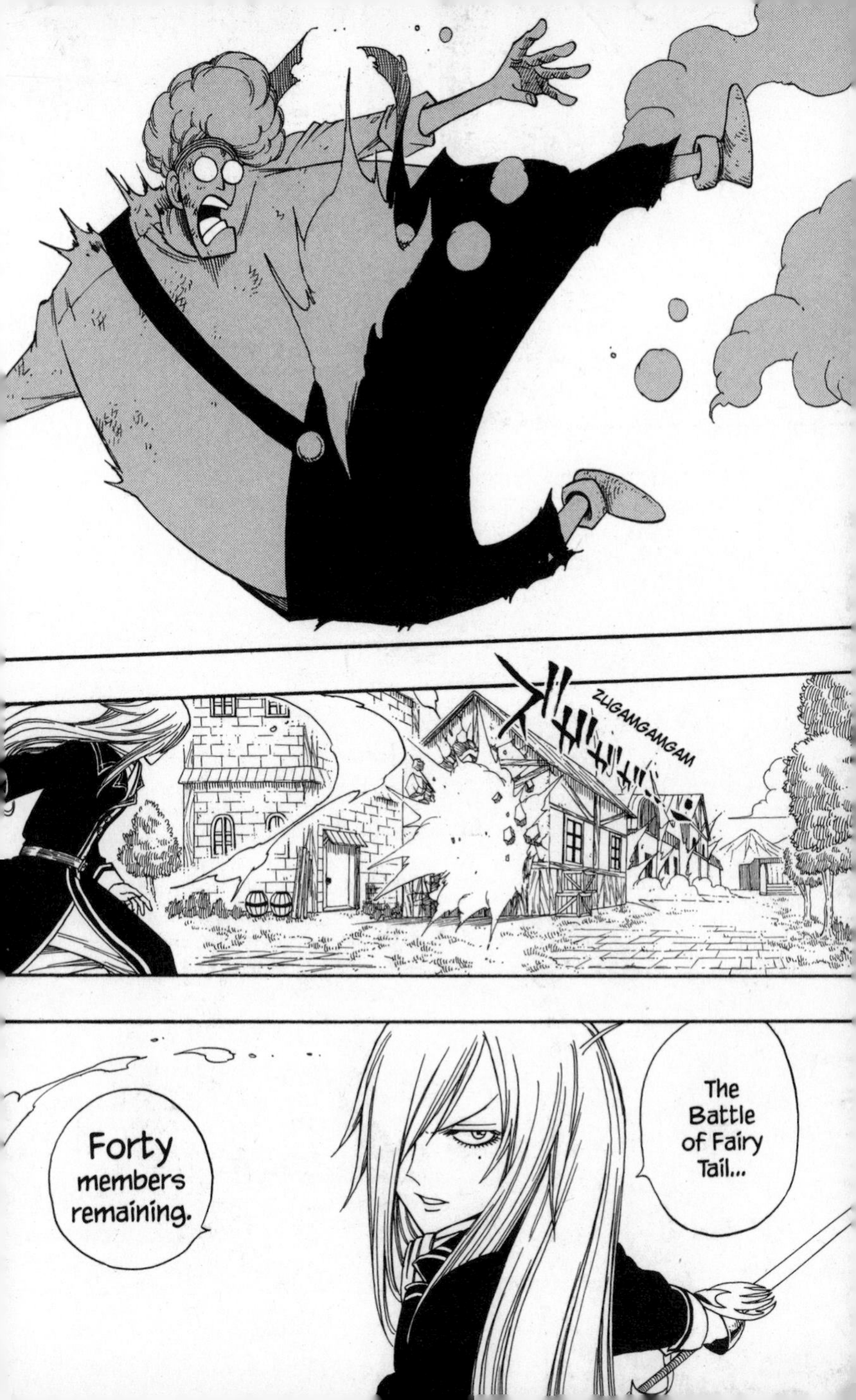
ZUGAMGAMGAM
The Battle of Fairy Tail...
Forty members remaining.

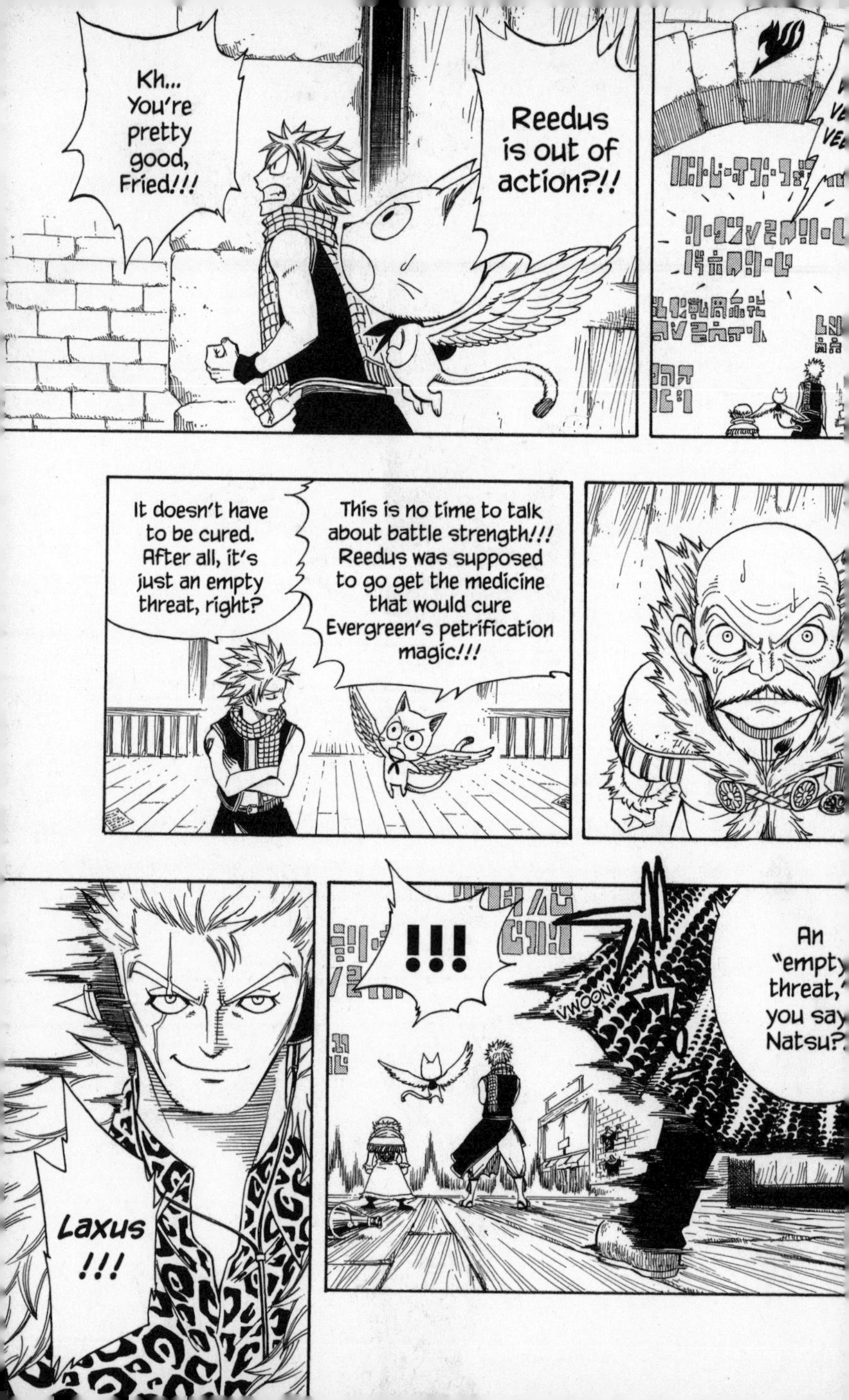
Reedus is out of action?!!
Kh... You're pretty good, Fried!!!
This is no time to talk about battle strength!!! Reedus was supposed to go get the medicine that would cure Evergreen's petrification magic!!!
It doesn't have to be cured. After all, it's just an empty threat, right?
An "empty threat," you say Natsu?
VWOON
!!!
Laxus!!!

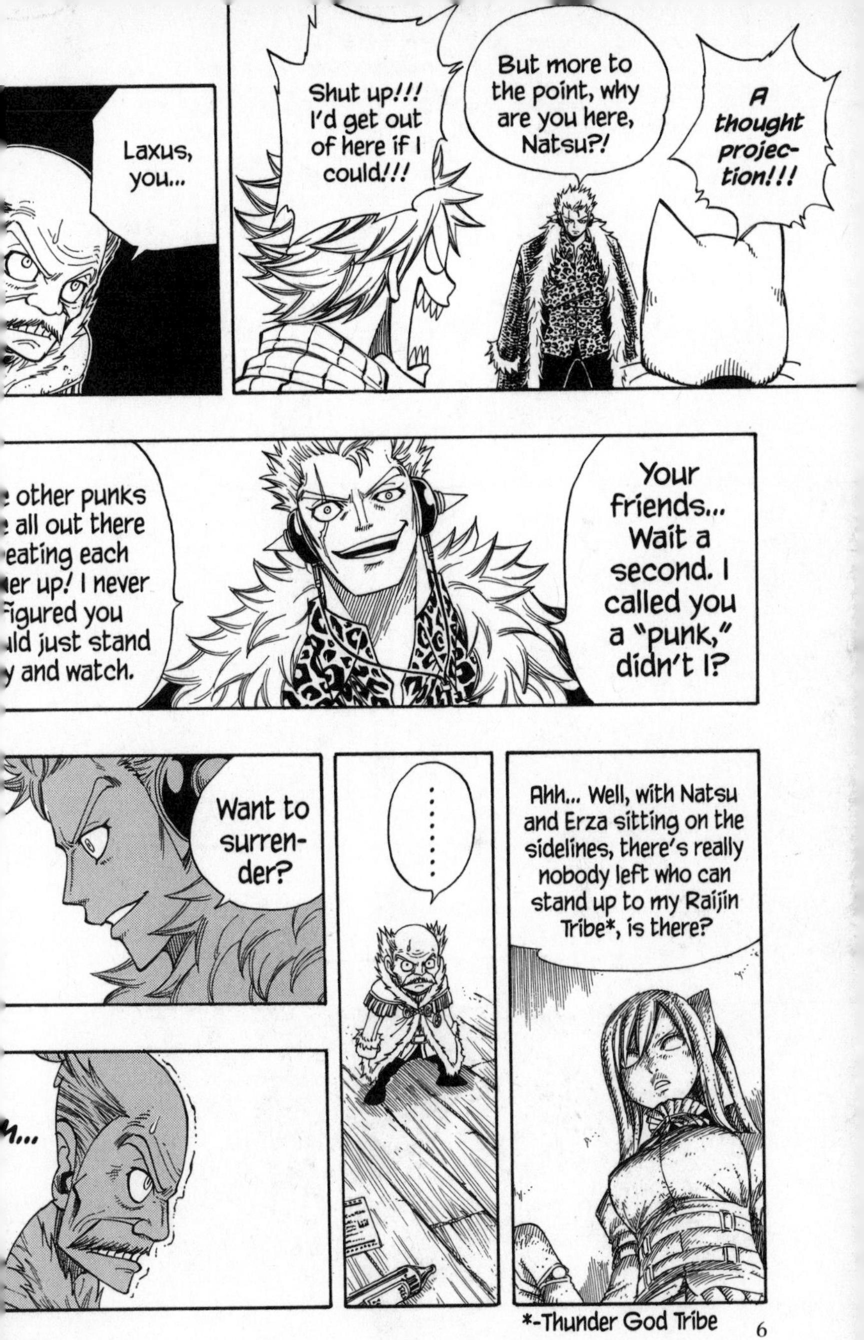
A thought projection!!!
But more to the point, why are you here, Natsu?!
Shut up!!! I'd get out of here if I could!!!
Laxus, you...
Your friends... Wait a second. I called you a "punk," didn't I?
other punks all out there eating each er up! I never figured you ld just stand y and watch.
Ahh... Well, with Natsu and Erza sitting on the sidelines, there's really nobody left who can stand up to my Raijin Tribe*, is there?
......
Want to surrender?

*-Thunder God Tribe

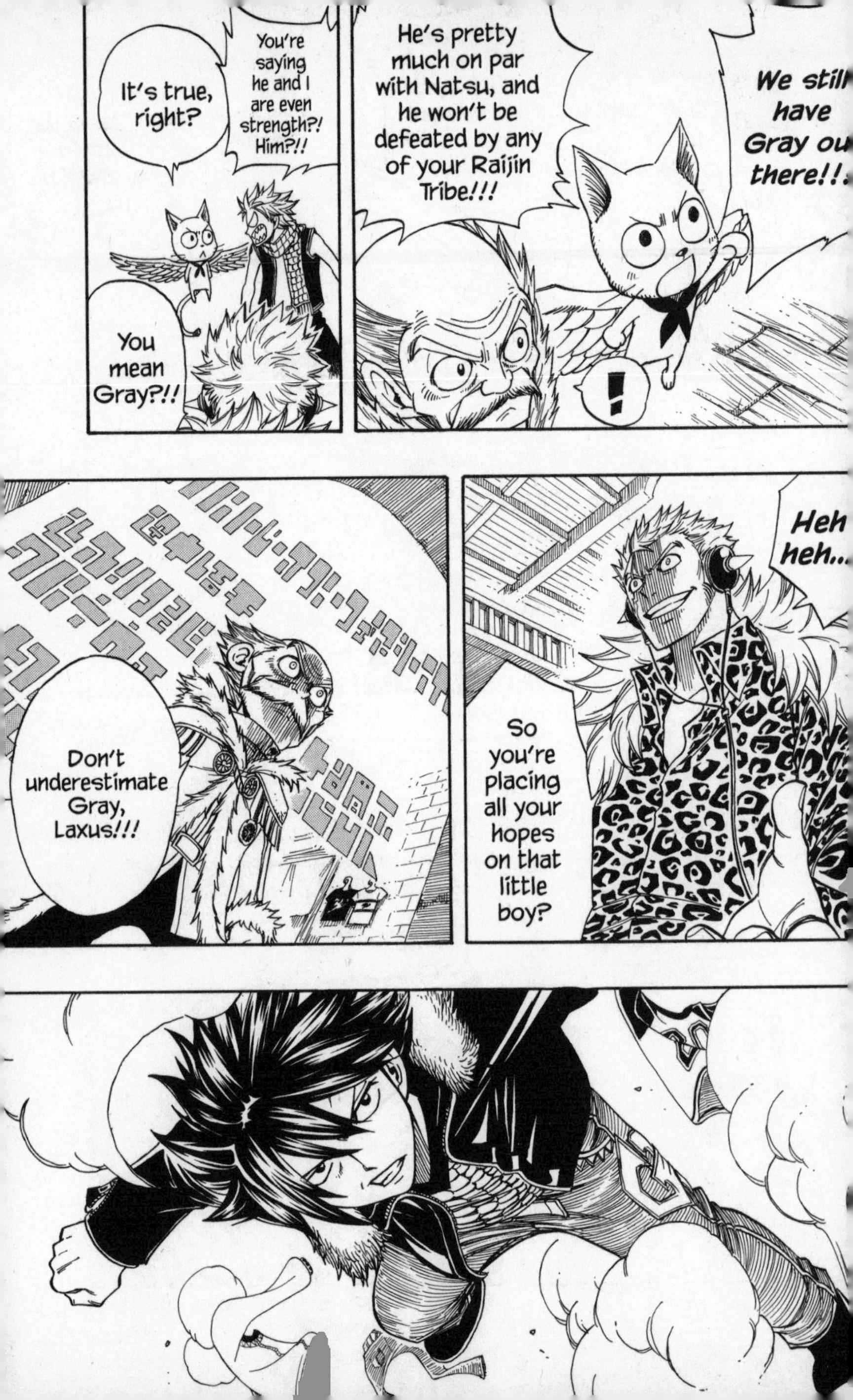
We stil have Gray ou there!!
He's pretty much on par with Natsu, and he won't be defeated by any of your Raijin Tribe!!!
!
You're saying he and I are even strength?! Him?!!
It's true, right?
You mean Gray?!!
Heh heh...
So you're placing all your hopes on that little boy?
Don't underestimate Gray, Laxus!!!

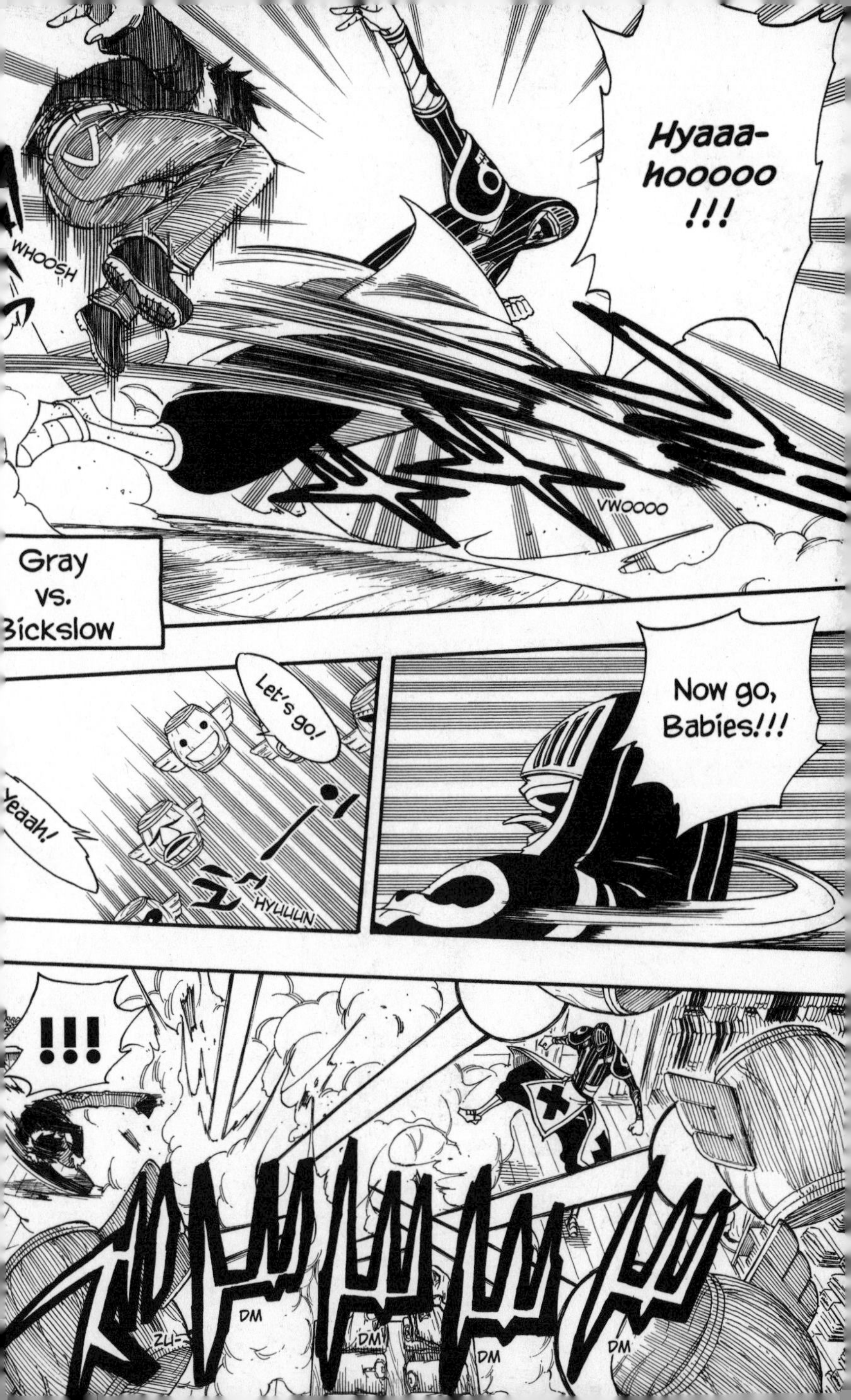

Hyaaa-hooooo!!!
VWOOOO
WHOOSH
Gray vs. Bickslow
Now go, Babies!!!
Let's go!
Yeaah!
HYUUUN
!!!
DM
DM
DM
DM
ZU-

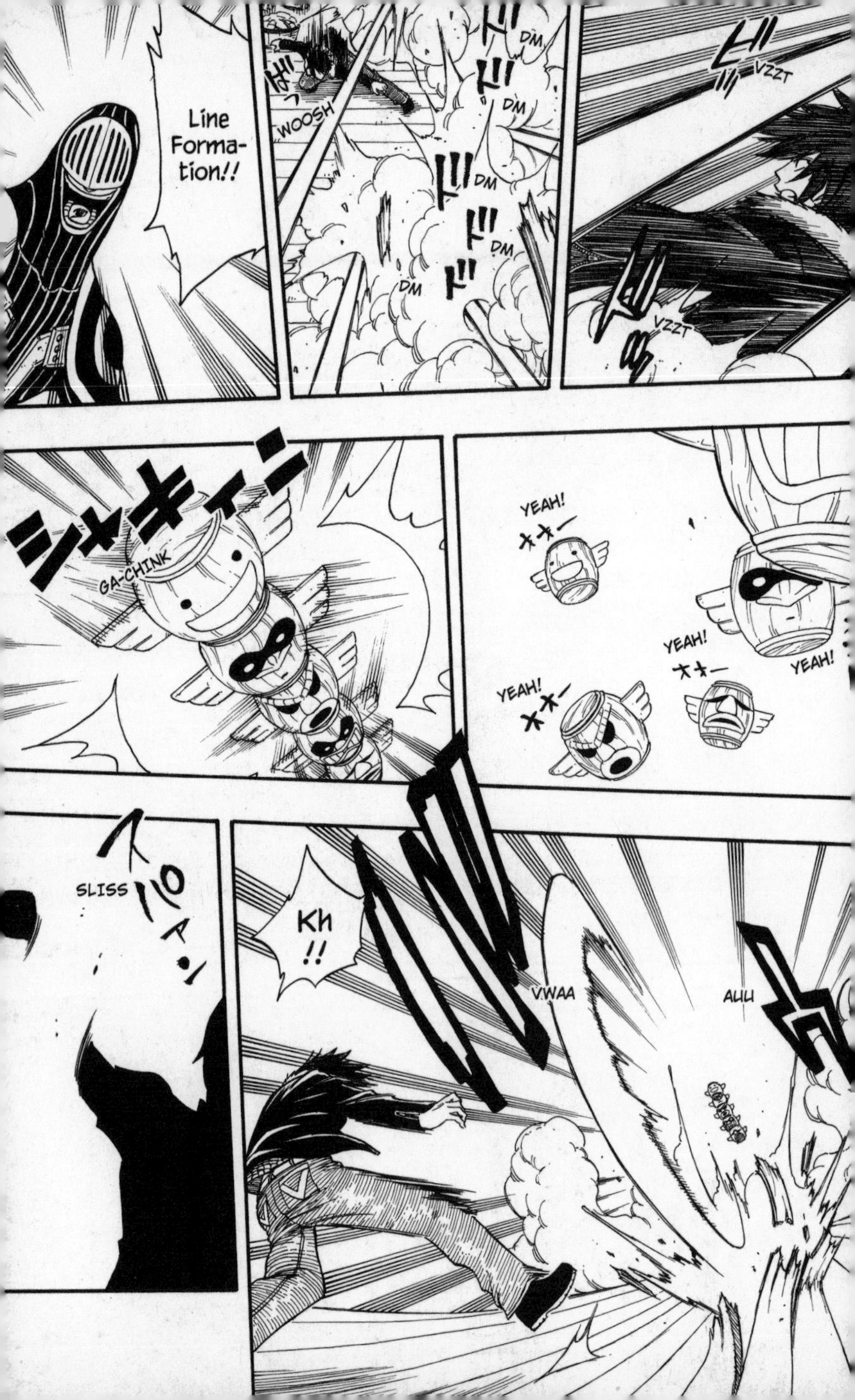
VZZT
VZZT
DM
DM
WOOSH
DM
DM
DM
Line Formation!!
YEAH!
YEAH!
YEAH!
YEAH!
GA-CHINK
AUU
VWAA
Kh!!
SLISS

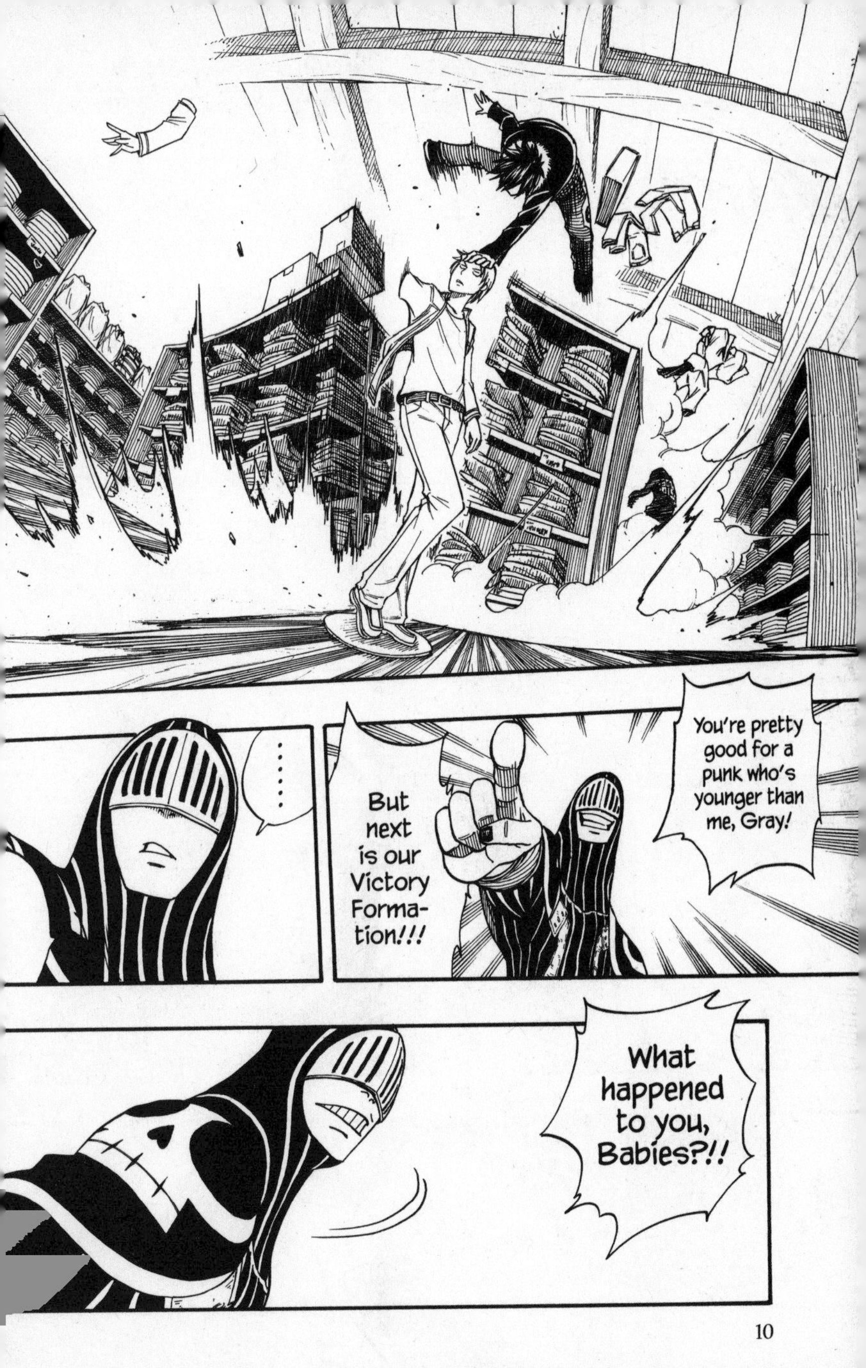
You're pretty good for a punk who's younger than me, Gray!
But next is our Victory Forma-tion!!!
......
What happened to you, Babies?!!

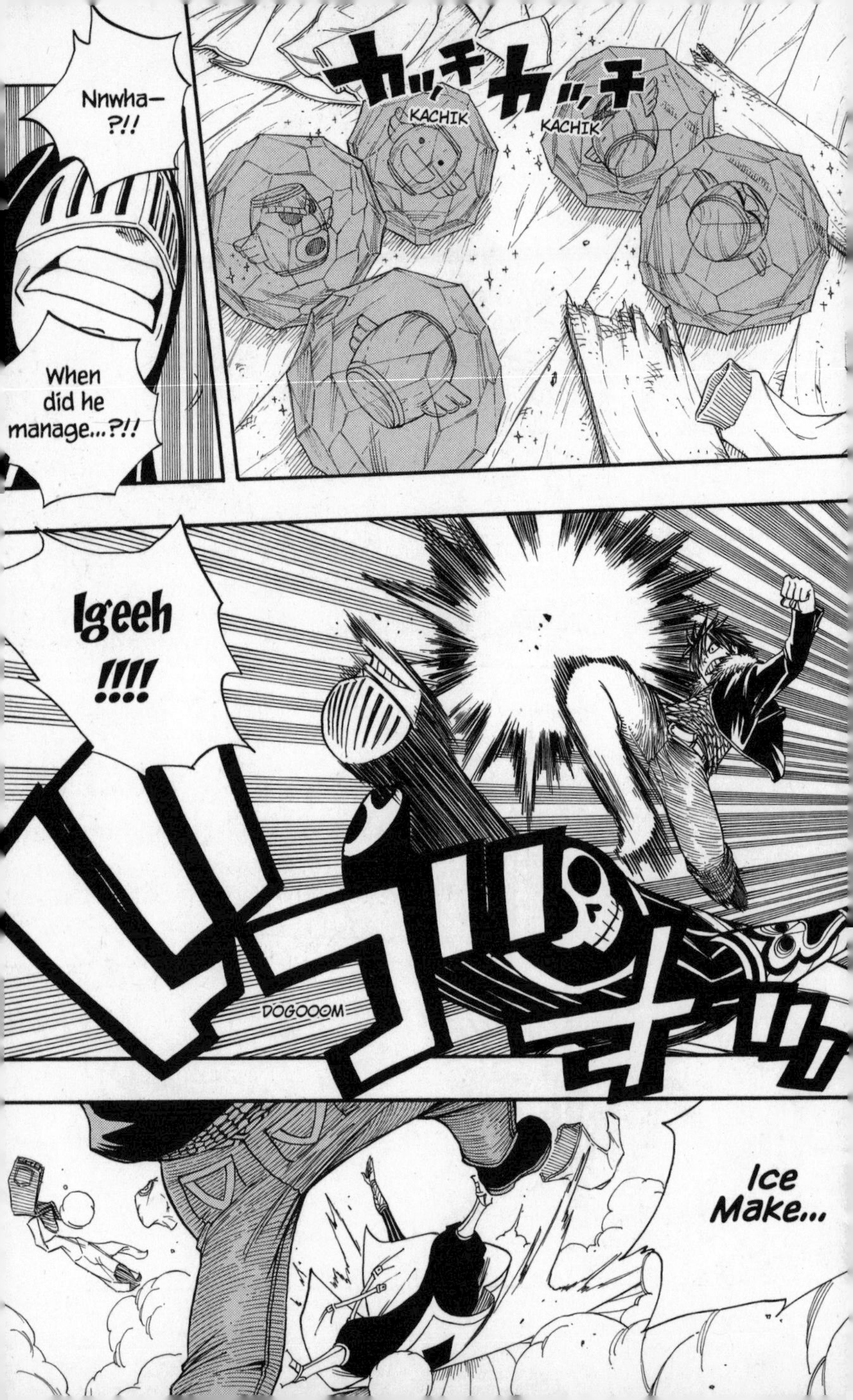
KACHIK
KACHIK
Nnwha– ?!!
When did he manage...?!!
Igeeh !!!!
DOGOOOM
Ice Make...

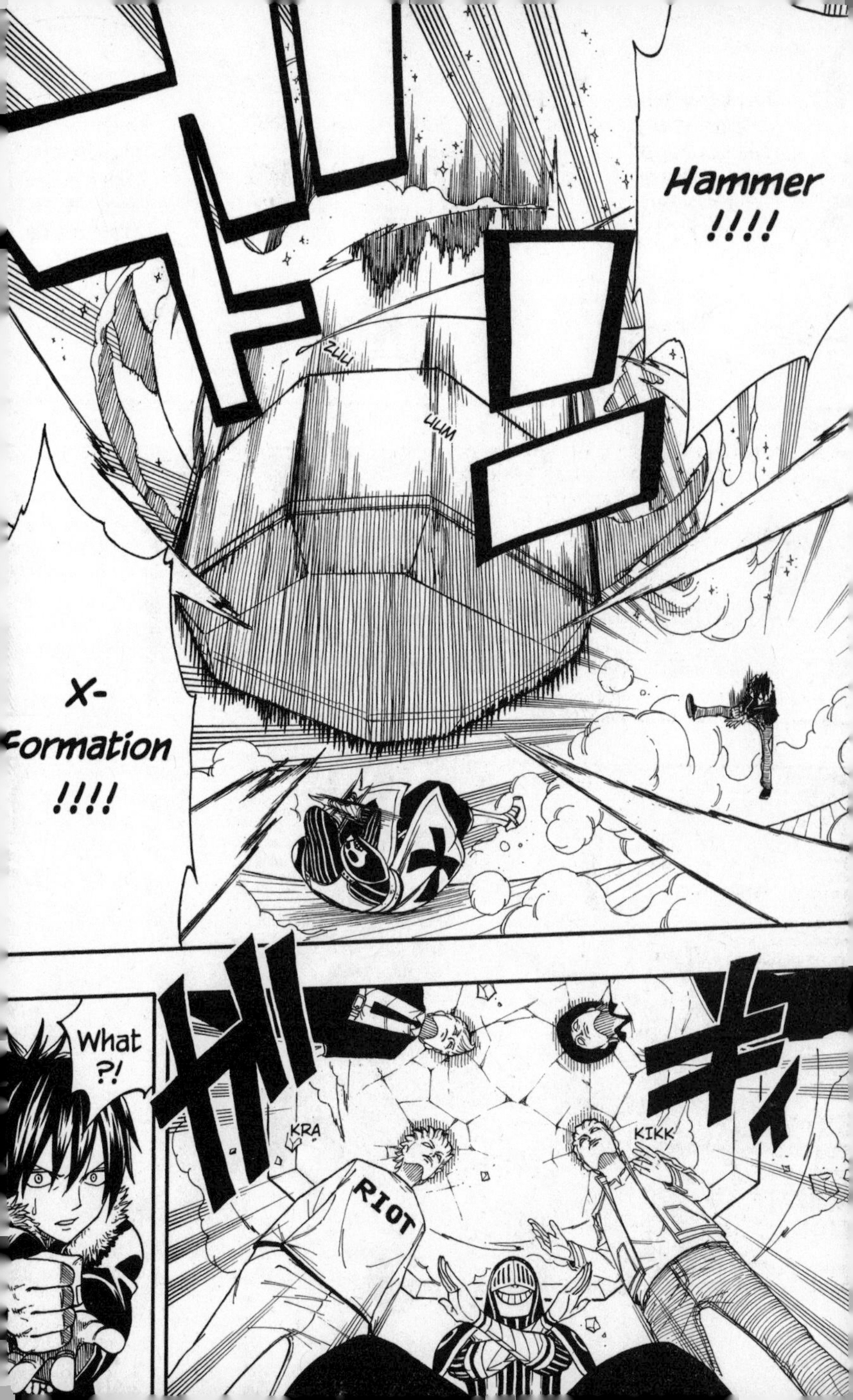
Hammer !!!!
ZUU
UUM
X-Formation !!!!
KIKK
What ?!
KRA
RIOT

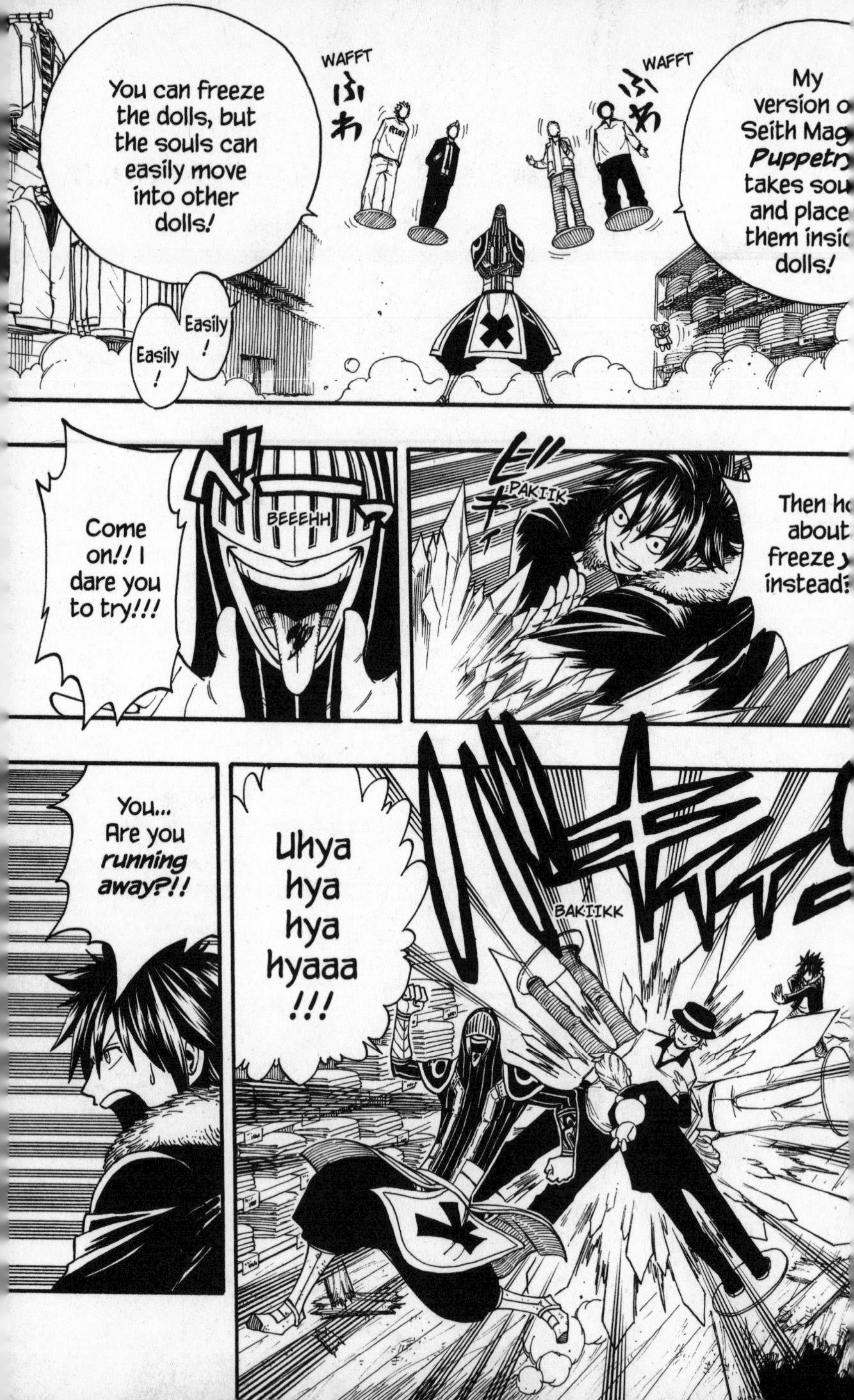
My version o Seith Mag Puppetry takes sou and place them insic dolls!
WAFFT
WAFFT
You can freeze the dolls, but the souls can easily move into other dolls!
Easily!
Easily!
PAKIIK
Then h about freeze y instead!?
BEEEHH
Come on!! I dare you to try!!!
BAKIIKK
Uhya hya hya hyaaa!!!
You... Are you running away?!!

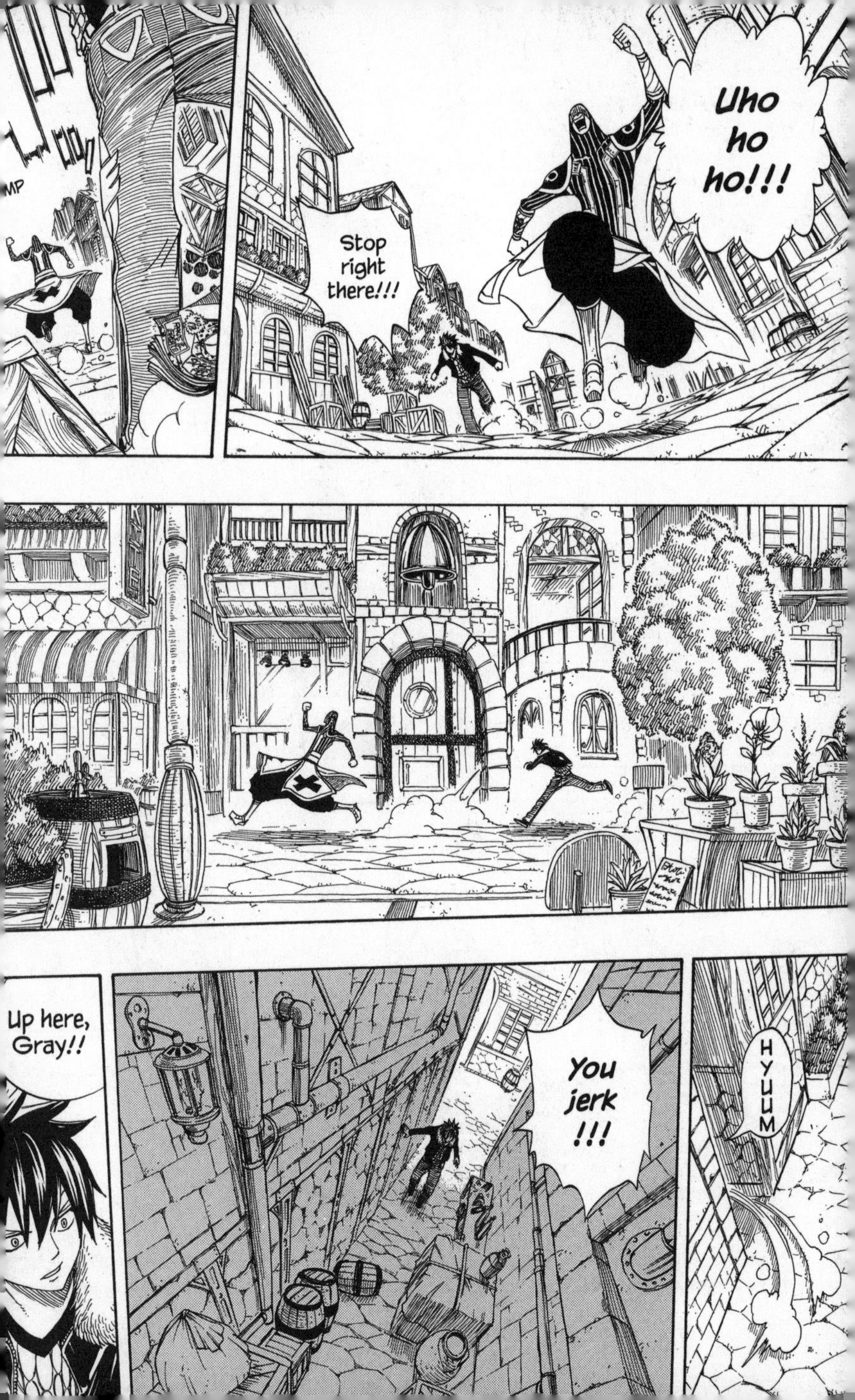
Uho ho ho!!!
Stop right there!!!
HYUUM
You jerk!!!
Up here, Gray!!

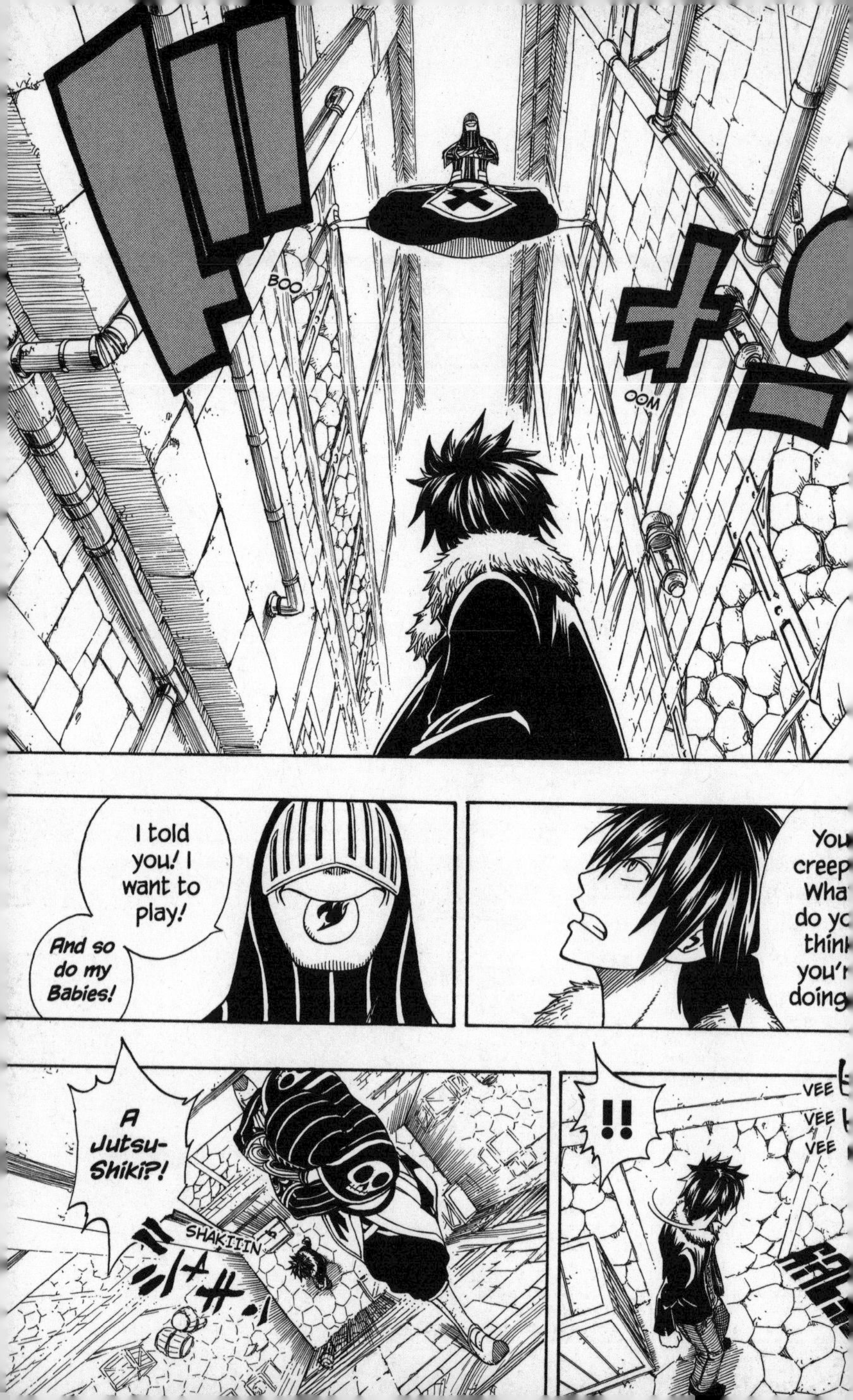
BOO
OOM
You creep Wha do yo think you'r doing
I told you! I want to play!
And so do my Babies!
!!
VEE
VEE
VEE
A Jutsu-Shiki?!
SHAKIIIN

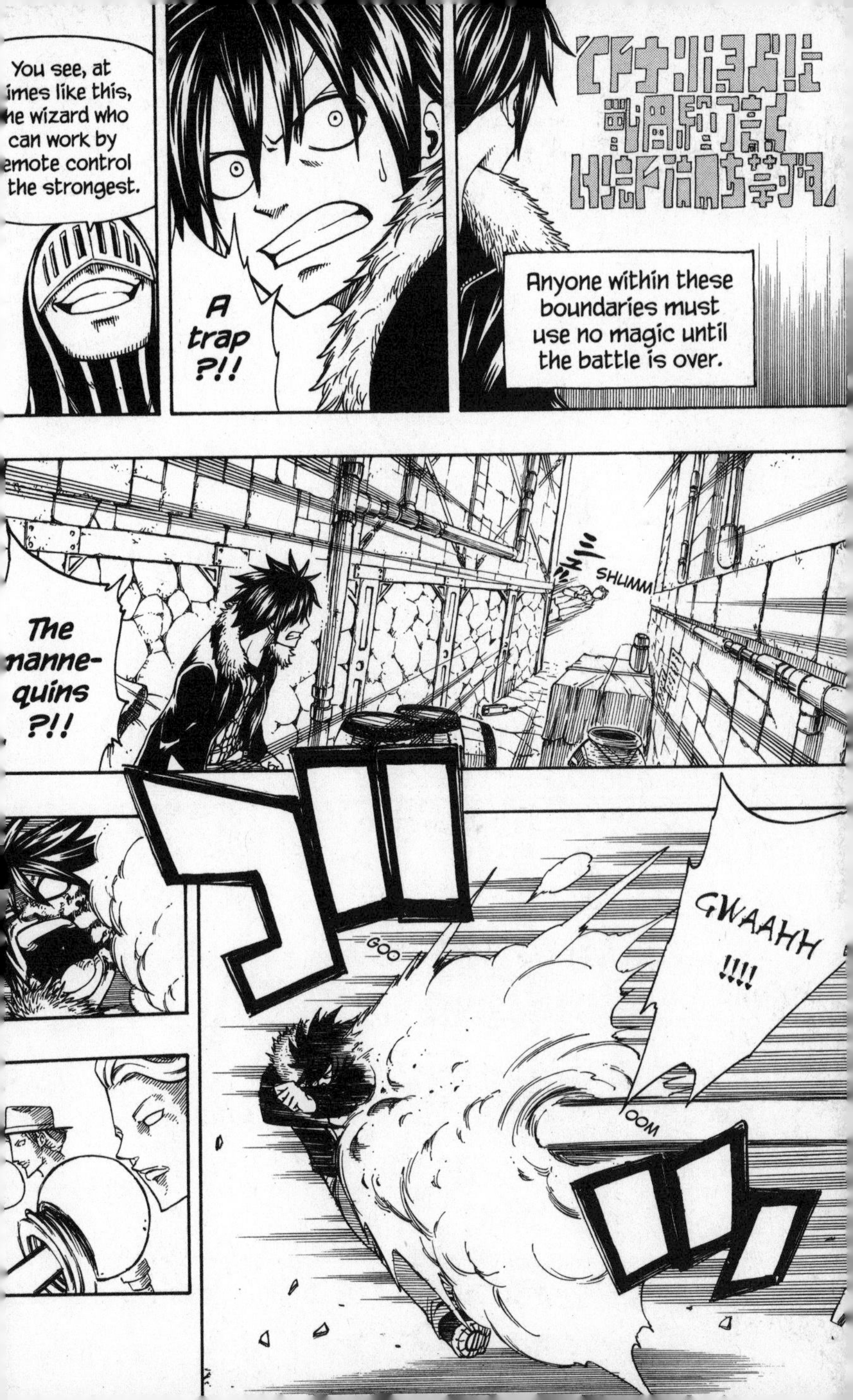
Anyone within these boundaries must use no magic until the battle is over.
A trap ?!!
You see, at imes like this, he wizard who can work by emote control the strongest.
SHUMM
The nanne-quins ?!!
GWAAHH !!!!
GOO
OOM

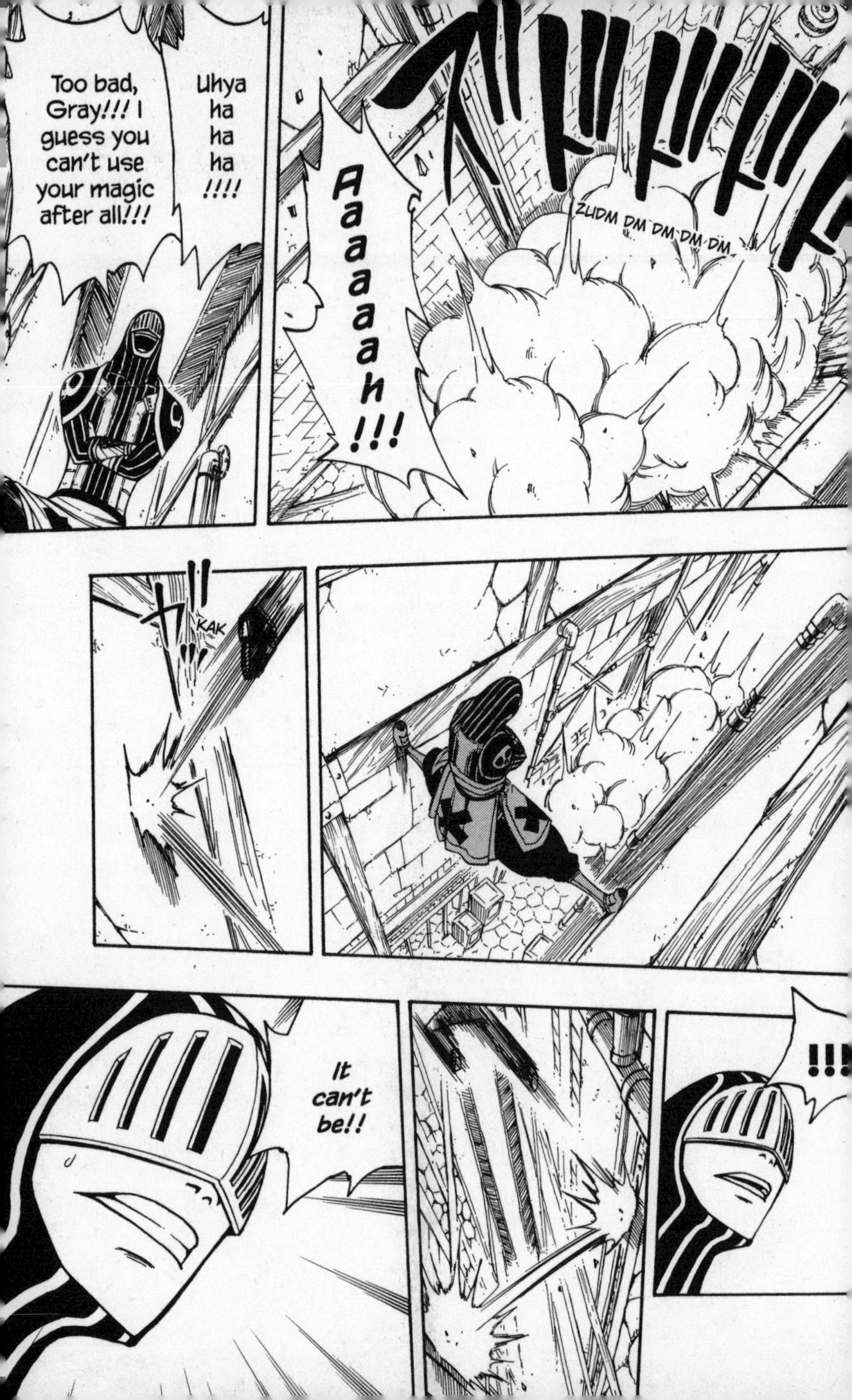
ZUDM DM DM DM DM
Aaaaaah!!!
Uhya ha ha ha!!!!
Too bad, Gray!!! I guess you can't use your magic after all!!!
KAK
!!!
It can't be!!

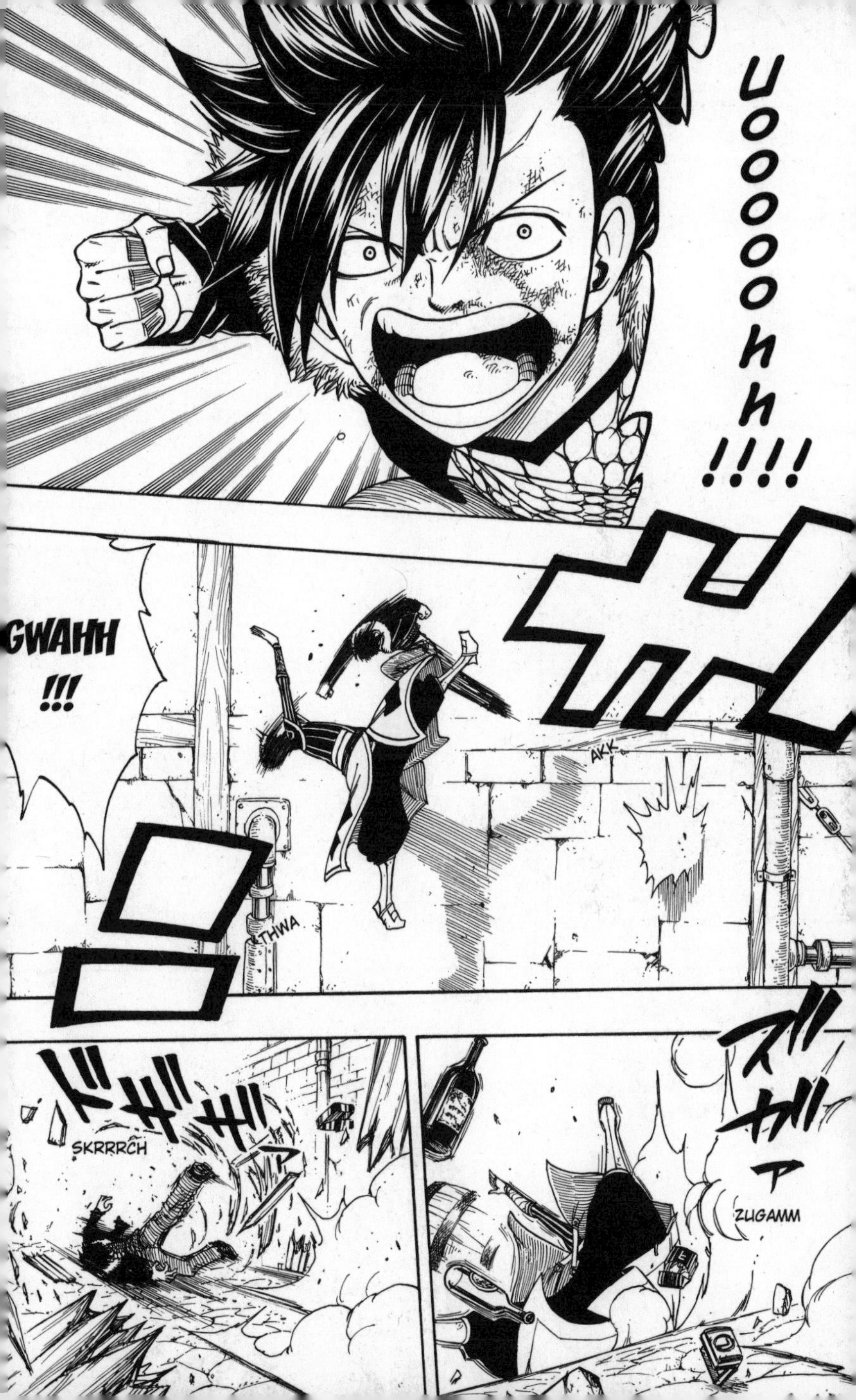
Uooooohh!!!!
AKK
THWA
GWAHH!!!
ZUGAMM
SKRRRCH

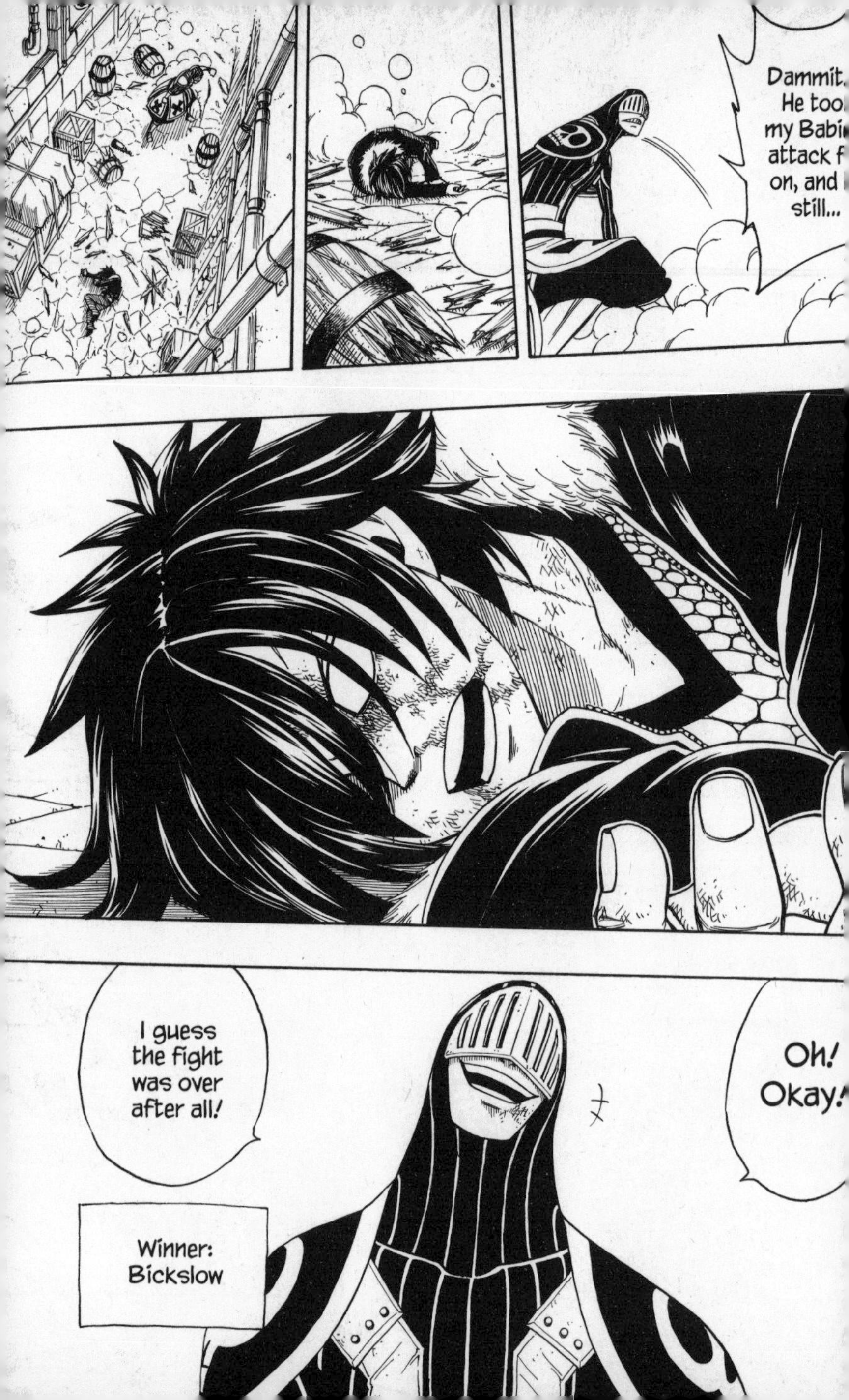
Dammit. He too my Babi attack f on, and still...
Oh! Okay!
I guess the fight was over after all!
Winner: Bickslow

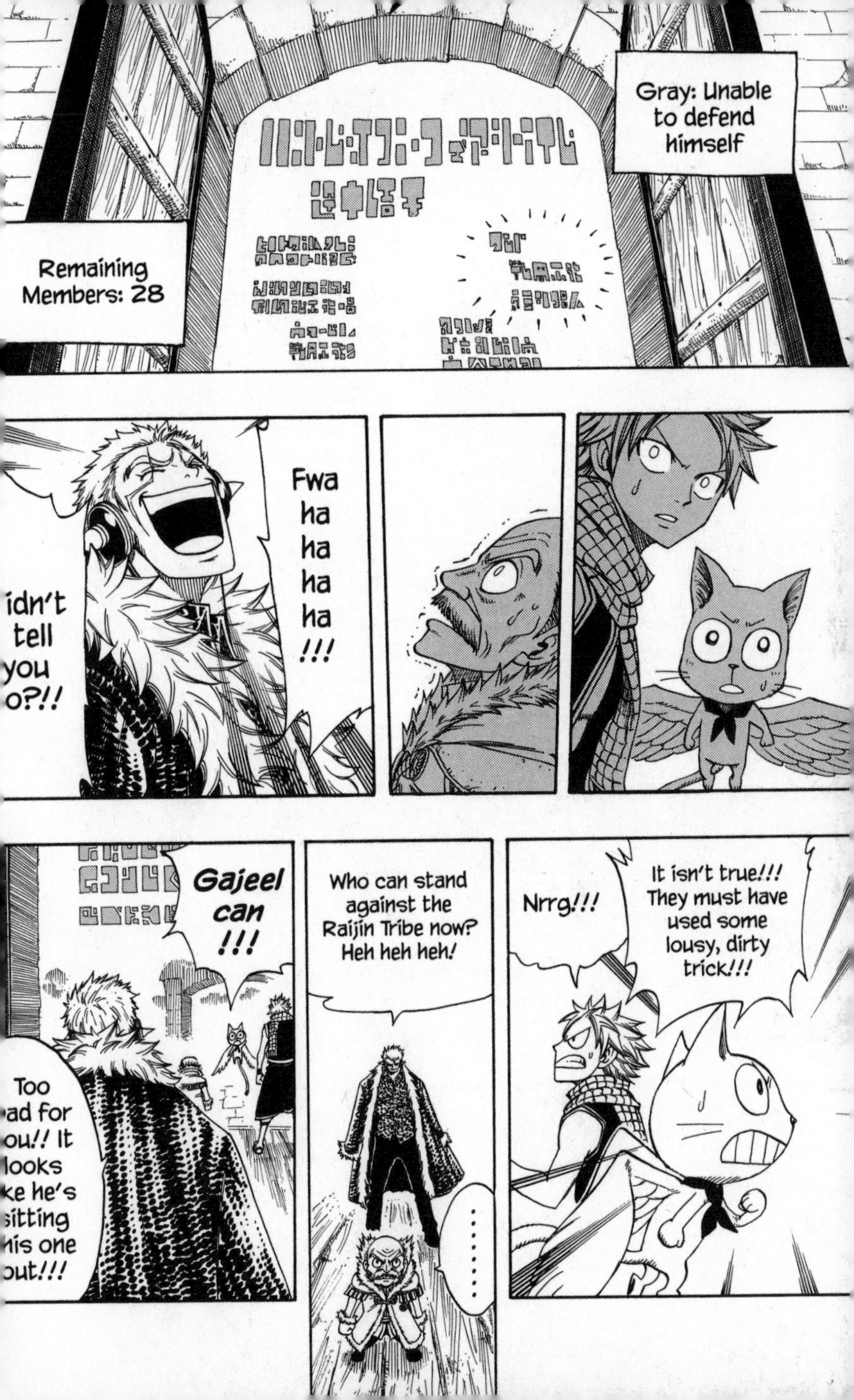

Gray: Unable to defend himself
Remaining Members: 28
Fwa ha ha ha ha!!!
idn't tell you o?!!
It isn't true!!! They must have used some lousy, dirty trick!!!
Nrrg!!!
Who can stand against the Raijin Tribe now? Heh heh heh!
......
Gajeel can!!!
Too ad for ou!! It looks ke he's sitting his one out!!!

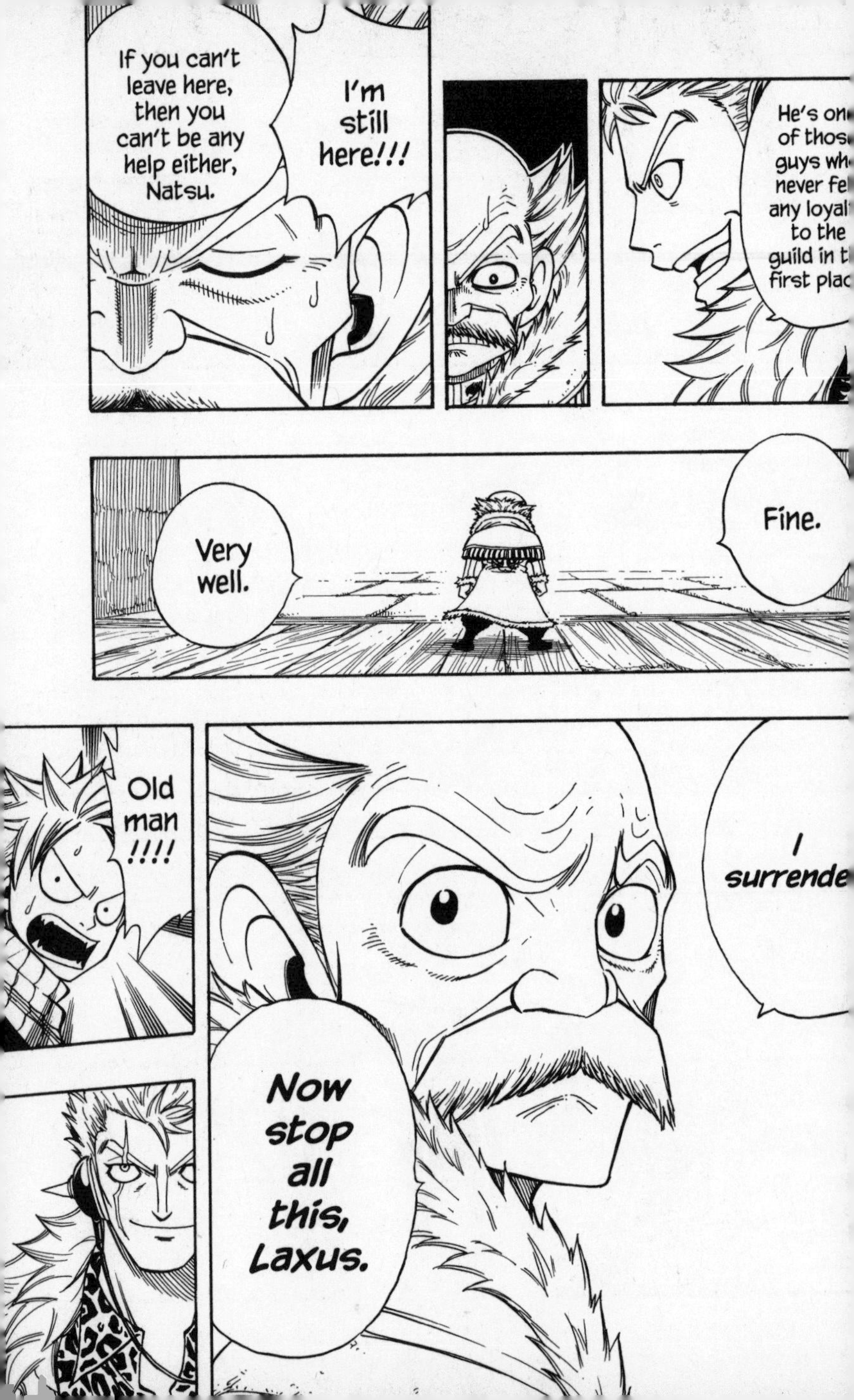
He's on of thos guys wh never fel any loyal to the guild in t first plac
I'm still here!!!
If you can't leave here, then you can't be any help either, Natsu.
Fine.
Very well.
I surrende
Now stop all this, Laxus.
Old man!!!!

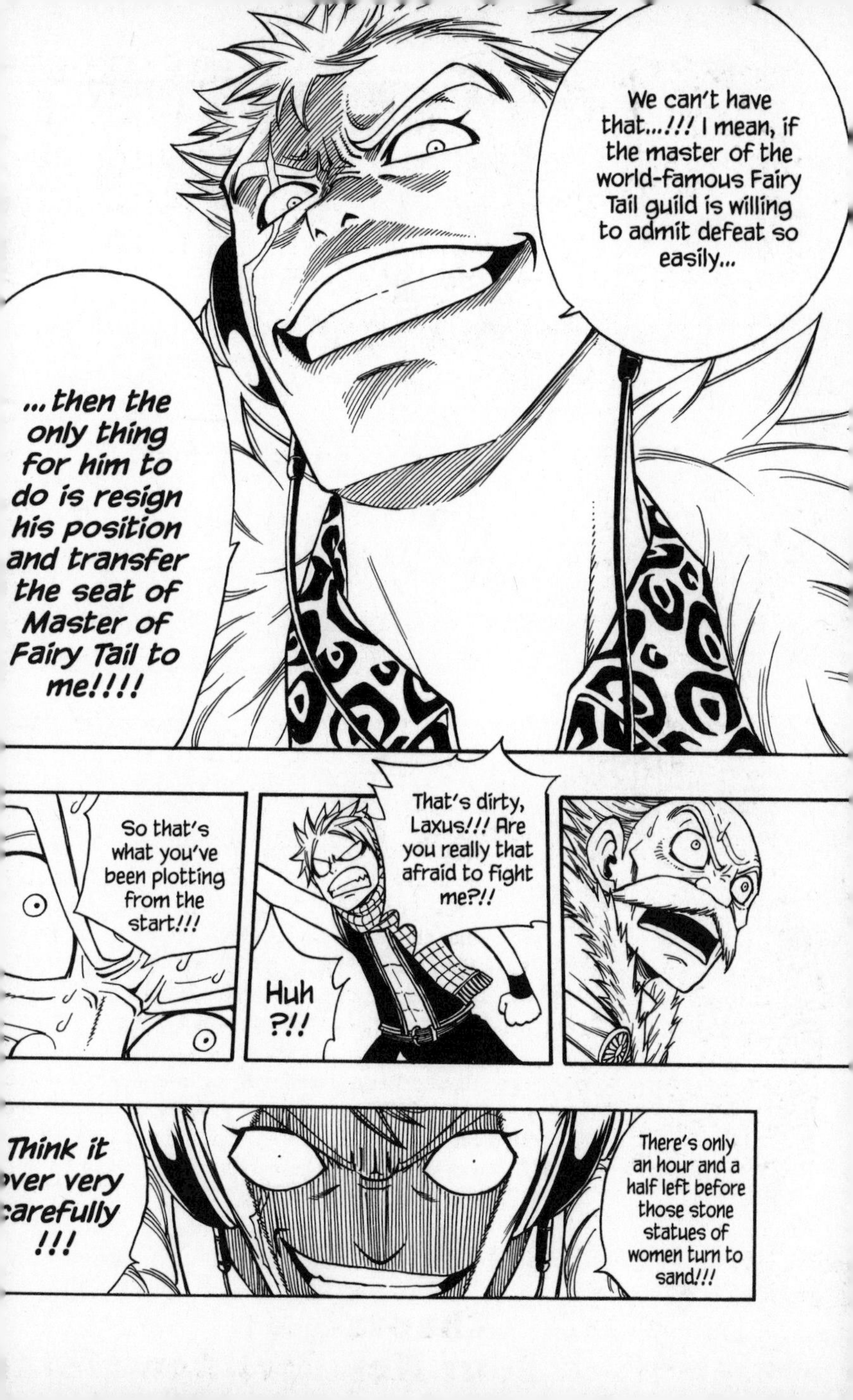
We can't have that...!!! I mean, if the master of the world-famous Fairy Tail guild is willing to admit defeat so easily...
...then the only thing for him to do is resign his position and transfer the seat of Master of Fairy Tail to me!!!!
That's dirty, Laxus!!! Are you really that afraid to fight me?!!
Huh ?!!
So that's what you've been plotting from the start!!!
There's only an hour and a half left before those stone statues of women turn to sand!!!
Think it ver very arefully !!!

FAIRY TAIL

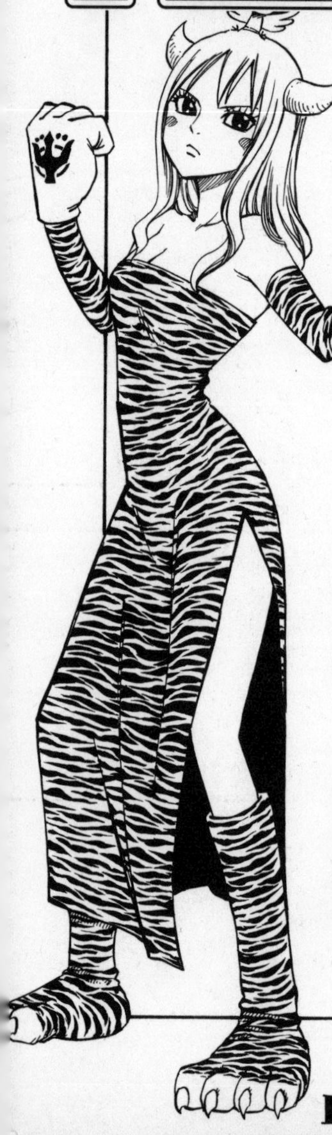

FAIRY TAIL

Name: Mickey Chickentiger **Age:** 18 yrs

Magic: Magic Bird & Martial Arts

Likes: Birds **Dislikes:** Boredom

Remarks

She uses a magic that controls the bird (Pii-chan) who is always with her. The bird is a Magic Bird that can turn into a fireball, become a shield, or deliver mail for her. (By the way, it can talk.)

However, Mickey's main weapon is her martial arts. Pii-chan is usually just along for the ride on most of her jobs. She's the leader and core of the team Young Mega-Death, but the team members are all afraid of Mickey, and they gave her the nickname Demon Princess. She rather likes the name, and has accessorized her hair with horns to match the "Demon Princess" character.

Chapter 111: Four Members Remaining

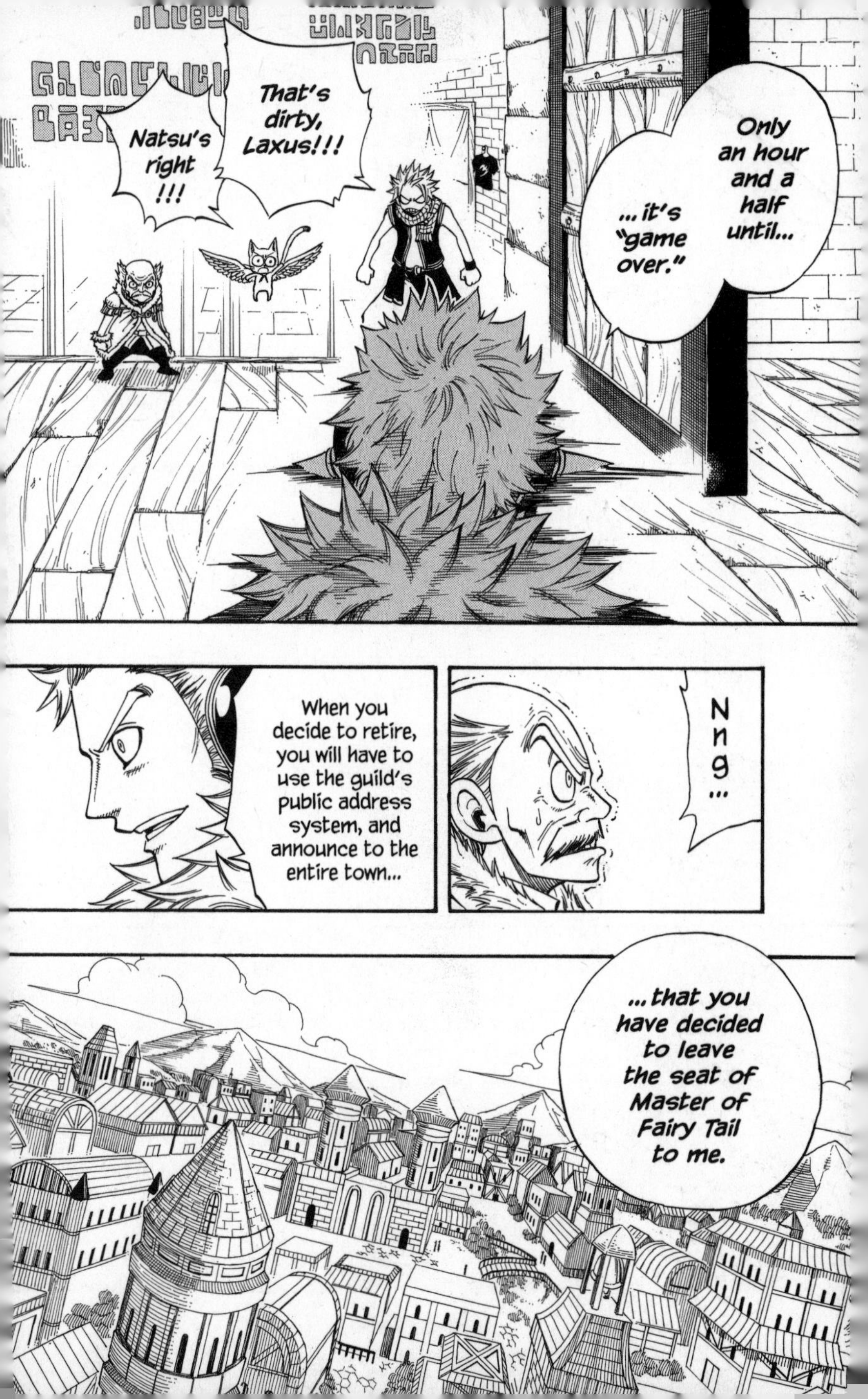
Only an hour and a half until...
...it's "game over."
That's dirty, Laxus!!!
Natsu's right!!!
Nng...
When you decide to retire, you will have to use the guild's public address system, and announce to the entire town...
...that you have decided to leave the seat of Master of Fairy Tail to me.

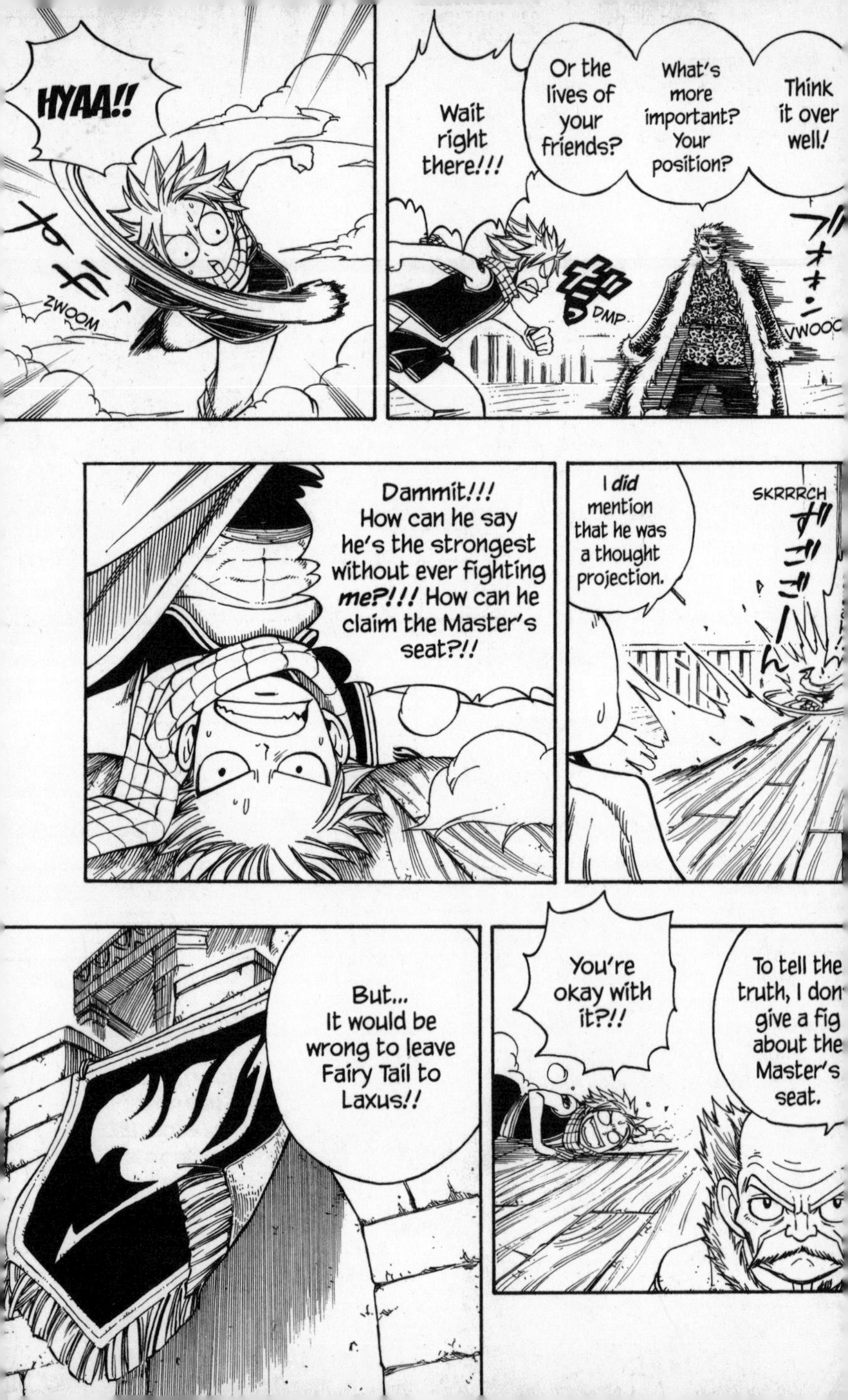

Think it over well!
What's more important? Your position?
Or the lives of your friends?
Wait right there!!!
VWOO
DMP
HYAA!!
ZWOOM
SKRRRCH
I *did* mention that he was a thought projection.
Dammit!!! How can he say he's the strongest without ever fighting *me?!!!* How can he claim the Master's seat?!!
To tell the truth, I don give a fig about the Master's seat.
You're okay with it?!!
But... It would be wrong to leave Fairy Tail to Laxus!!

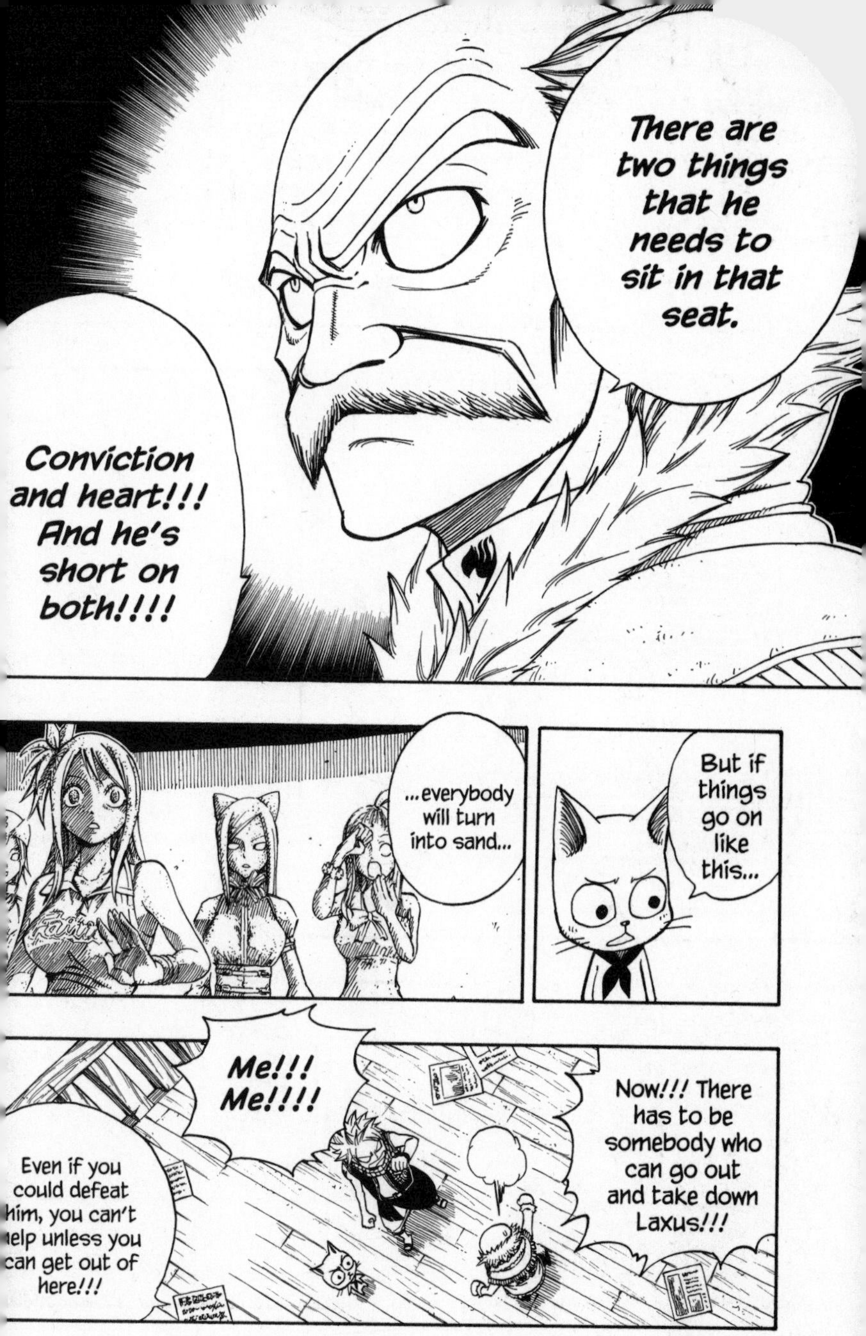
There are two things that he needs to sit in that seat.
Conviction and heart!!! And he's short on both!!!!
But if things go on like this...
...everybody will turn into sand...
Now!!! There has to be somebody who can go out and take down Laxus!!!
Me!!! Me!!!!
Even if you could defeat him, you can't help unless you can get out of here!!!

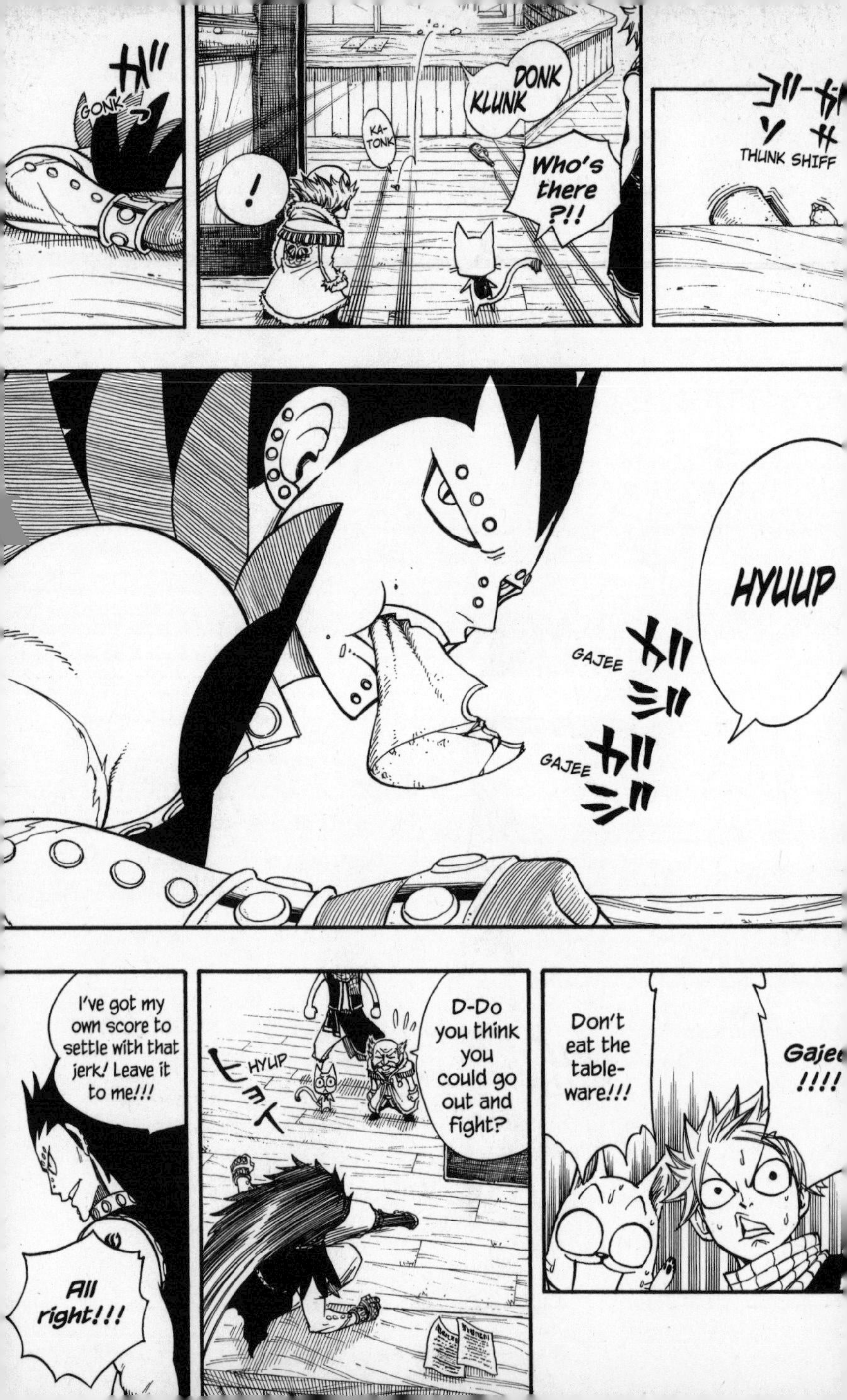
THUNK SHIFF
DONK KLUNK
KA-TONK
Who's there?!!
!
GONK
HYUUP
GAJEE
GAJEE
Gajee!!!!
Don't eat the tableware!!!
D-Do you think you could go out and fight?
HYUP
I've got my own score to settle with that jerk! Leave it to me!!!
All right!!!

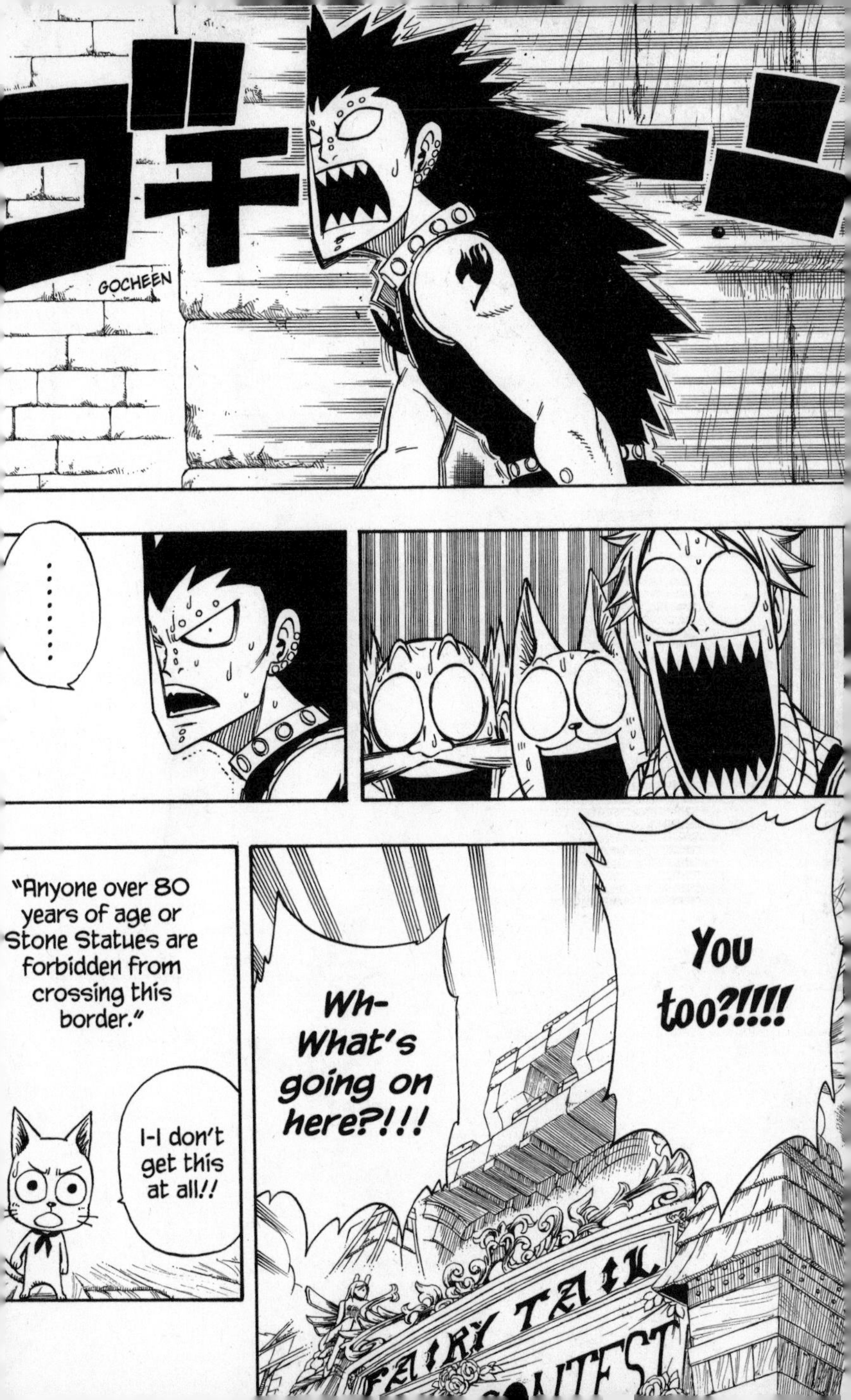
ゴチーン
GOCHEEN
......
You too?!!!!
Wh-What's going on here?!!!
FAIRY TAIL
"Anyone over 80 years of age or Stone Statues are forbidden from crossing this border."
I-I don't get this at all!!

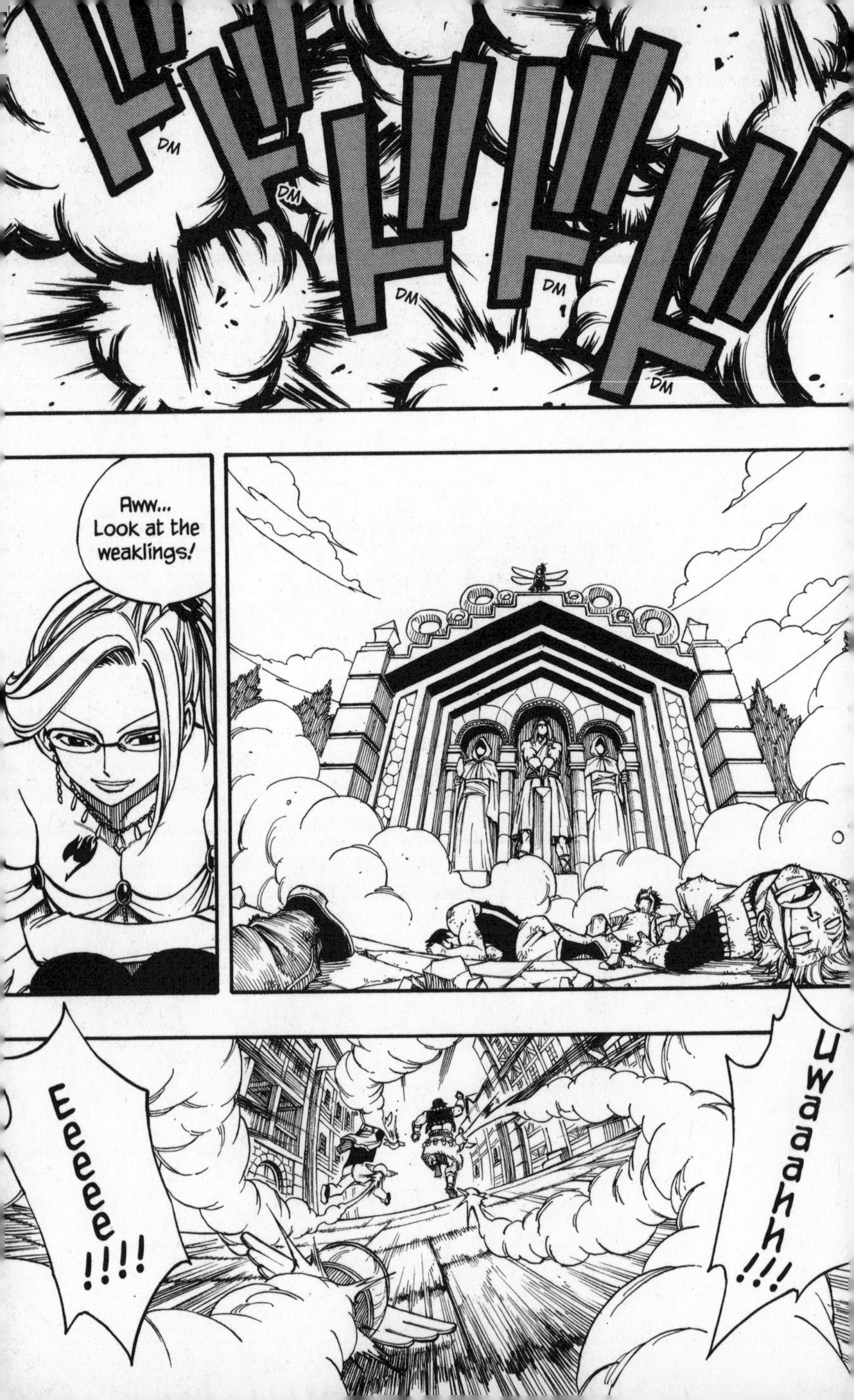
DM
DM
DM
DM
DM
Aww... Look at the weaklings!
Uwaaaahh!!!
Eeeee!!!!

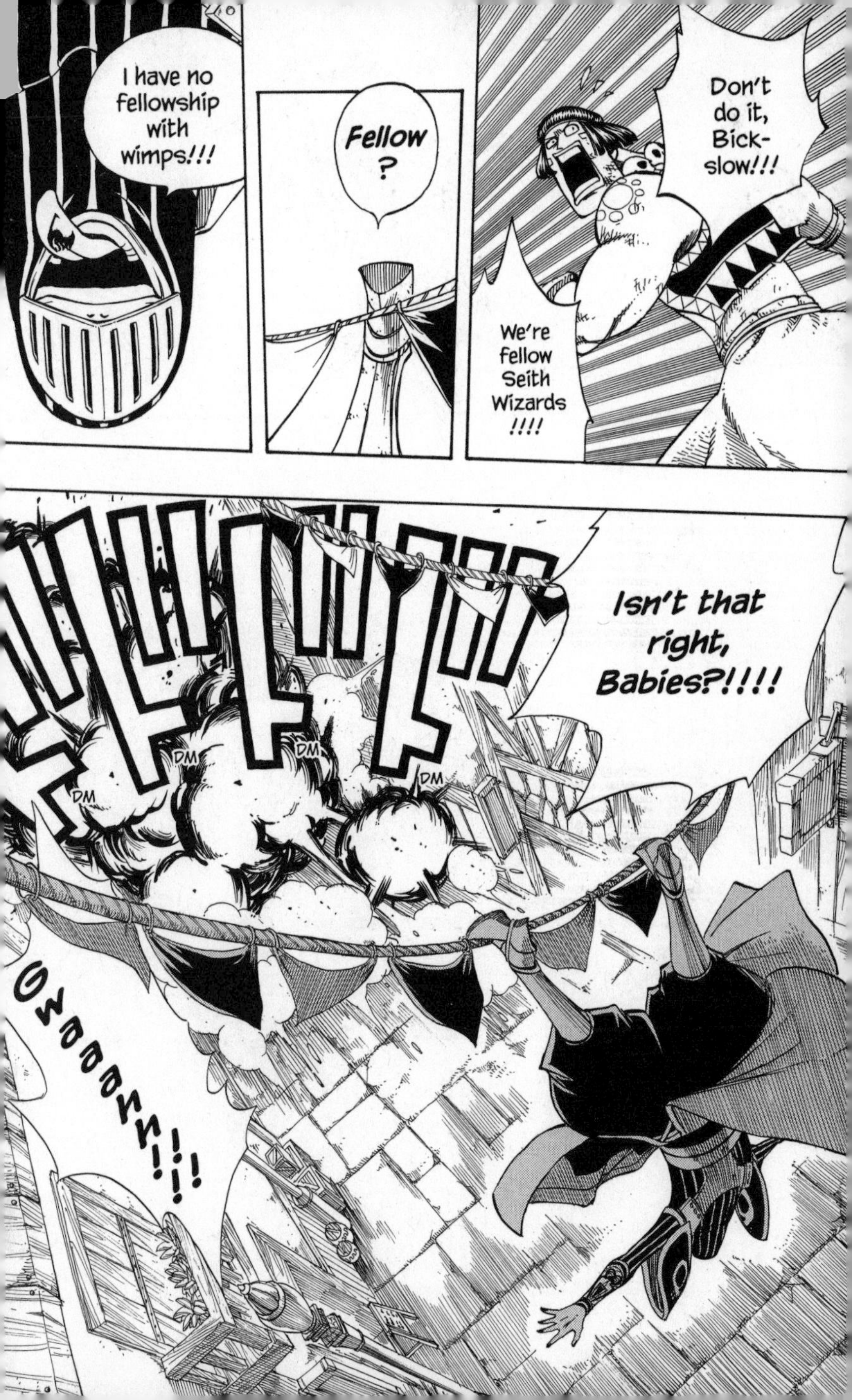

Don't do it, Bick-slow!!!
We're fellow Seith Wizards!!!!
Fellow?
I have no fellowship with wimps!!!
Isn't that right, Babies?!!!!
DM
DM
DM
DM
Gwaaanh!!!

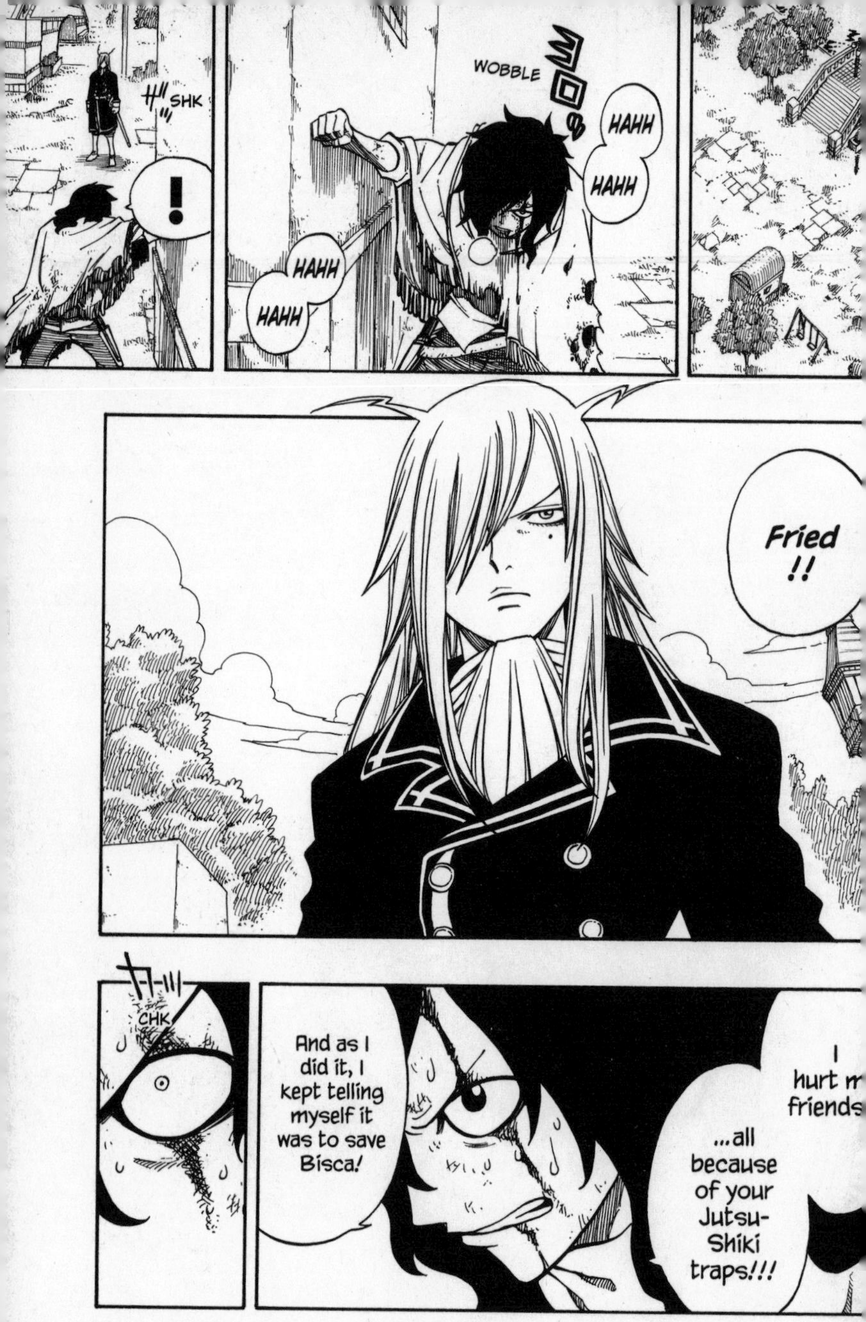
WOBBLE
HAHH HAHH
HAHH HAHH
SHK
!
Fried!!
I hurt m friends
...all because of your Jutsu-Shiki traps!!!
And as I did it, I kept telling myself it was to save Bisca!
CHK

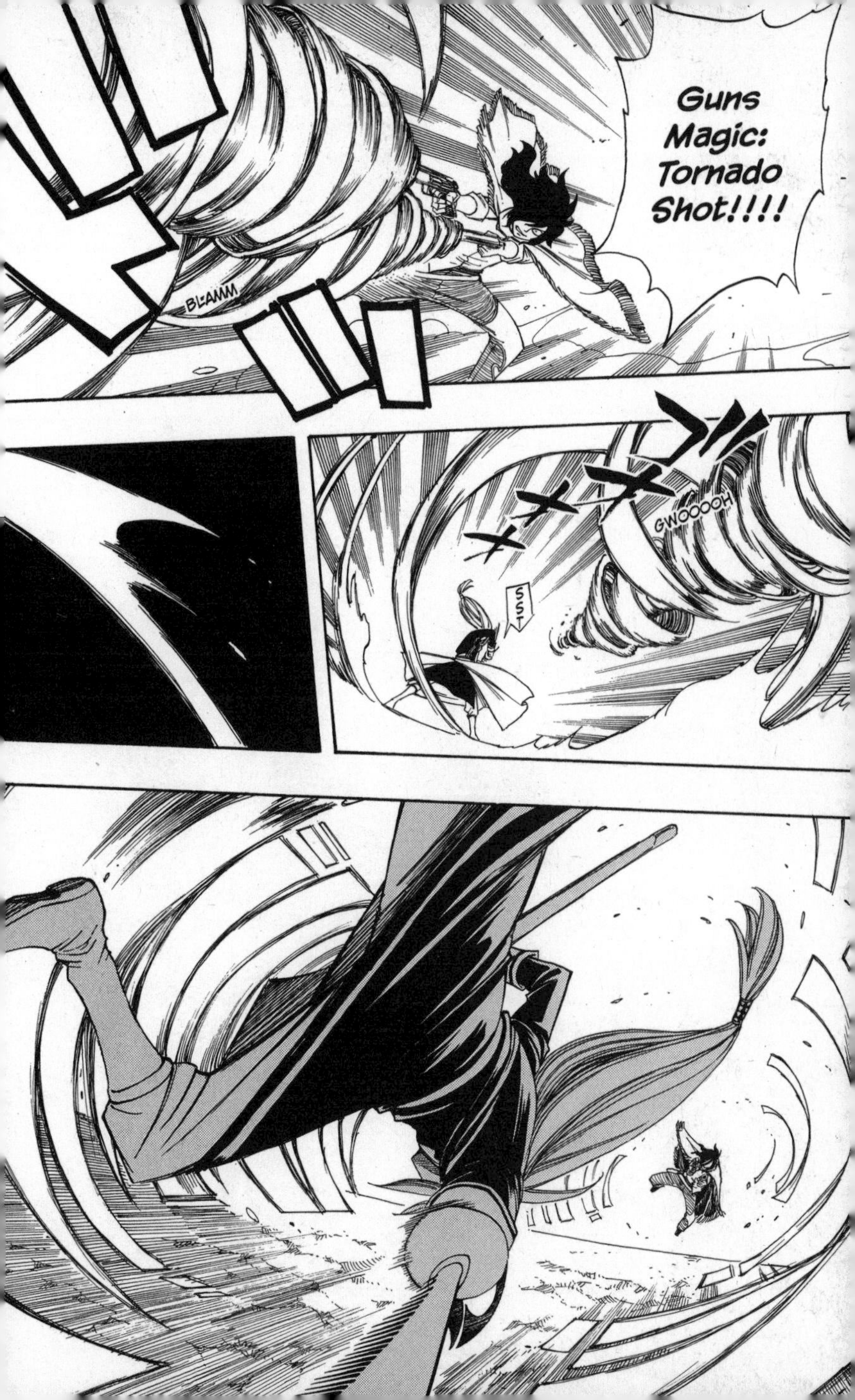
Guns Magic: Tornado Shot!!!!
BLAMM
GWOOOOH
SST

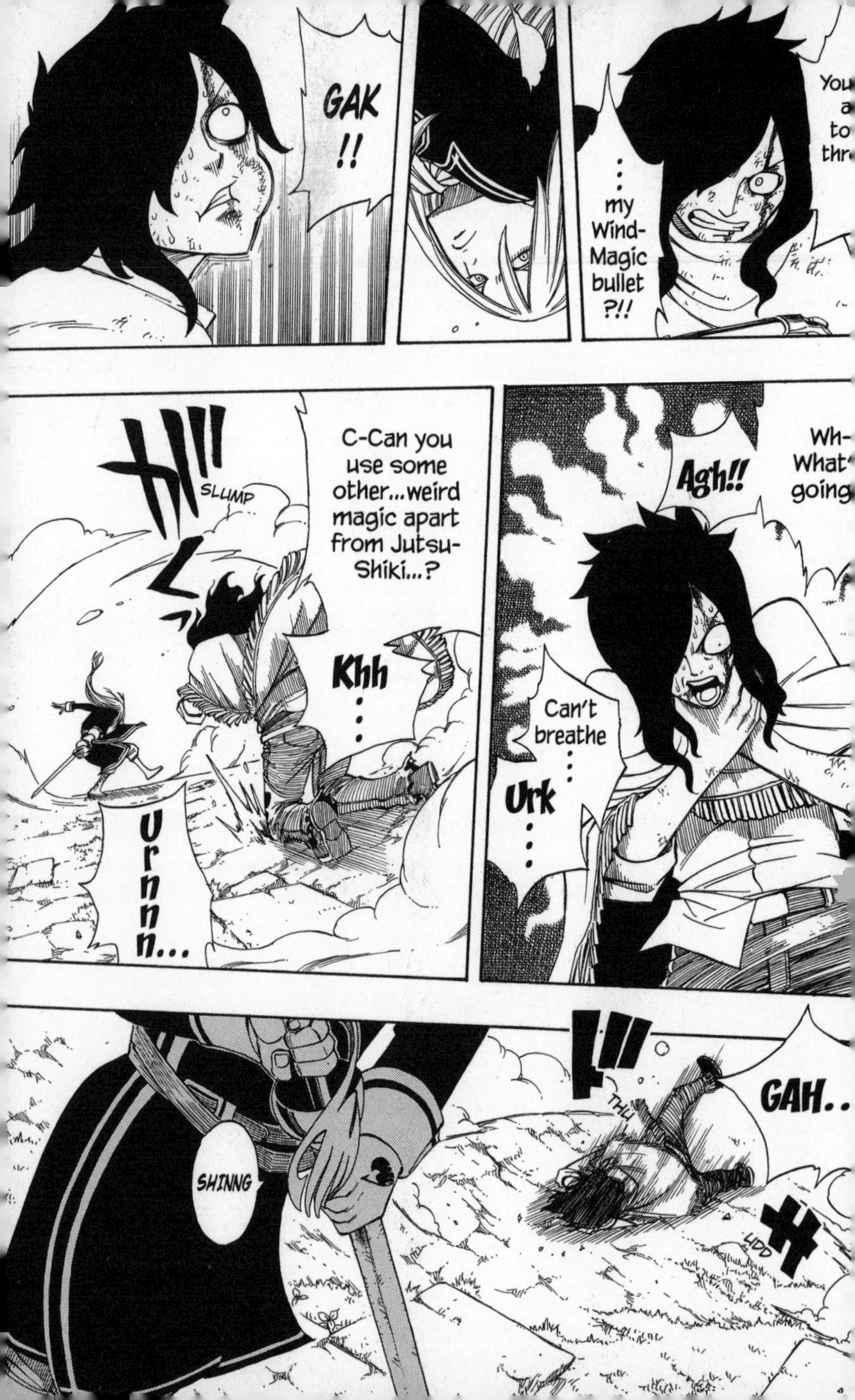
You
...my Wind-Magic bullet?!!
GAK!!
Agh!!
Can't breathe...
Urk...
C-Can you use some other...weird magic apart from Jutsu-Shiki...?
SLUMP
Khh...
Urnnn...
GAH..
THU
SHINNG

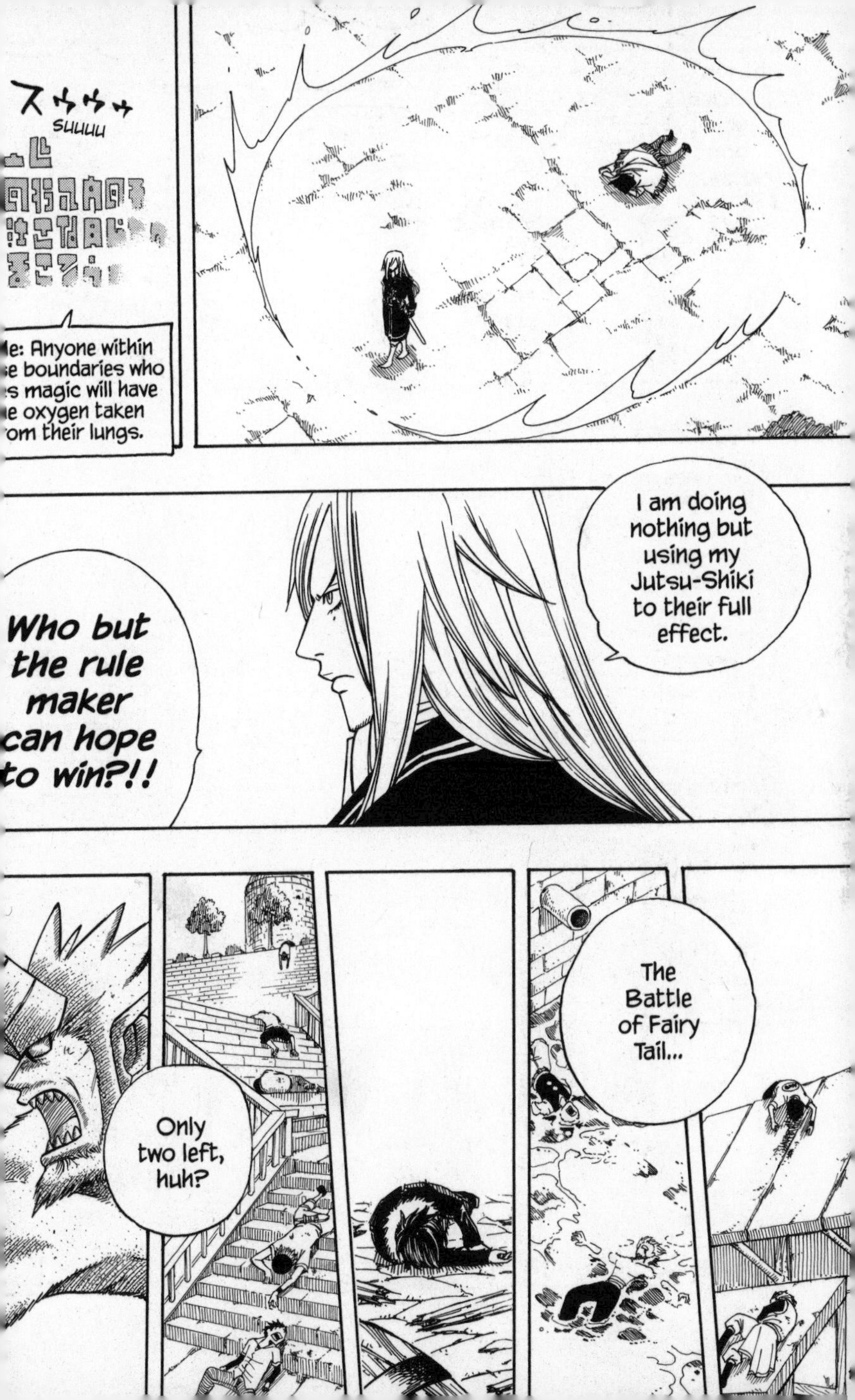
スゥゥゥ
SUUUU
e: Anyone within se boundaries who s magic will have e oxygen taken om their lungs.
I am doing nothing but using my Jutsu-Shiki to their full effect.
Who but the rule maker can hope to win?!!
The Battle of Fairy Tail...
Only two left, huh?

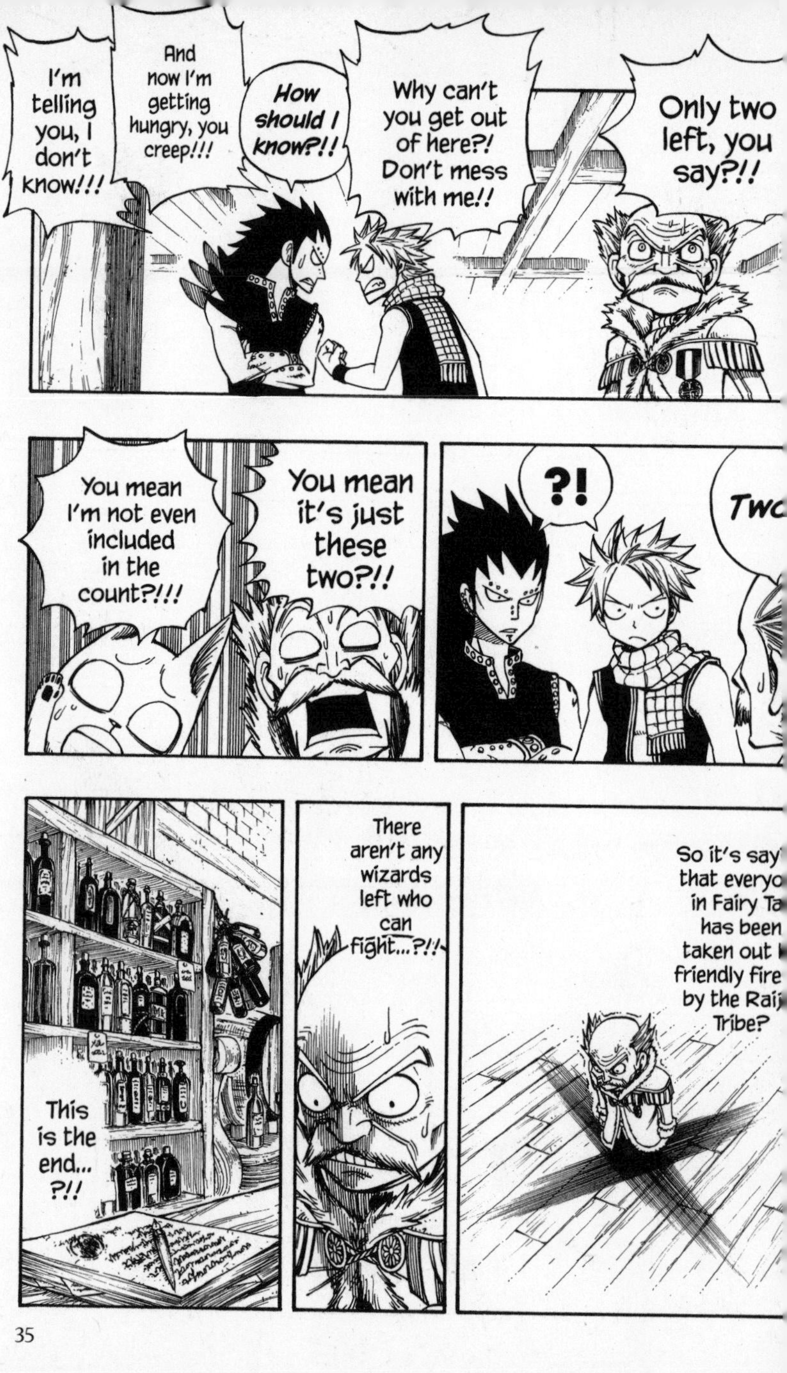
Only two left, you say?!!
Why can't you get out of here?! Don't mess with me!!
How should I know?!!
And now I'm getting hungry, you creep!!!
I'm telling you, I don't know!!!
Tw
?!
You mean it's just these two?!!
You mean I'm not even included in the count?!!!
So it's say that everyo in Fairy Ta has been taken out friendly fire by the Raij Tribe?
There aren't any wizards left who can fight...?!!
This is the end...?!!

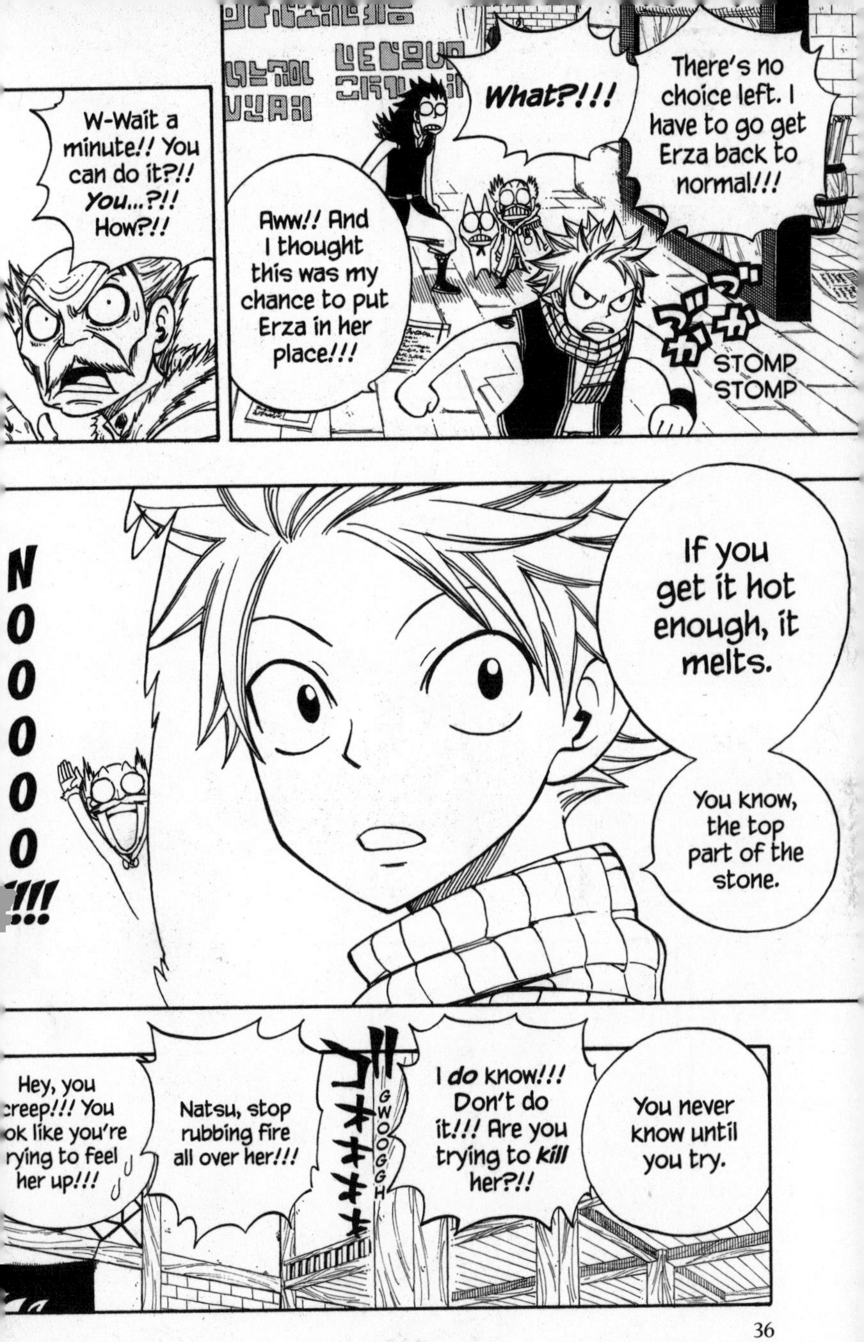
There's no choice left. I have to go get Erza back to normal!!!
What?!!!
STOMP STOMP
Aww!! And I thought this was my chance to put Erza in her place!!!
W-Wait a minute!! You can do it?!! You...?!! How?!!
If you get it hot enough, it melts.
You know, the top part of the stone.
NOOOOOO!!!
You never know until you try.
I do know!!! Don't do it!!! Are you trying to kill her?!!
GWOOOGGH
Natsu, stop rubbing fire all over her!!!
Hey, you creep!!! You ok like you're rying to feel her up!!!

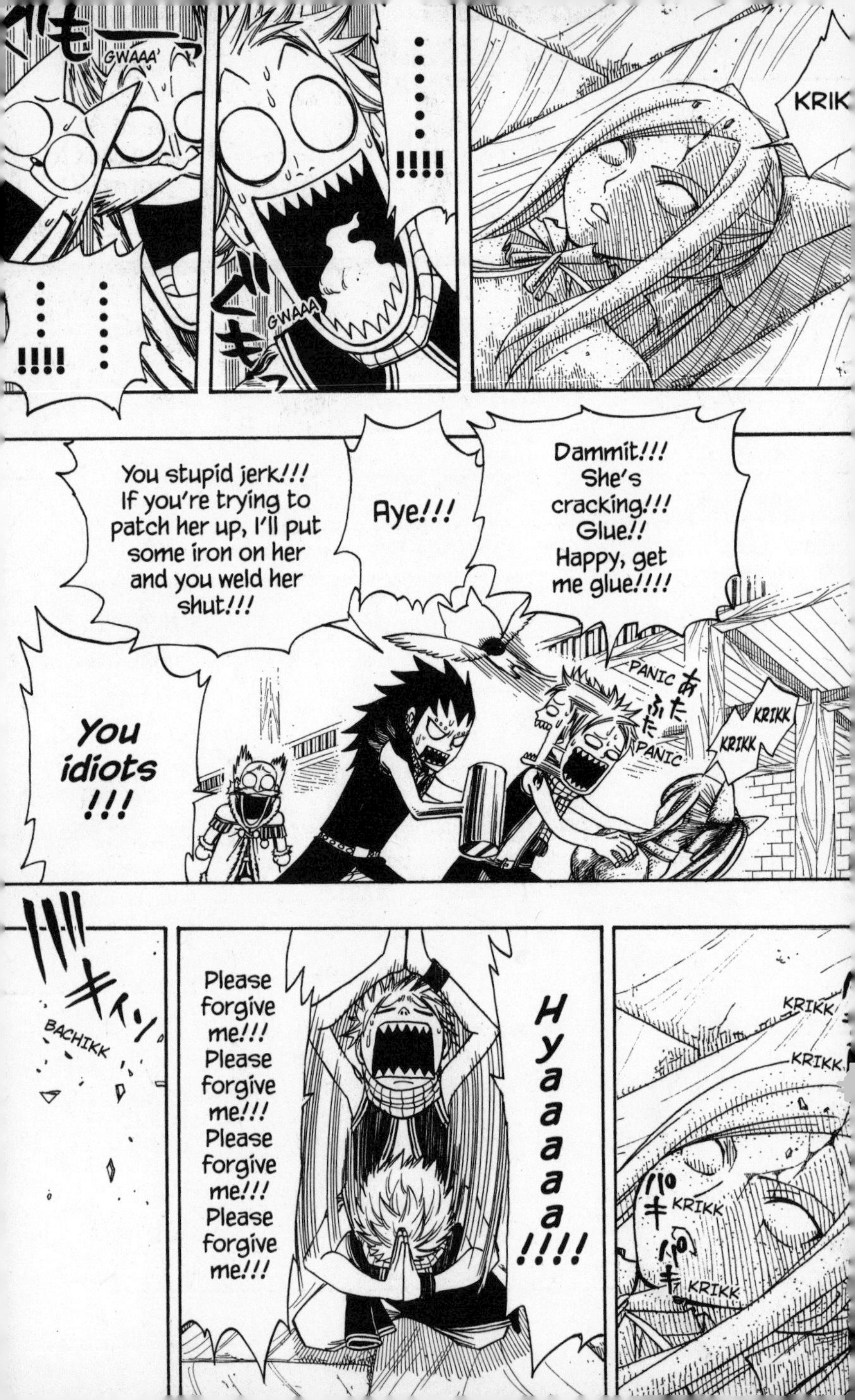
KRIK
....!!!!
GWAAA
GWAAA'
....
....
!!!!
Dammit!!! She's cracking!!! Glue!! Happy, get me glue!!!!
Aye!!!
You stupid jerk!!! If you're trying to patch her up, I'll put some iron on her and you weld her shut!!!
PANIC
あたふた
PANIC
KRIKK
KRIKK
You idiots!!!
KRIKK
KRIKK
KRIKK
KRIKK
Hyaaaaa!!!!
Please forgive me!!! Please forgive me!!! Please forgive me!!! Please forgive me!!!
BACHIKK

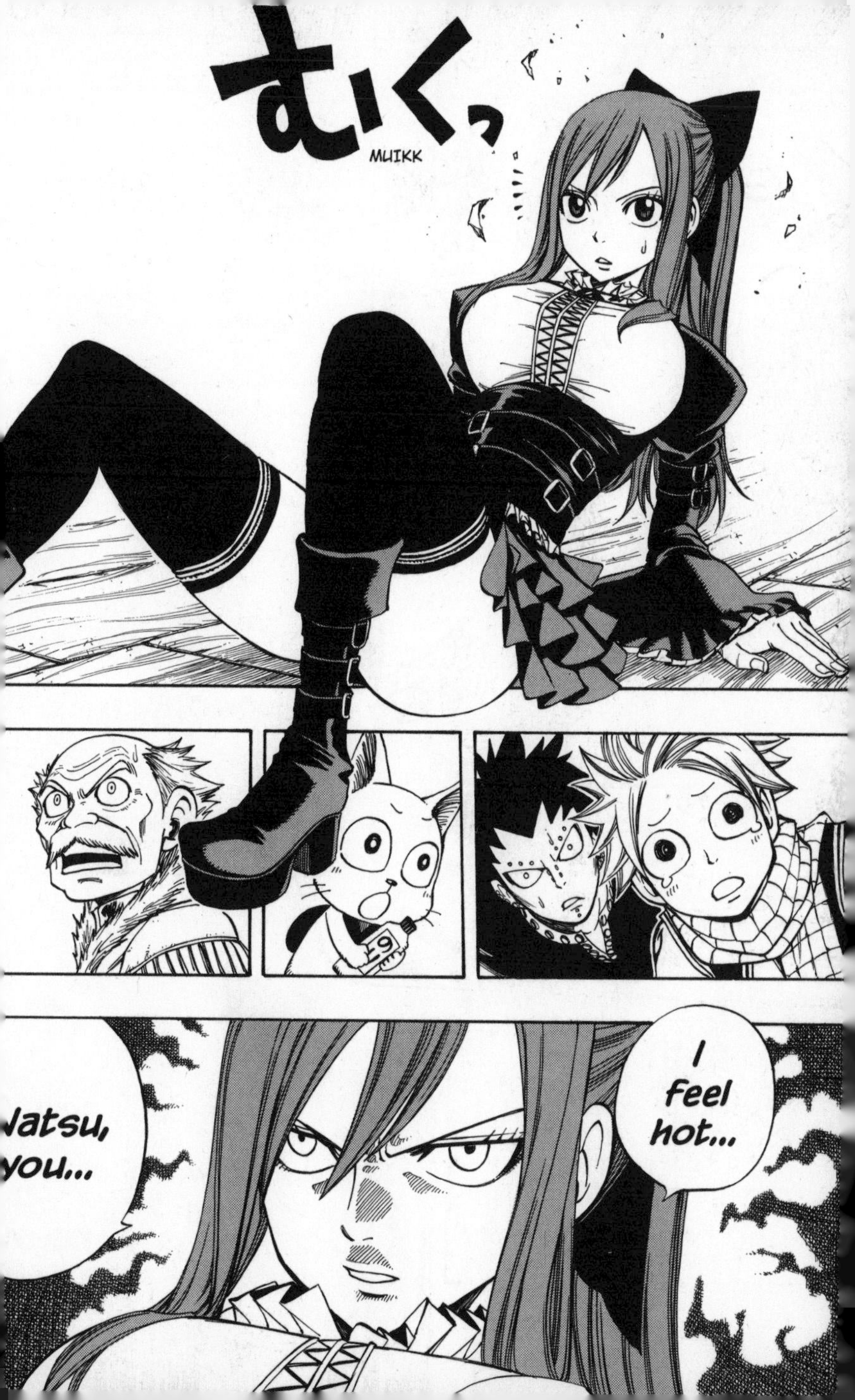
むくっ
MUIKK
I feel hot...
Natsu, you...

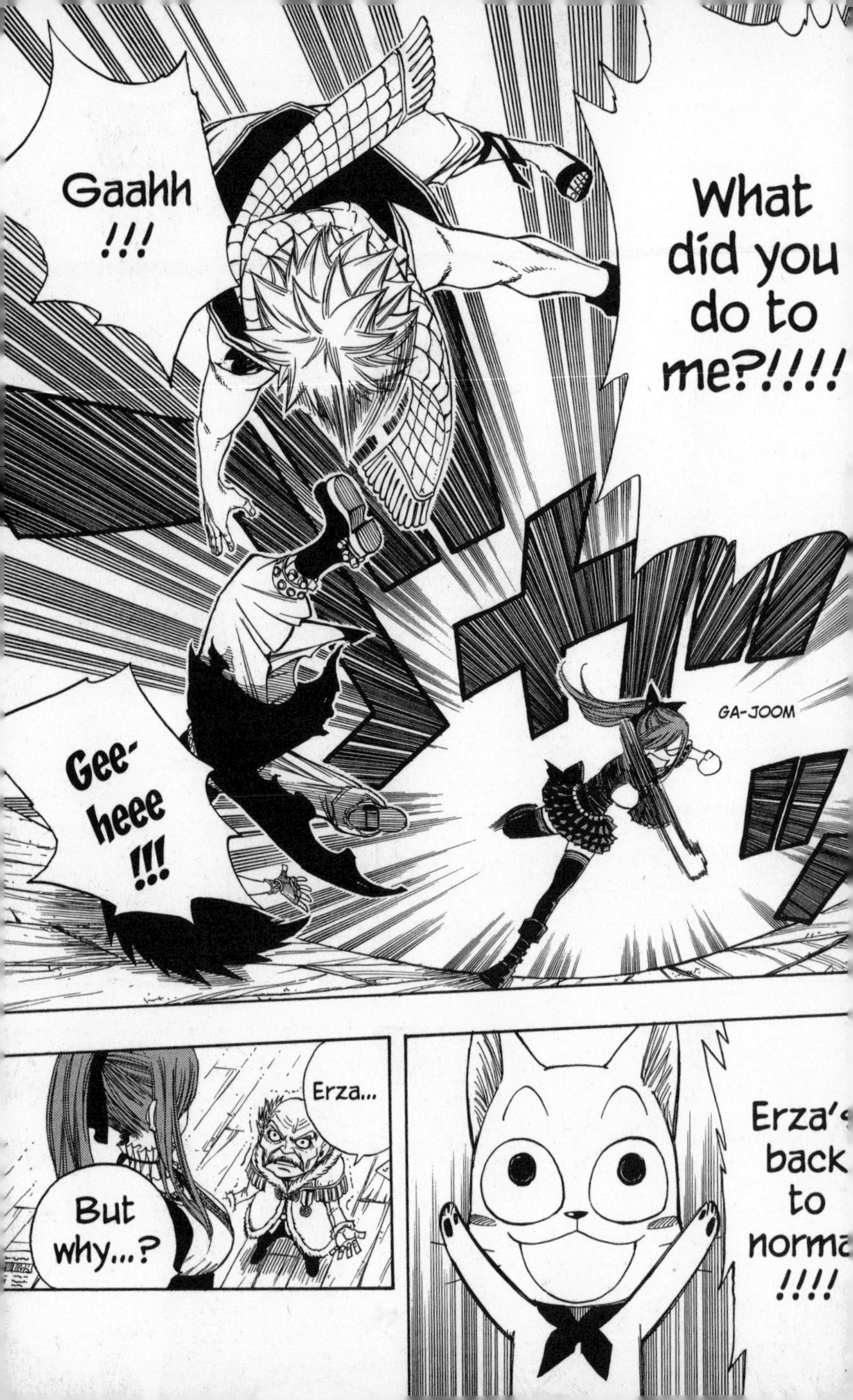
What did you do to me?!!!!
Gaahh!!!
GA-JOOM
Gee-heee!!!
Erza's back to norma
!!!!
Erza...
But why...?

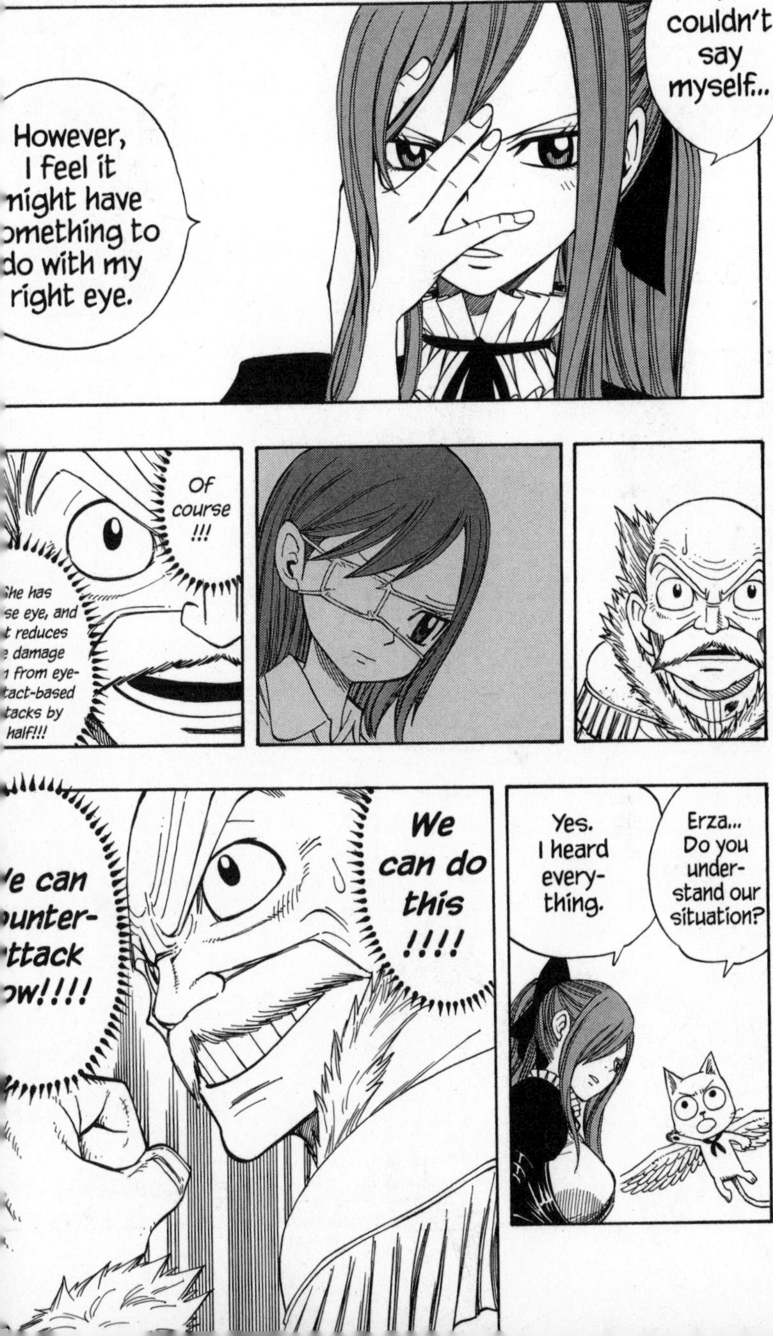

I couldn't say myself...
However, I feel it night have omething to do with my right eye.
Of course!!!
She has se eye, and t reduces e damage n from eye- tact-based tacks by half!!!
Erza... Do you under- stand our situation?
Yes. I heard every- thing.
We can do this!!!!
'e can ounter- ttack ow!!!!

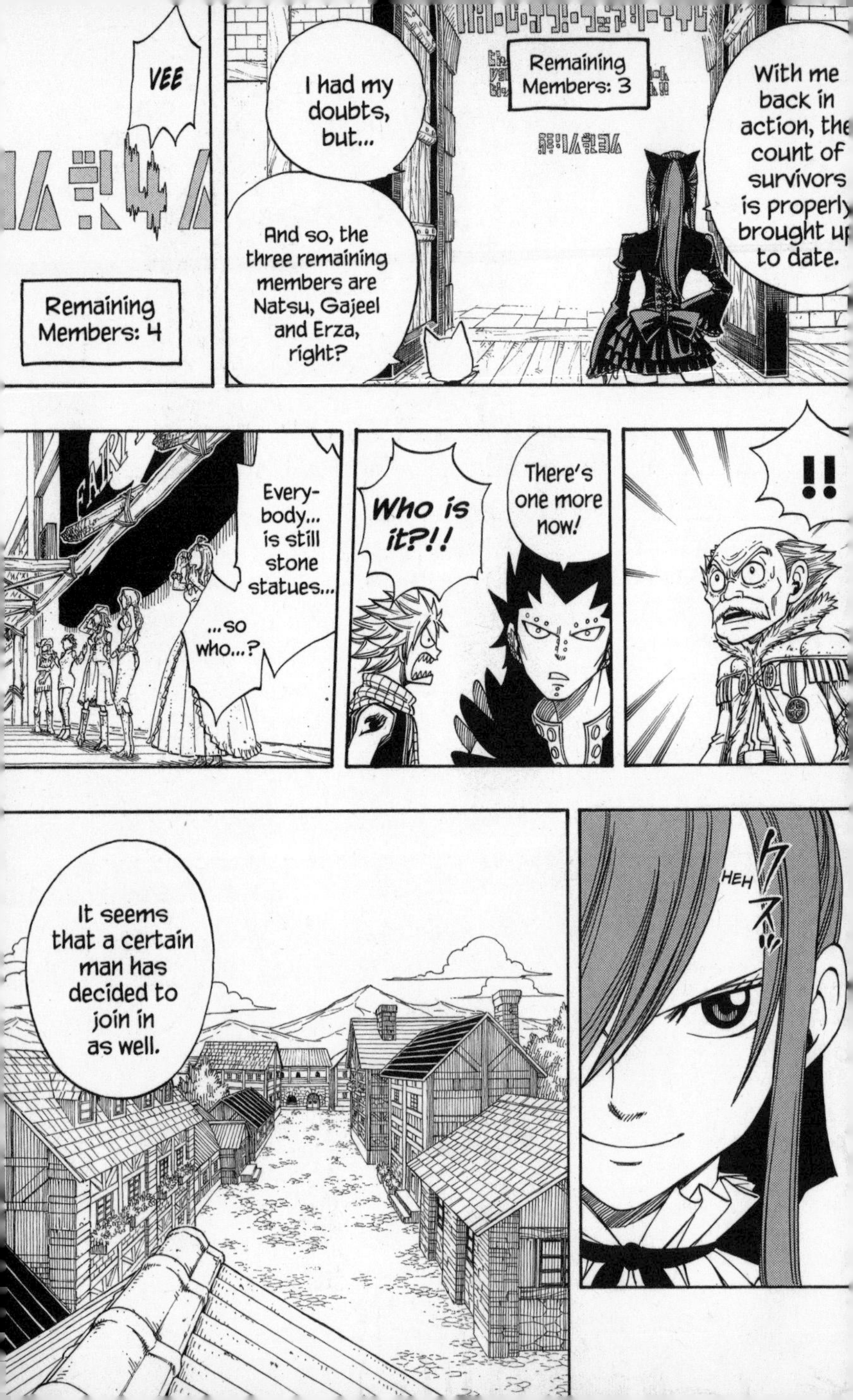
With me back in action, the count of survivors is properly brought up to date.
Remaining Members: 3
I had my doubts, but...
And so, the three remaining members are Natsu, Gajeel and Erza, right?
VEE
Remaining Members: 4
!!
There's one more now!
Who is it?!!
Everybody... is still stone statues...
...so who...?
HEH
It seems that a certain man has decided to join in as well.

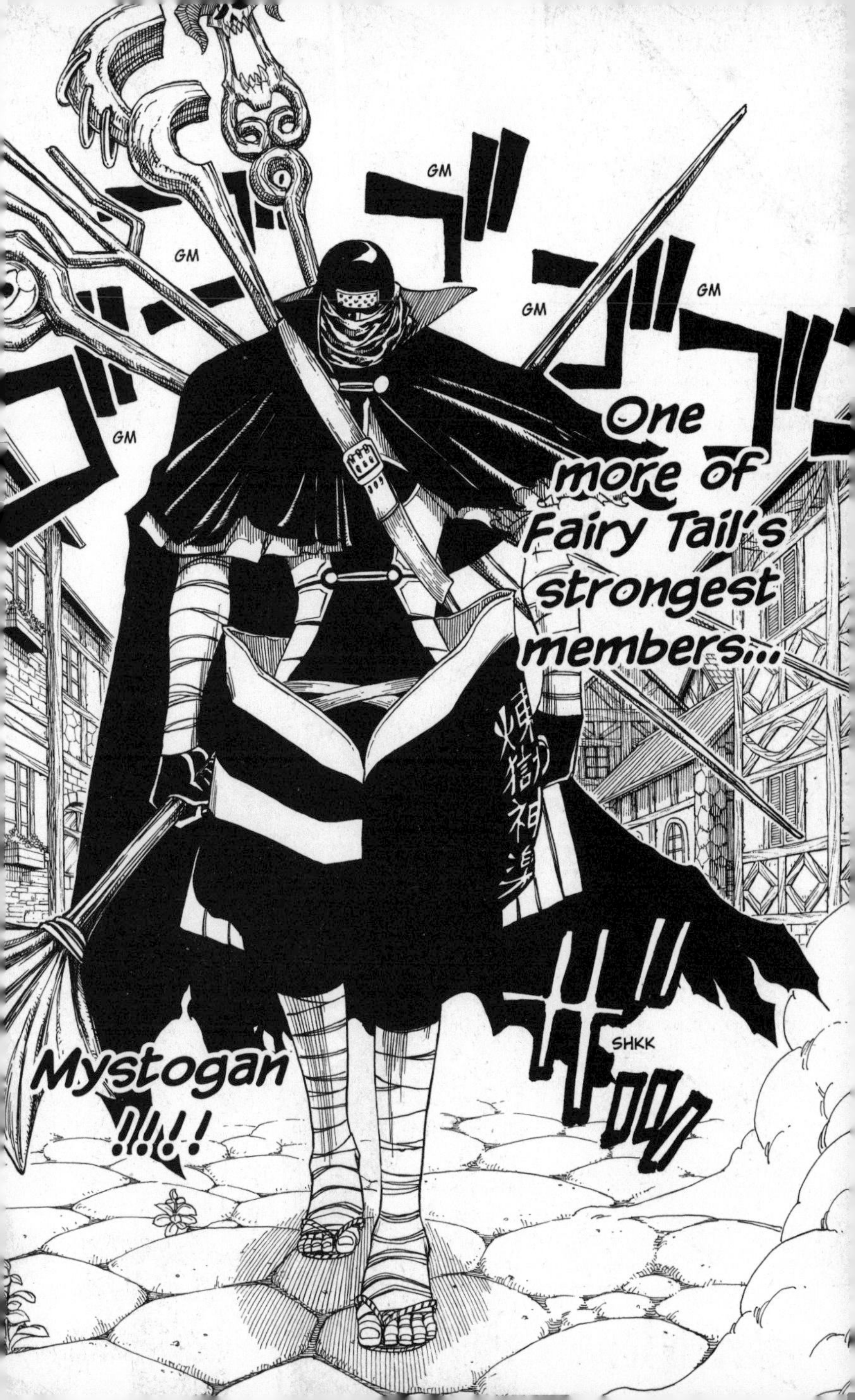
GM
GM
GM
One more of Fairy Tail's strongest members...
GM
GM
SHKK
Mystogan !!!!!

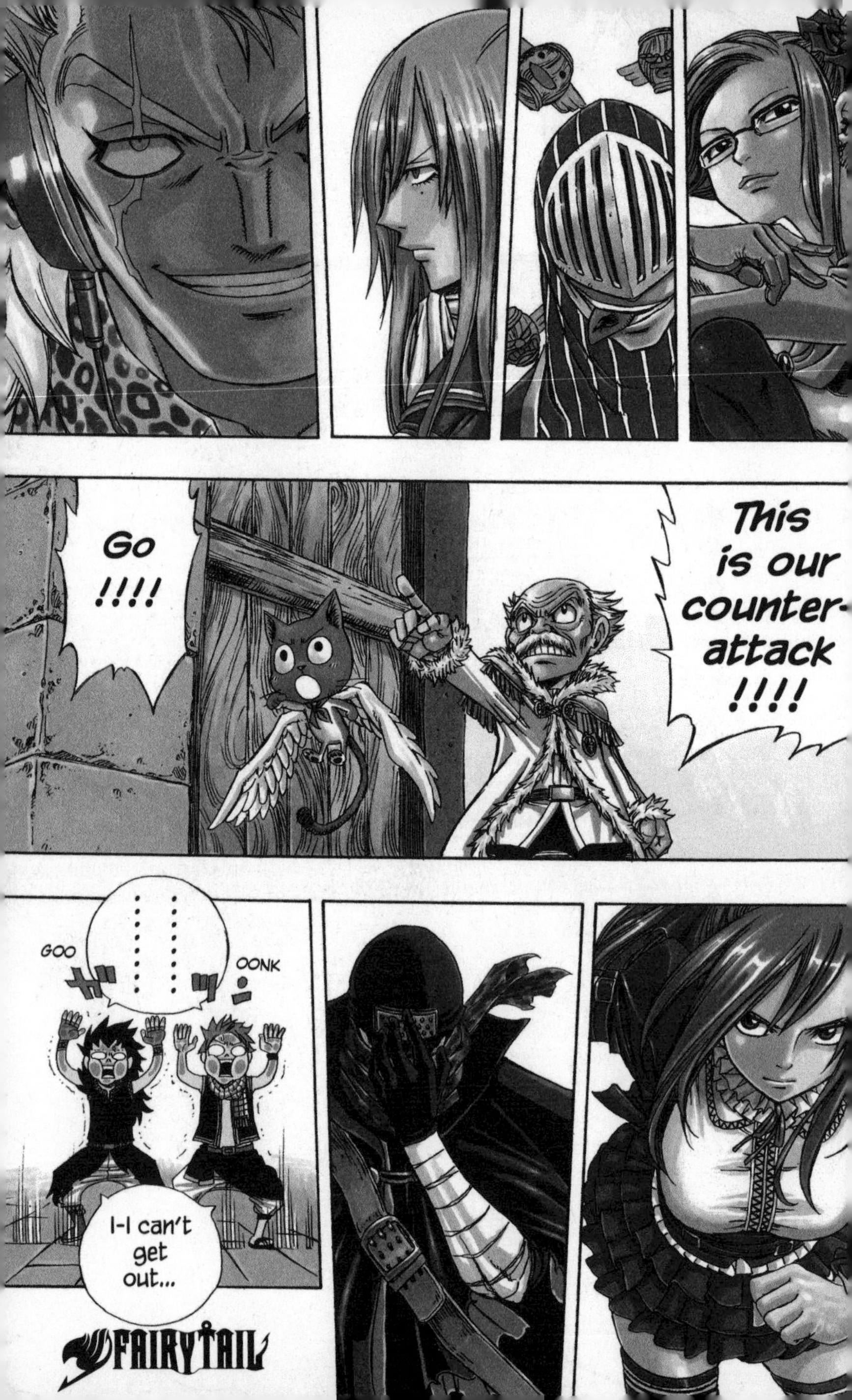
This is our counter-attack !!!!
Go !!!!
......
OONK
GOO
I-I can't get out...
FAIRY TAIL

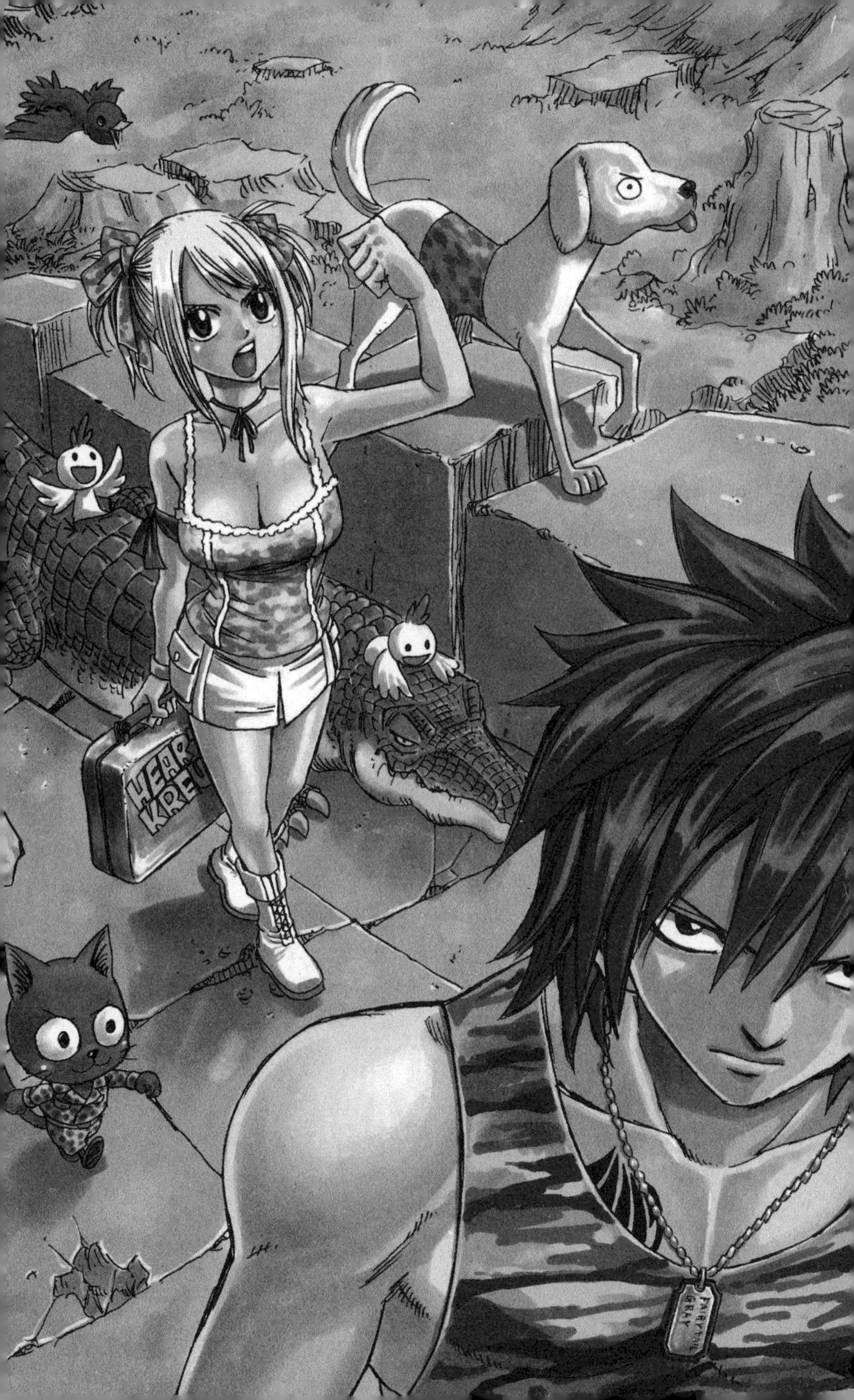
FAIRY TAIL
GRAY

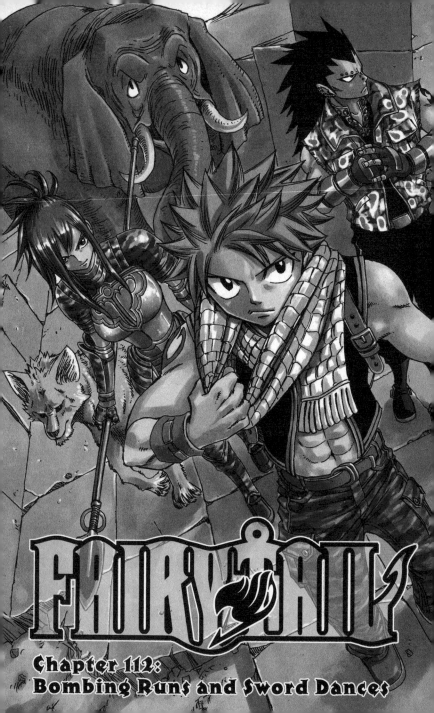

FAIRY TAIL

Chapter 112:
Bombing Runs and Sword Dances

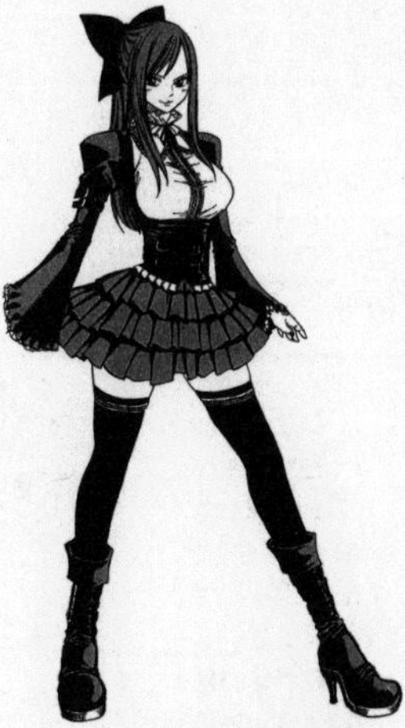

FAIRY TAIL

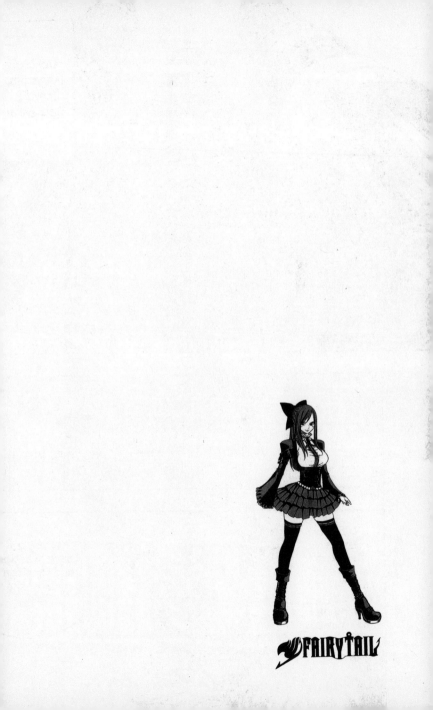

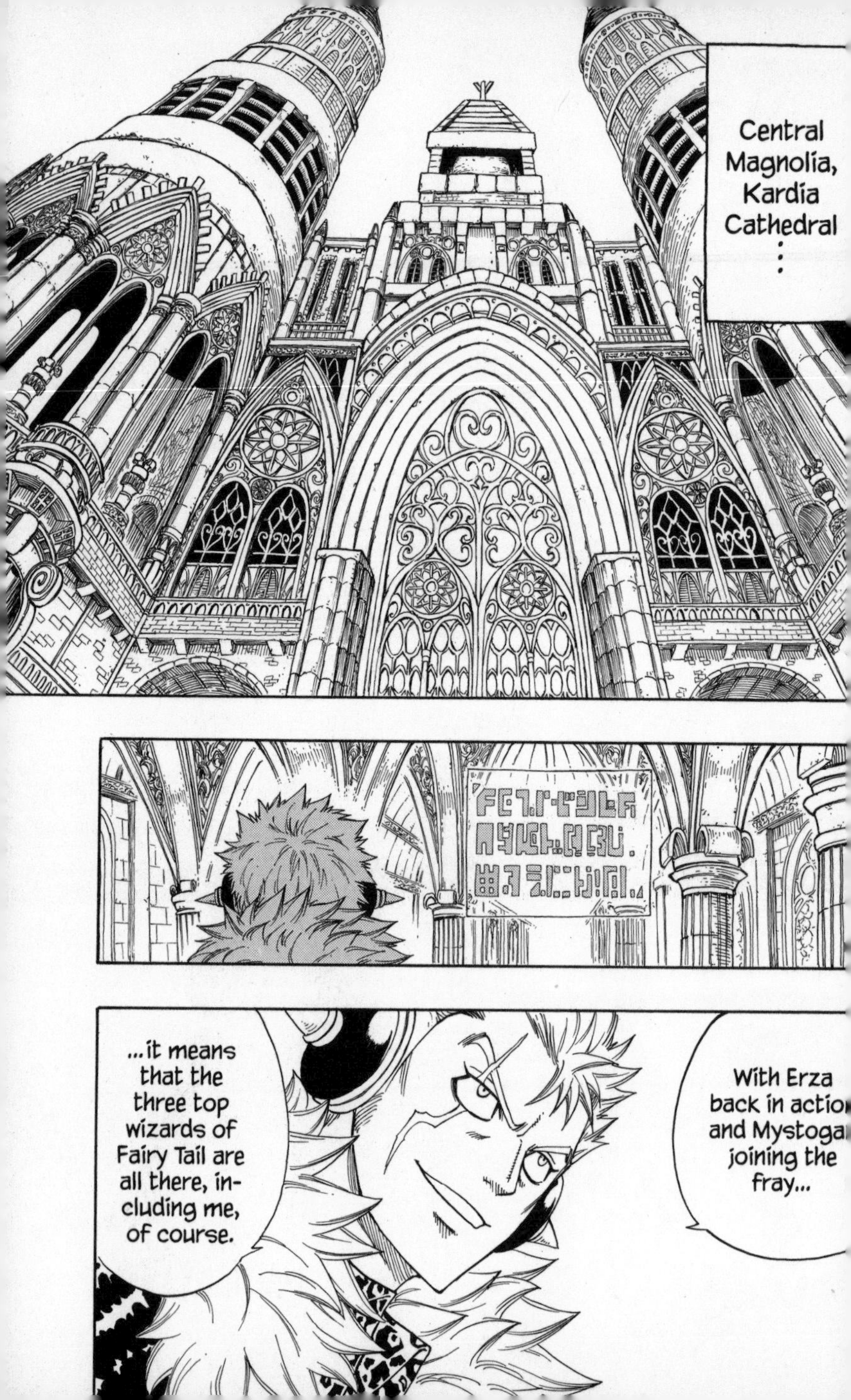
Central Magnolia, Kardia Cathedral
With Erza back in actio and Mystoga joining the fray...
...it means that the three top wizards of Fairy Tail are all there, including me, of course.

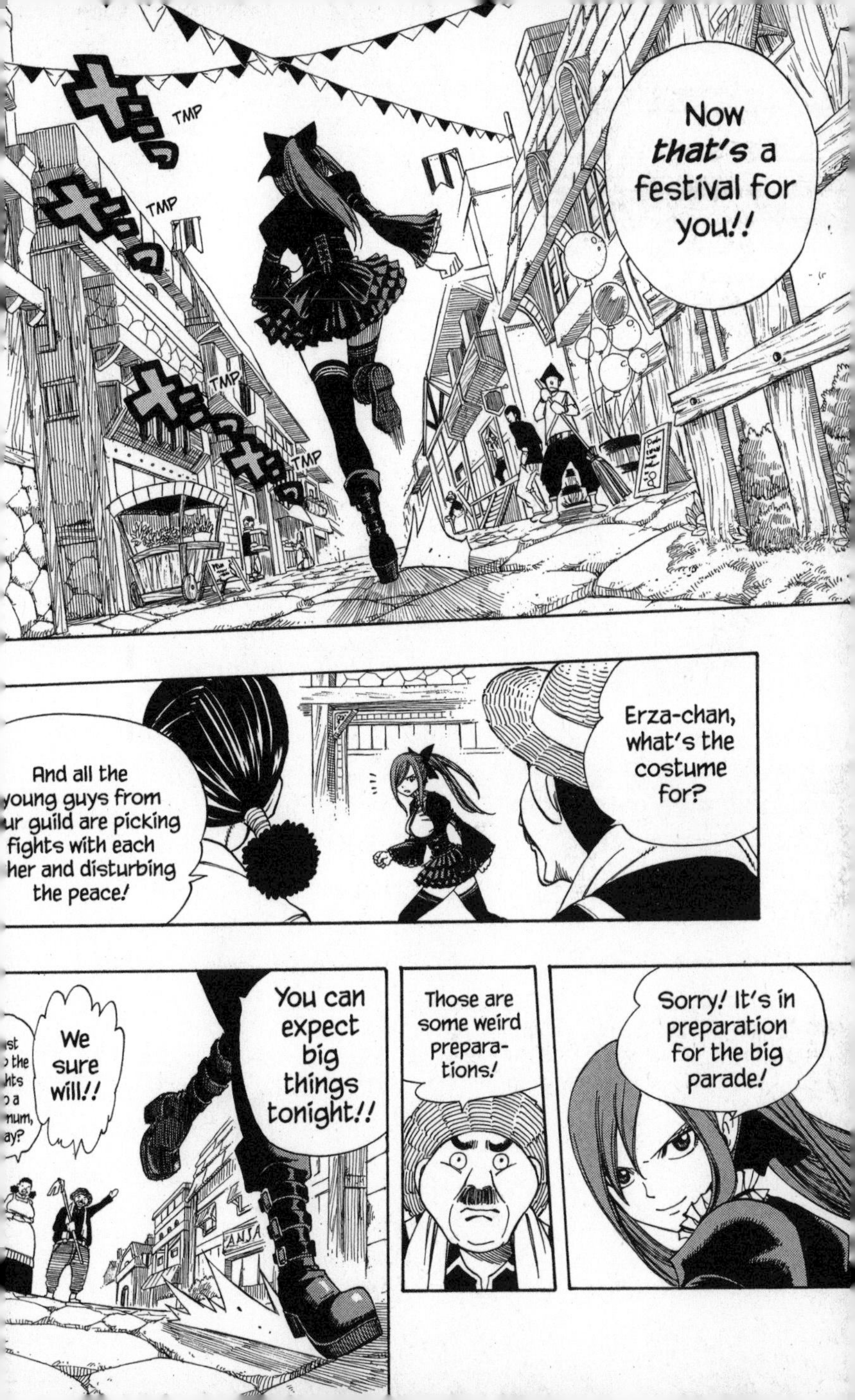
TMP
TMP
TMP
TMP
Now that's a festival for you!!
Erza-chan, what's the costume for?
And all the young guys from ur guild are picking fights with each her and disturbing the peace!
Sorry! It's in preparation for the big parade!
Those are some weird prepara-tions!
You can expect big things tonight!!
We sure will!!

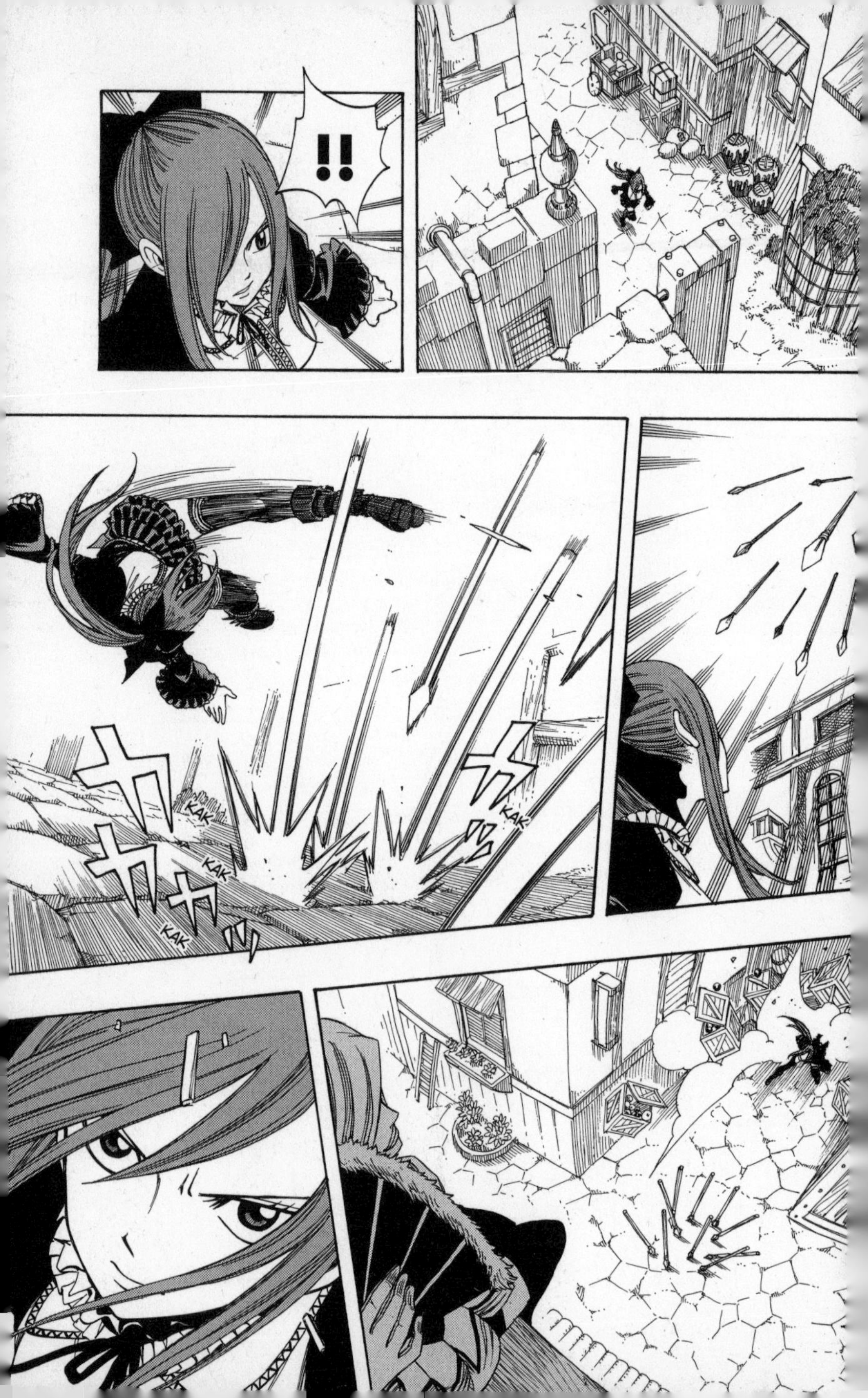
!!
KAK
KAK
KAK
KAK

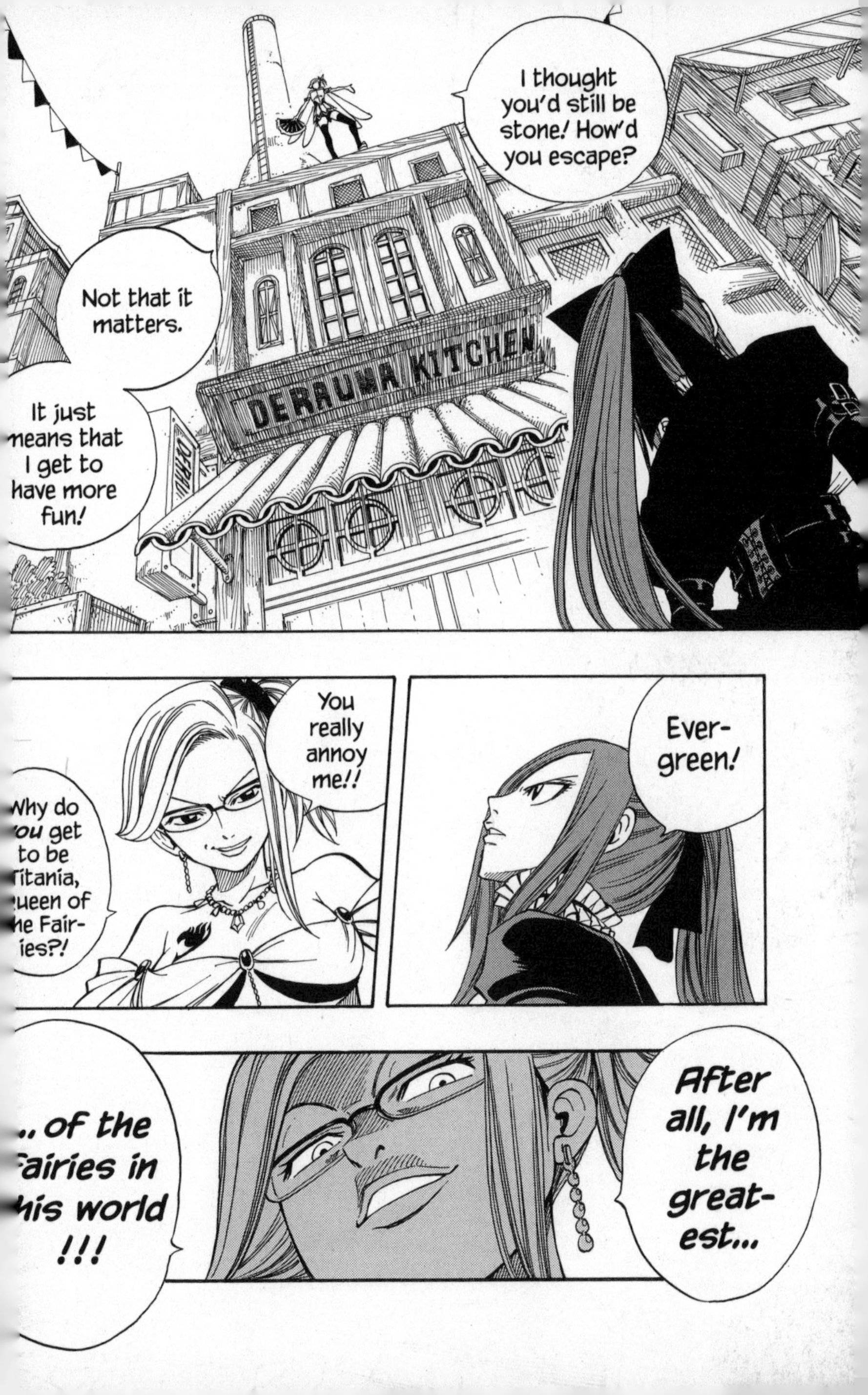
I thought you'd still be stone! How'd you escape?
DERRUMA KITCHEN
Not that it matters.
It just means that I get to have more fun!
Ever-green!
You really annoy me!!
Why do you get to be Titania, queen of the Fair-ies?!
After all, I'm the great-est...
...of the Fairies in this world!!!

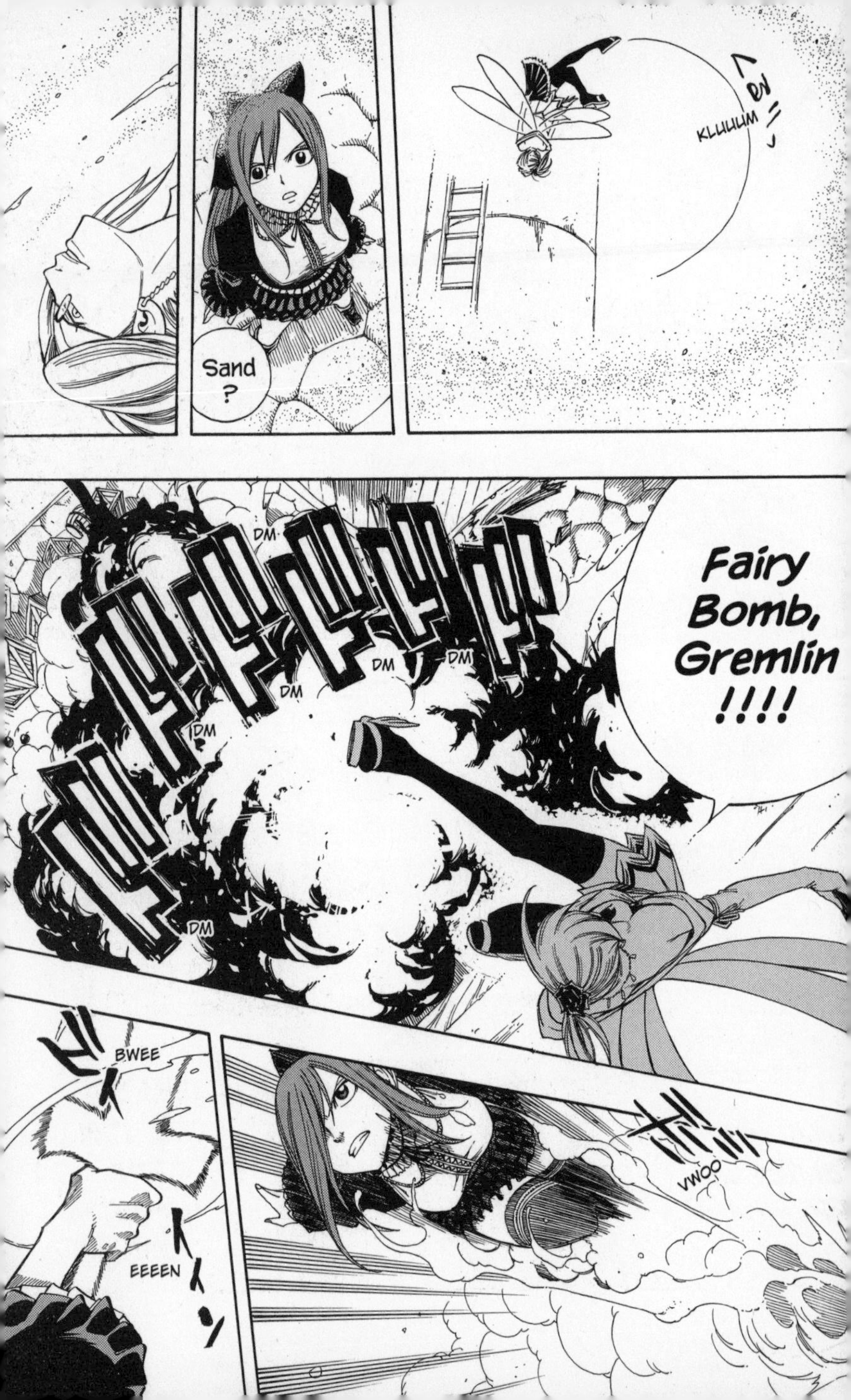
KLUUUM
Sand ?
Fairy Bomb, Gremlin !!!!
DM
DM
DM
DM
DM
DM
VWOO
BWEE
EEEEN

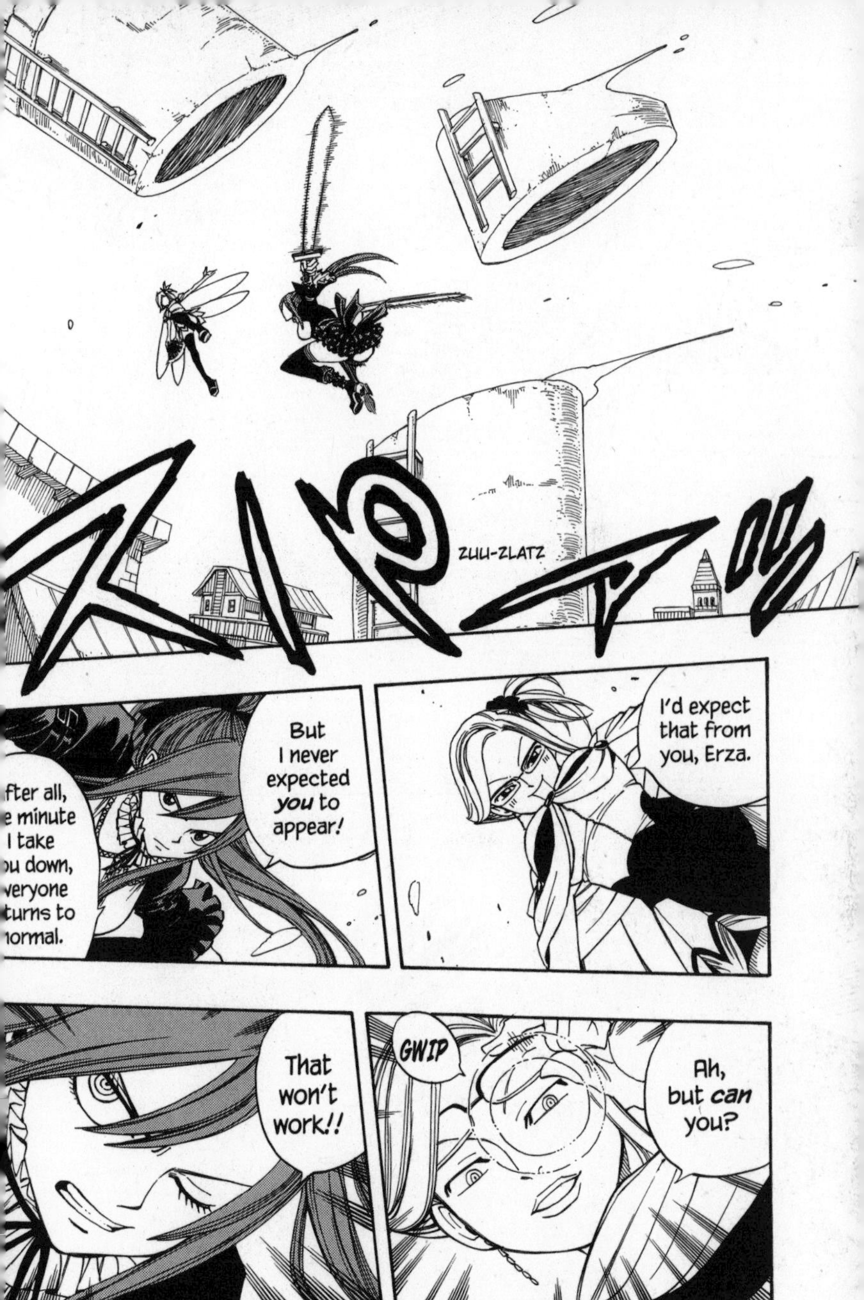
ZUU-ZLATZ
I'd expect that from you, Erza.
But I never expected *you* to appear!
fter all, e minute I take u down, veryone turns to normal.
GWIP
Ah, but *can* you?
That won't work!!

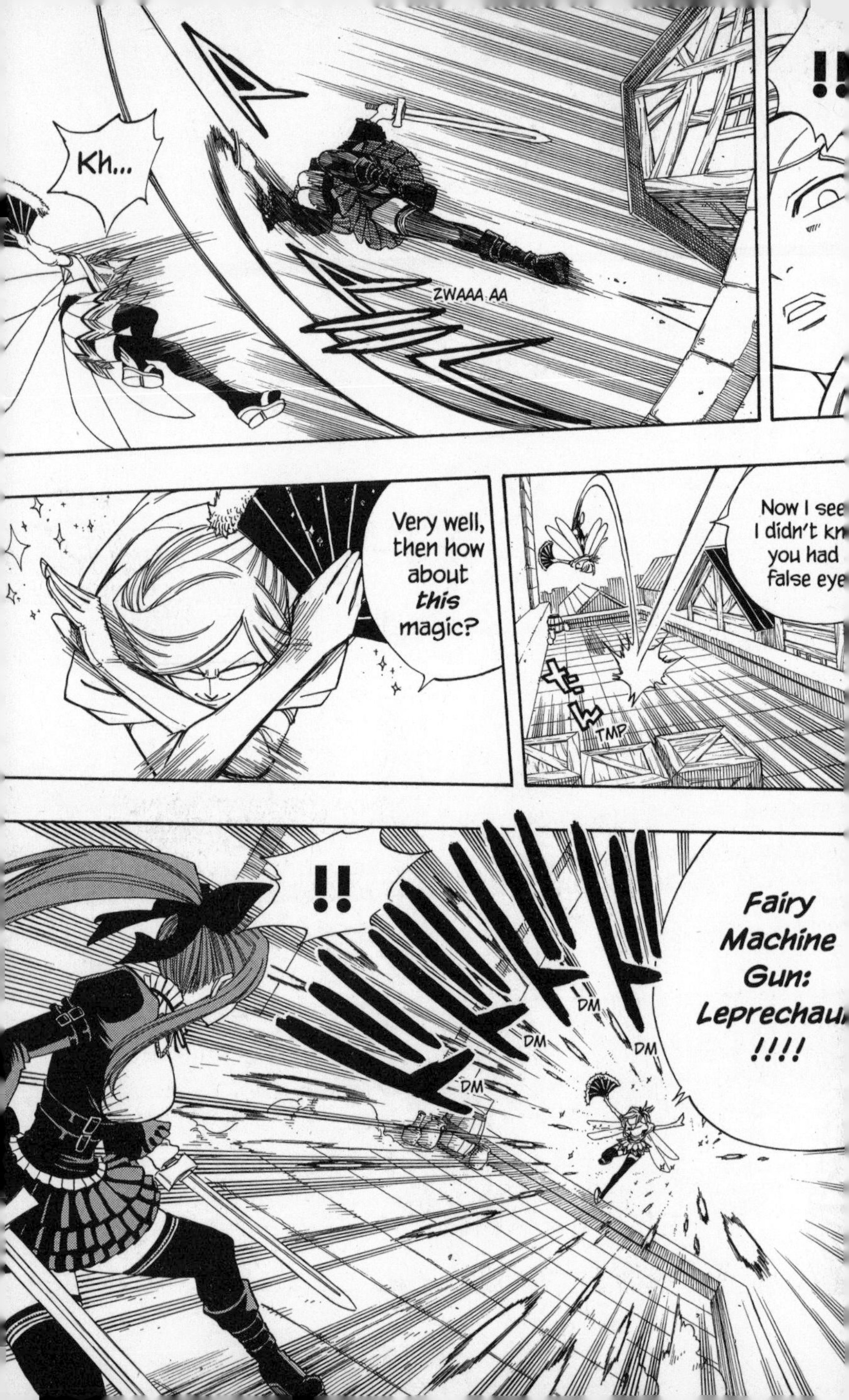
!!
Kh...
ZWAAA AA
Now I see I didn't kn you had false eye
TMP
Very well, then how about *this* magic?
Fairy Machine Gun: Leprechau !!!!
!!
DM
DM
DM
DM

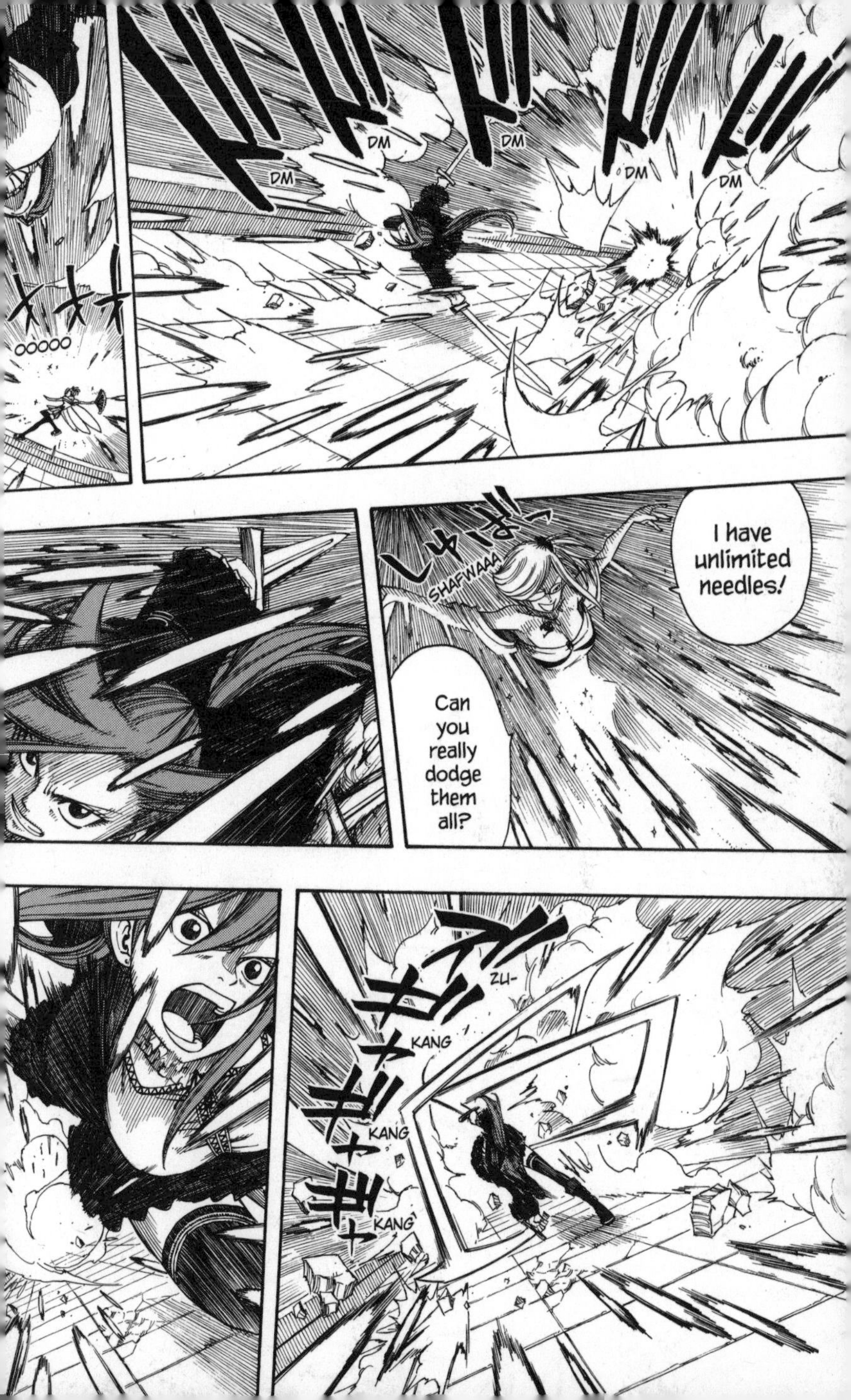
DM
DM
DM
DM
DM
ooooo
SHAFWAAA
I have unlimited needles!
Can you really dodge them all?
ZU-
KANG
KANG
KANG

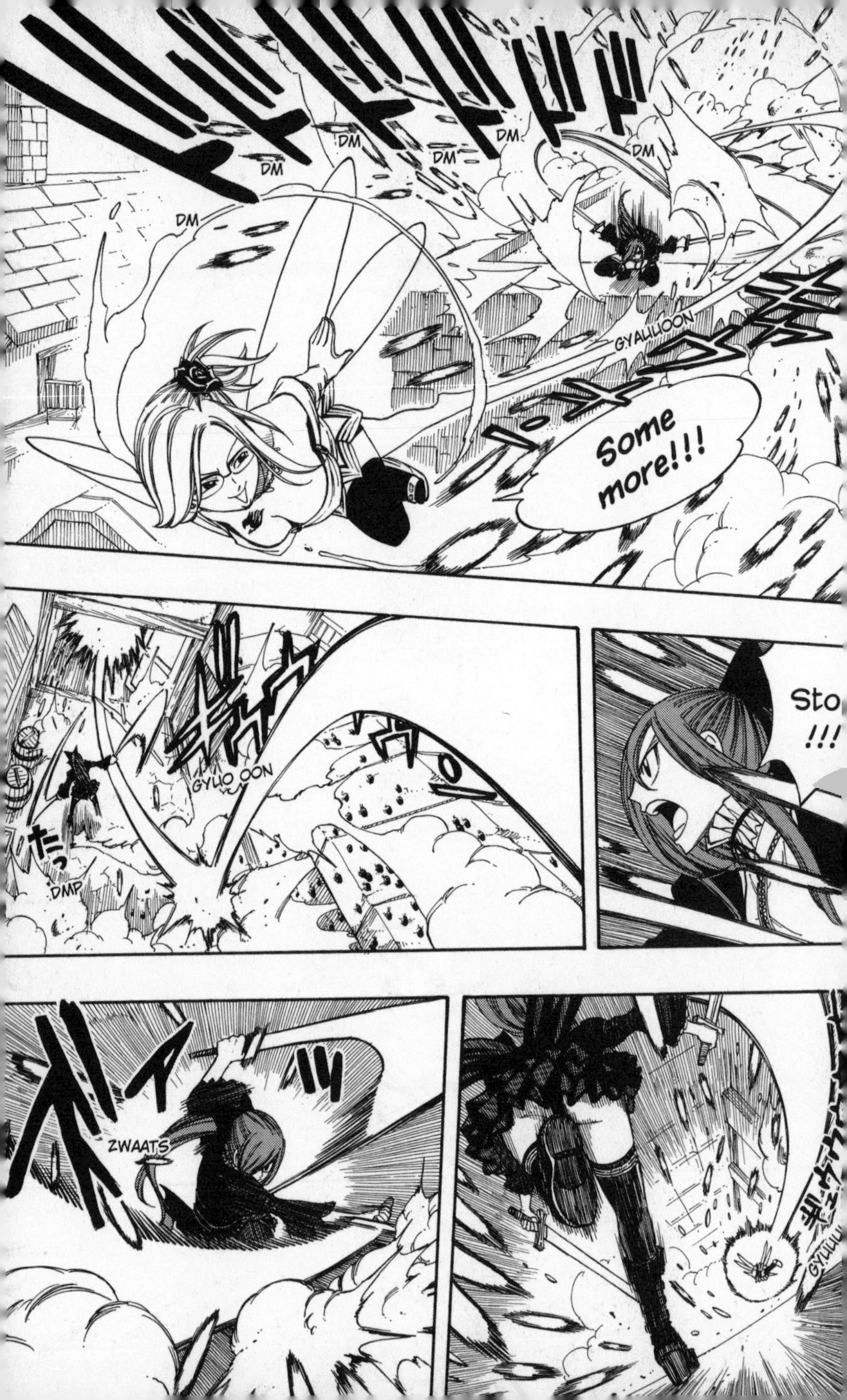
DM
DM
DM
DM
DM
DM
GYAUUOON
Some more!!!
Sto
!!!
GYUO OON
DMP
GYUUU
ZWAATS

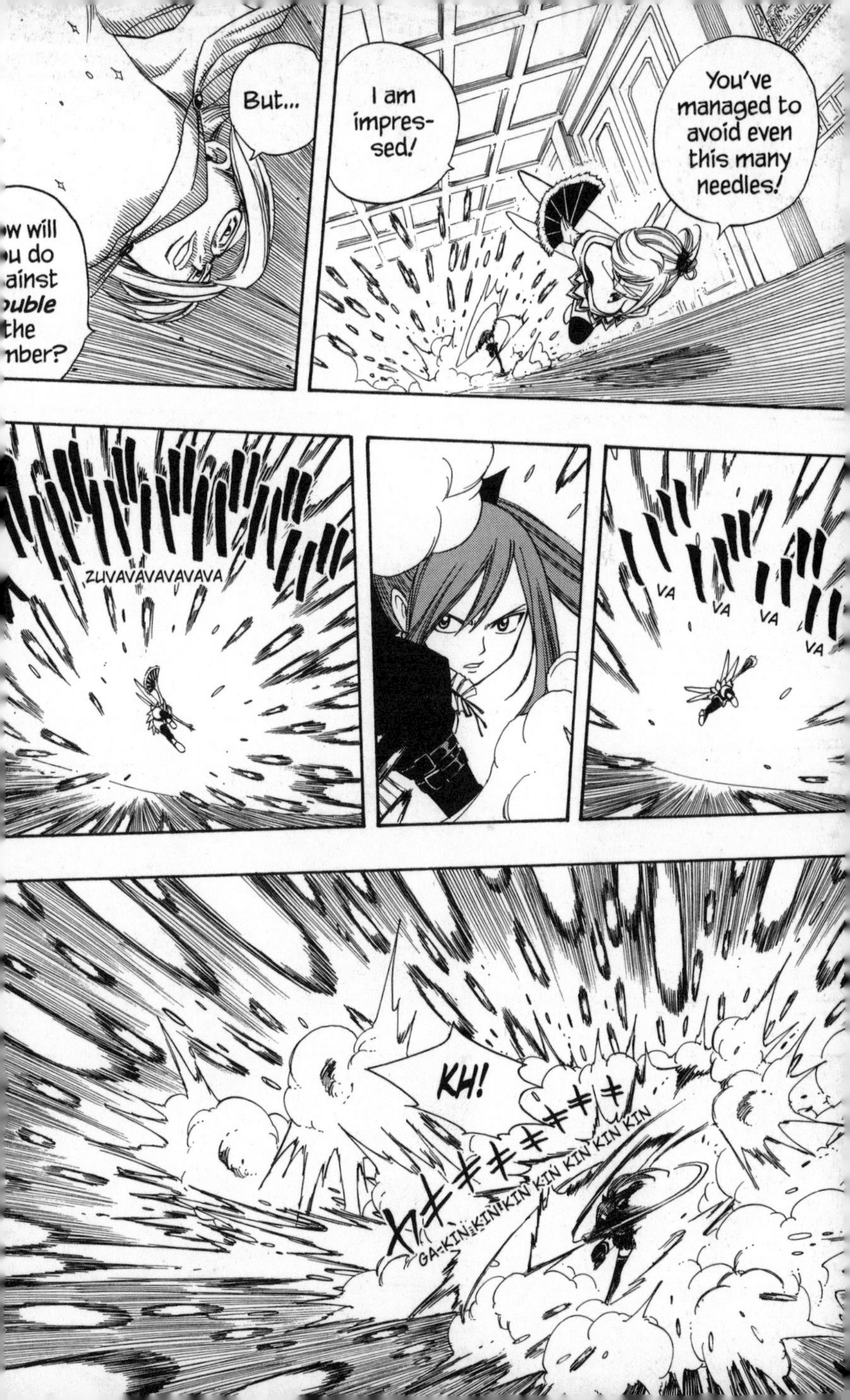
You've managed to avoid even this many needles!
I am impressed!
But...
w will u do ainst uble the nber?
VA VA VA VA
ZUVAVAVAVAVAVA
KH!
GA-KIN KIN KIN KIN KIN KIN

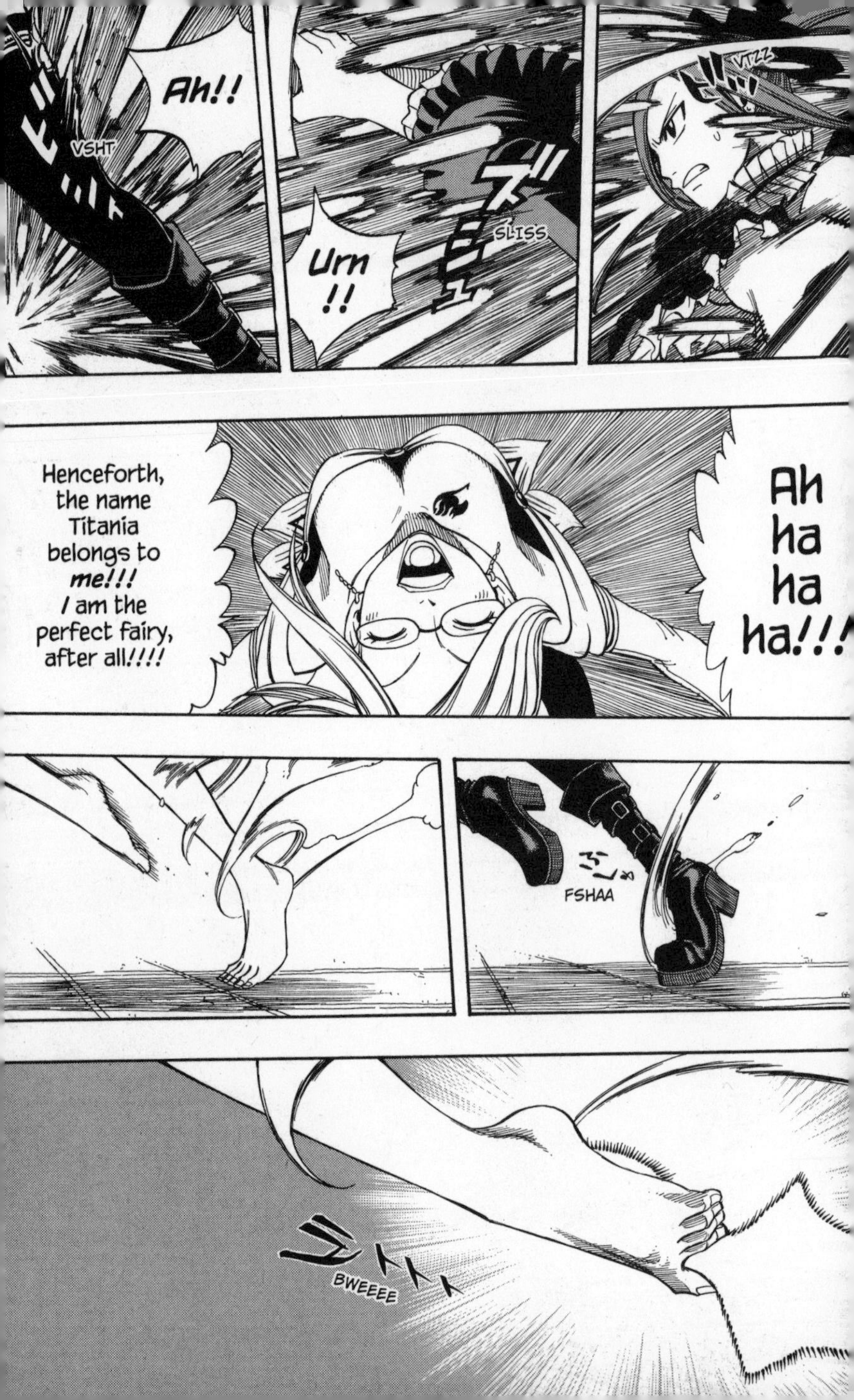
VTZZ
Urn!!
SLISS
Ah!!
VSHT
Ah ha ha ha!!!
Henceforth, the name Titania belongs to *me!!!* I am the perfect fairy, after all!!!!
FSHAA
BWEEEE

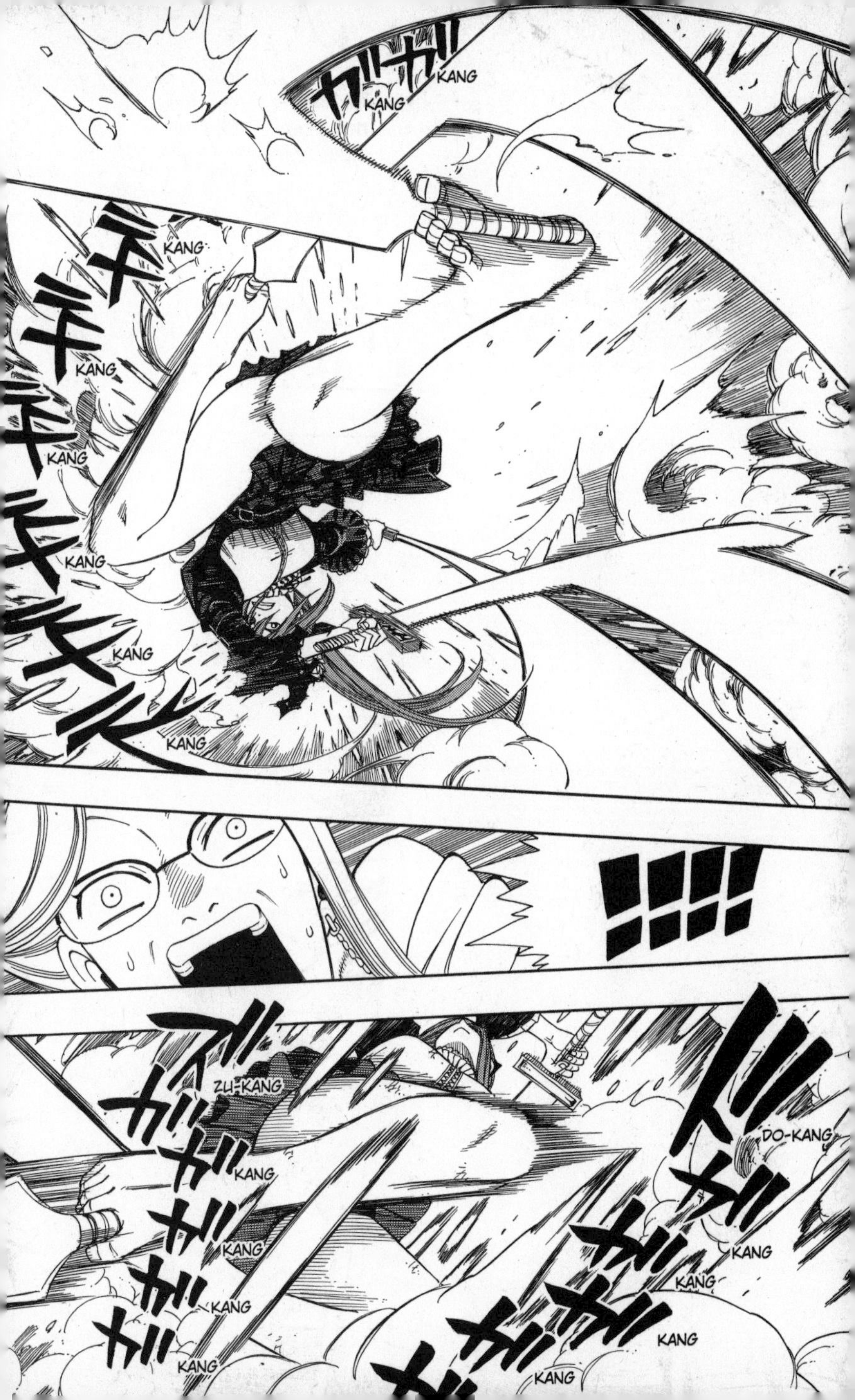
KANG
KANG
KANG
KANG
KANG
KANG
KANG
KANG
!!!!!
DO-KANG
KANG
KANG
KANG
KANG
ZU-KANG
KANG
KANG
KANG
KANG

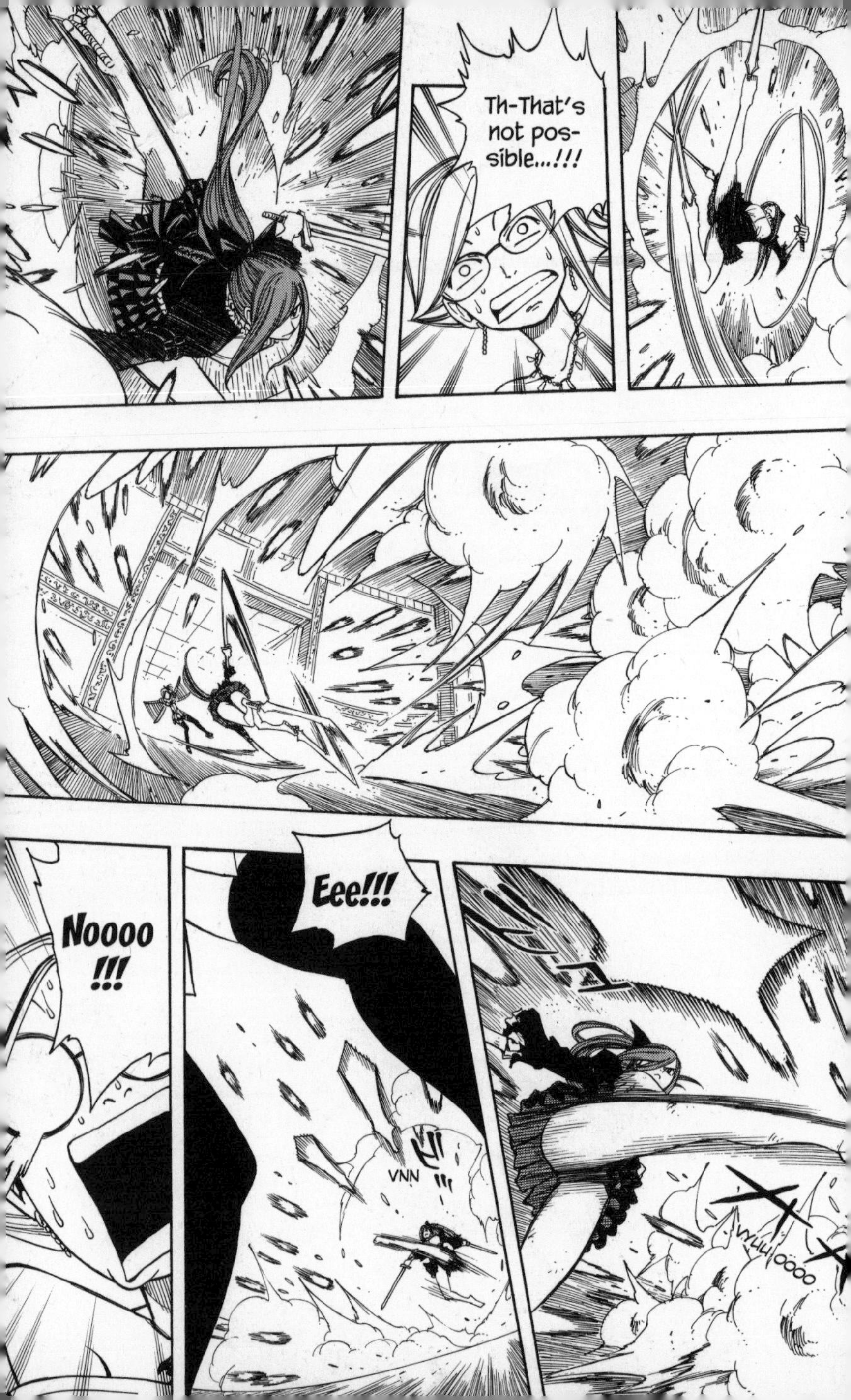
Th-That's not pos-sible...!!!
VVUUOOOO
VNN
Eee!!!
Noooo !!!

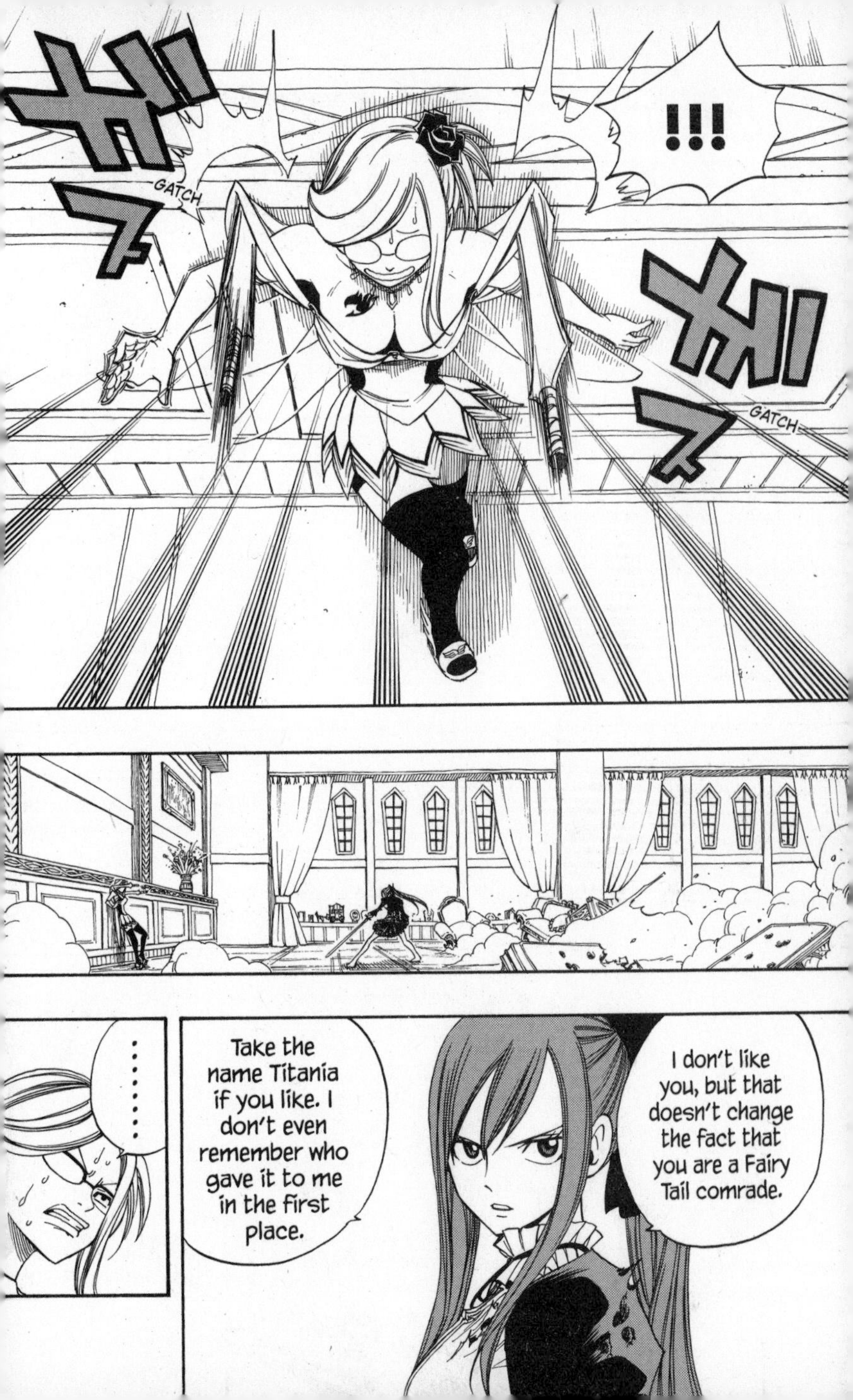
!!!
GATCH
GATCH
I don't like you, but that doesn't change the fact that you are a Fairy Tail comrade.
Take the name Titania if you like. I don't even remember who gave it to me in the first place.
......

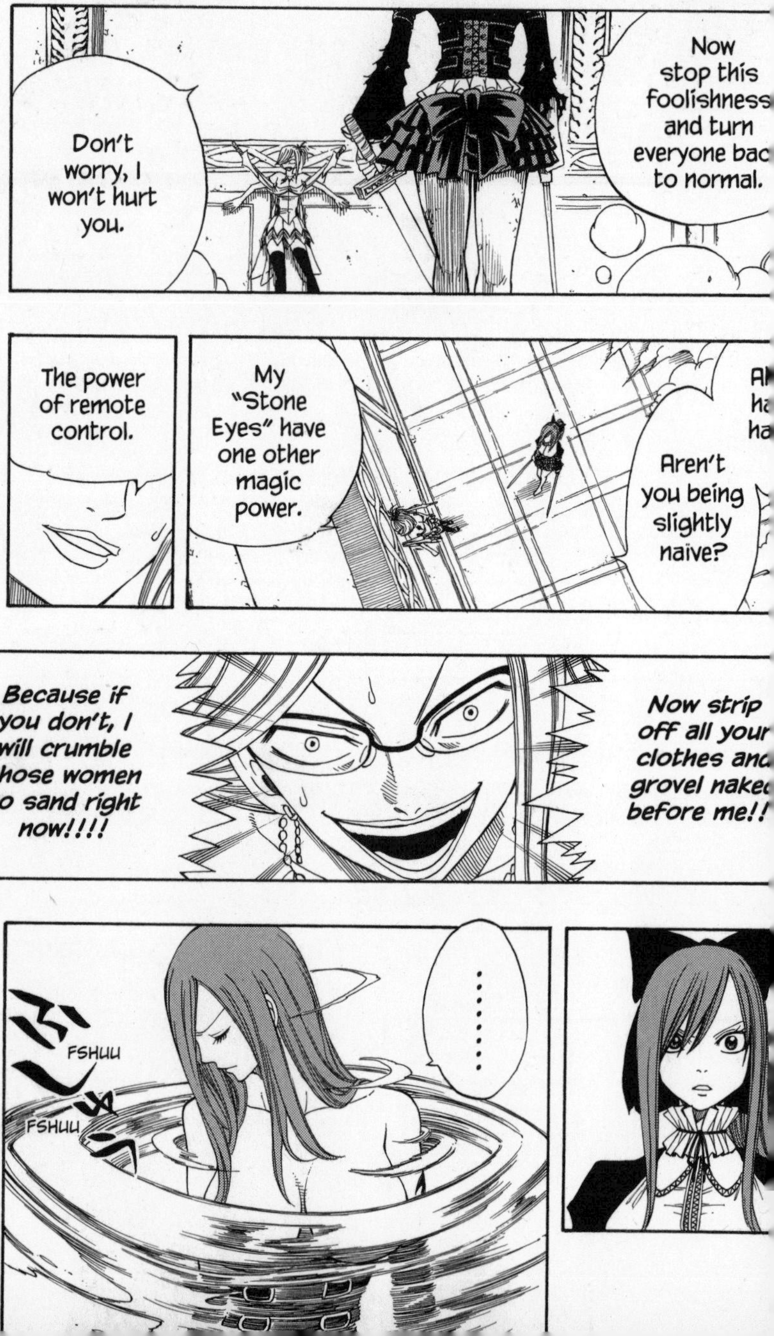
Now stop this foolishness and turn everyone bac to normal.
Don't worry, I won't hurt you.
Aren't you being slightly naïve?
My "Stone Eyes" have one other magic power.
The power of remote control.
Now strip off all your clothes and grovel nake before me!!
Because if you don't, I will crumble those women to sand right now!!!!
......
FSHUU
FSHUU

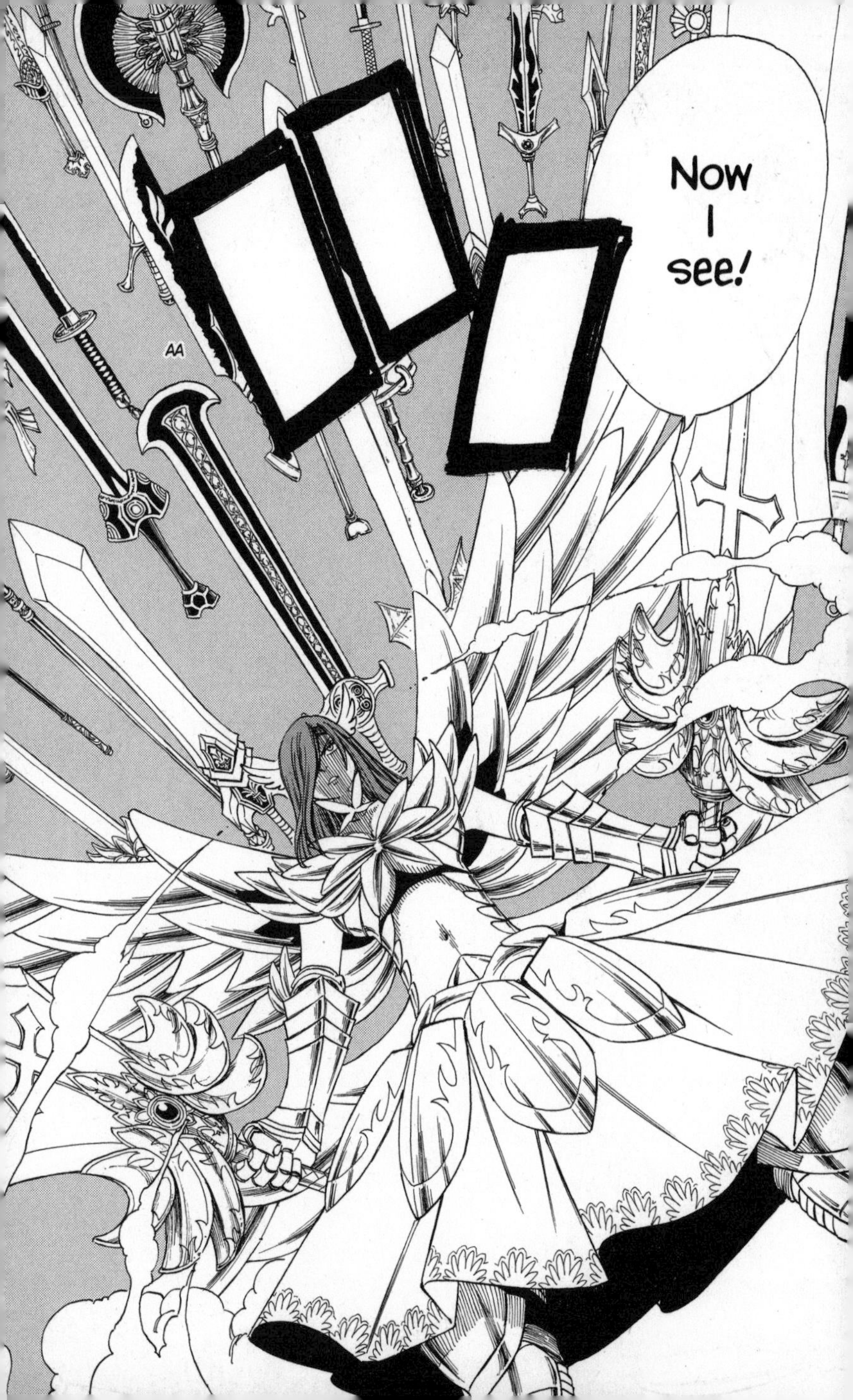
Now I see!
AA

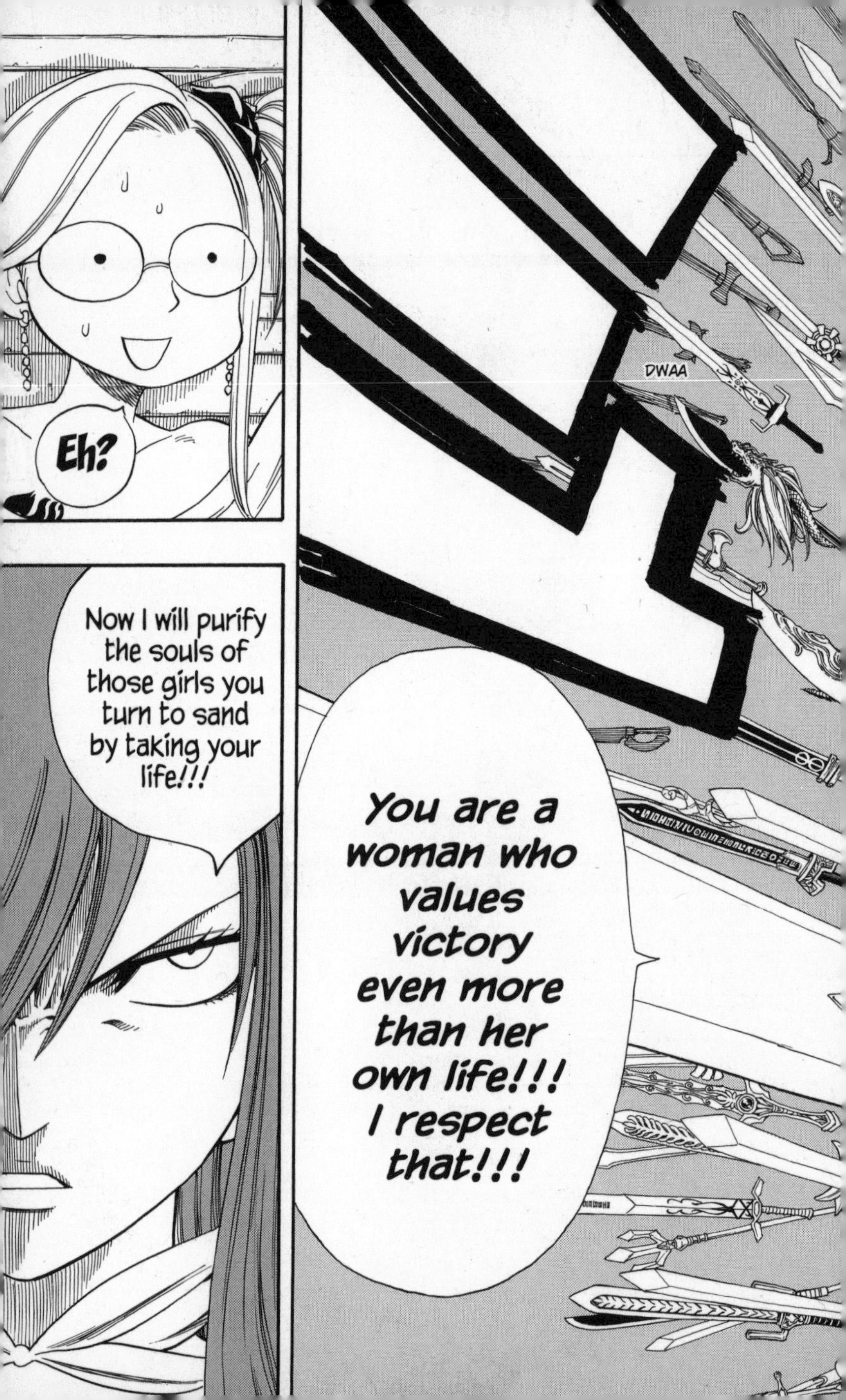
DWAA
You are a woman who values victory even more than her own life!!! I respect that!!!
Eh?
Now I will purify the souls of those girls you turn to sand by taking your life!!!

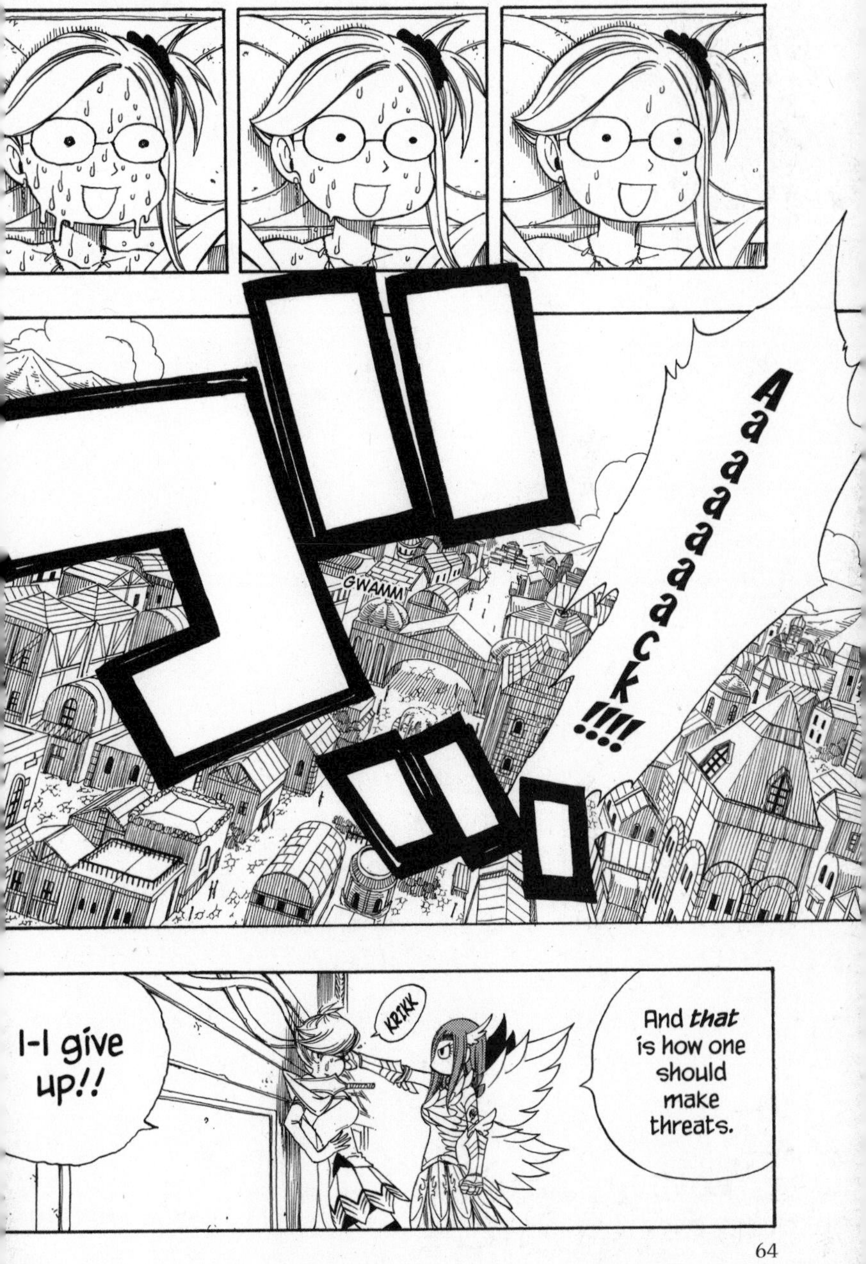
Aaaaaaaack!!!!
GWAMM
And *that* is how one should make threats.
KRIKK
I-I give up!!

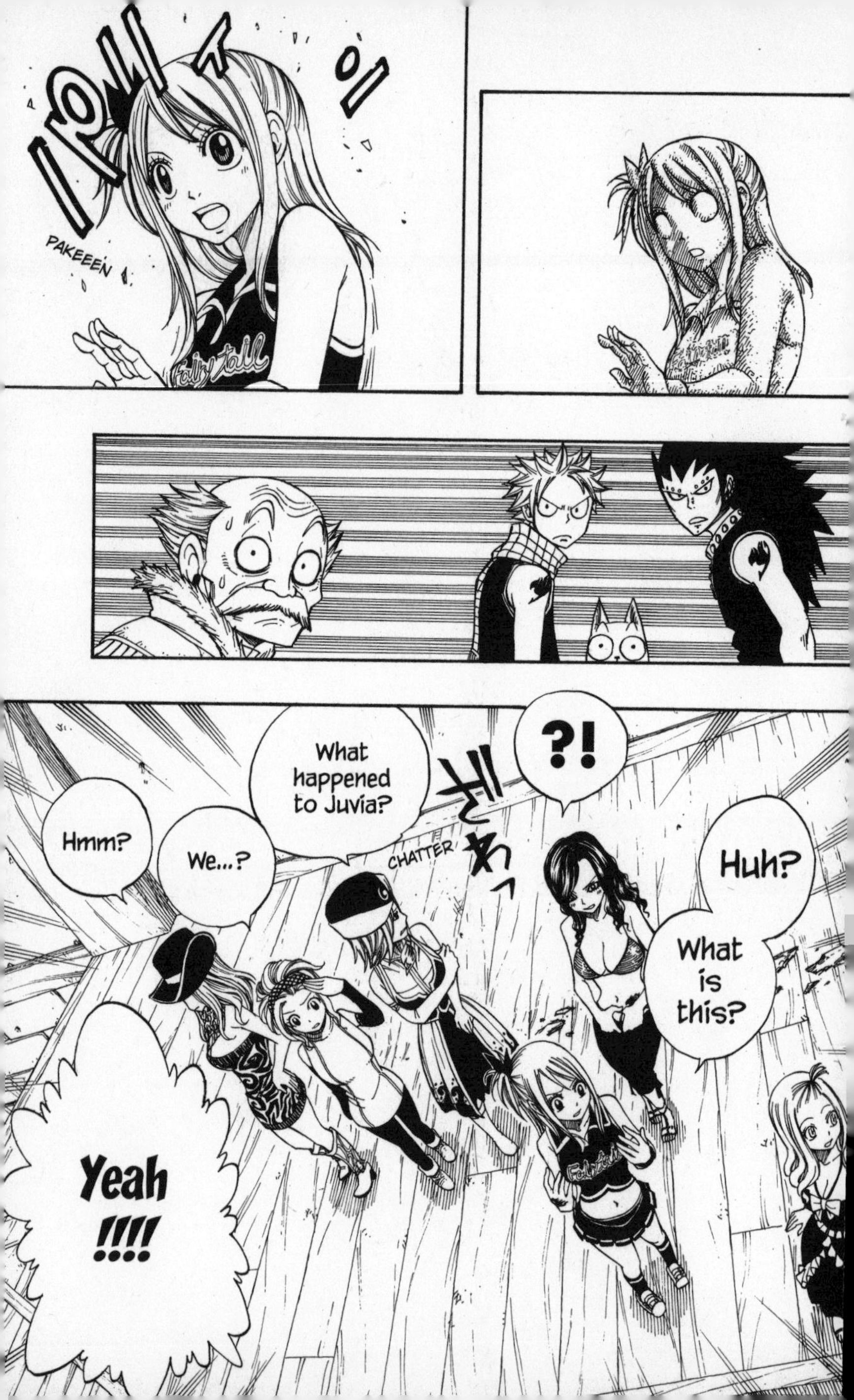
PAKEEEN
?!
Huh?
What happened to Juvia?
CHATTER
What is this?
We...?
Hmm?
Yeah !!!!

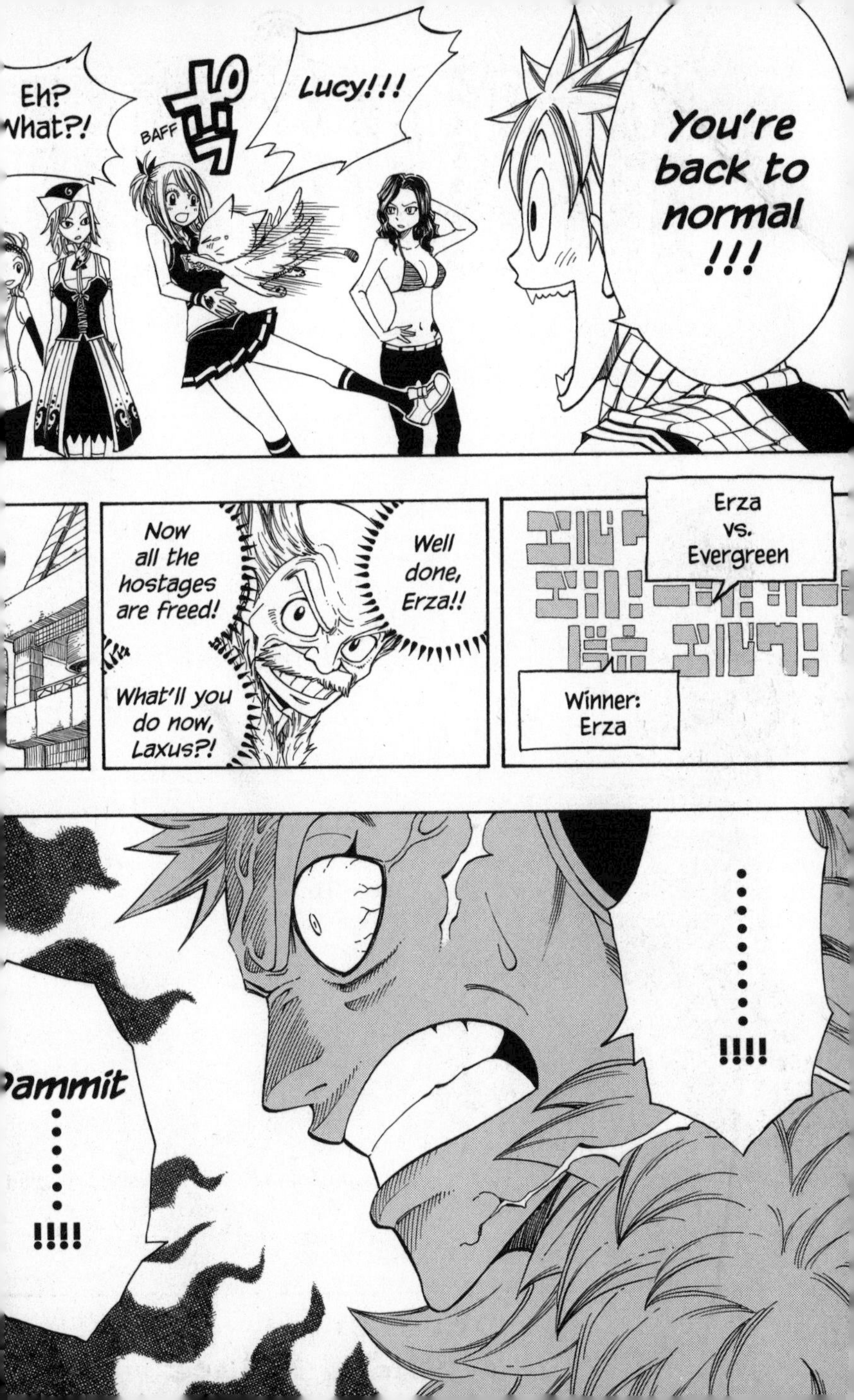
You're back to normal !!!
Lucy!!!
BAFF
Eh? What?!
Erza vs. Evergreen
Winner: Erza
Well done, Erza!!
Now all the hostages are freed!
What'll you do now, Laxus?!
......!!!!
Dammit ......!!!!

FAIRY TAIL

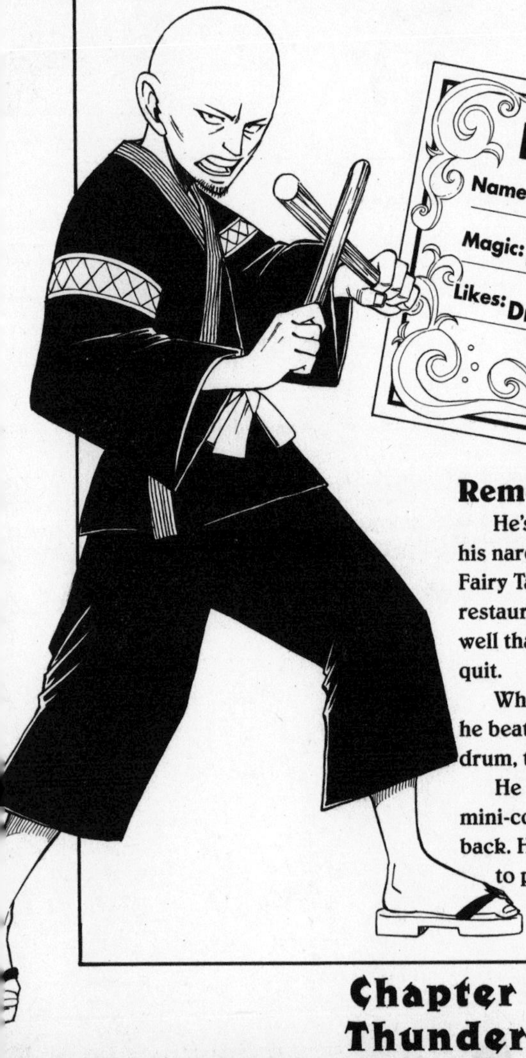

FAIRY TAIL

Name: Mikuni Shin **Age:** 16 yrs.

Magic: Earth Magic

Likes: Drums **Dislikes:** Rats

WIZARD GUILD X633

Remarks

He's a man whose appearance belies his narcissistic name. Before he entered Fairy Tail, he used to work at a sushi restaurant, and he fit the atmosphere so well that the owner begged him not to quit.

When performing his Earth Magic, he beats the ground with his sticks like a drum, thus doubling his power.

He loves the drums, and at a recent mini-concert by Mira, he couldn't hold back. He barged onto the stage and had to perform on the drum set. His dream is to one day be a producer for idol singers.

Chapter 113: Thunder Palace

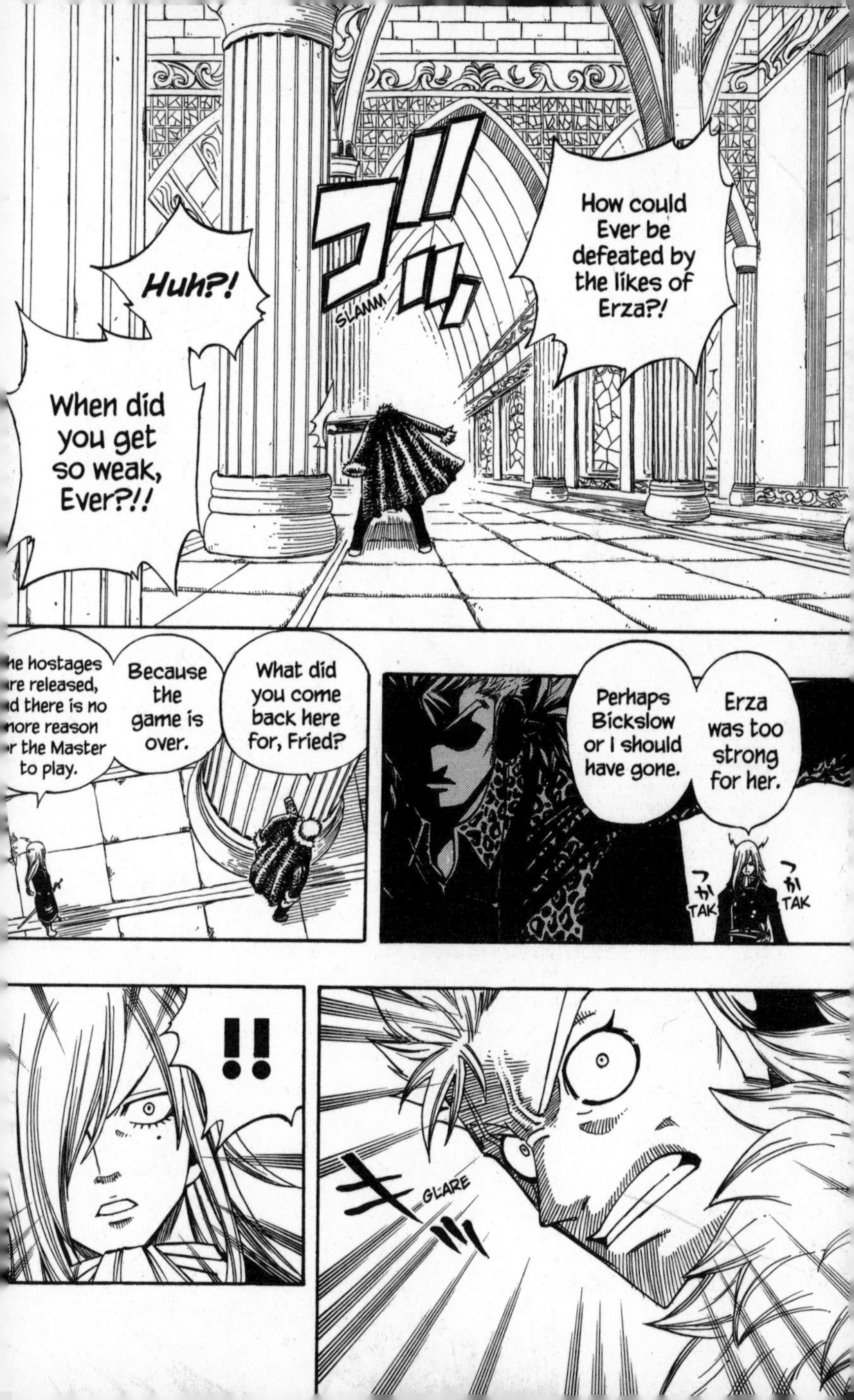

How could Ever be defeated by the likes of Erza?!
SLAMM
Huh?!
When did you get so weak, Ever?!!
Erza was too strong for her.
Perhaps Bickslow or I should have gone.
TAK
TAK
What did you come back here for, Fried?
Because the game is over.
he hostages re released, d there is no nore reason r the Master to play.
GLARE
!!

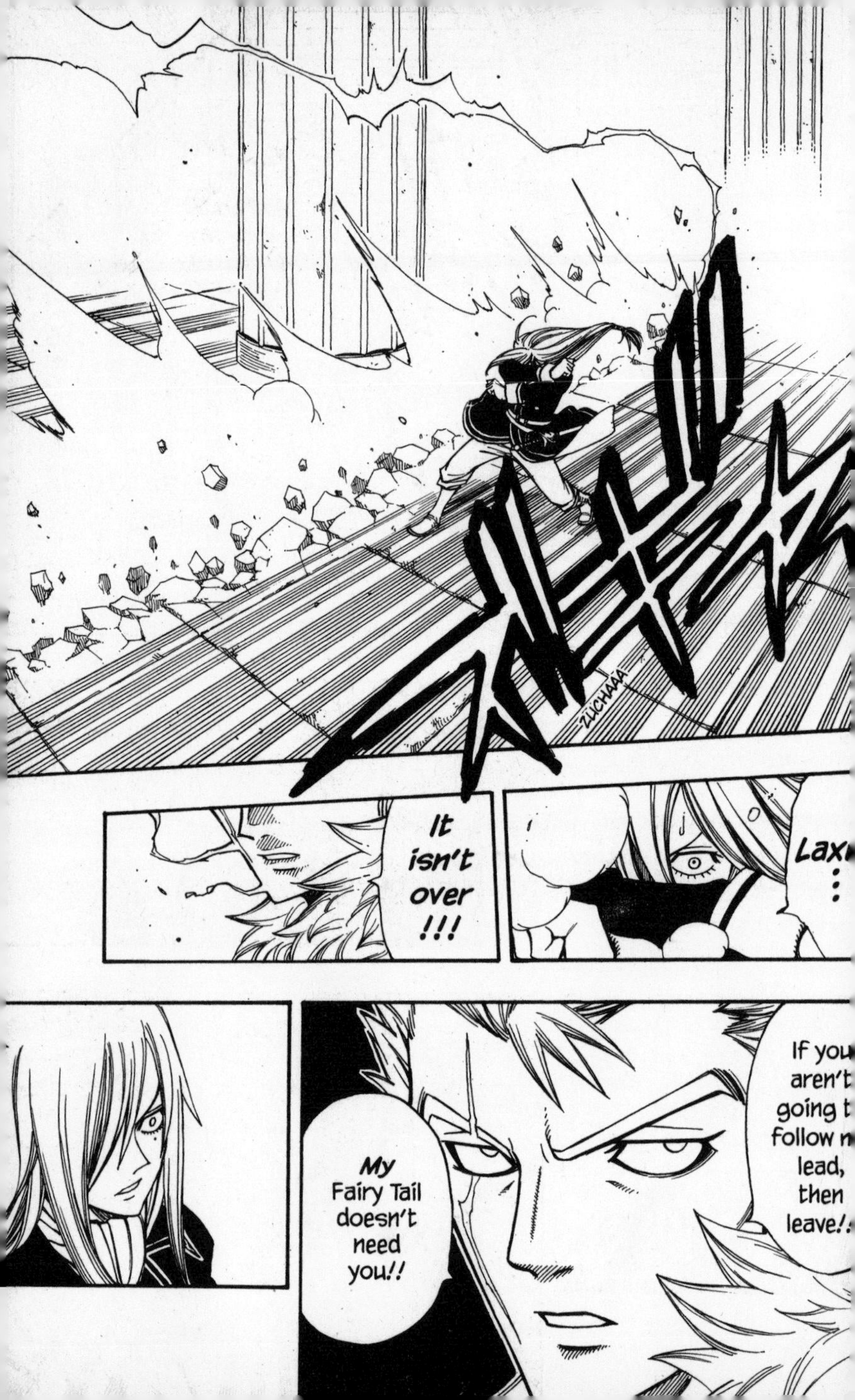
ZUCHAAA
Lax...
It isn't over!!!
If you aren't going t follow m lead, then leave!!
My Fairy Tail doesn't need you!!

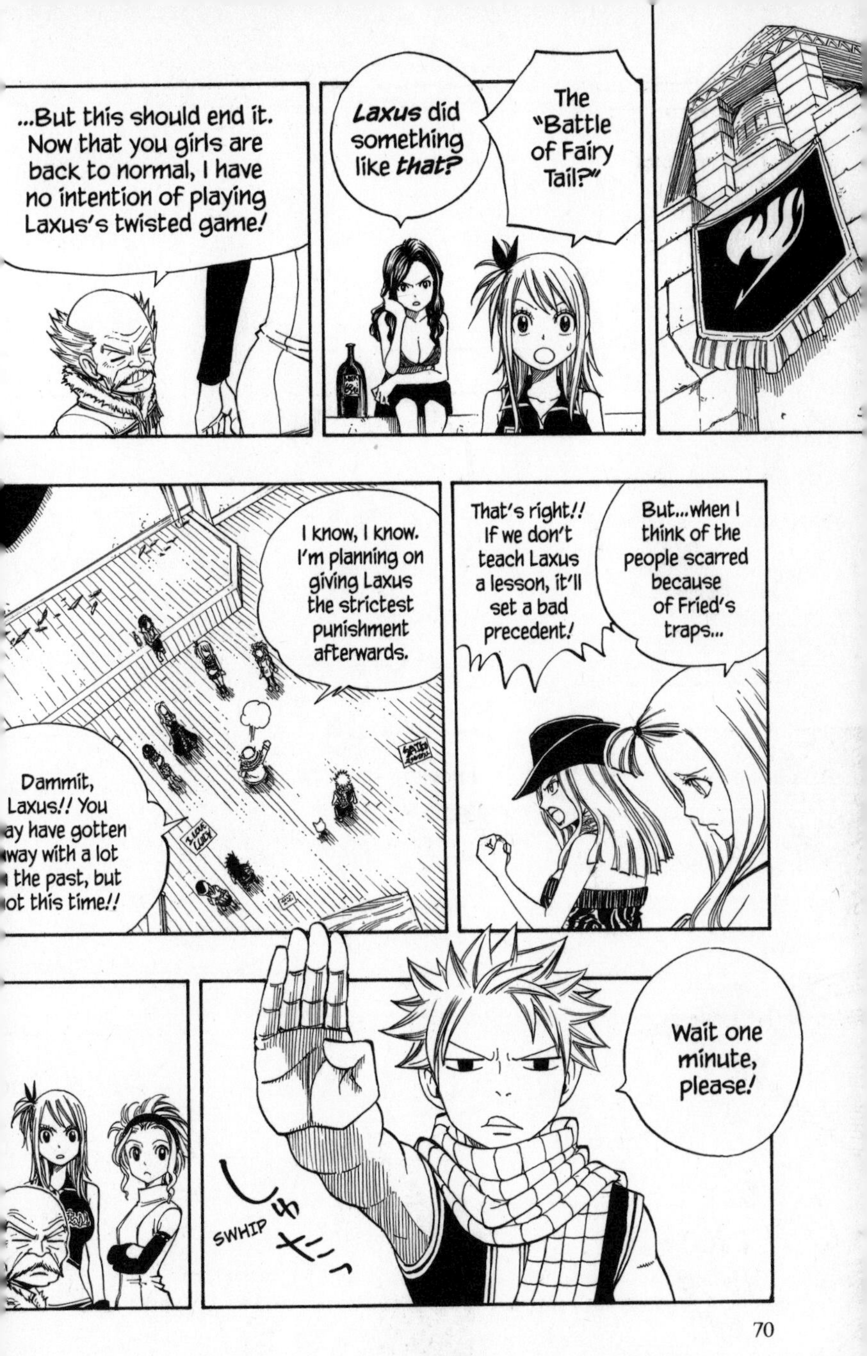

The "Battle of Fairy Tail?"
Laxus did something like that?
...But this should end it. Now that you girls are back to normal, I have no intention of playing Laxus's twisted game!
But...when I think of the people scarred because of Fried's traps...
That's right!! If we don't teach Laxus a lesson, it'll set a bad precedent!
I know, I know. I'm planning on giving Laxus the strictest punishment afterwards.
Dammit, Laxus!! You ay have gotten way with a lot the past, but ot this time!!
Wait one minute, please!
SWHIP

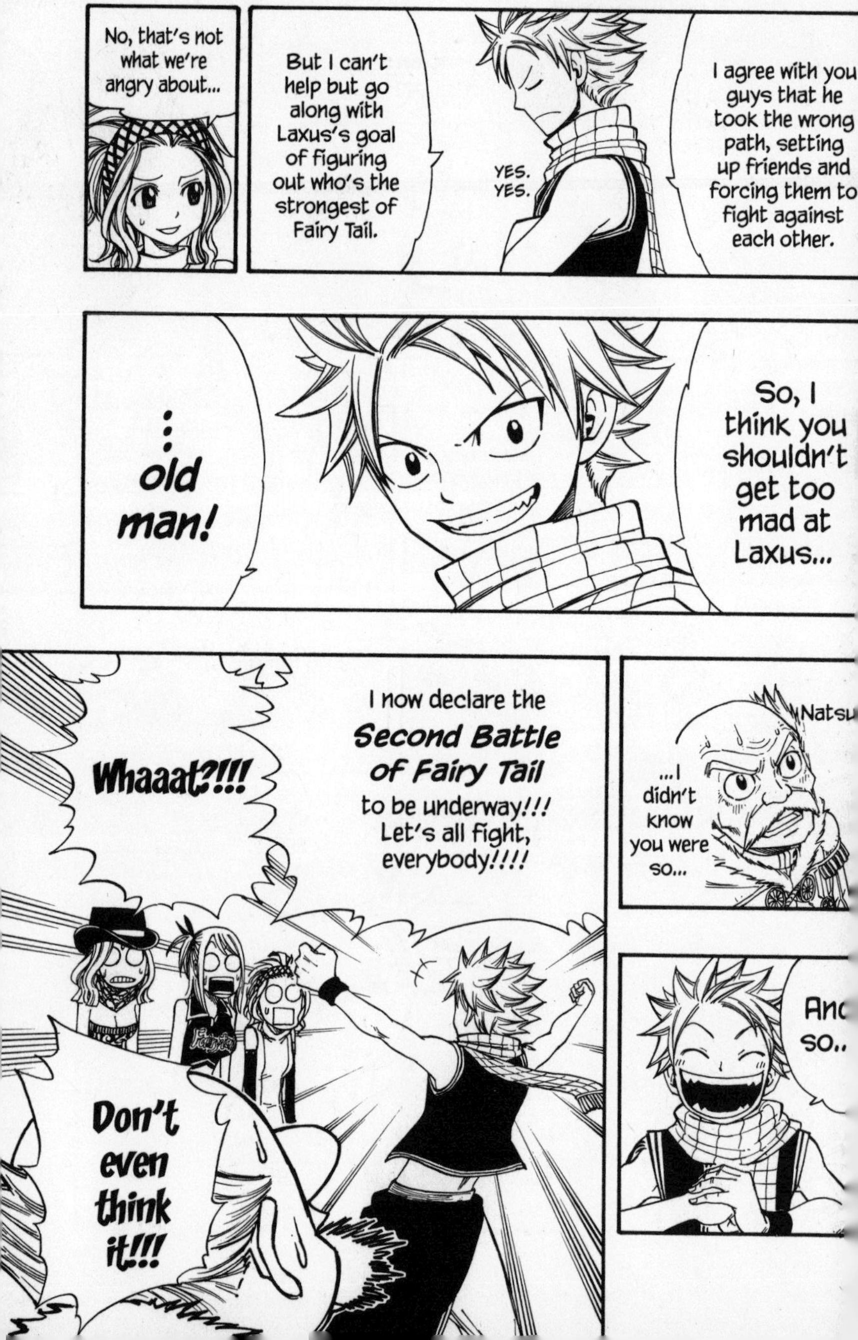

I agree with you guys that he took the wrong path, setting up friends and forcing them to fight against each other.
YES. YES.
But I can't help but go along with Laxus's goal of figuring out who's the strongest of Fairy Tail.
No, that's not what we're angry about...
So, I think you shouldn't get too mad at Laxus...
...old man!
Natsu
...I didn't know you were so...
And so..
I now declare the *Second Battle of Fairy Tail* to be underway!!! Let's all fight, everybody!!!!
Whaaat?!!!
Don't even think it!!!

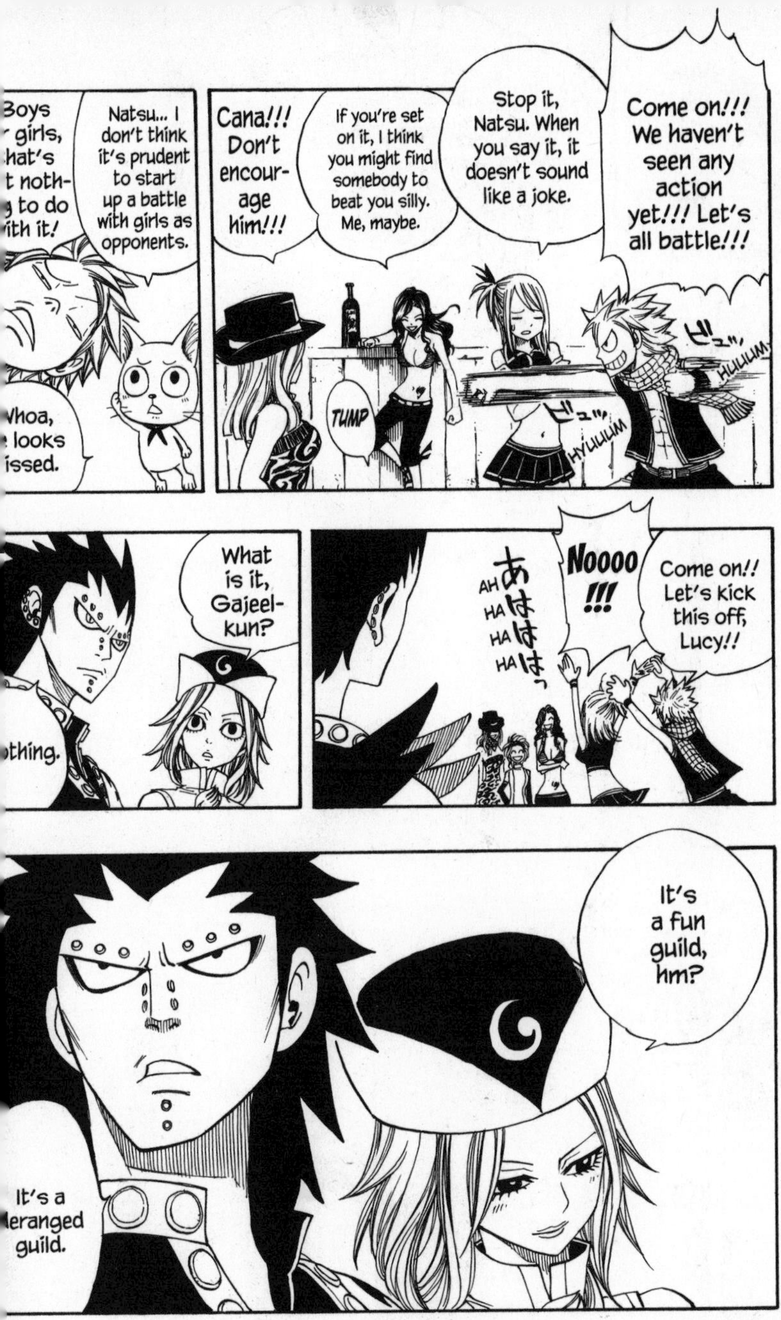

Come on!!! We haven't seen any action yet!!! Let's all battle!!!
Stop it, Natsu. When you say it, it doesn't sound like a joke.
HUUUM
HYUUUM
If you're set on it, I think you might find somebody to beat you silly. Me, maybe.
Cana!!! Don't encourage him!!!
TUMP
Natsu... I don't think it's prudent to start up a battle with girls as opponents.
Boys
girls,
hat's
t noth-
g to do
ith it!
hoa,
looks
issed.
Come on!! Let's kick this off, Lucy!!
Noooo!!!
あははは AH HA HA HA
What is it, Gajeel-kun?
othing.
It's a fun guild, hm?
It's a
eranged
guild.

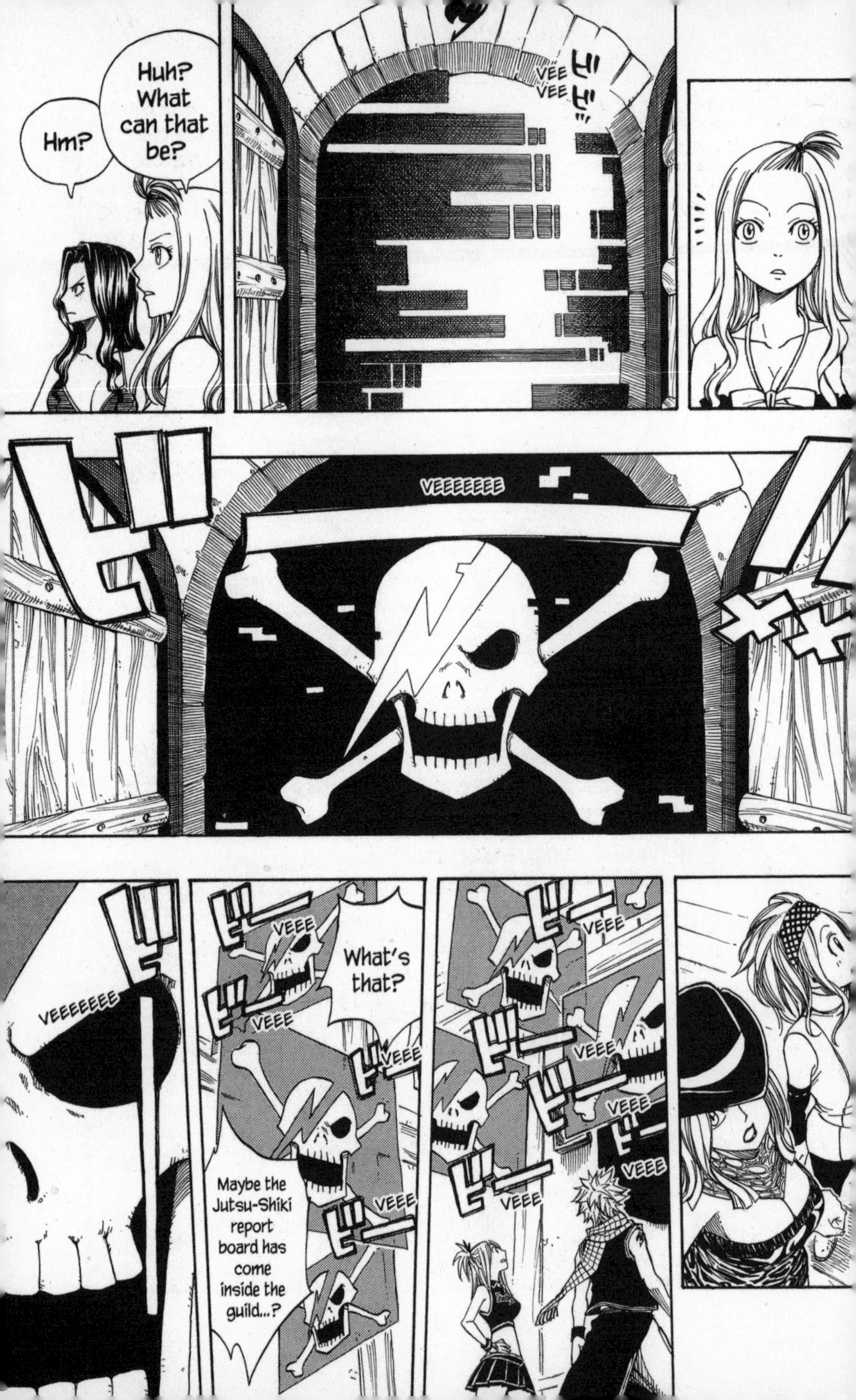
VEE
VEE
Huh? What can that be?
Hm?
VEEEEEEE
VEEE
VEEE
VEEE
VEEE
VEEE
VEEE
VEEE
VEEE
VEEE
What's that?
VEEE
VEEE
Maybe the Jutsu-Shiki report board has come inside the guild...?
VEEEEEEE

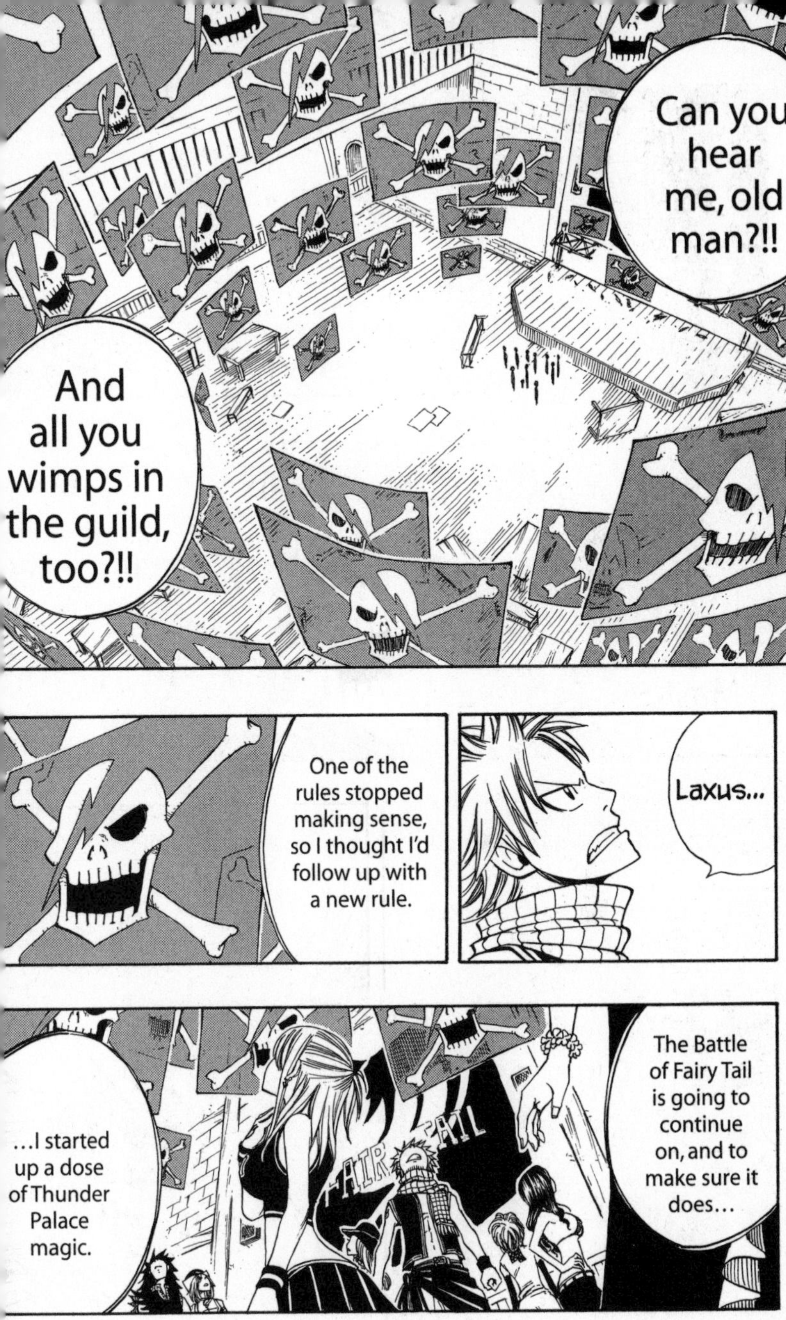
Can you hear me, old man?!!
And all you wimps in the guild, too?!!
Laxus...
One of the rules stopped making sense, so I thought I'd follow up with a new rule.
The Battle of Fairy Tail is going to continue on, and to make sure it does…
…I started up a dose of Thunder Palace magic.

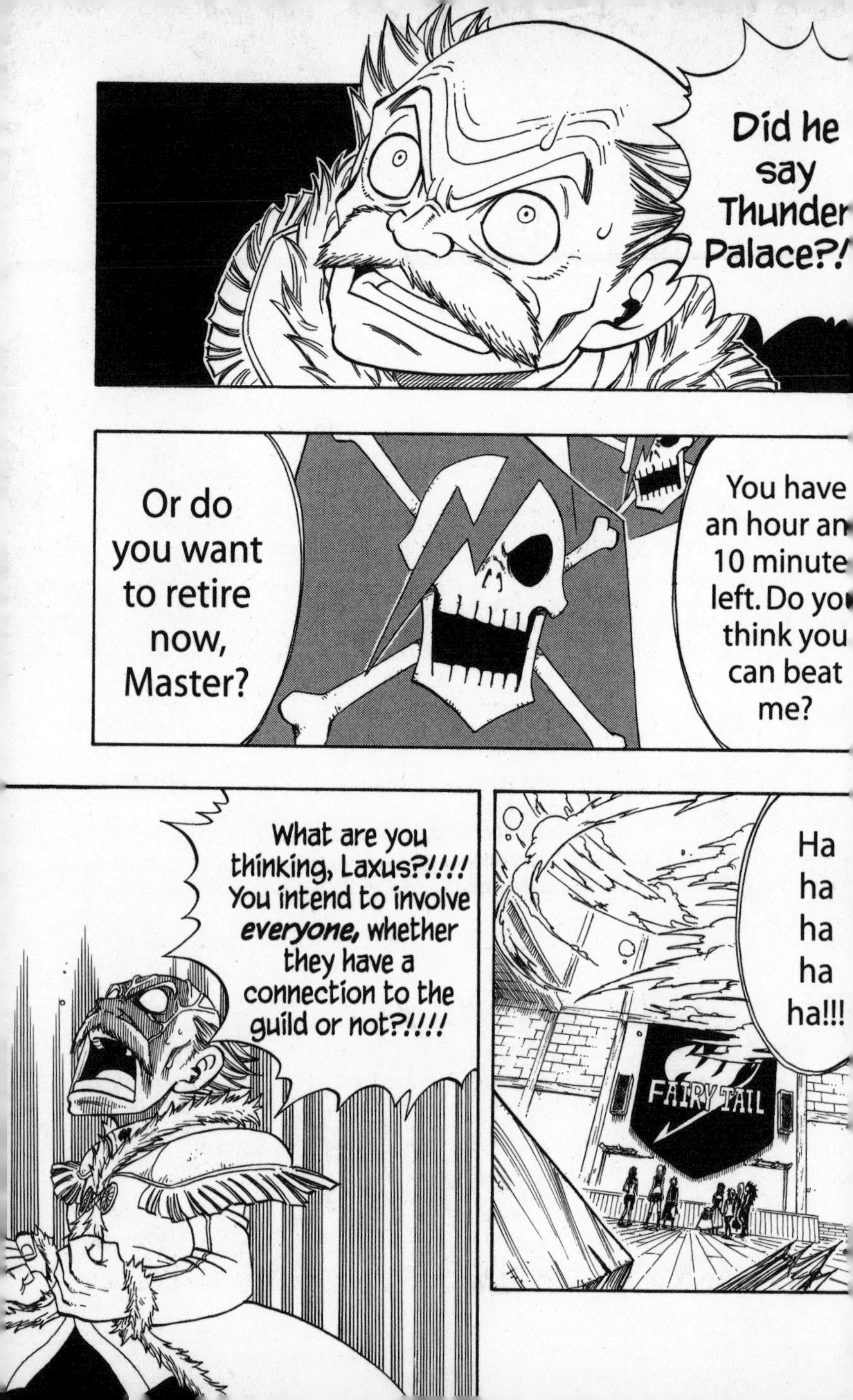
Did he say Thunder Palace?!
You have an hour an 10 minute left. Do yo think you can beat me?
Or do you want to retire now, Master?
Ha ha ha ha ha!!!
FAIRY TAIL
What are you thinking, Laxus?!!!! You intend to involve *everyone,* whether they have a connection to the guild or not?!!!!

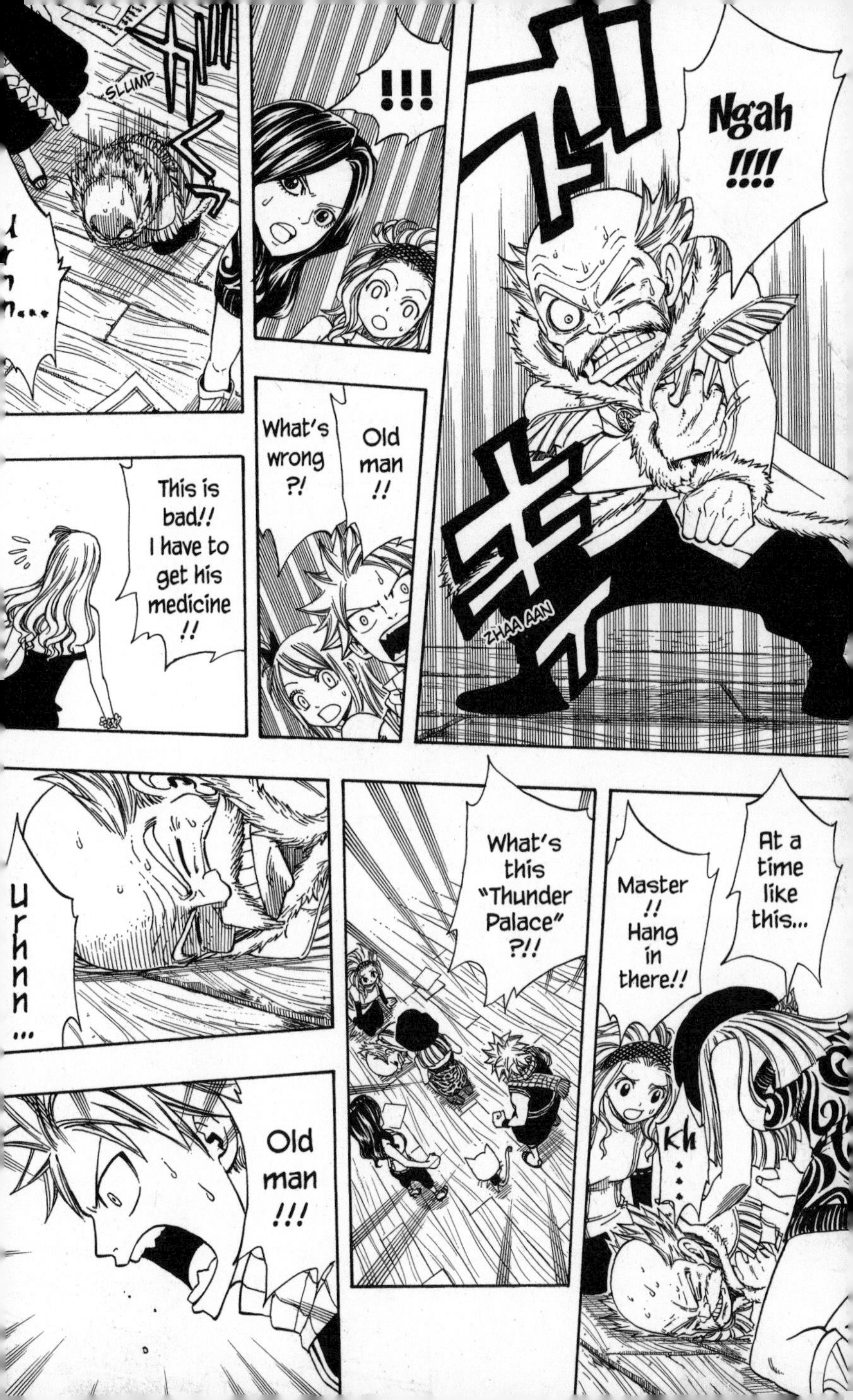
Ngah !!!!
ZHAA AAN
!!!
Old man !!
What's wrong ?!
SLUMP
This is bad!! I have to get his medicine !!
At a time like this...
Master !! Hang in there!!
Kh...
What's this "Thunder Palace" ?!!
Urhnn...
Old man !!!

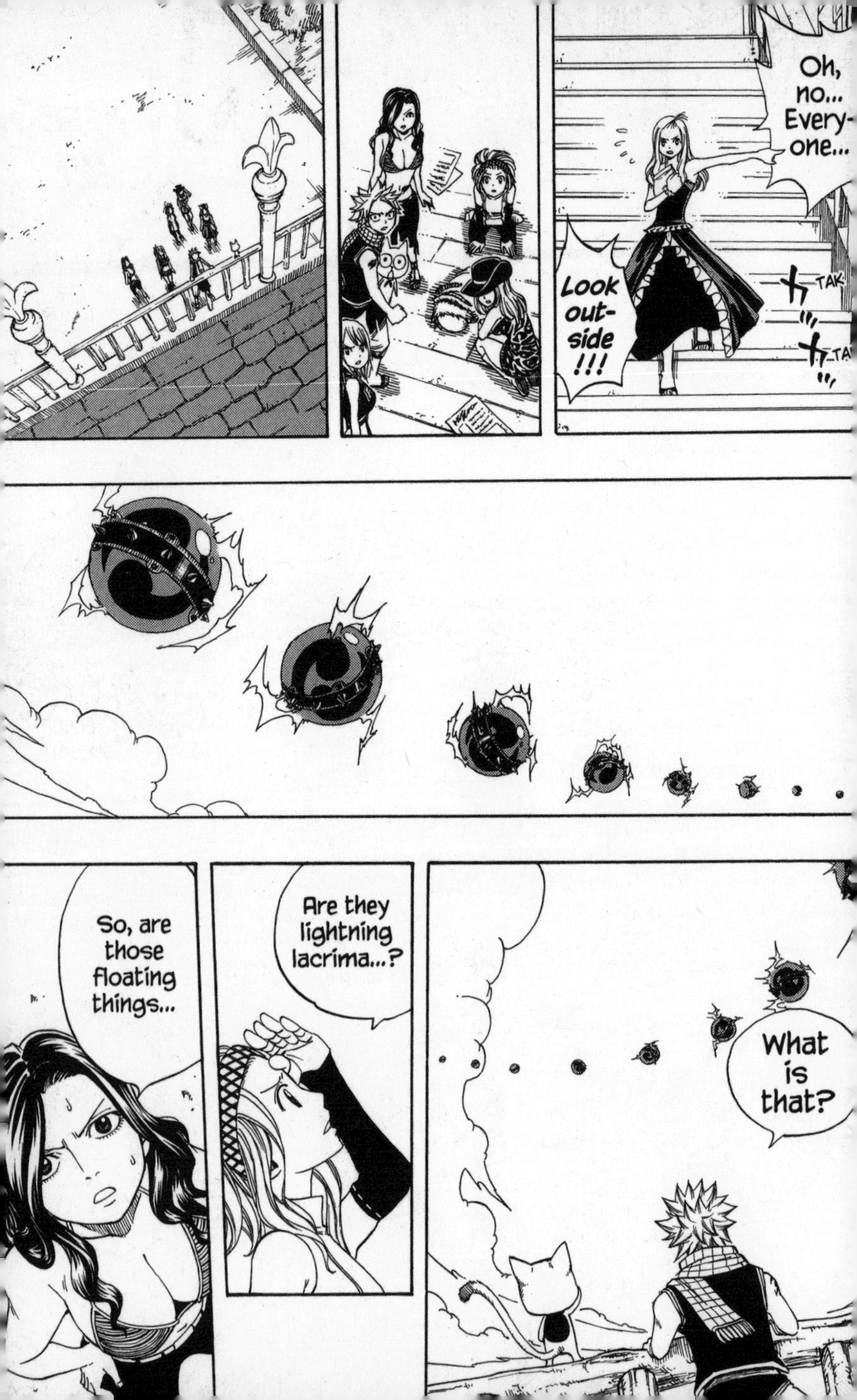
Oh, no... Every-one...
Look out-side!!!
TAK
TAK
What is that?
Are they lightning lacrima...?
So, are those floating things...

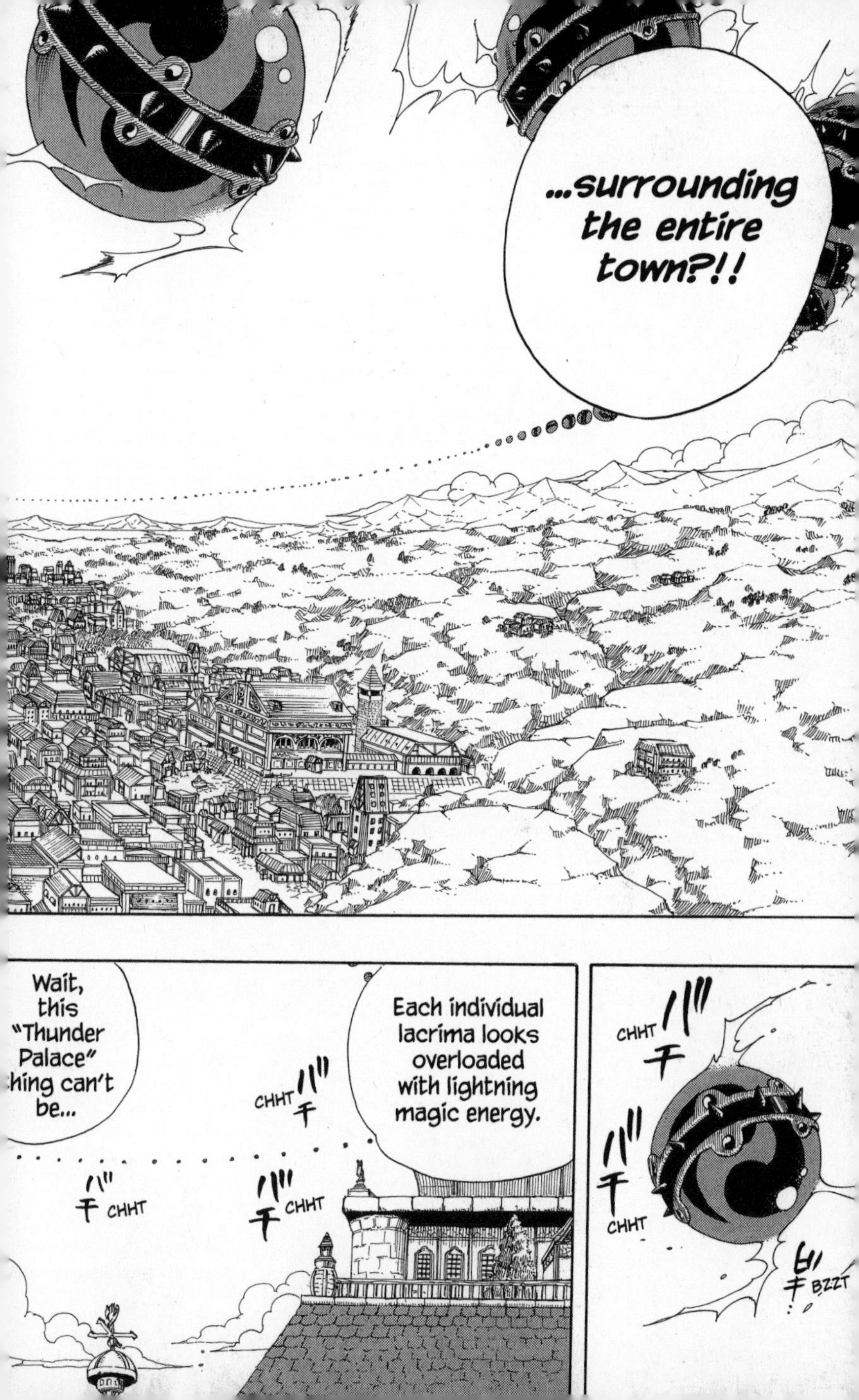
...surrounding the entire town?!!
CHHT
CHHT
BZZT
Each individual lacrima looks overloaded with lightning magic energy.
CHHT
CHHT
Wait, this "Thunder Palace" hing can't be...
CHHT

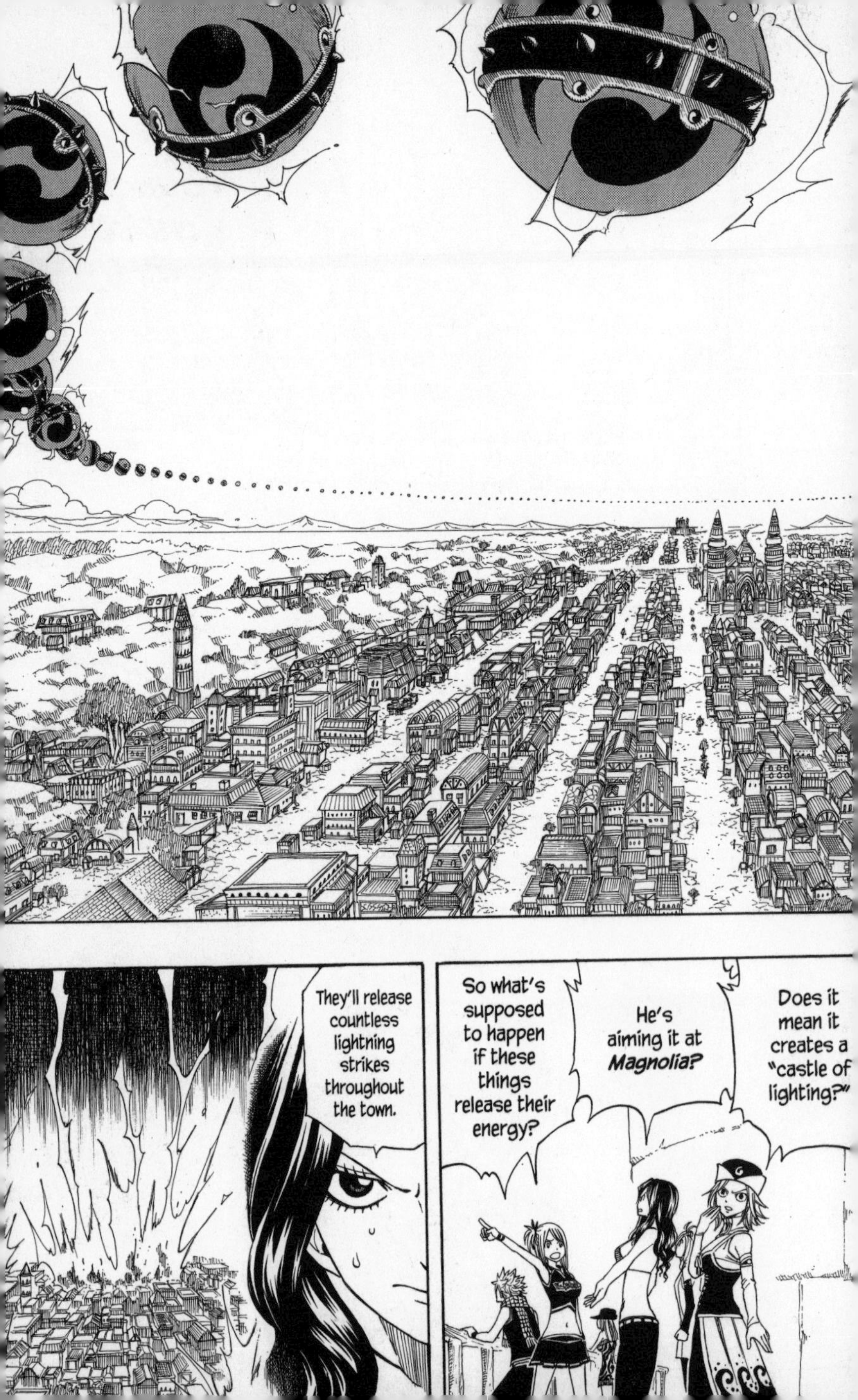
Does it mean it creates a "castle of lighting?"
He's aiming it at *Magnolia?*
So what's supposed to happen if these things release their energy?
They'll release countless lightning strikes throughout the town.

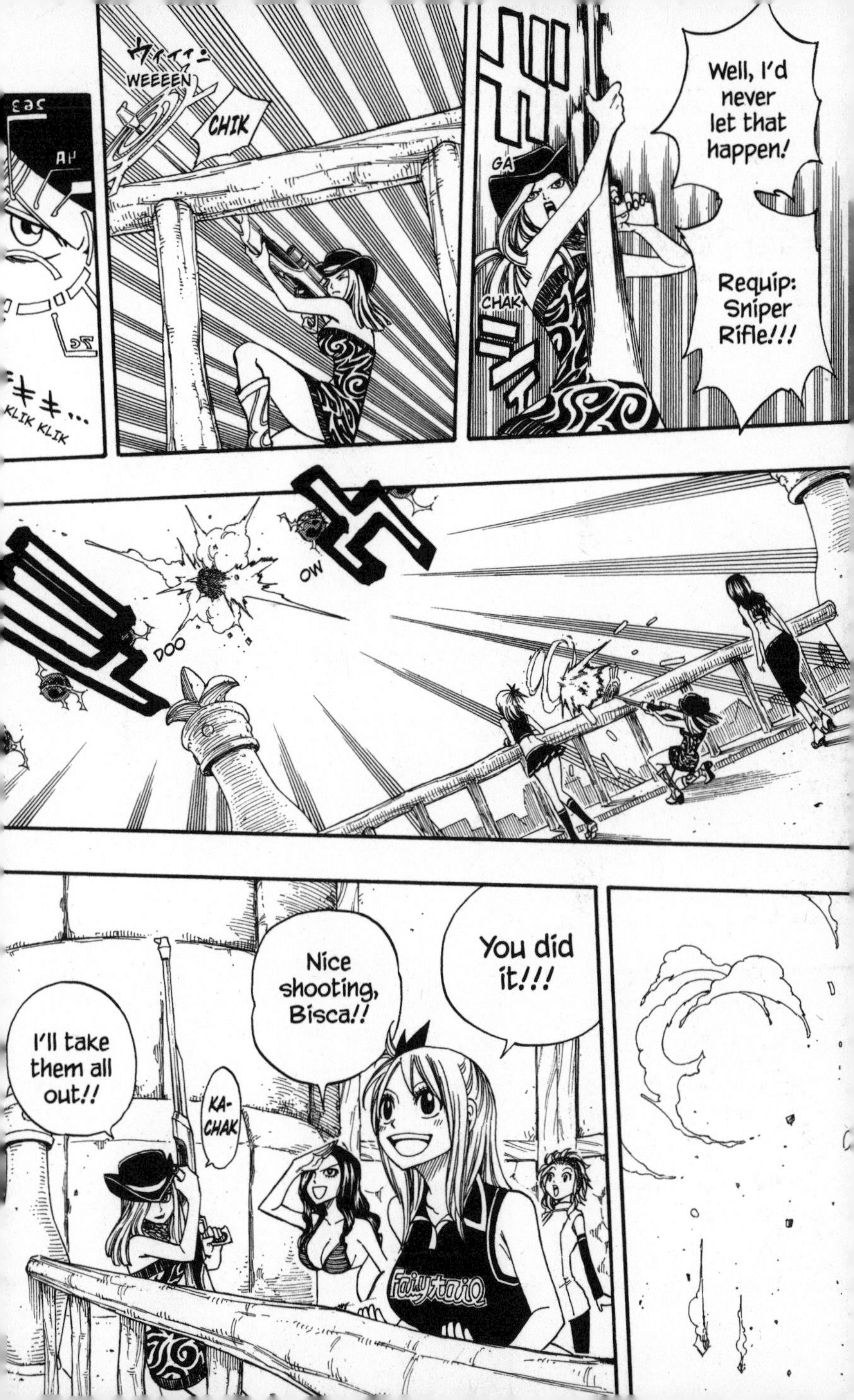
Well, I'd never let that happen!
Requip: Sniper Rifle!!!
GA
CHAK
ウィィィー
WEEEEN
CHIK
キキ…
KLIK KLIK
OW
DOO
You did it!!!
Nice shooting, Bisca!!
KA-CHAK
I'll take them all out!!
Fairy tail

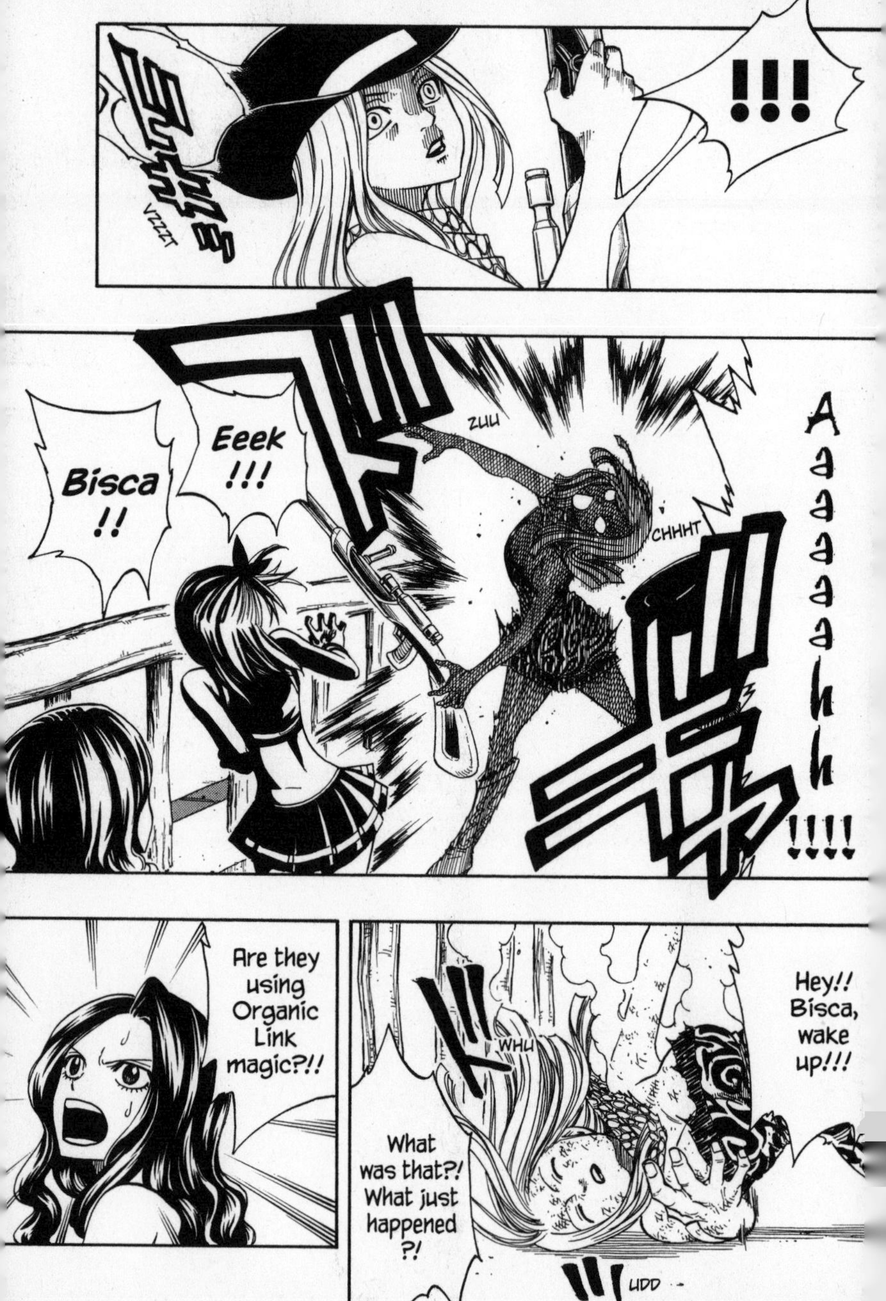
!!!
VZZZT
Aaaaaaahh!!!!
CHHHT
ZUU
Eeek!!!
Bisca!!
Hey!! Bisca, wake up!!!
WHU
What was that?! What just happened?!
UDD
Are they using Organic Link magic?!!

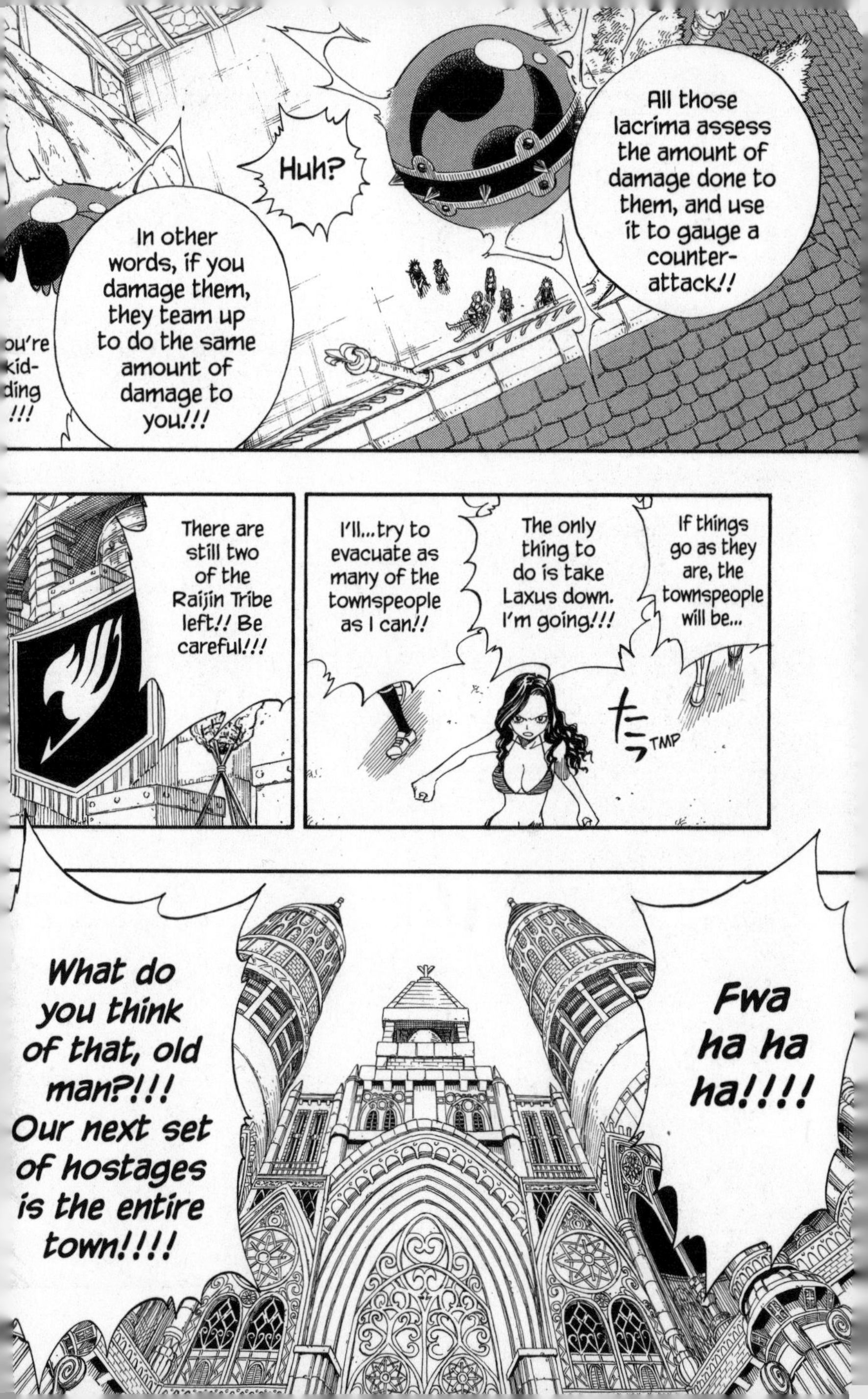
All those lacrima assess the amount of damage done to them, and use it to gauge a counter-attack!!
Huh?
In other words, if you damage them, they team up to do the same amount of damage to you!!!
ou're kid-ding !!!
If things go as they are, the townspeople will be...
The only thing to do is take Laxus down. I'm going!!!
I'll...try to evacuate as many of the townspeople as I can!!
TMP
There are still two of the Raijin Tribe left!! Be careful!!!
Fwa ha ha ha!!!!
What do you think of that, old man?!!! Our next set of hostages is the entire town!!!!

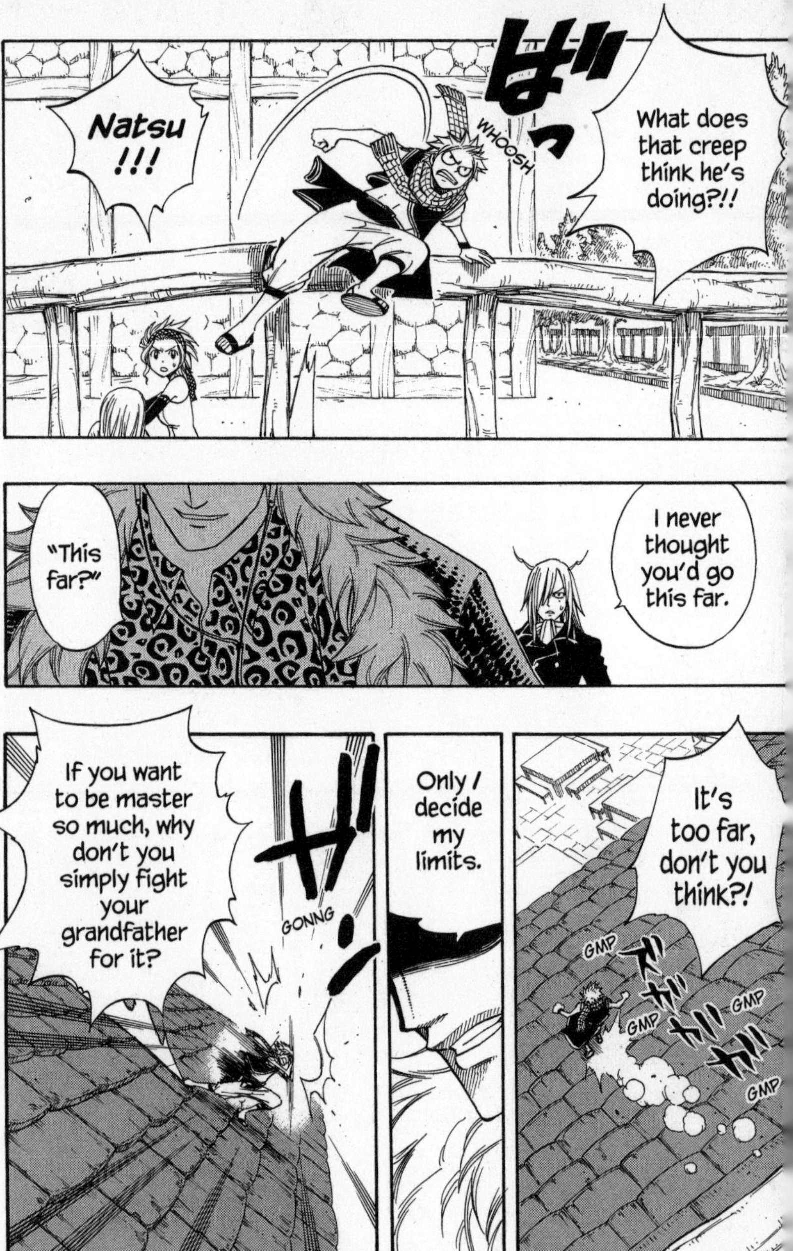
What does that creep think he's doing?!!
ばっ
WHOOSH
Natsu !!!
I never thought you'd go this far.
"This far?"
It's too far, don't you think?!
GMP
GMP
GMP
GMP
Only I decide my limits.
If you want to be master so much, why don't you simply fight your grandfather for it?
GONNG

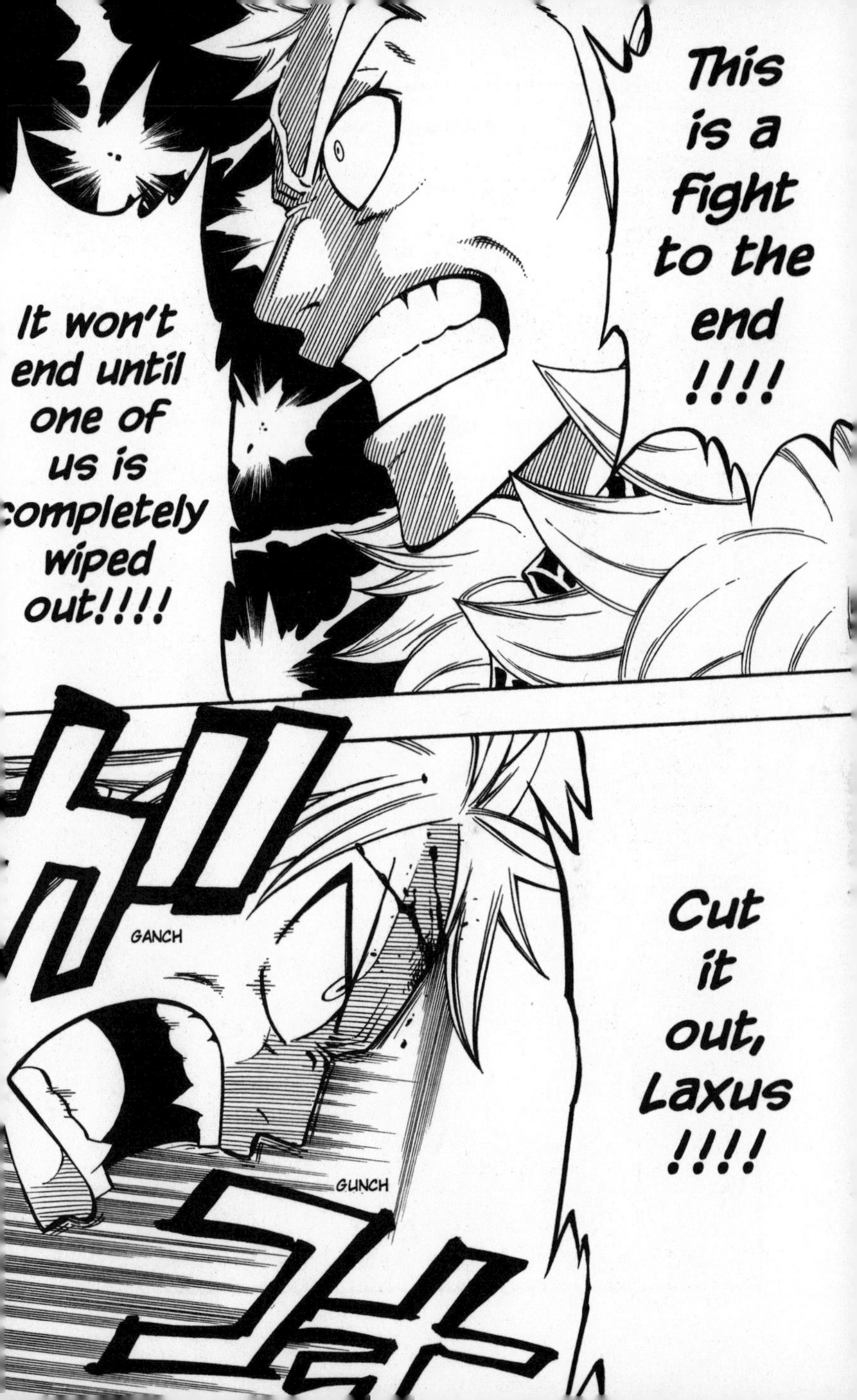
This is a fight to the end!!!!
It won't end until one of us is completely wiped out!!!!
Cut it out, Laxus!!!!
GANCH
GUNCH

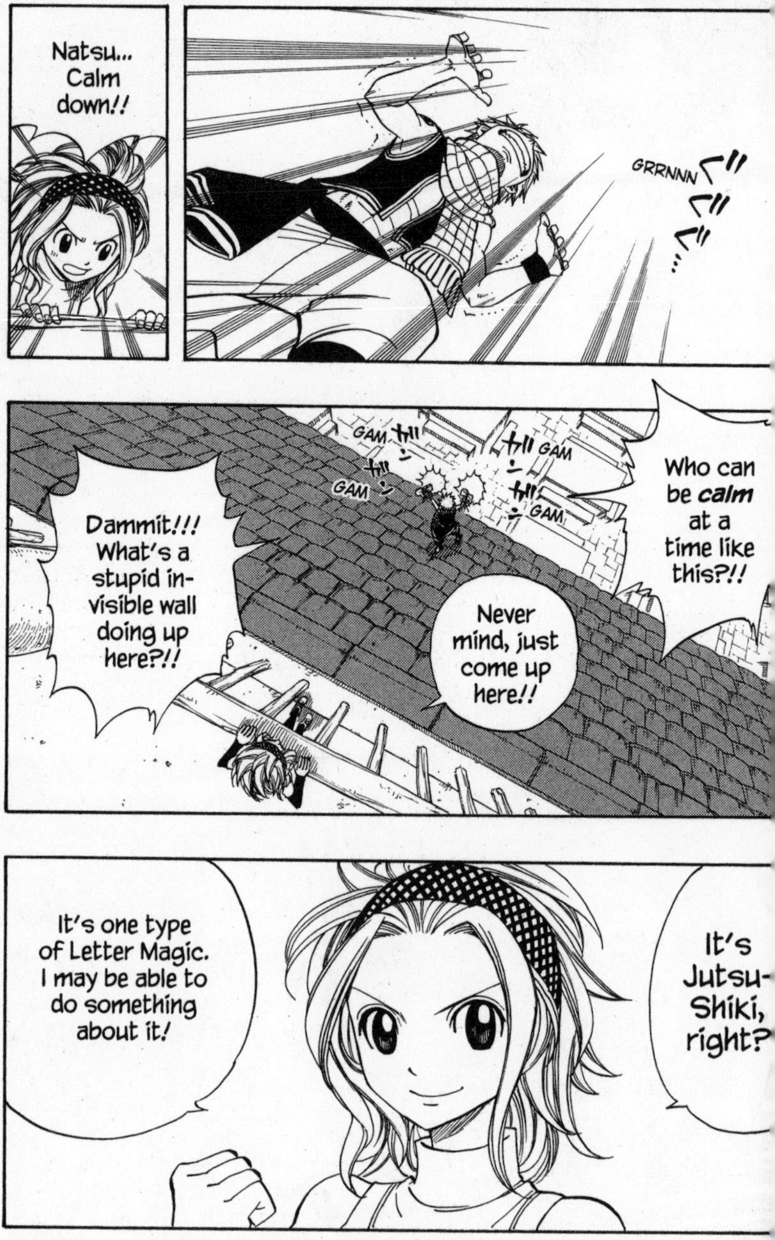
GRRNNN
Natsu... Calm down!!
Who can be *calm* at a time like this?!!
GAM
GAM
GAM
GAM
Dammit!!! What's a stupid invisible wall doing up here?!!
Never mind, just come up here!!
It's Jutsu-Shiki, right?
It's one type of Letter Magic. I may be able to do something about it!

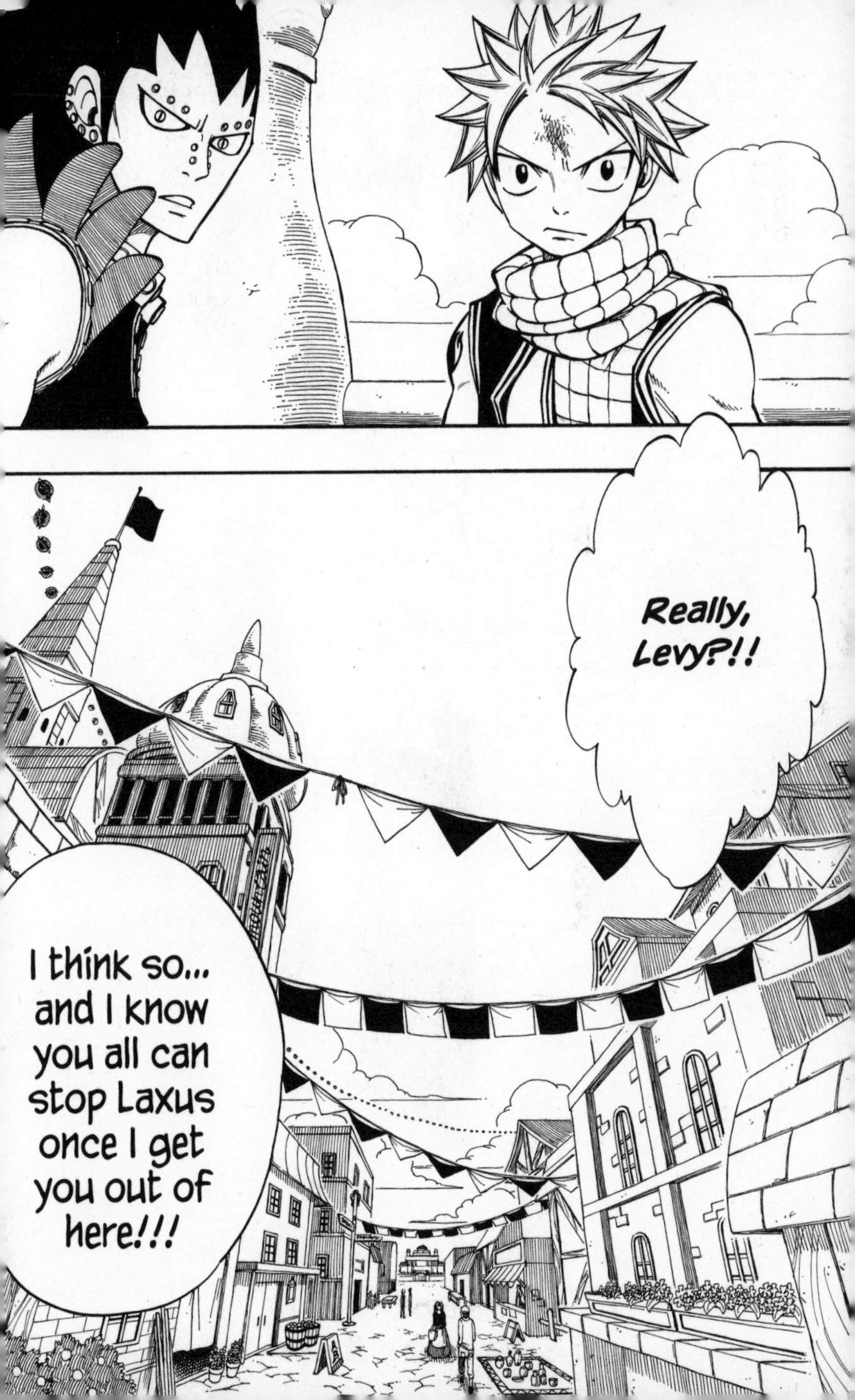
Really, Levy?!!
I think so... and I know you all can stop Laxus once I get you out of here!!!

FAIRY TAIL

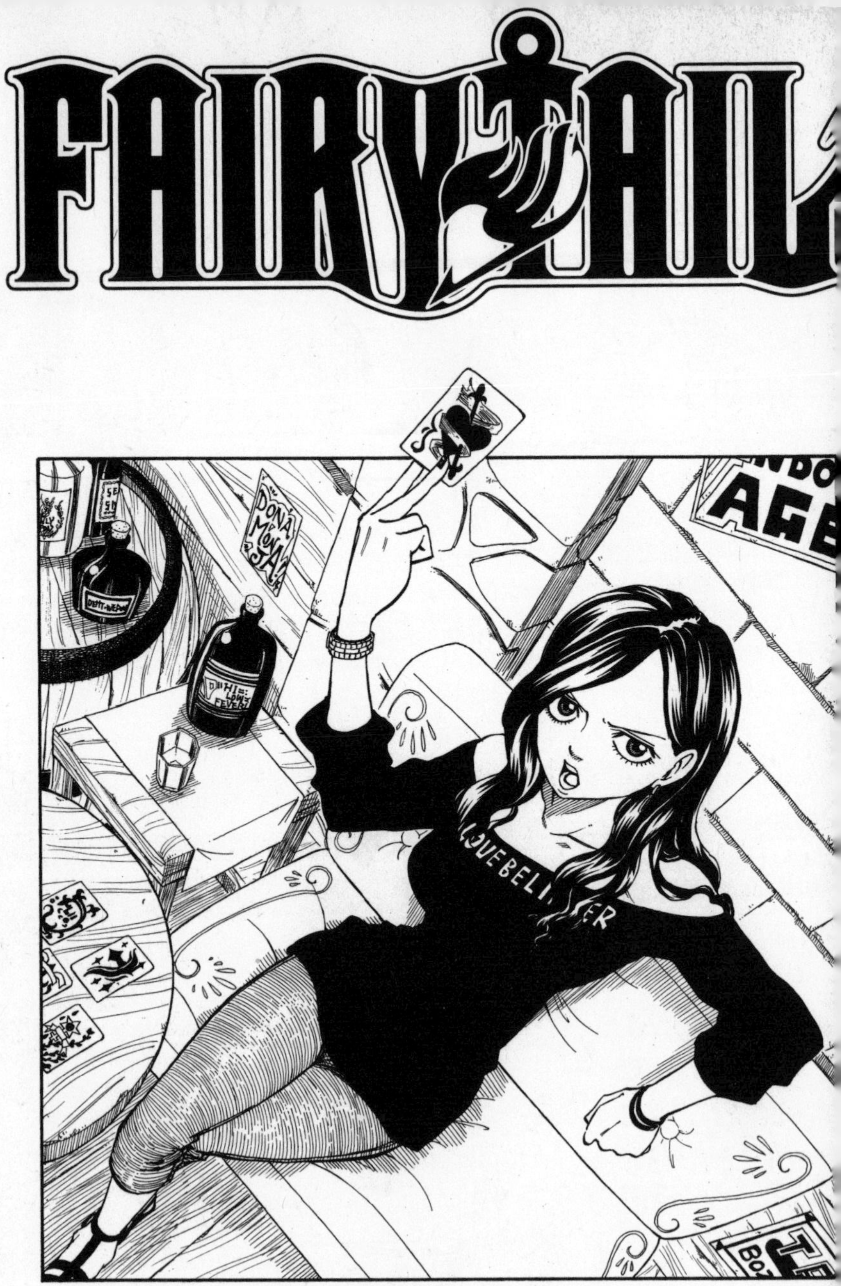

Chapter 114:
Love Breaks Down Walls

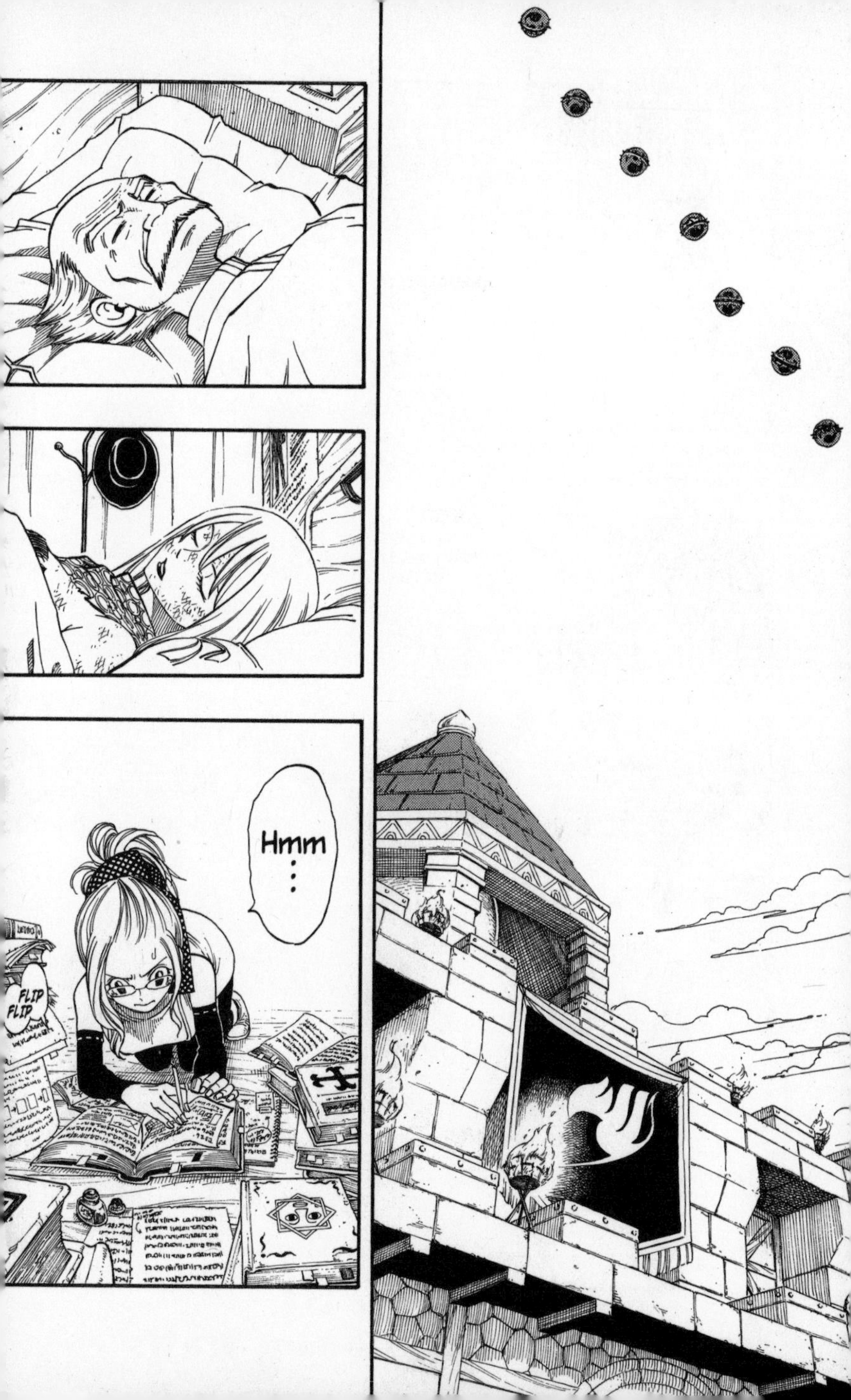
Hmm...
FLIP FLIP

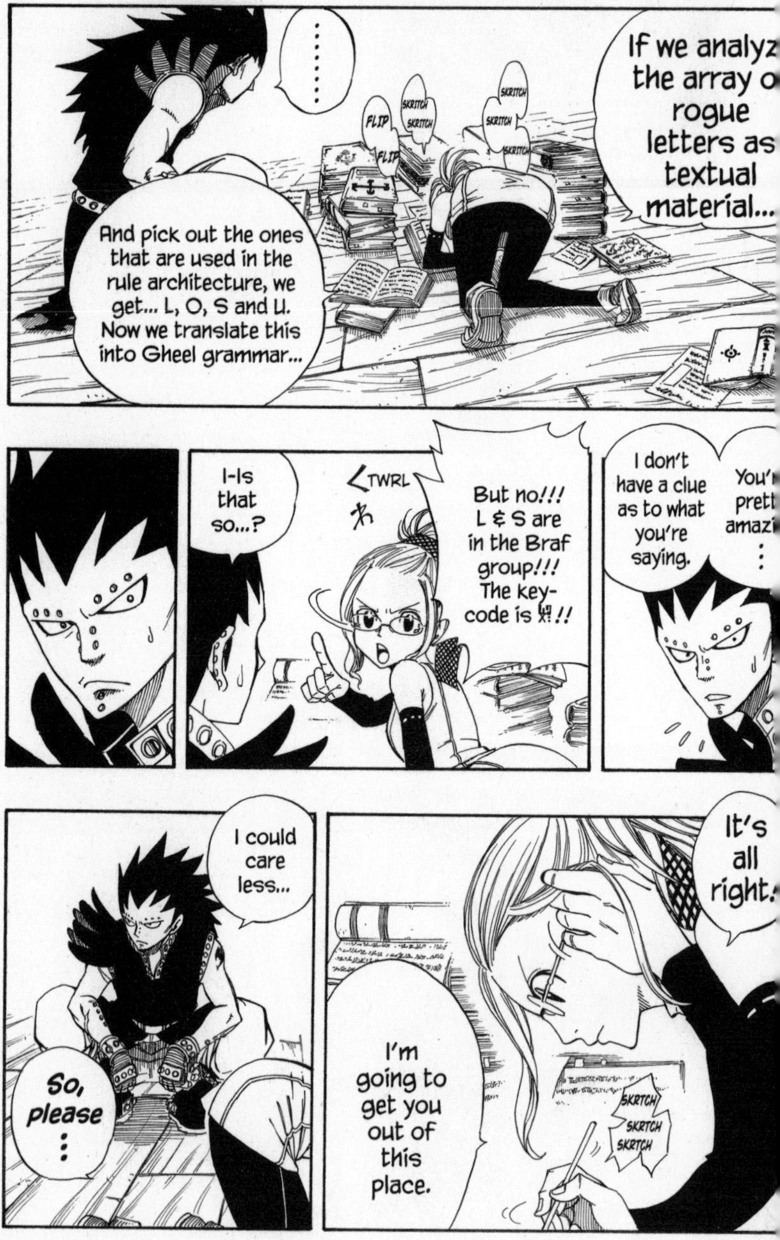

If we analyz the array o rogue letters as textual material...
SKRITCH
SKRITCH
SKRITCH
SKRITCH
SKRITCH
FLIP
FLIP
......
And pick out the ones that are used in the rule architecture, we get... L, O, S and U. Now we translate this into Gheel grammar...
You'r prett amazi...
I don't have a clue as to what you're saying.
But no!!! L & S are in the Braf group!!! The key-code is !!
TWRL
I-Is that so...?
It's all right.
I'm going to get you out of this place.
SKRTCH
SKRTCH
SKRTCH
I could care less...
So, please...

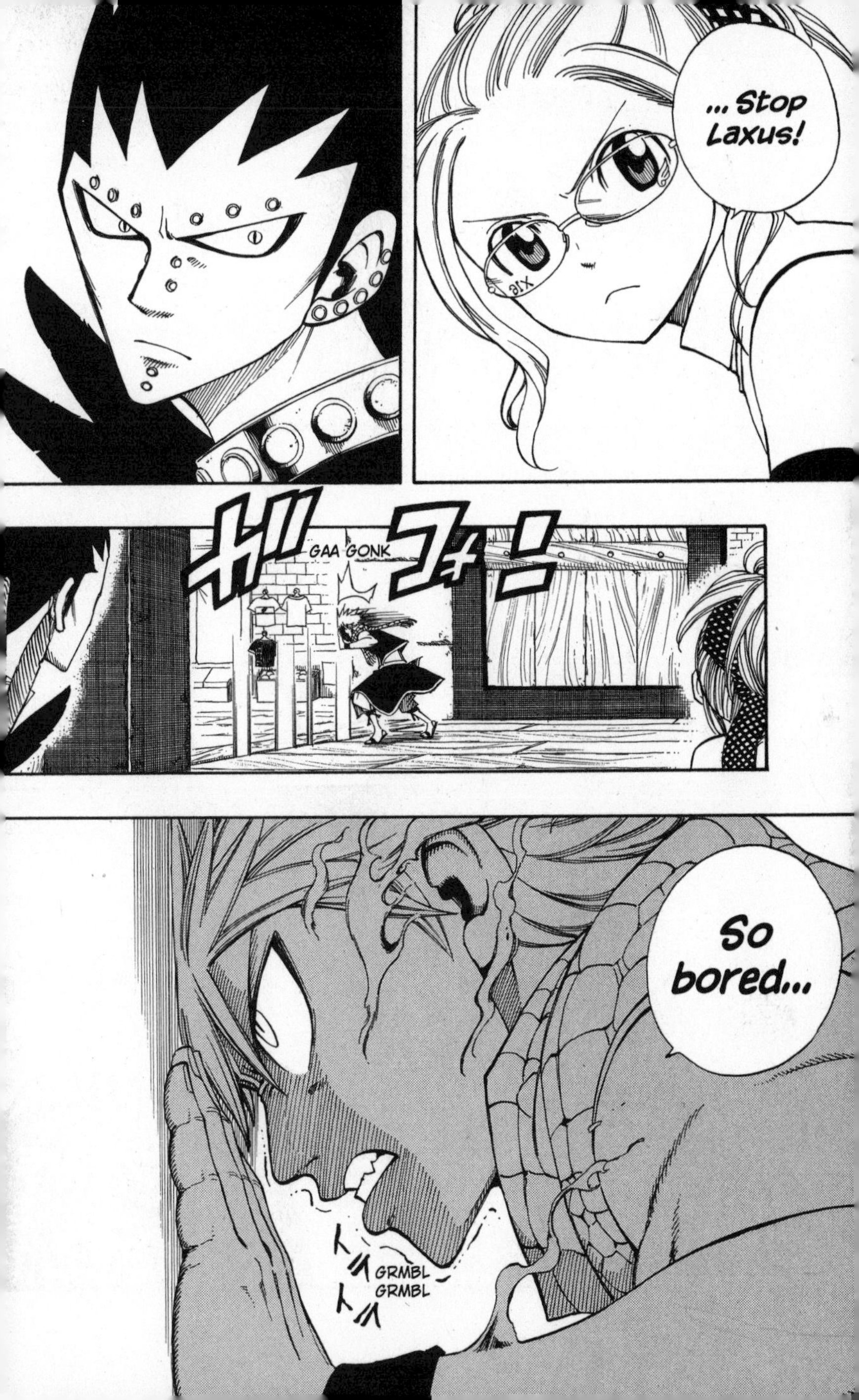
...Stop Laxus!
GAA GONK
So bored...
GRMBL GRMBL

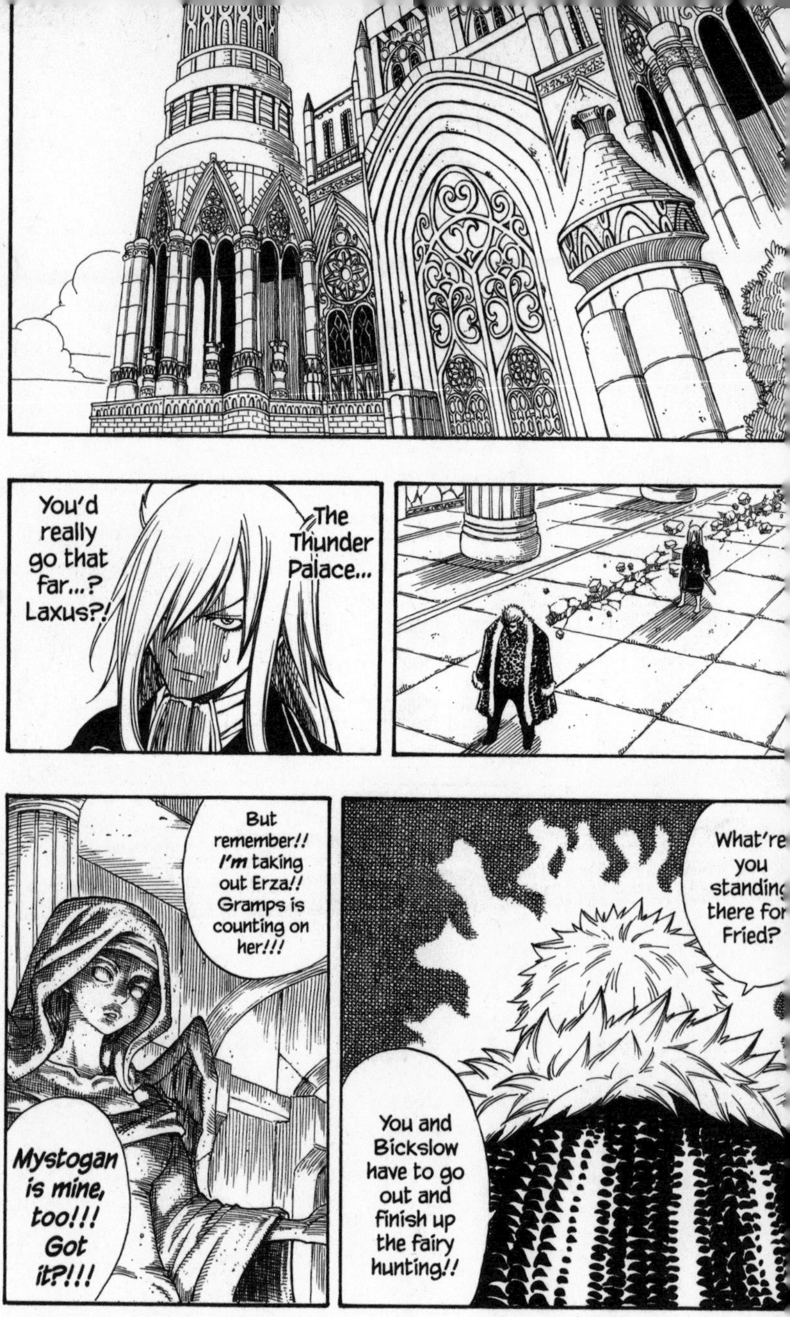

The Thunder Palace...
You'd really go that far...? Laxus?!
What're you standing there for Fried?
You and Bickslow have to go out and finish up the fairy hunting!!
But remember!! *I'm* taking out Erza!! Gramps is counting on her!!!
Mystogan is mine, too!!! Got it?!!!

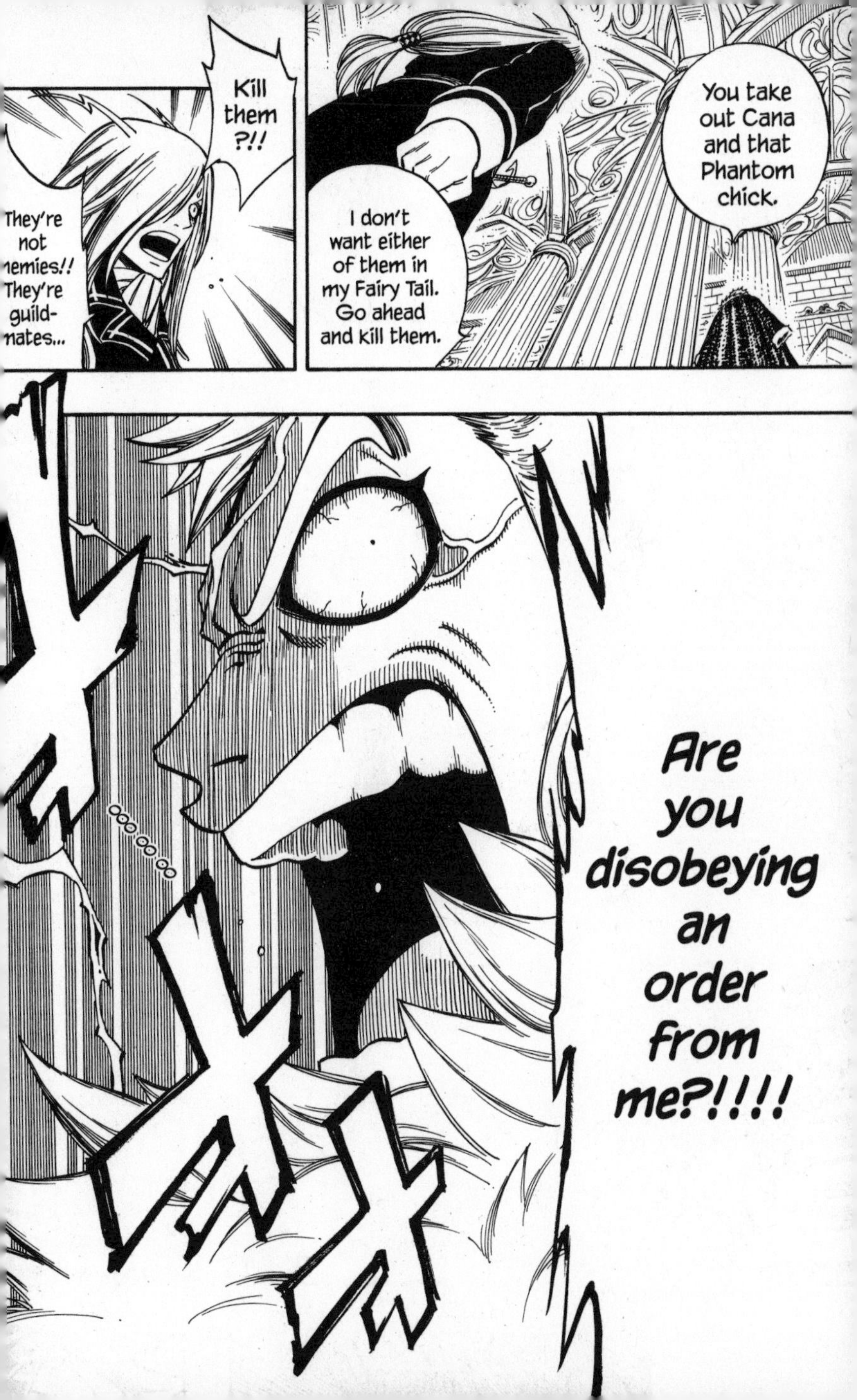
You take out Cana and that Phantom chick.
I don't want either of them in my Fairy Tail. Go ahead and kill them.
Kill them ?!!
They're not nemies!! They're guild- nates...
Are you disobeying an order from me?!!!!

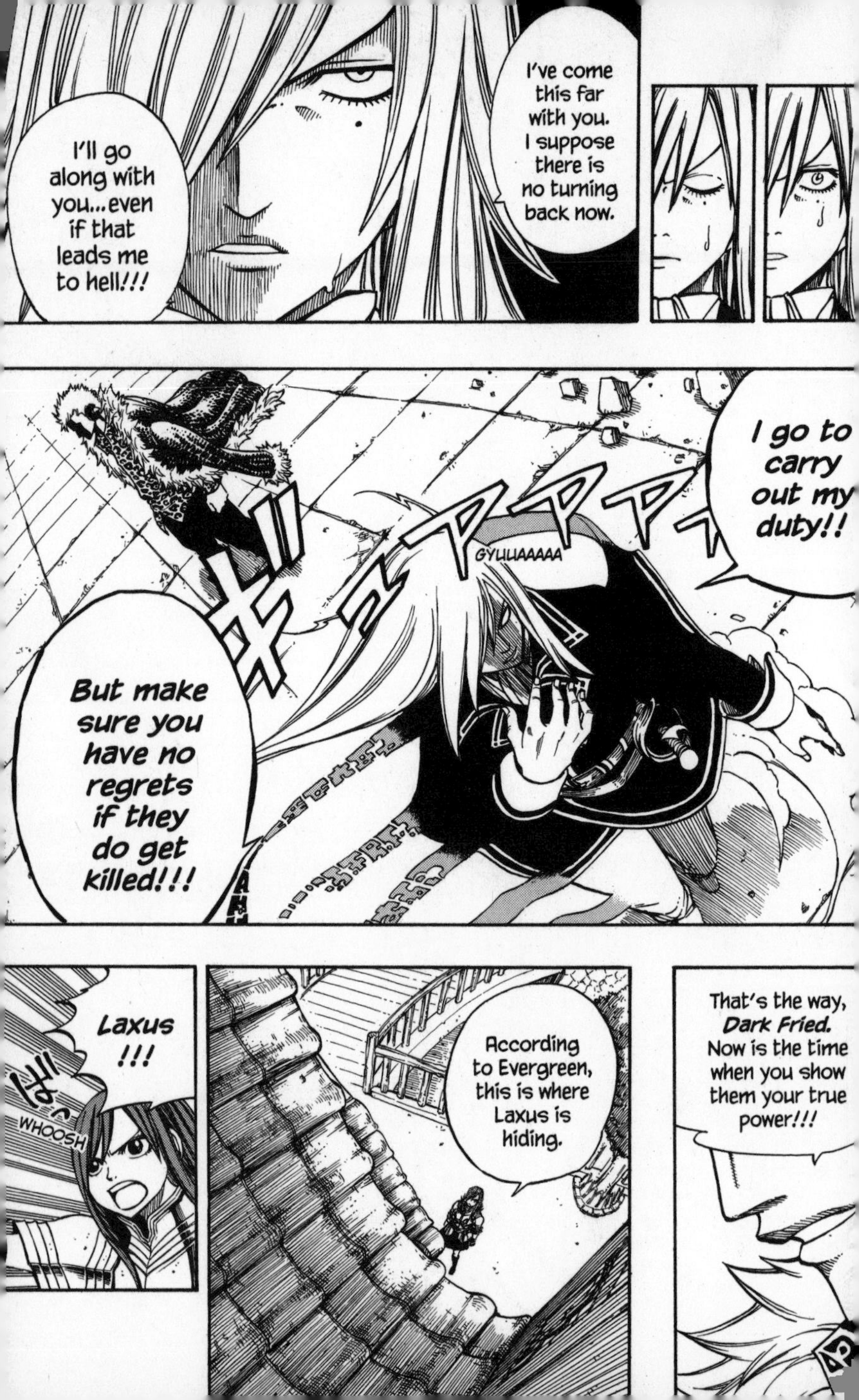
I've come this far with you. I suppose there is no turning back now.
I'll go along with you...even if that leads me to hell!!!
I go to carry out my duty!!
GYUUAAAAA
But make sure you have no regrets if they do get killed!!!
That's the way, *Dark Fried.* Now is the time when you show them your true power!!!
According to Evergreen, this is where Laxus is hiding.
Laxus !!!
WHOOSH

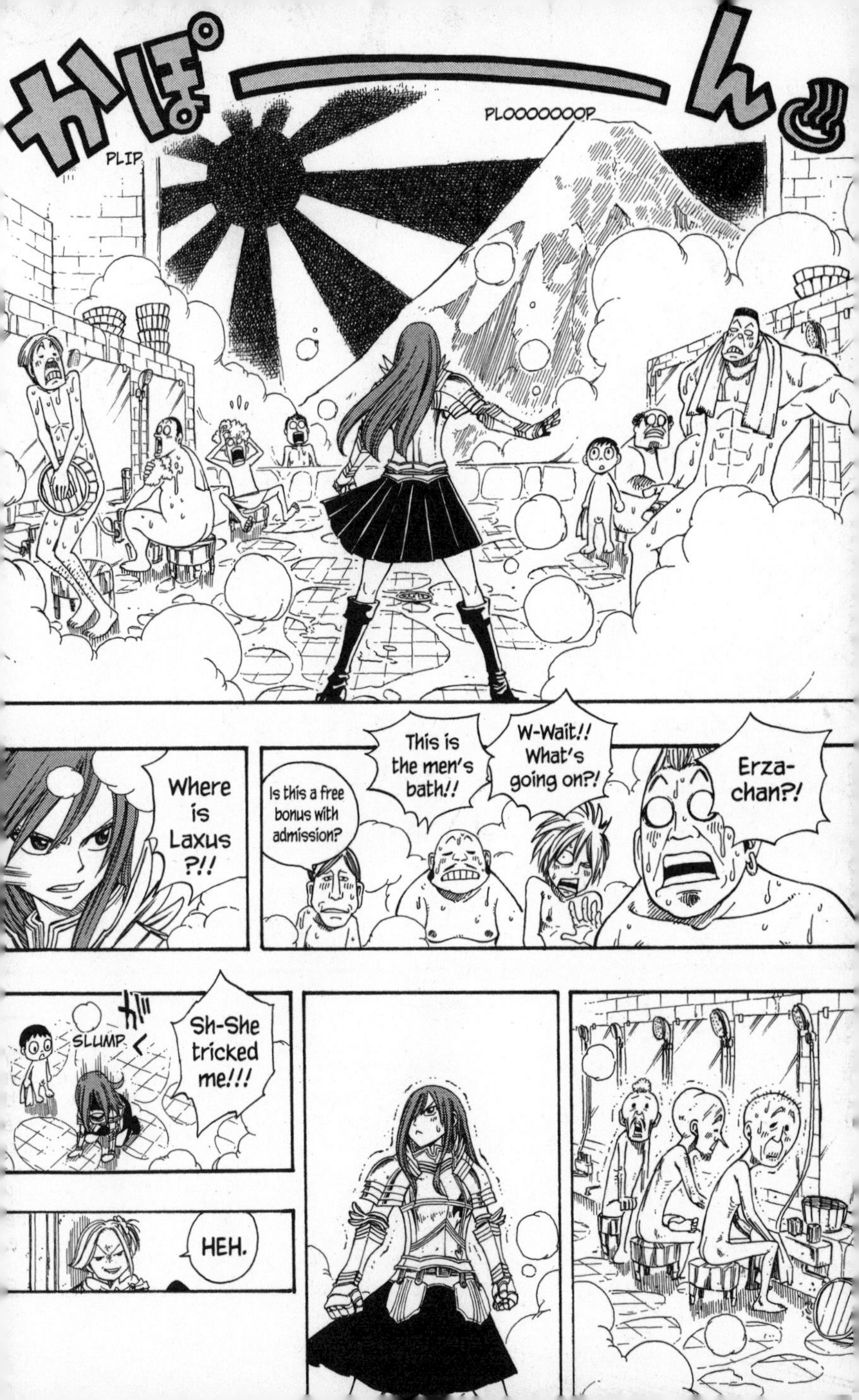
かぽーーーーーん
PLOOOOOOOP
PLIP
Erza-chan?!
W-Wait!! What's going on?!
This is the men's bath!!
Is this a free bonus with admission?
Where is Laxus?!!
Sh-She tricked me!!!
ガく
SLUMP
HEH.

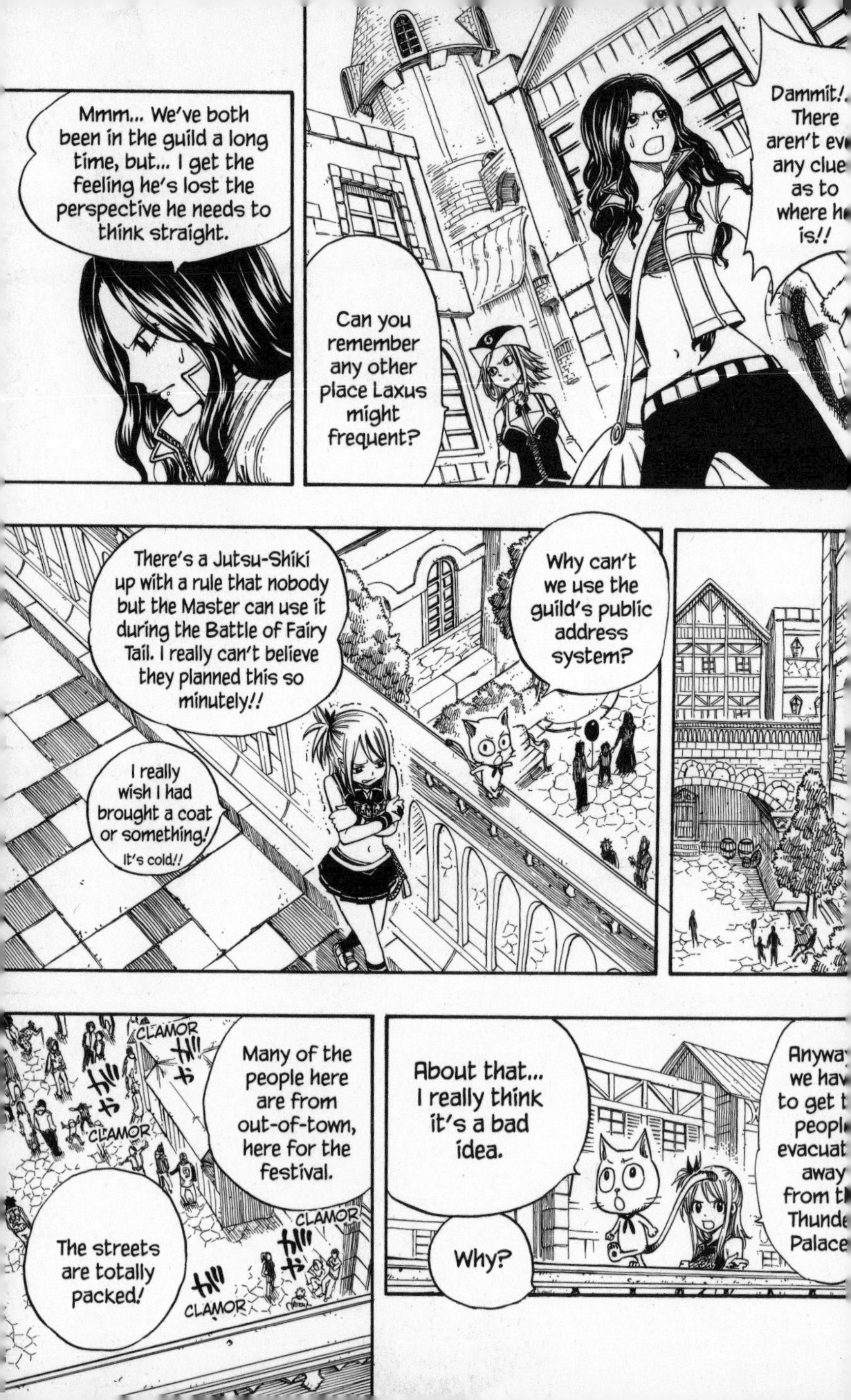
Dammit!! There aren't ev any clue as to where h is!!
Can you remember any other place Laxus might frequent?
Mmm... We've both been in the guild a long time, but... I get the feeling he's lost the perspective he needs to think straight.
Why can't we use the guild's public address system?
There's a Jutsu-Shiki up with a rule that nobody but the Master can use it during the Battle of Fairy Tail. I really can't believe they planned this so minutely!!
I really wish I had brought a coat or something!
It's cold!!
Anywa we hav to get t peopl evacuat away from t Thunde Palace
About that... I really think it's a bad idea.
Why?
CLAMOR
CLAMOR
Many of the people here are from out-of-town, here for the festival.
CLAMOR
The streets are totally packed!
CLAMOR

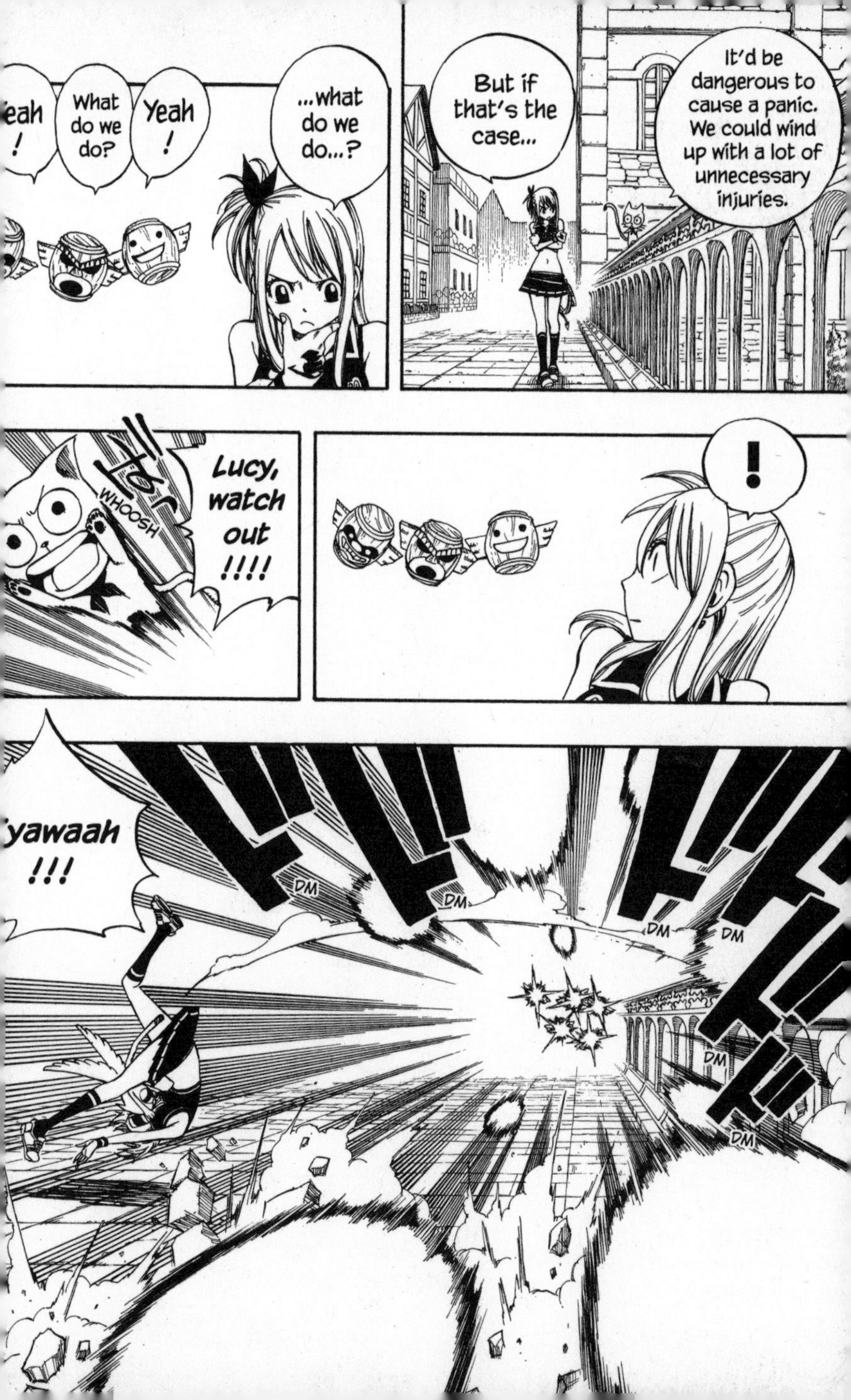

It'd be dangerous to cause a panic. We could wind up with a lot of unnecessary injuries.
But if that's the case...
...what do we do...?
Yeah!
What do we do?
eah!
!
Lucy, watch out!!!!
WHOOSH
yawaah!!!
DM
DM
DM
DM
DM
DM

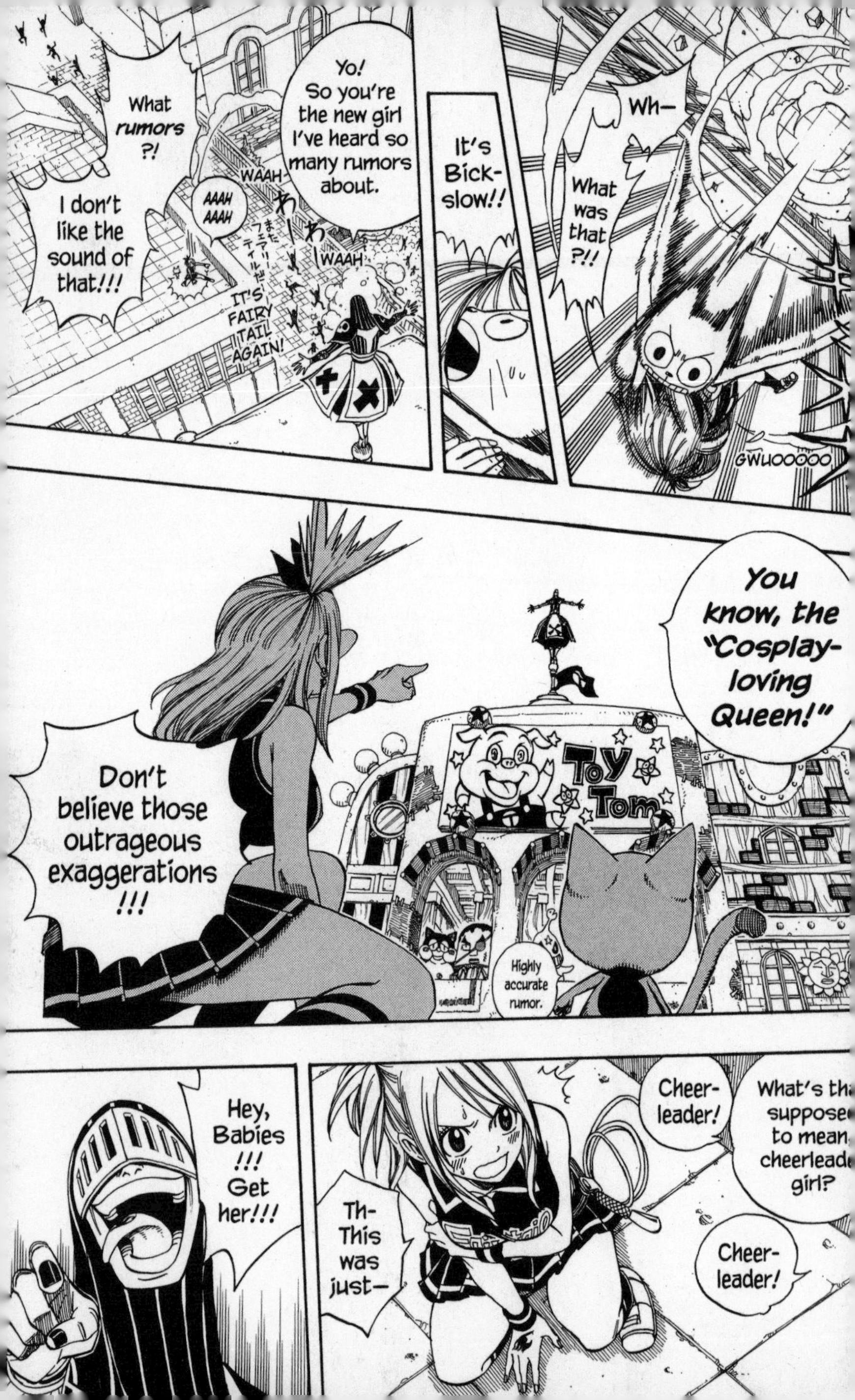

Wh—
What was that ?!!
GWUOOOOO
It's Bick-slow!!
Yo! So you're the new girl I've heard so many rumors about.
What rumors ?!
I don't like the sound of that!!!
WAAH
わーわー
WAAH
AAAH AAAH
またフェアリーテイルだー
IT'S FAIRY TAIL AGAIN!
You know, the "Cosplay-loving Queen!"
Don't believe those outrageous exaggerations !!!
Toy Tom
Highly accurate rumor.
What's tha supposed to mean, cheerleade girl?
Cheer-leader!
Cheer-leader!
Th-This was just—
Hey, Babies !!! Get her!!!

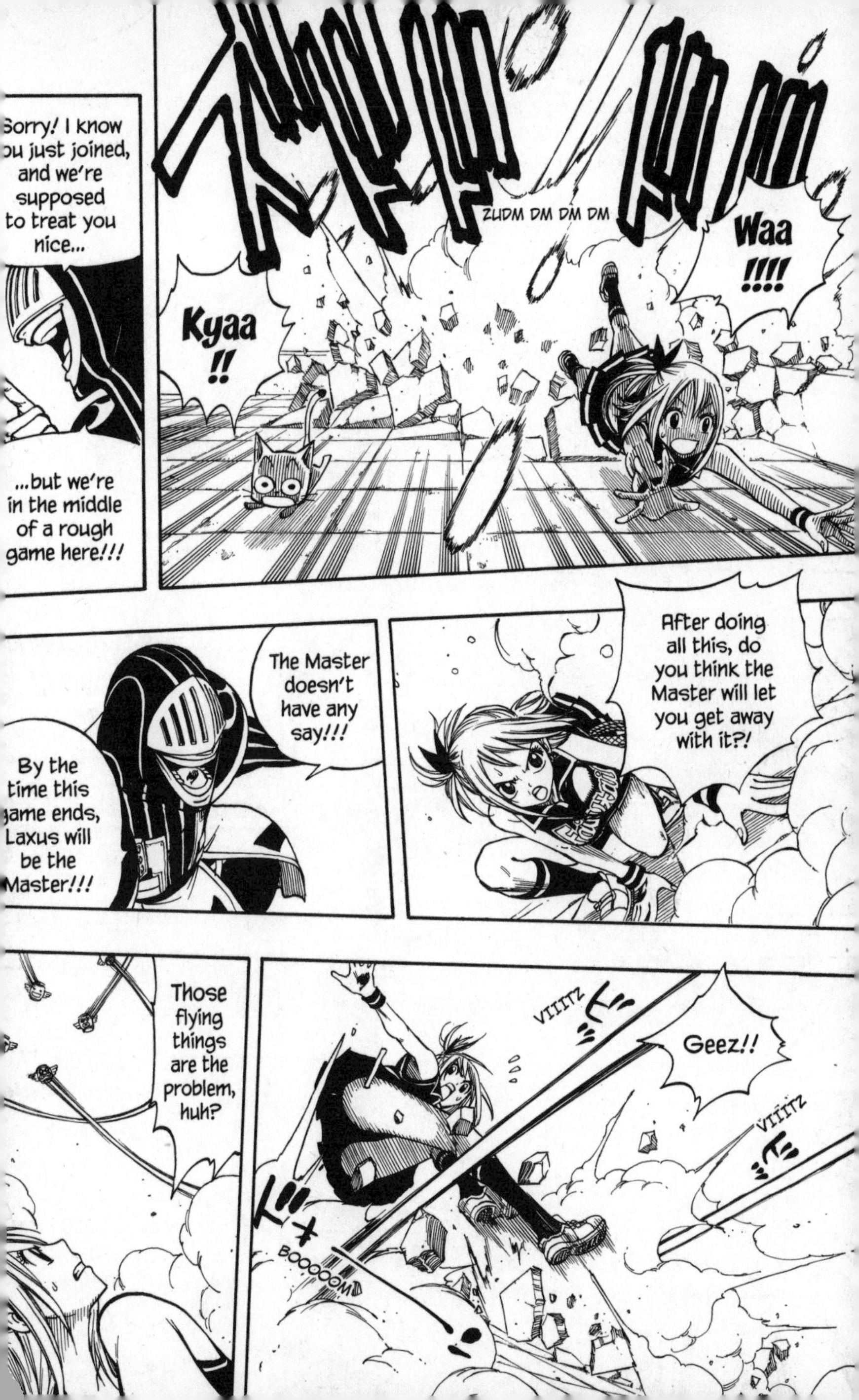
ZUDM DM DM DM
Waa !!!!
Kyaa !!
Sorry! I know ou just joined, and we're supposed to treat you nice...
...but we're in the middle of a rough game here!!!
After doing all this, do you think the Master will let you get away with it?!
The Master doesn't have any say!!!
By the time this game ends, Laxus will be the Master!!!
VIIITZ
Geez!!
VIIITZ
BOOOOOM
Those flying things are the problem, huh?

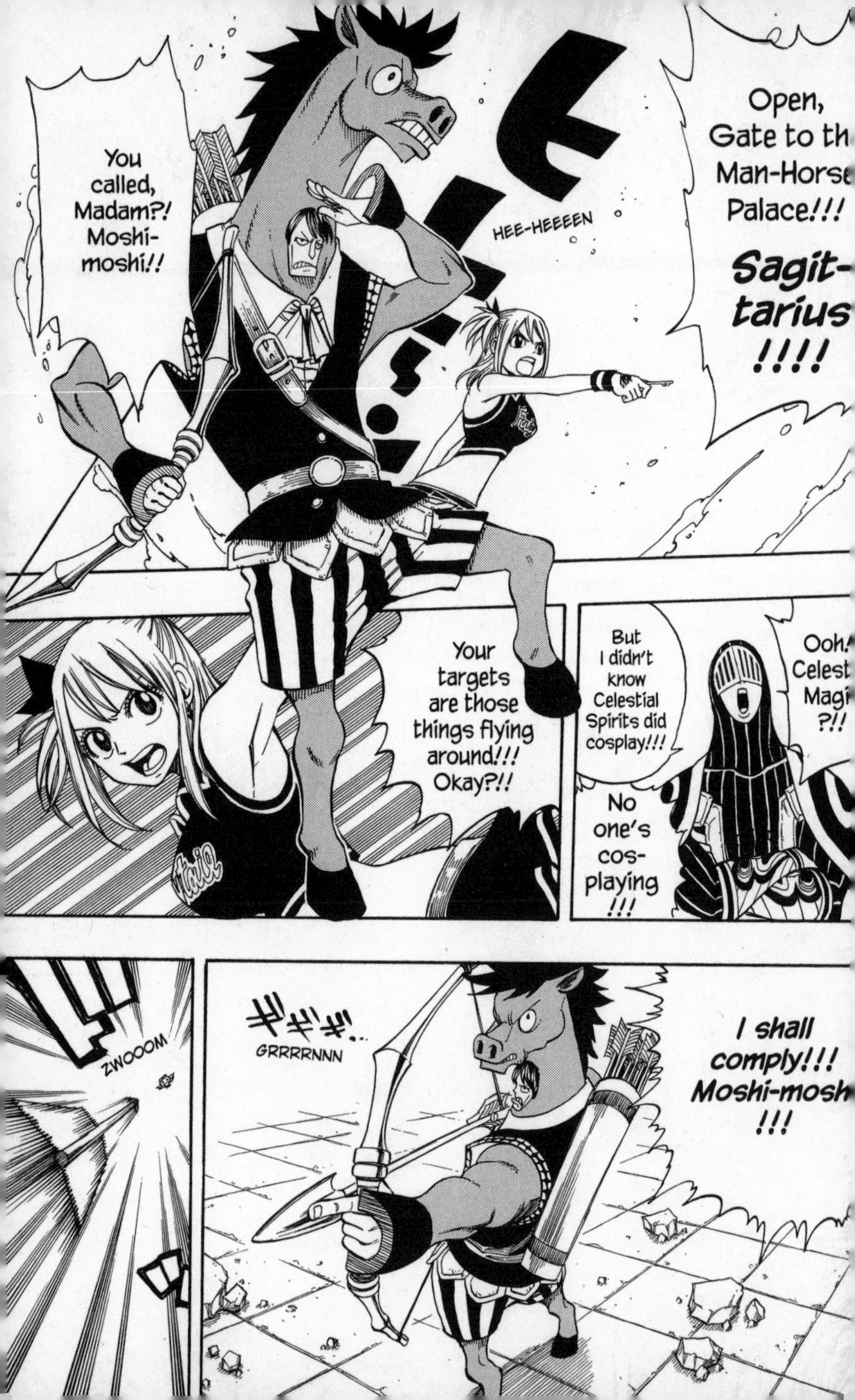
Open, Gate to th Man-Horse Palace!!!
Sagit-tarius !!!!
HEE-HEEEEN
You called, Madam?! Moshi-moshi!!
Ooh! Celest Magi ?!!
But I didn't know Celestial Spirits did cosplay!!!
No one's cos-playing !!!
Your targets are those things flying around!!! Okay?!!
I shall comply!!! Moshi-mosh !!!
ギギギ...
GRRRRNNN
ZWOOOM

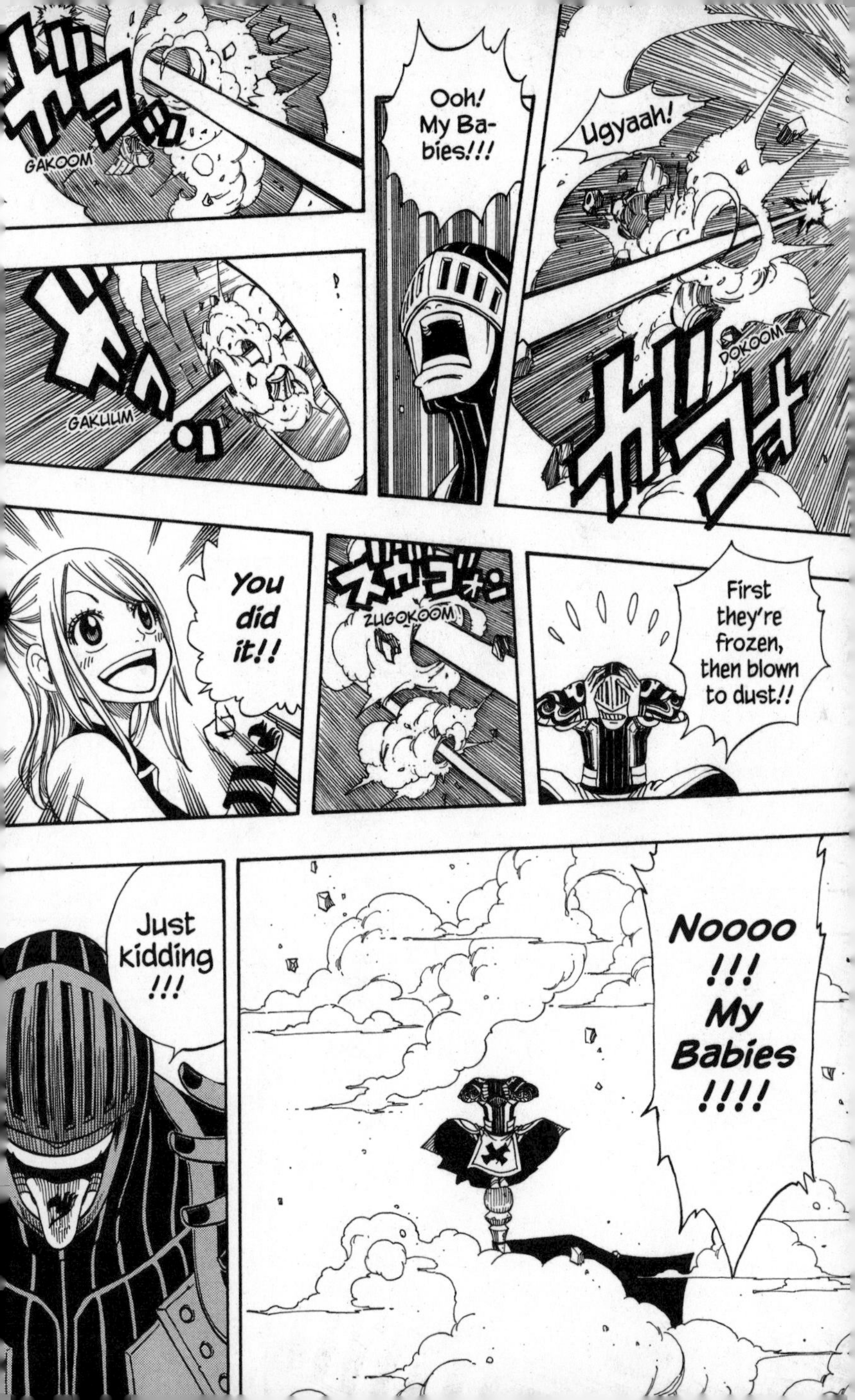
Ugyaah!
DOKOOM
Ooh! My Ba-bies!!!
GAKOOM
GAKUUM
First they're frozen, then blown to dust!!
ZUGOKOOM
You did it!!
Noooo!!! My Babies!!!!
Just kidding!!!

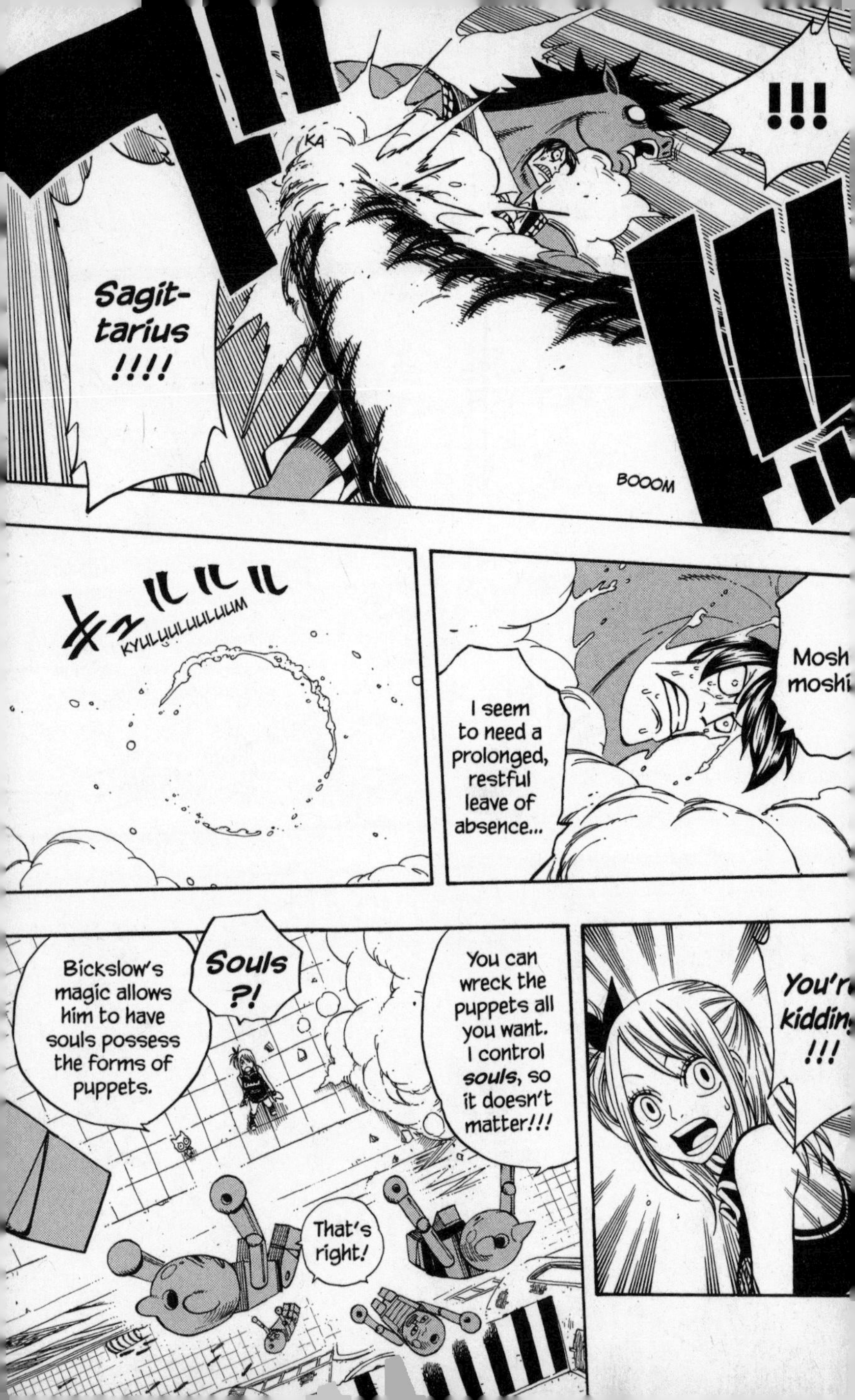
!!!
KA
Sagit-tarius !!!!
BOOOM
Mosh moshi
I seem to need a prolonged, restful leave of absence...
KYULULULULUM
You'r kiddin !!!
You can wreck the puppets all you want. I control souls, so it doesn't matter!!!
Souls ?!
Bickslow's magic allows him to have souls possess the forms of puppets.
That's right!

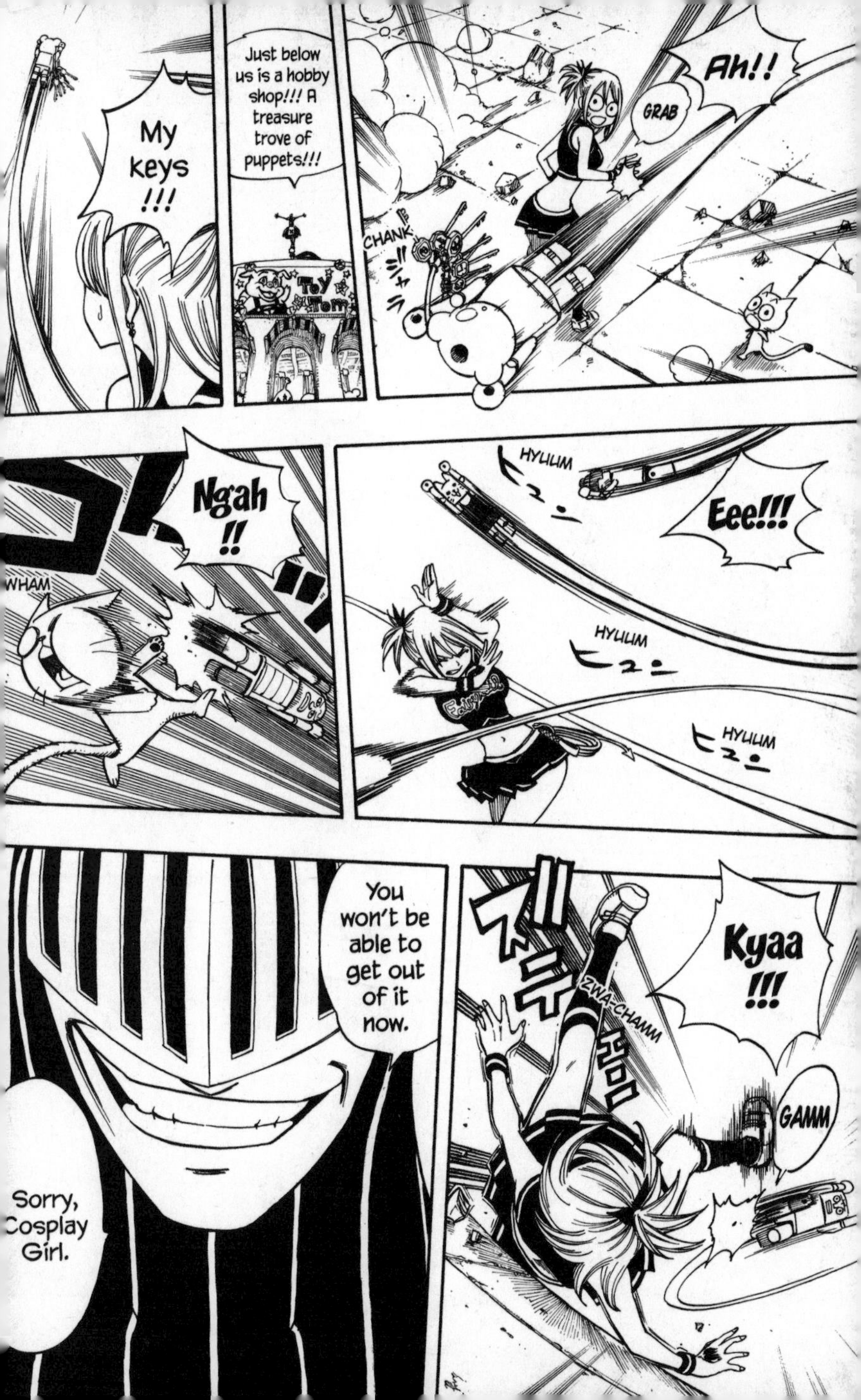
Ah!!
GRAB
CHANK
Just below us is a hobby shop!!! A treasure trove of puppets!!!
My keys !!!
HYUUM
Eee!!!
HYUUM
HYUUM
Ngah !!
WHAM
Kyaa !!!
ZWA-CHAMM
GAMM
You won't be able to get out of it now.
Sorry, Cosplay Girl.

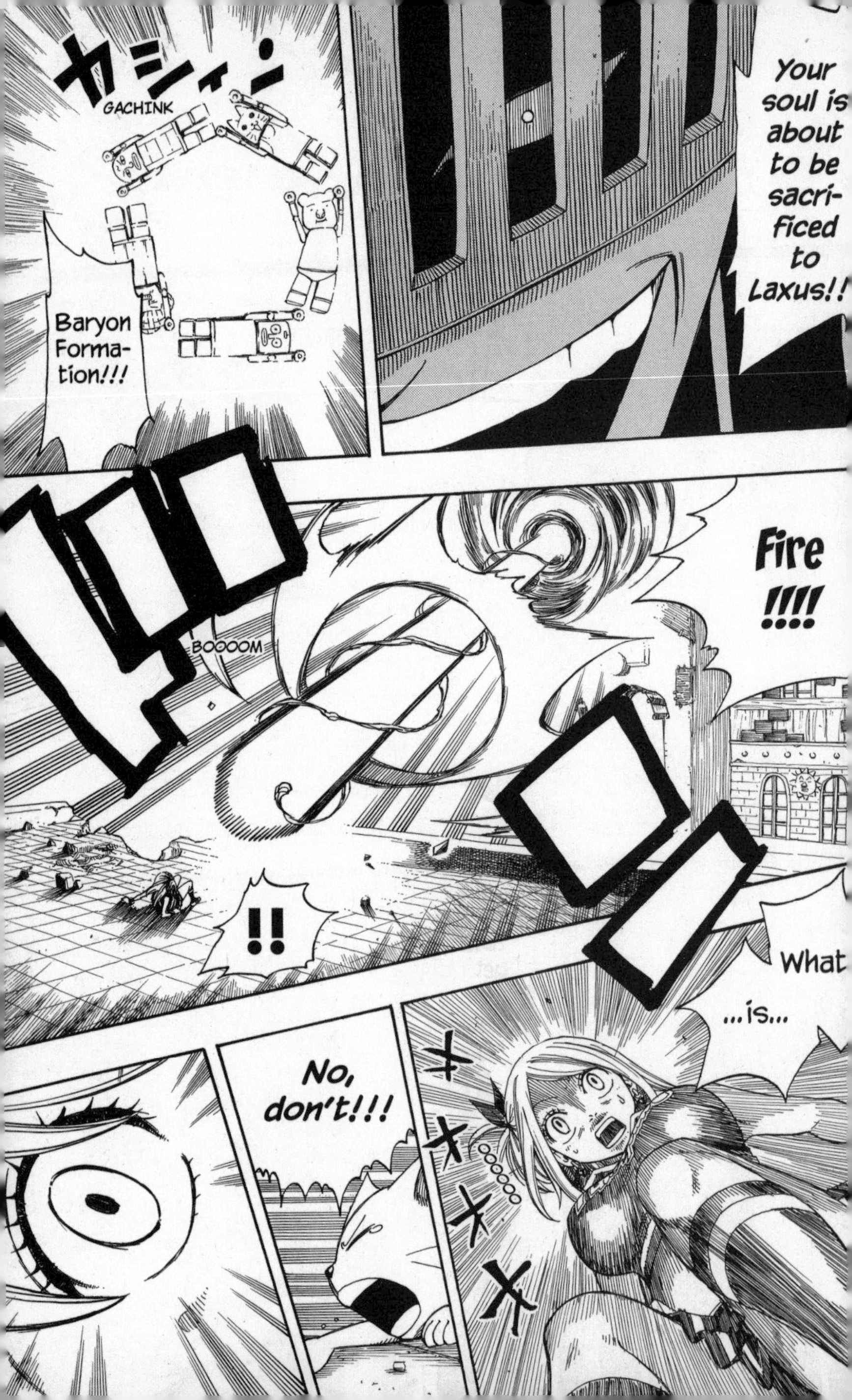

Your soul is about to be sacrificed to Laxus!!
カシィン
GACHINK
Baryon Formation!!!
Fire!!!!
BOOOOM
!!
What
...is...
No, don't!!!

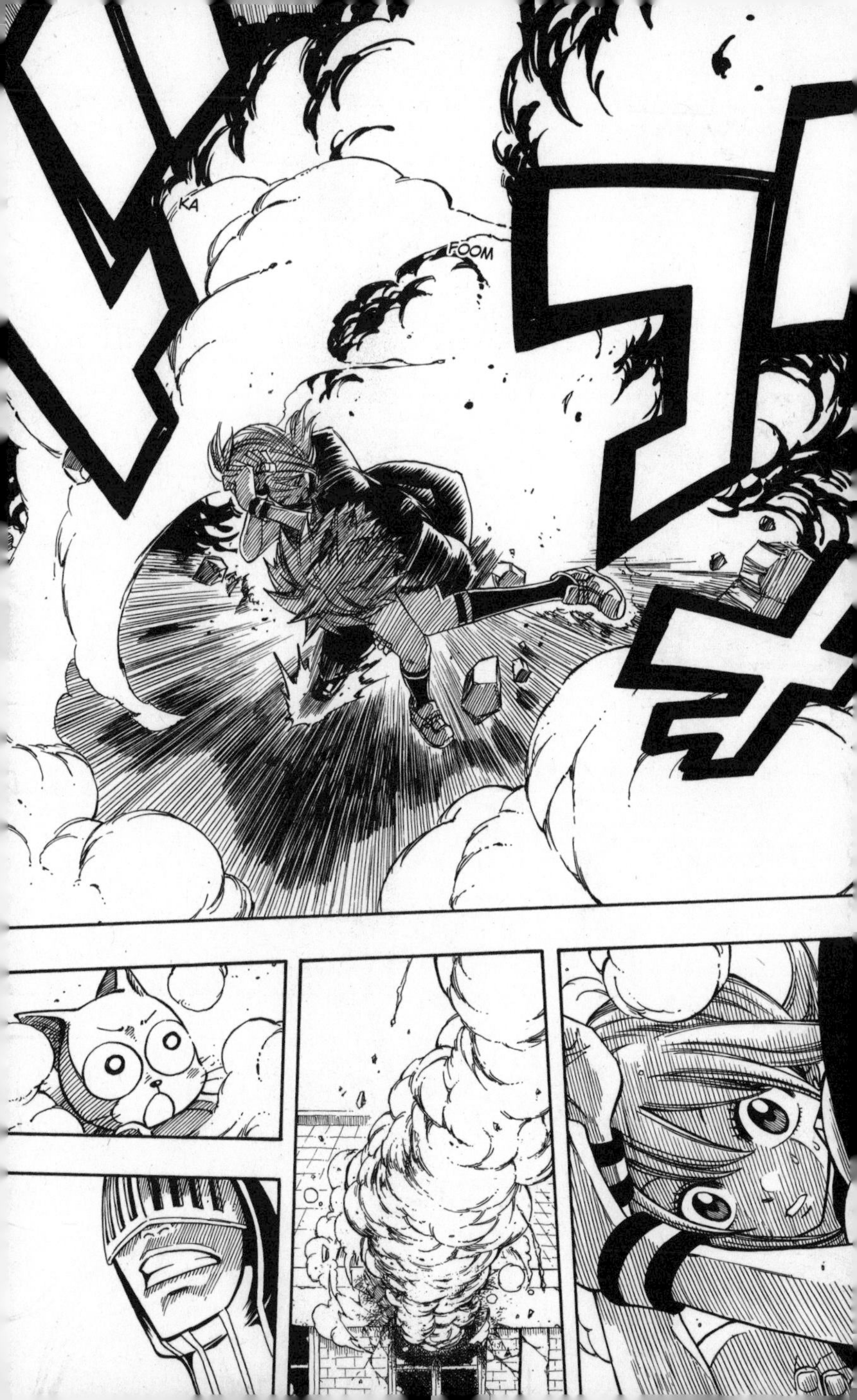
FOOM
KA

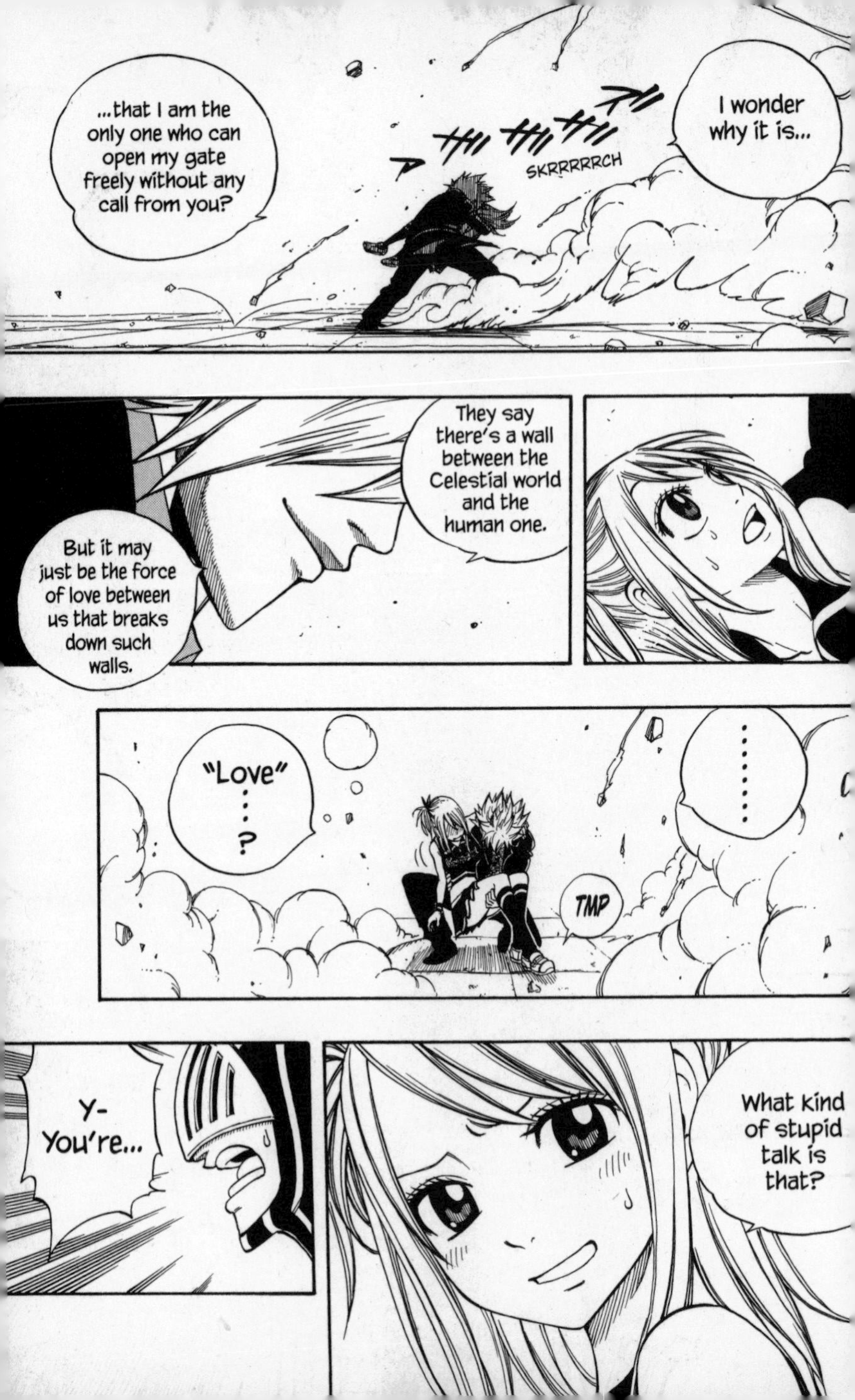

I wonder why it is...
SKRRRRCH
...that I am the only one who can open my gate freely without any call from you?
They say there's a wall between the Celestial world and the human one.
But it may just be the force of love between us that breaks down such walls.
....
"Love"...?
TMP
What kind of stupid talk is that?
Y- You're...

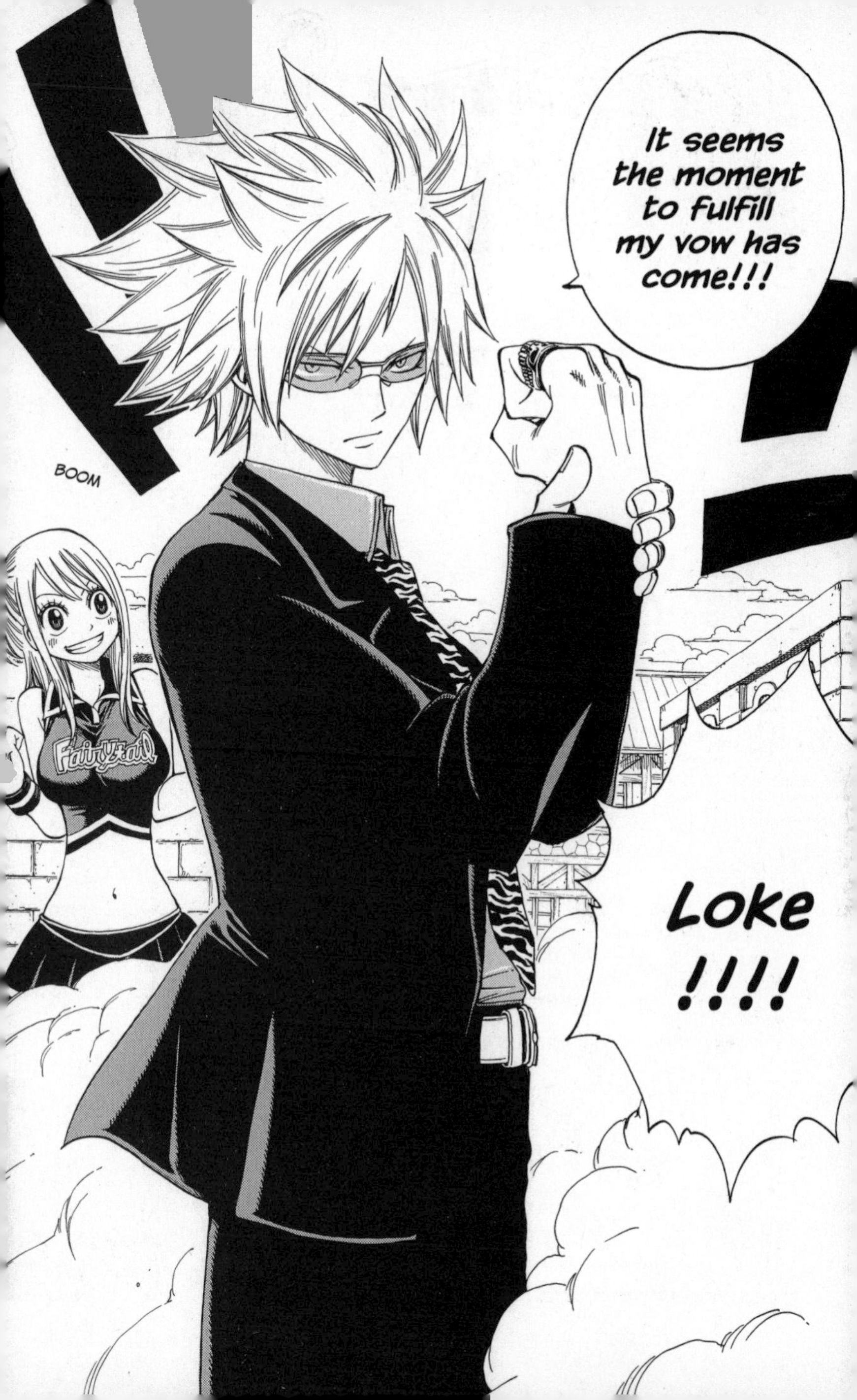
It seems the moment to fulfill my vow has come!!!
BOOM
Loke !!!!

FAIRY TAIL

Chapter 115: Regulus (The Light of the Lion)

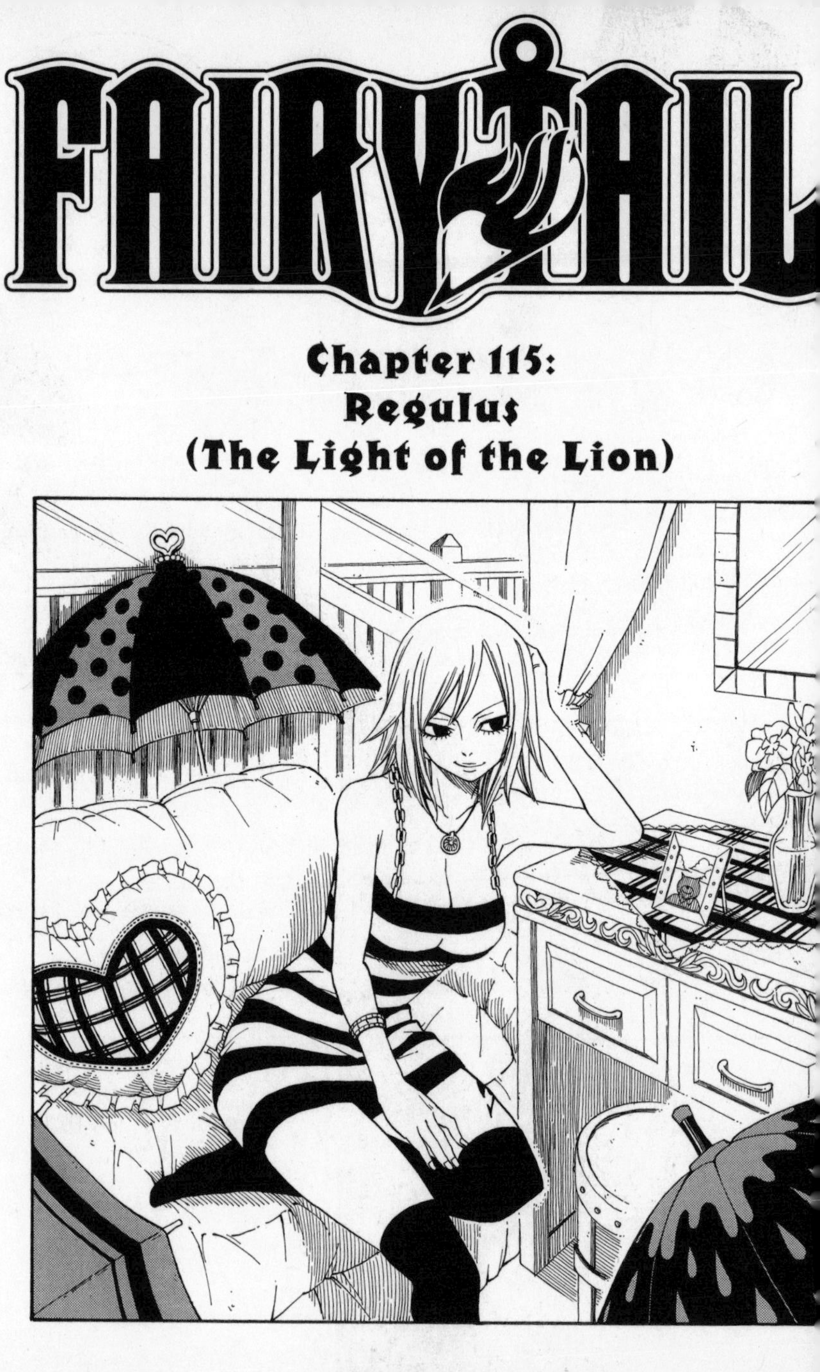

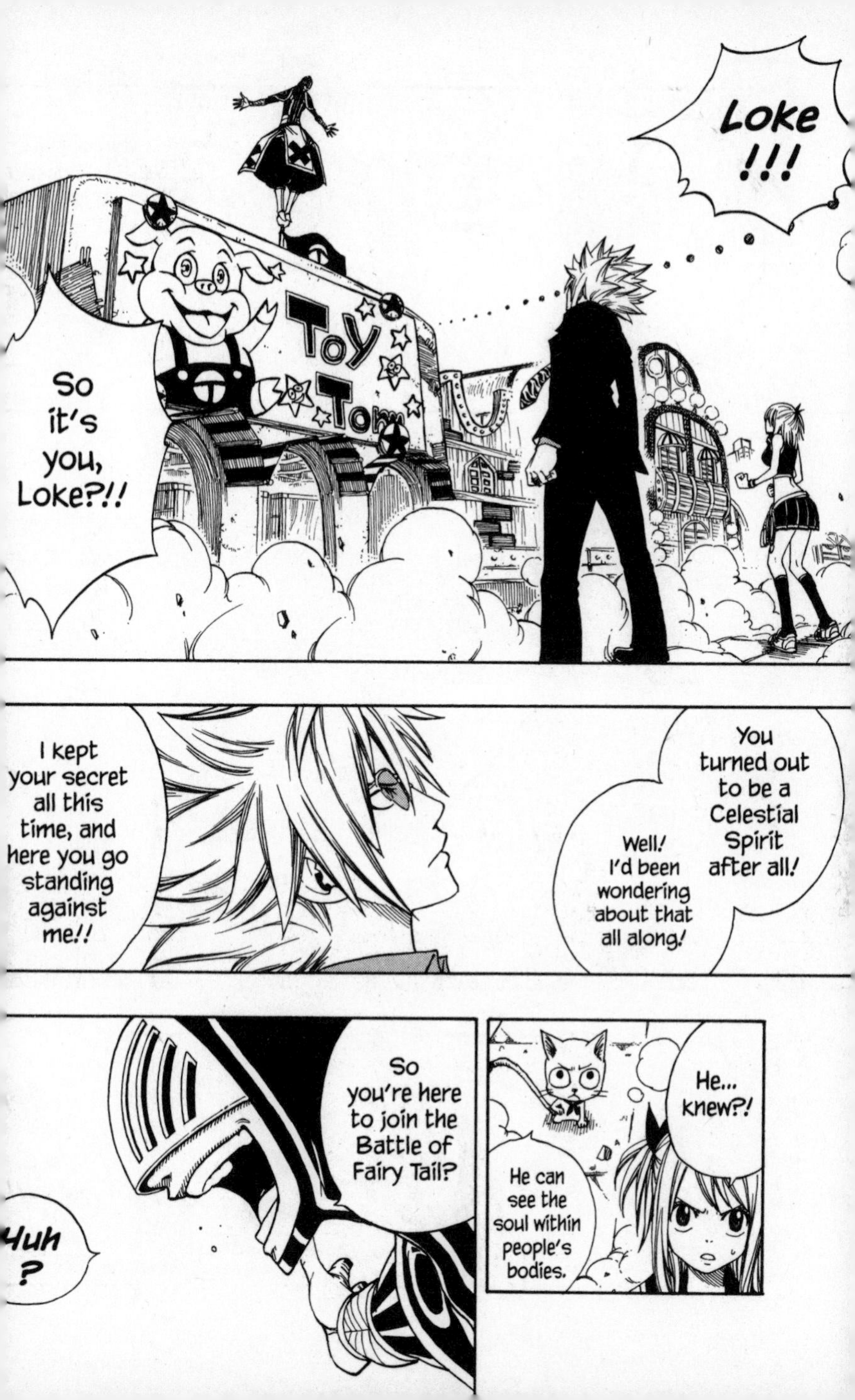
Loke!!!
Toy Tom
So it's you, Loke?!!
You turned out to be a Celestial Spirit after all!
Well! I'd been wondering about that all along!
I kept your secret all this time, and here you go standing against me!!
He... knew?!
He can see the soul within people's bodies.
So you're here to join the Battle of Fairy Tail?
Huh?

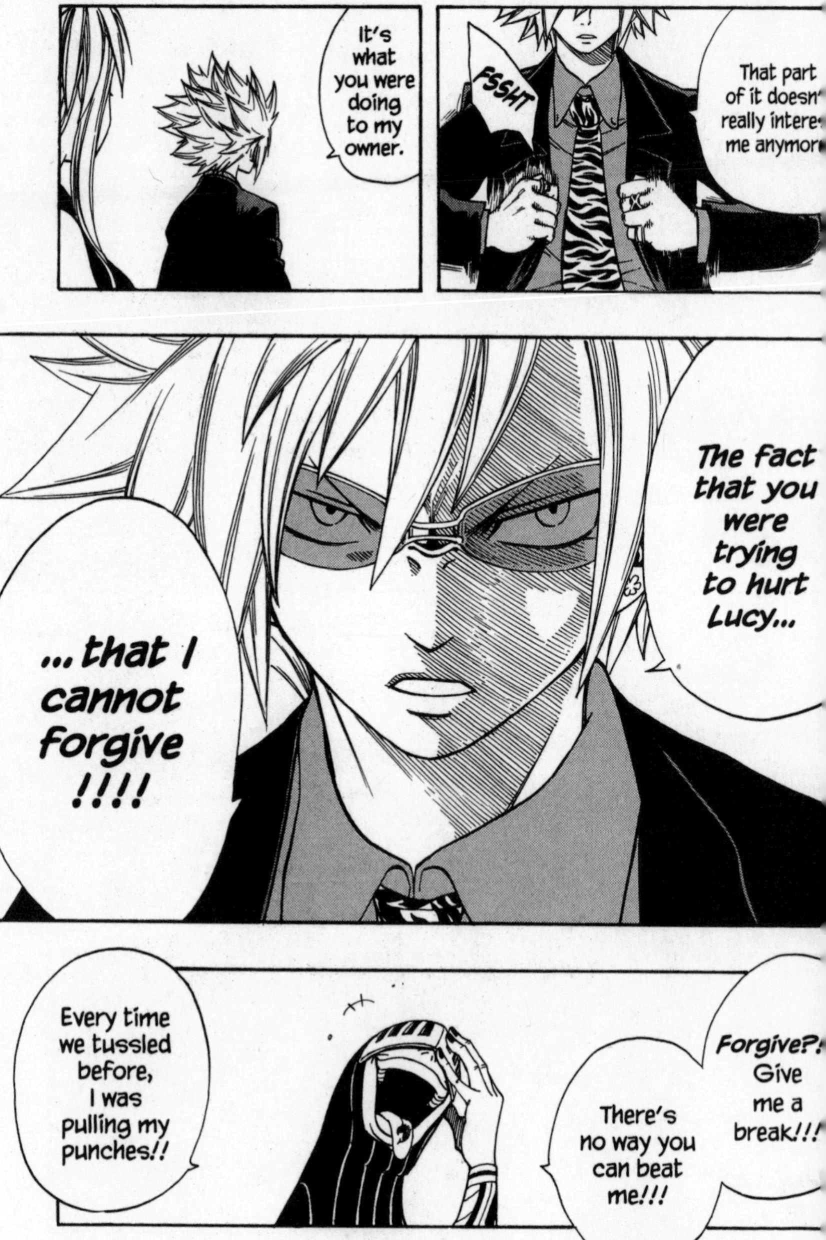
FSSHT
That part of it doesn' really interes me anymor
It's what you were doing to my owner.
The fact that you were trying to hurt Lucy...
...that I cannot forgive!!!!
Forgive?! Give me a break!!!
There's no way you can beat me!!!
Every time we tussled before, I was pulling my punches!!

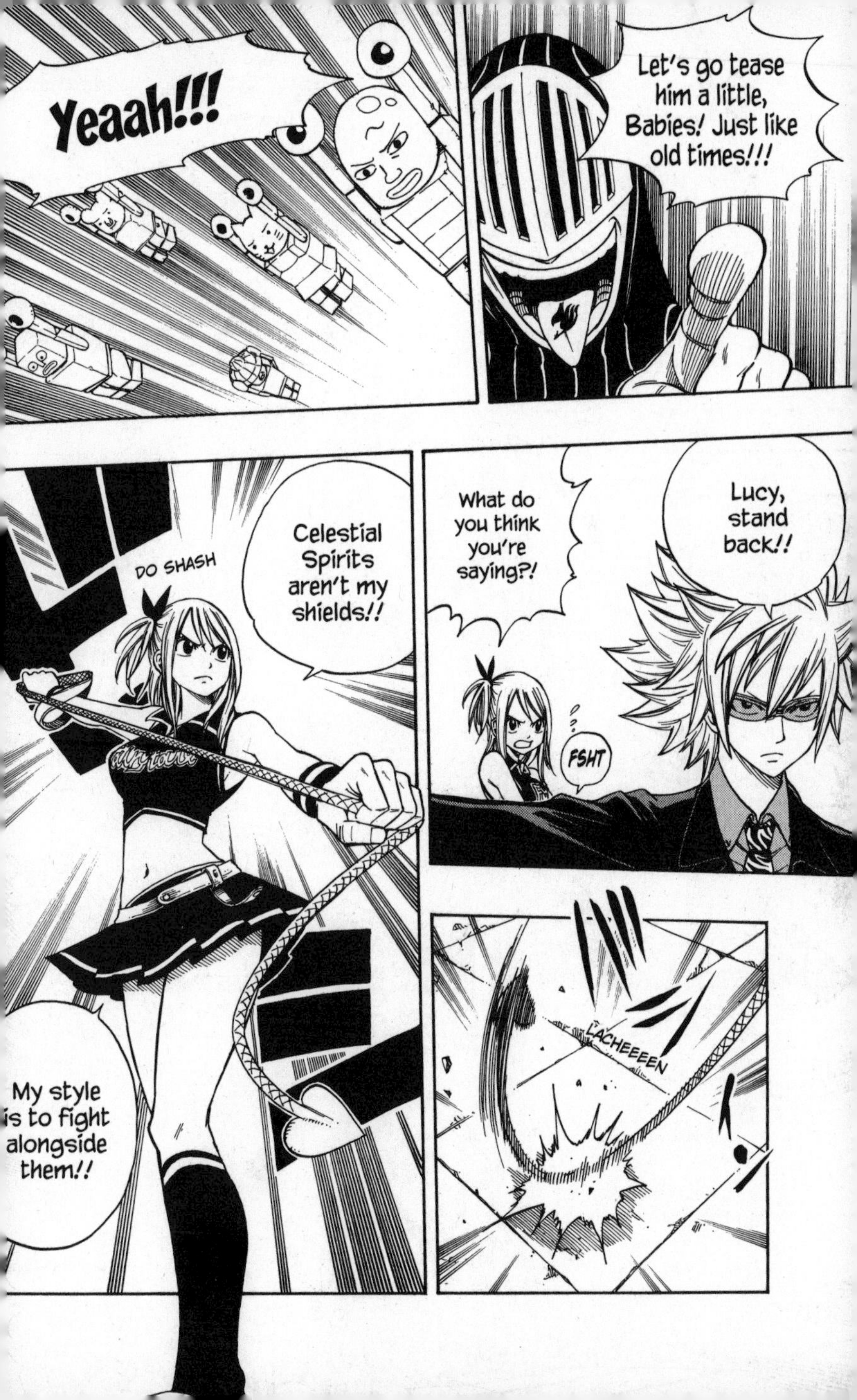
Let's go tease him a little, Babies! Just like old times!!!
Yeaah!!!
Lucy, stand back!!
What do you think you're saying?!
FSHT
LACHEEEEN
Celestial Spirits aren't my shields!!
DO SHASH
My style is to fight alongside them!!

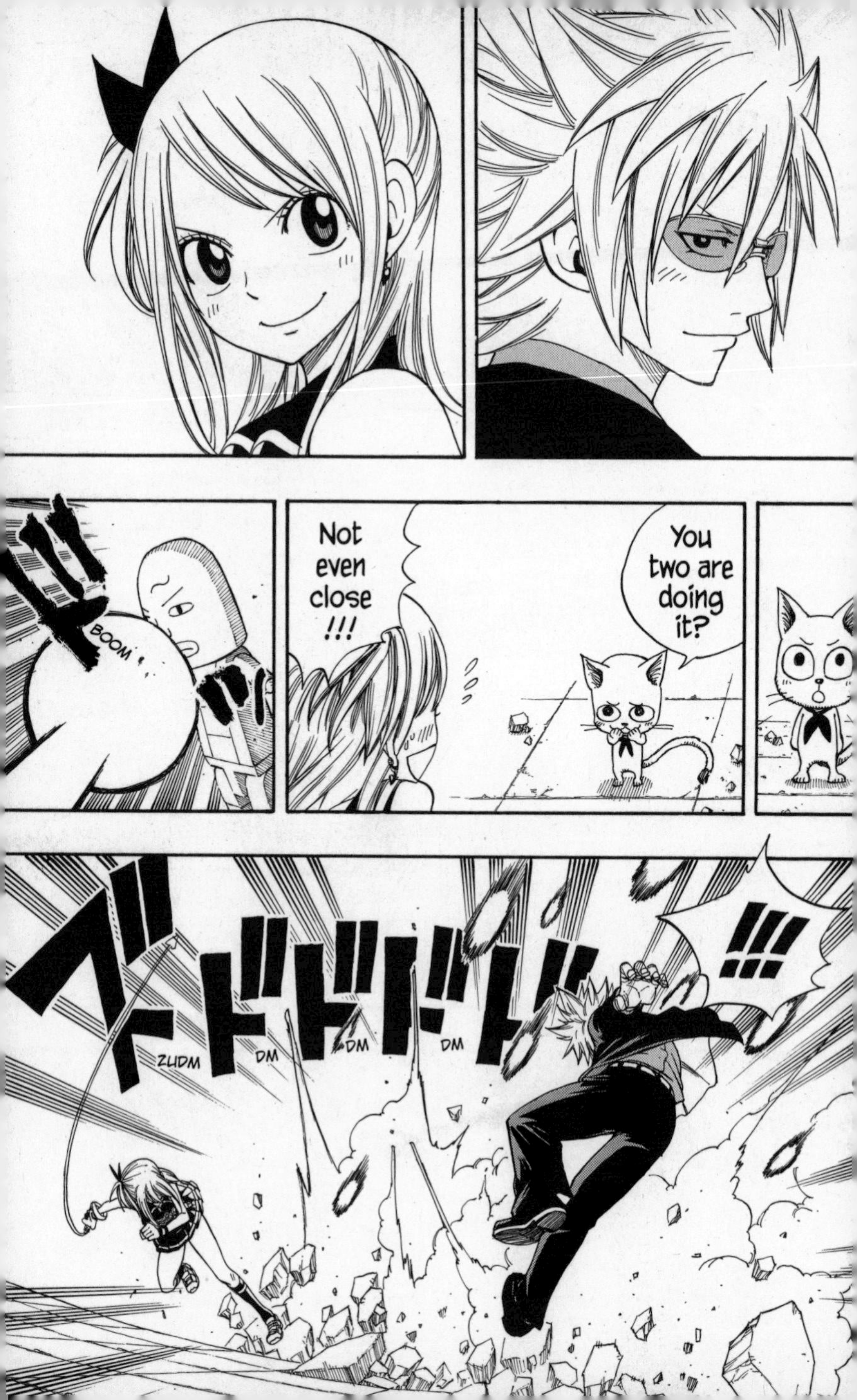
You two are doing it?
Not even close !!!
BOOM
!!!
DM
DM
DM
ZUDM

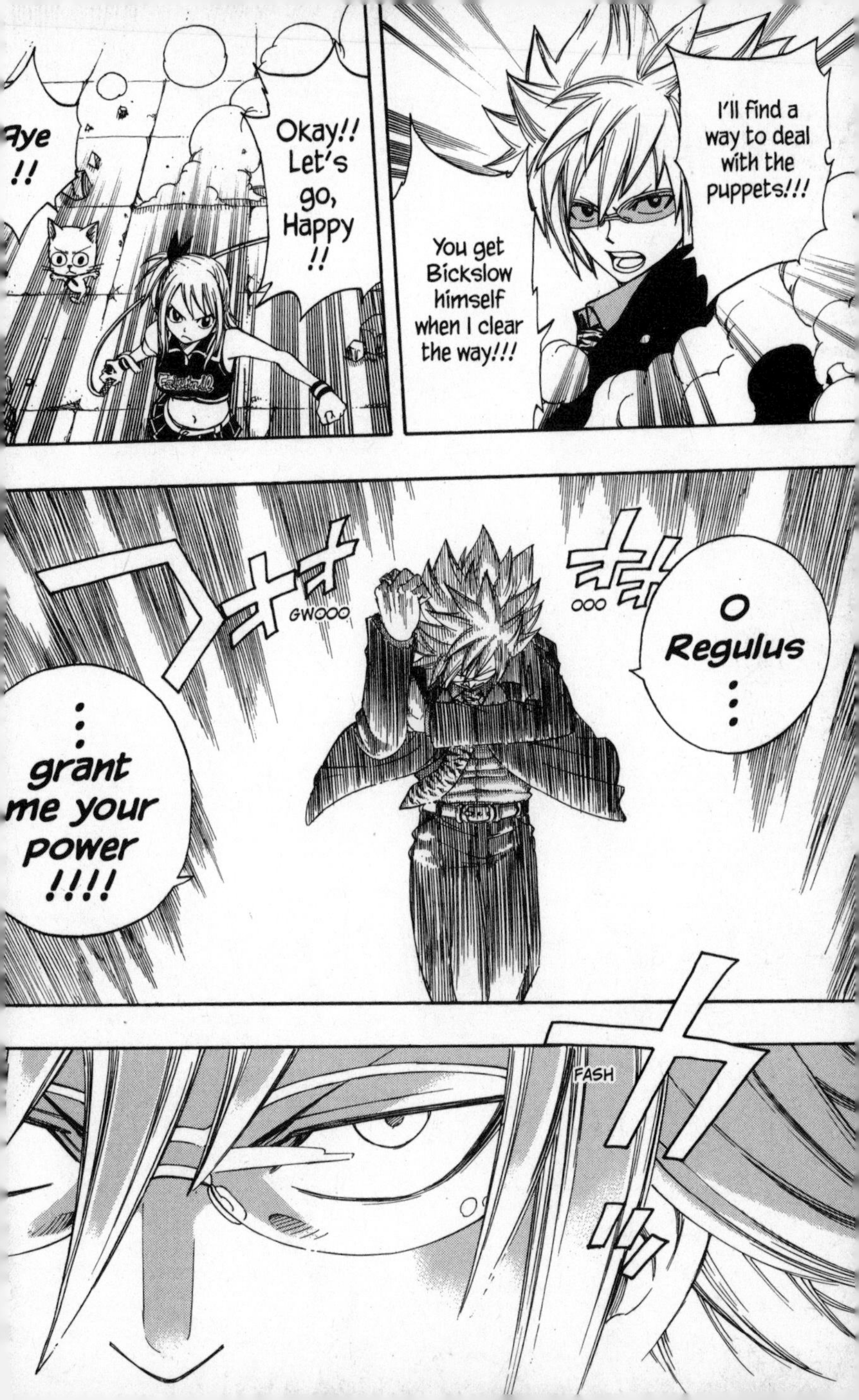
I'll find a way to deal with the puppets!!!
You get Bickslow himself when I clear the way!!!
Okay!! Let's go, Happy!!
Aye!!
GWOOO
OOO
O Regulus...
...grant me your power!!!!
FASH

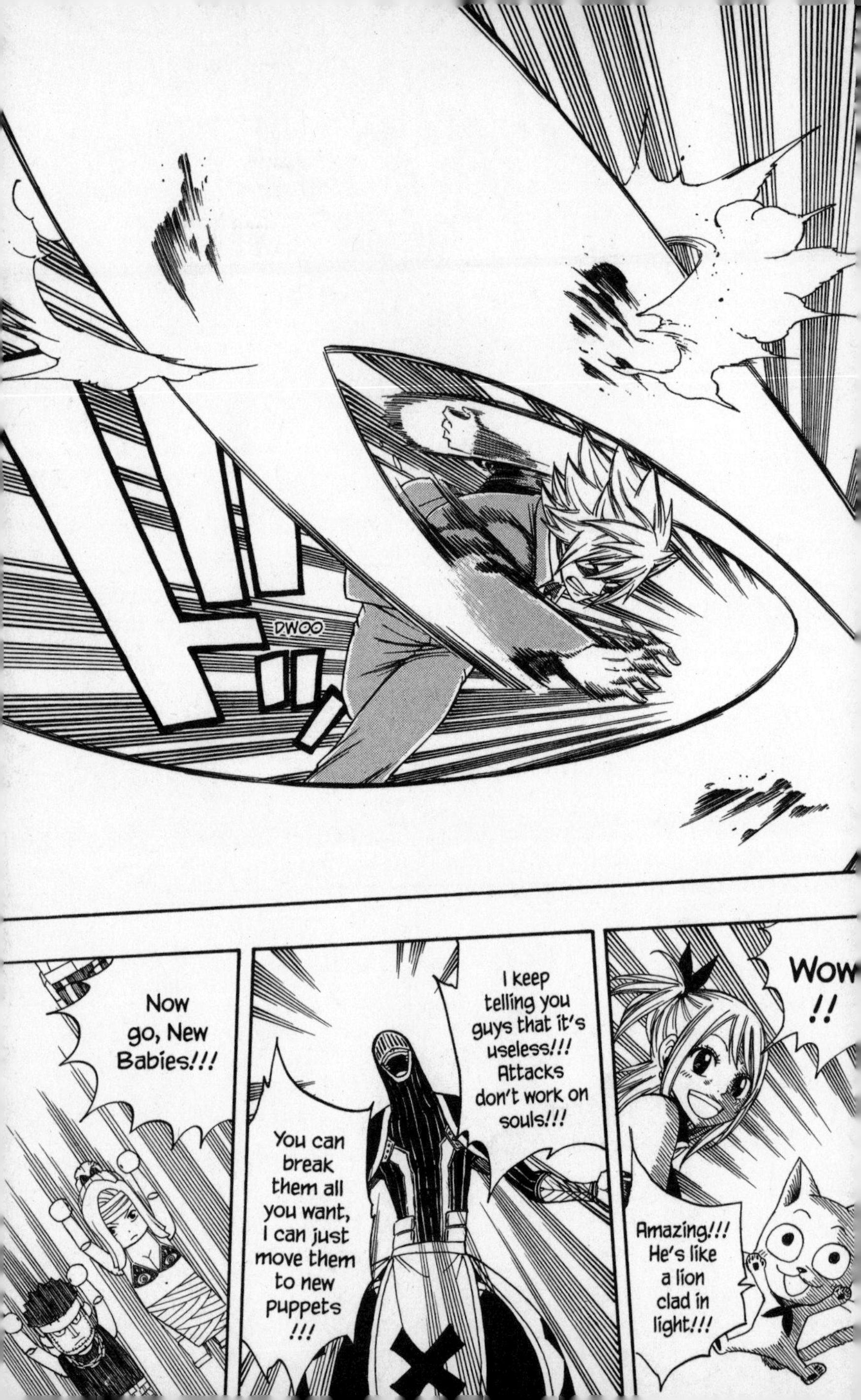
DWOO
Wow!!
Amazing!!! He's like a lion clad in light!!!
I keep telling you guys that it's useless!!! Attacks don't work on souls!!!
You can break them all you want, I can just move them to new puppets!!!
Now go, New Babies!!!

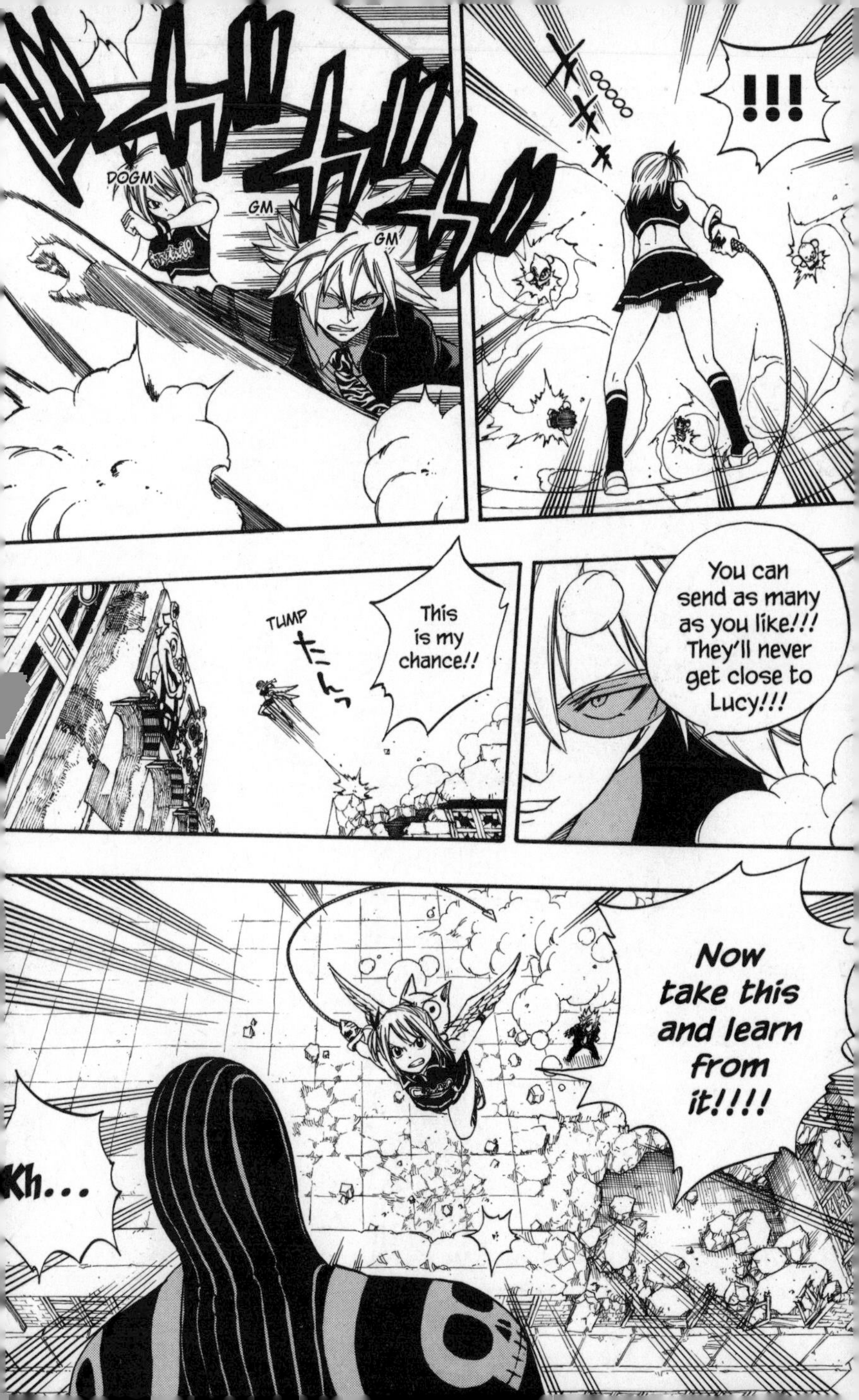
!!!
DOGM
GM
GM
You can send as many as you like!!! They'll never get close to Lucy!!!
This is my chance!!
TUMP
たんっ
Now take this and learn from it!!!!
Kh...

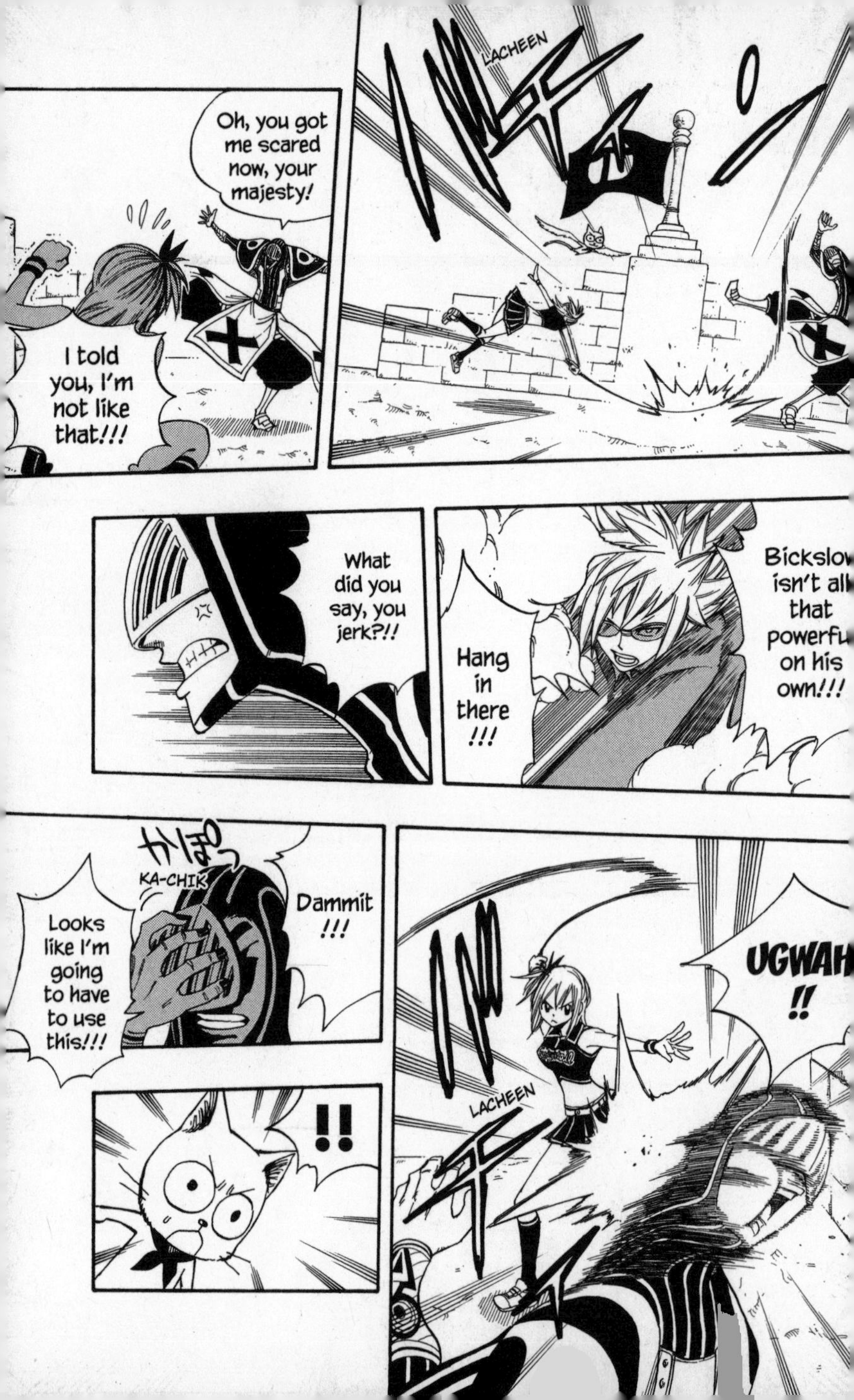
LACHEEN
Oh, you got me scared now, your majesty!
I told you, I'm not like that!!!
Bickslow isn't all that powerfu on his own!!!
Hang in there!!!
What did you say, you jerk?!!
UGWAH!!
LACHEEN
かぽっ
KA-CHIK
Dammit!!!
Looks like I'm going to have to use this!!!
!!

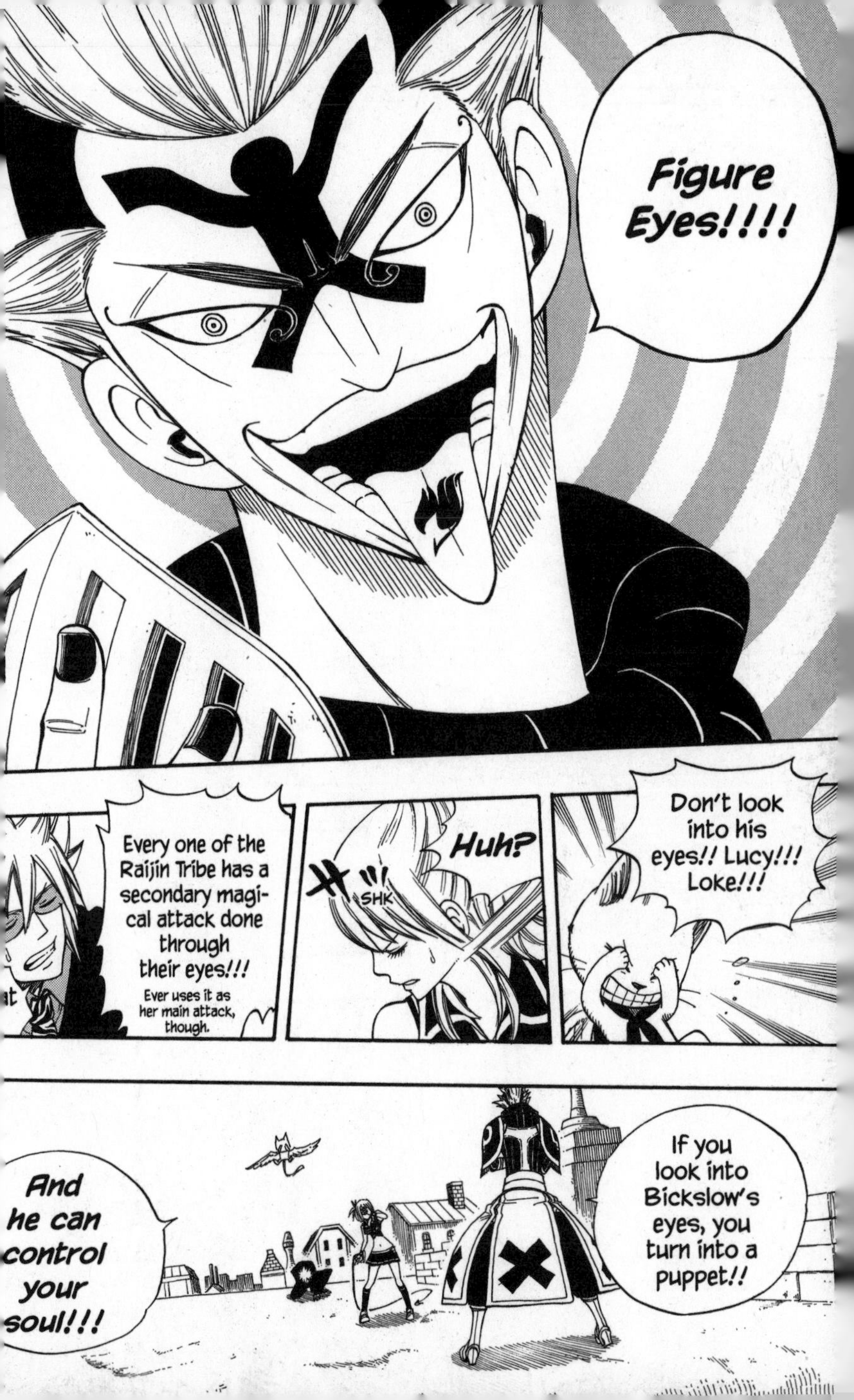
Figure Eyes!!!!
Don't look into his eyes!! Lucy!!! Loke!!!
Huh?
SHK
Every one of the Raijin Tribe has a secondary magical attack done through their eyes!!!
Ever uses it as her main attack, though.
If you look into Bickslow's eyes, you turn into a puppet!!
And he can control your soul!!!

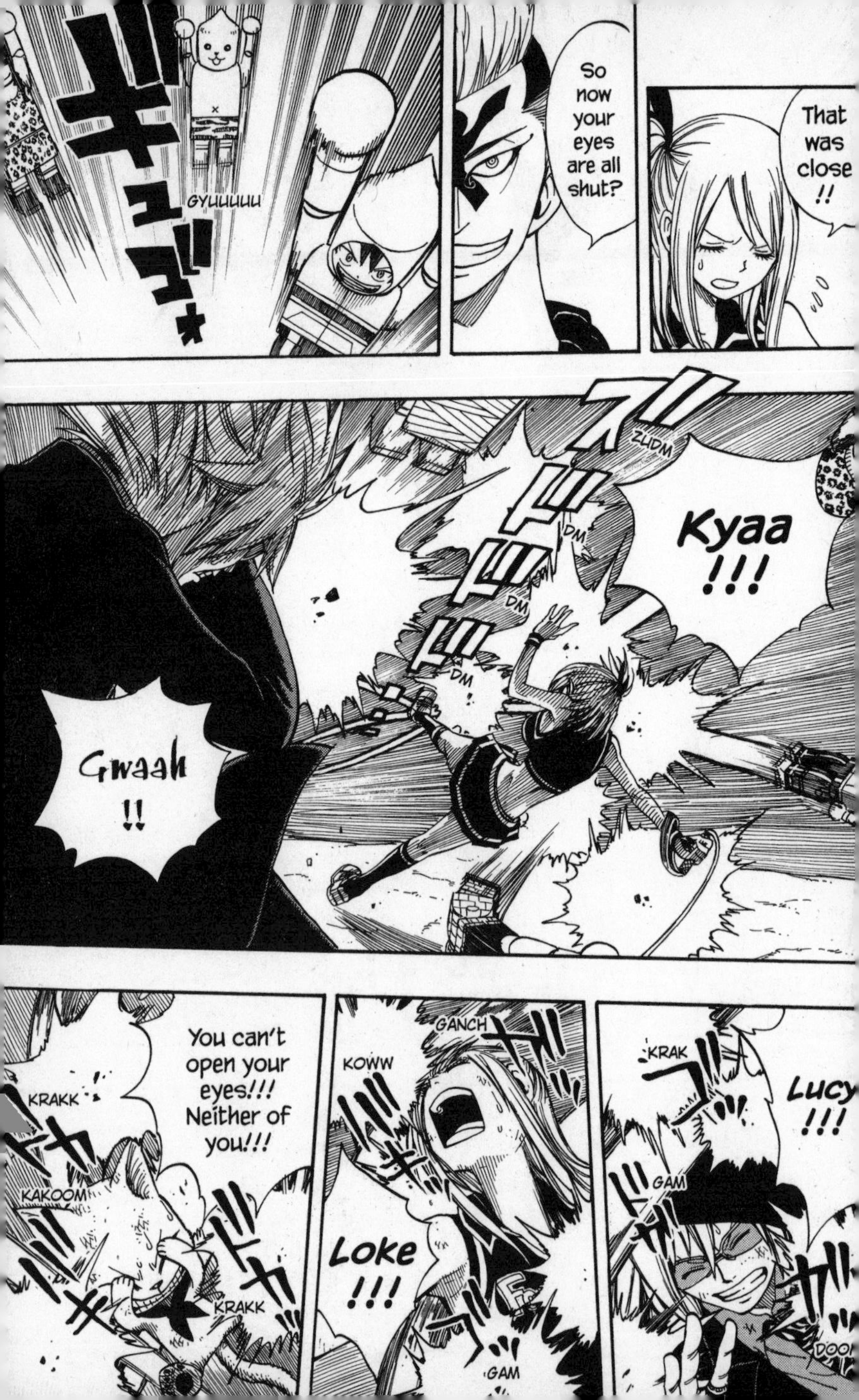
That was close!!
So now your eyes are all shut?
GYUUUUU
ZUDM
Kyaa!!!
DM
DM
DM
Gwaah!!
KRAK
Lucy!!!
GAM
DOO
GANCH
KOWW
Loke!!!
GAM
You can't open your eyes!!! Neither of you!!!
KRAKK
KAKOOM
KRAKK

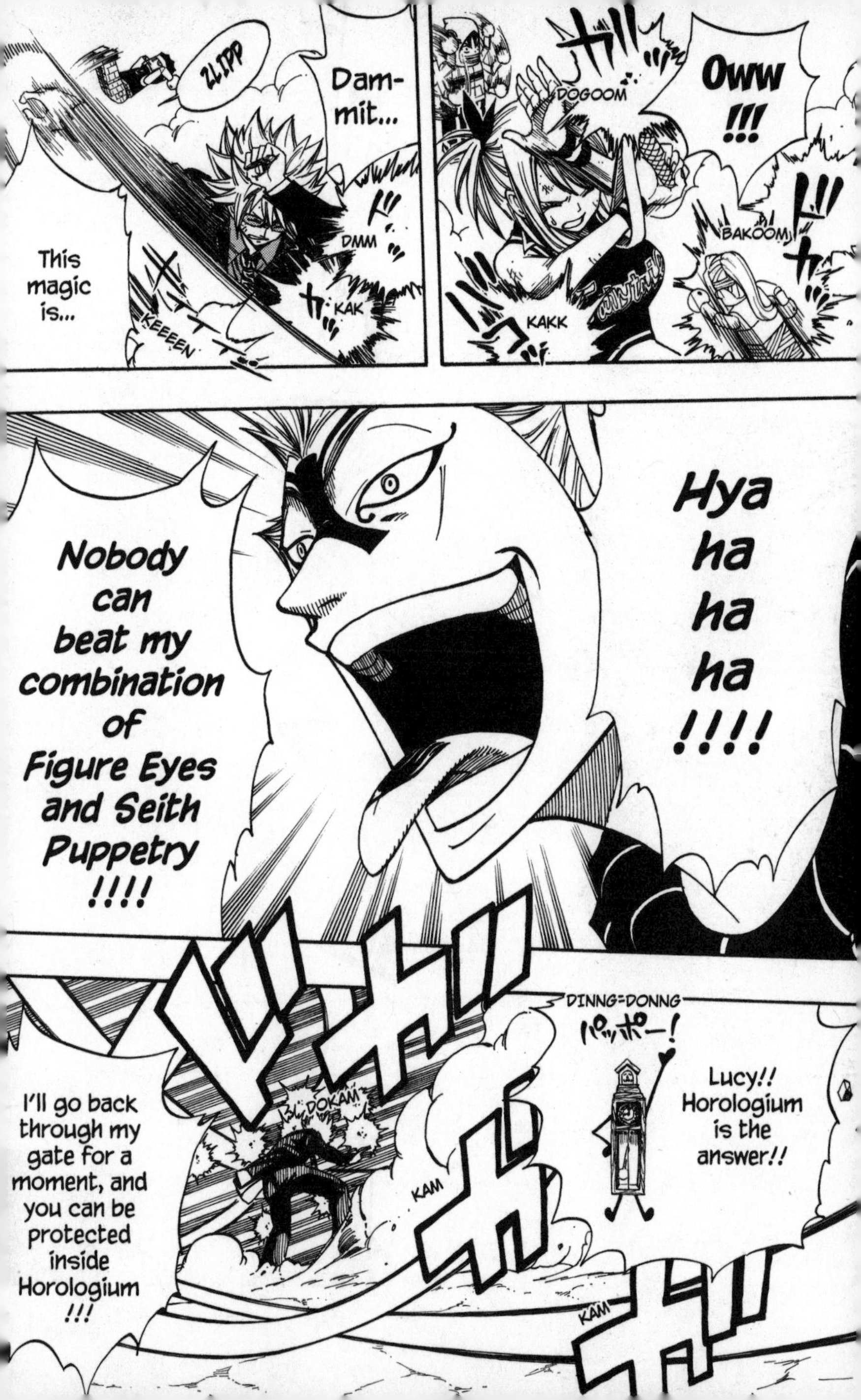
Oww!!!
DOGOOM
BAKOOM
KAKK
Dam-mit...
ZLIPP
DMM
KAK
KEEEEN
This magic is...
Hya ha ha ha!!!!
Nobody can beat my combination of Figure Eyes and Seith Puppetry!!!!
DINNG=DONNG
パッポー!
Lucy!! Horologium is the answer!!
KAM
DOKAM
I'll go back through my gate for a moment, and you can be protected inside Horologium!!!
KAM

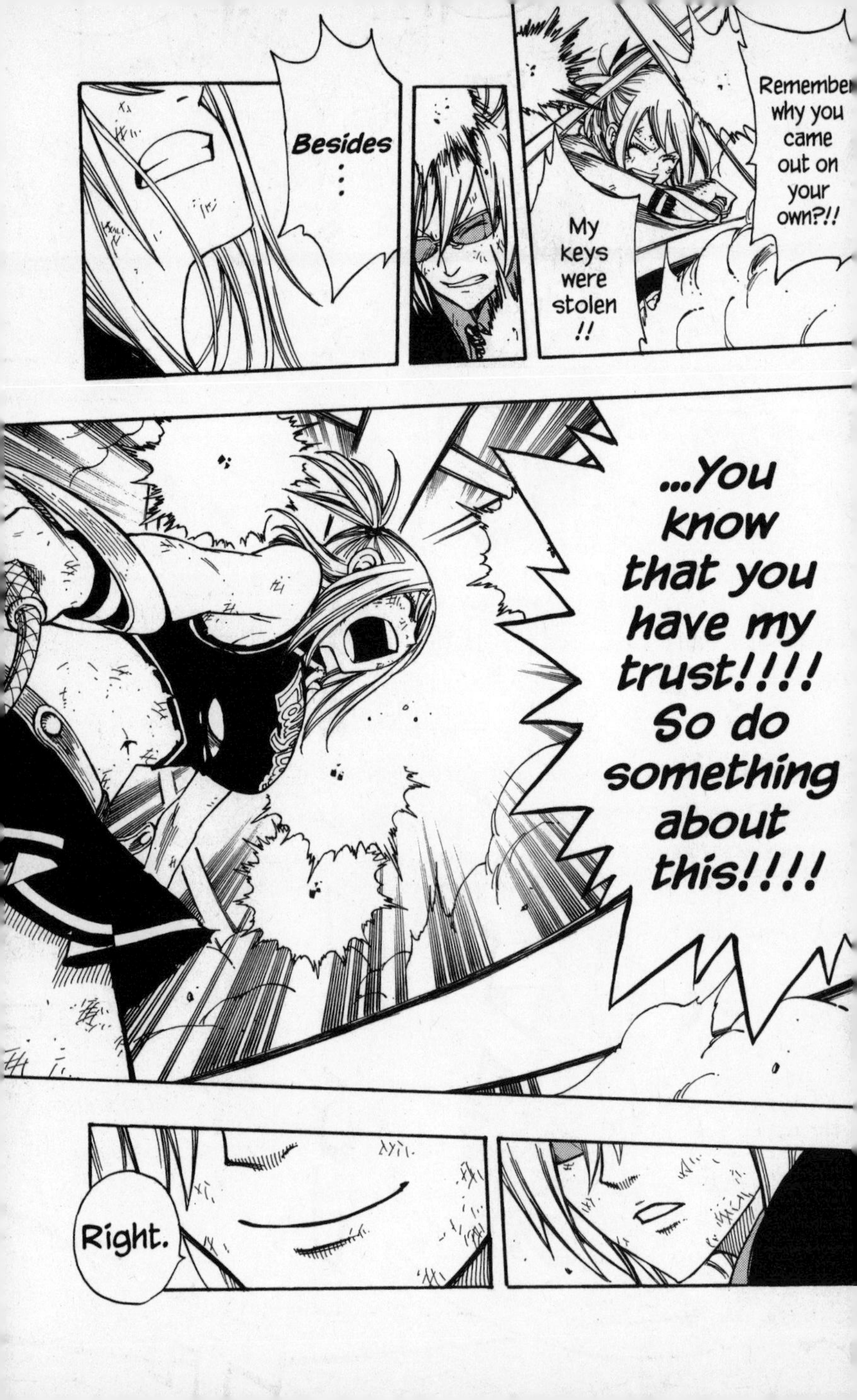

Remember why you came out on your own?!!
My keys were stolen!!
Besides...
...You know that you have my trust!!!! So do something about this!!!!
Right.

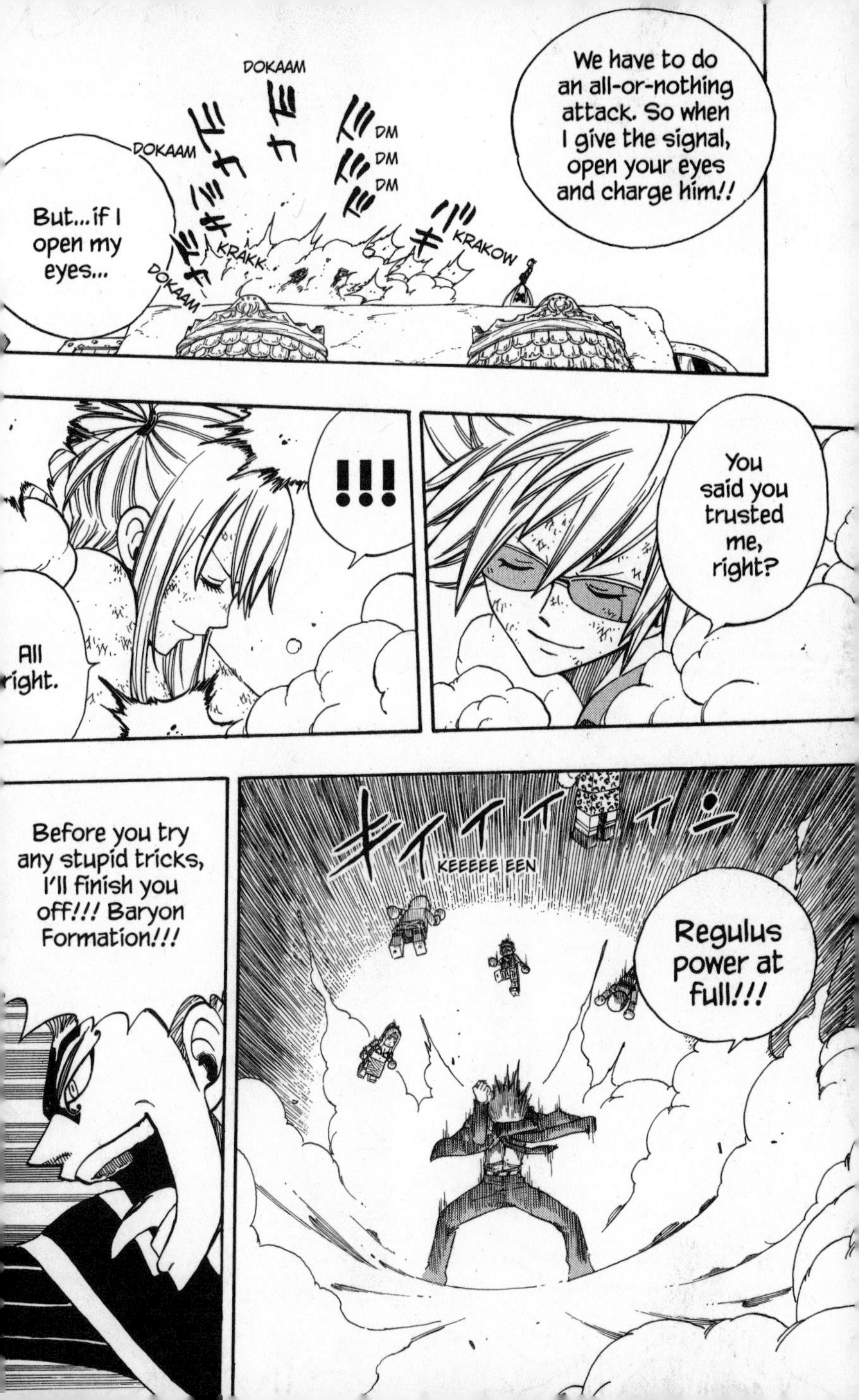
We have to do an all-or-nothing attack. So when I give the signal, open your eyes and charge him!!
DOKAAM
DM
DM
DM
KRAKOW
KRAKK
DOKAAM
DOKAAM
But...if I open my eyes...
You said you trusted me, right?
!!!
All right.
KEEEEE EEN
Regulus power at full!!!
Before you try any stupid tricks, I'll finish you off!!! Baryon Formation!!!

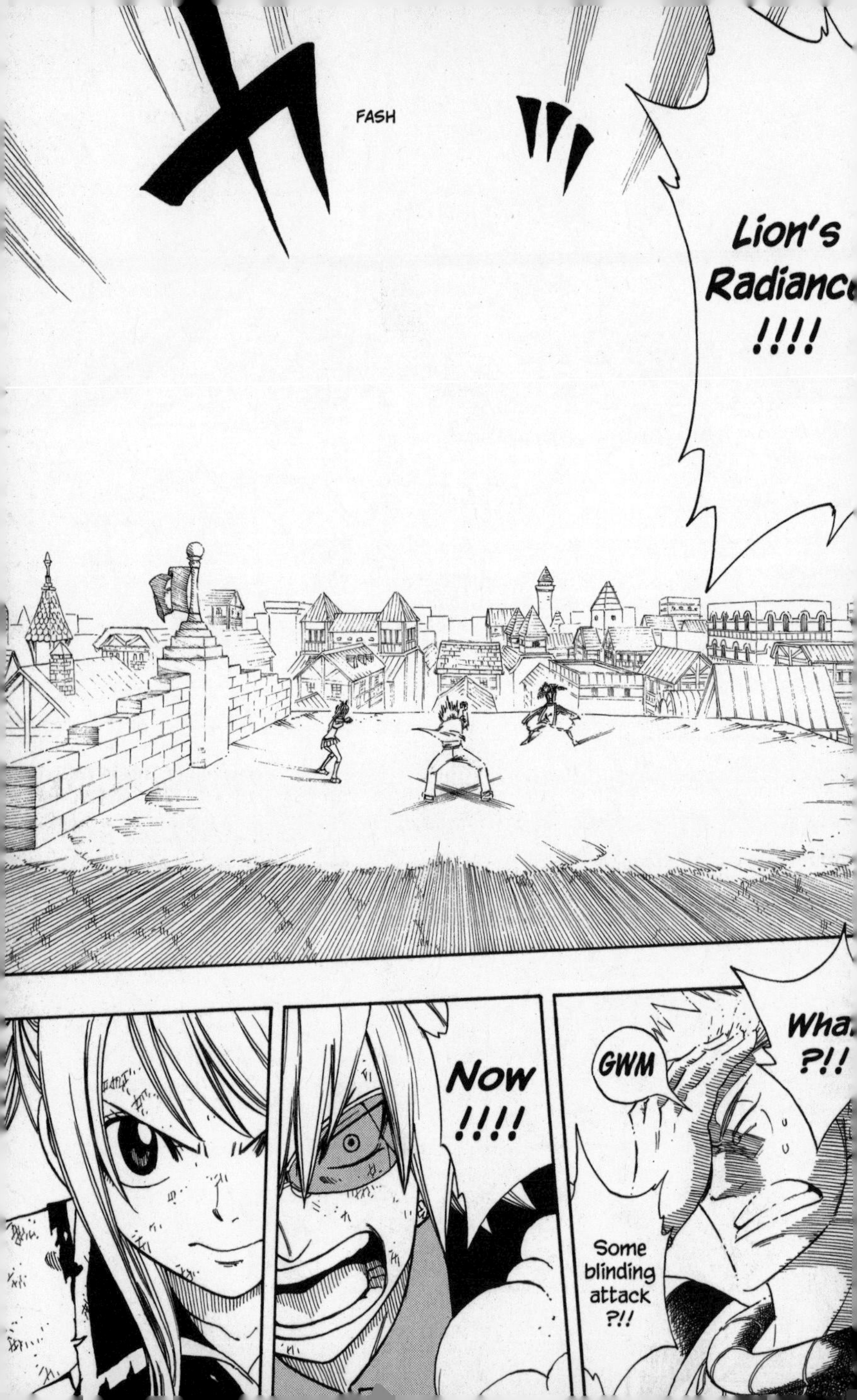
Lion's Radianc !!!!
FASH
Wha. ?!!
GWM
Some blinding attack ?!!
Now !!!!

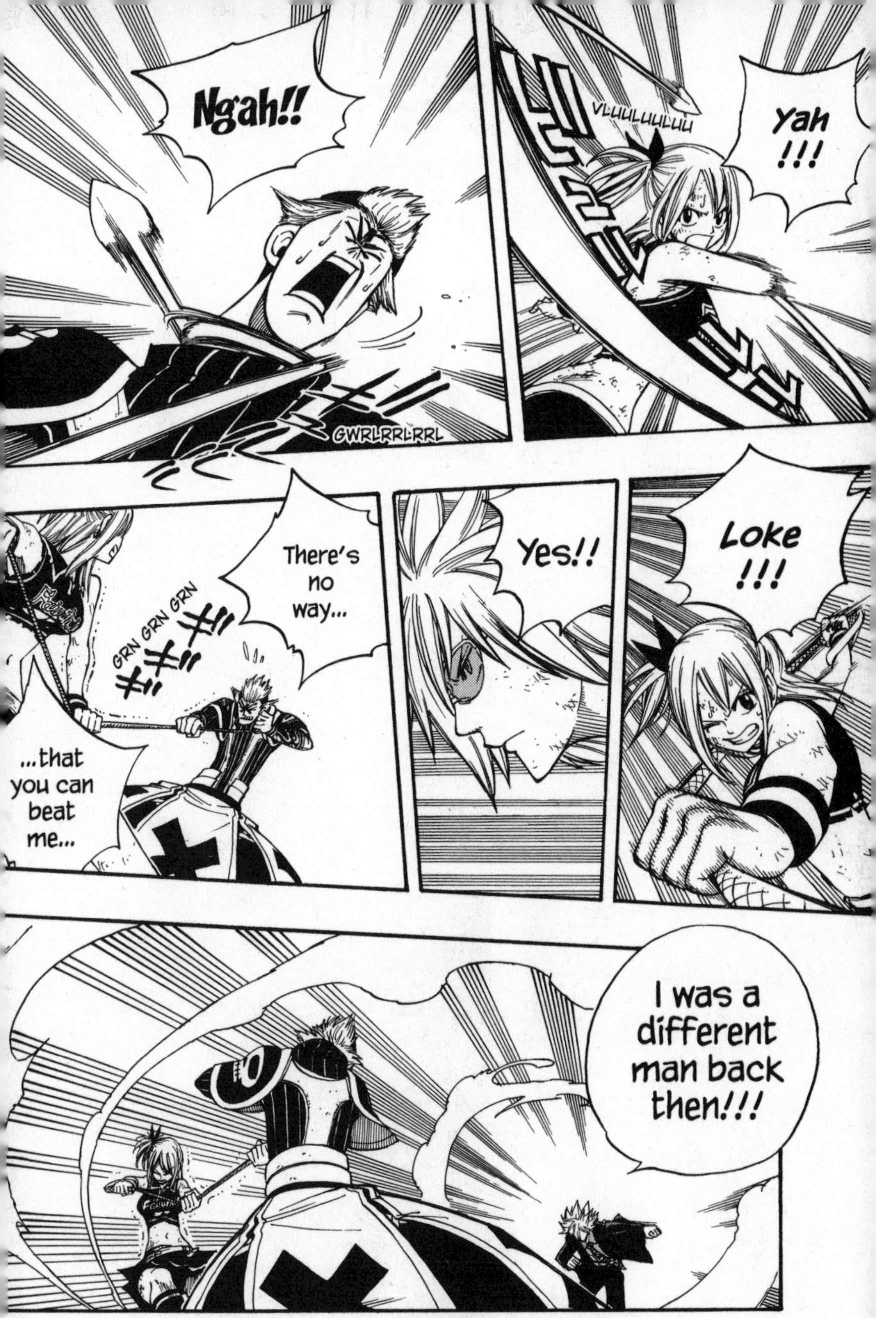
VLUULUULUU
Yah!!!
Ngah!!
GWRLRRLRRL
Loke!!!
Yes!!
There's no way...
GRN GRN GRN
...that you can beat me...
I was a different man back then!!!

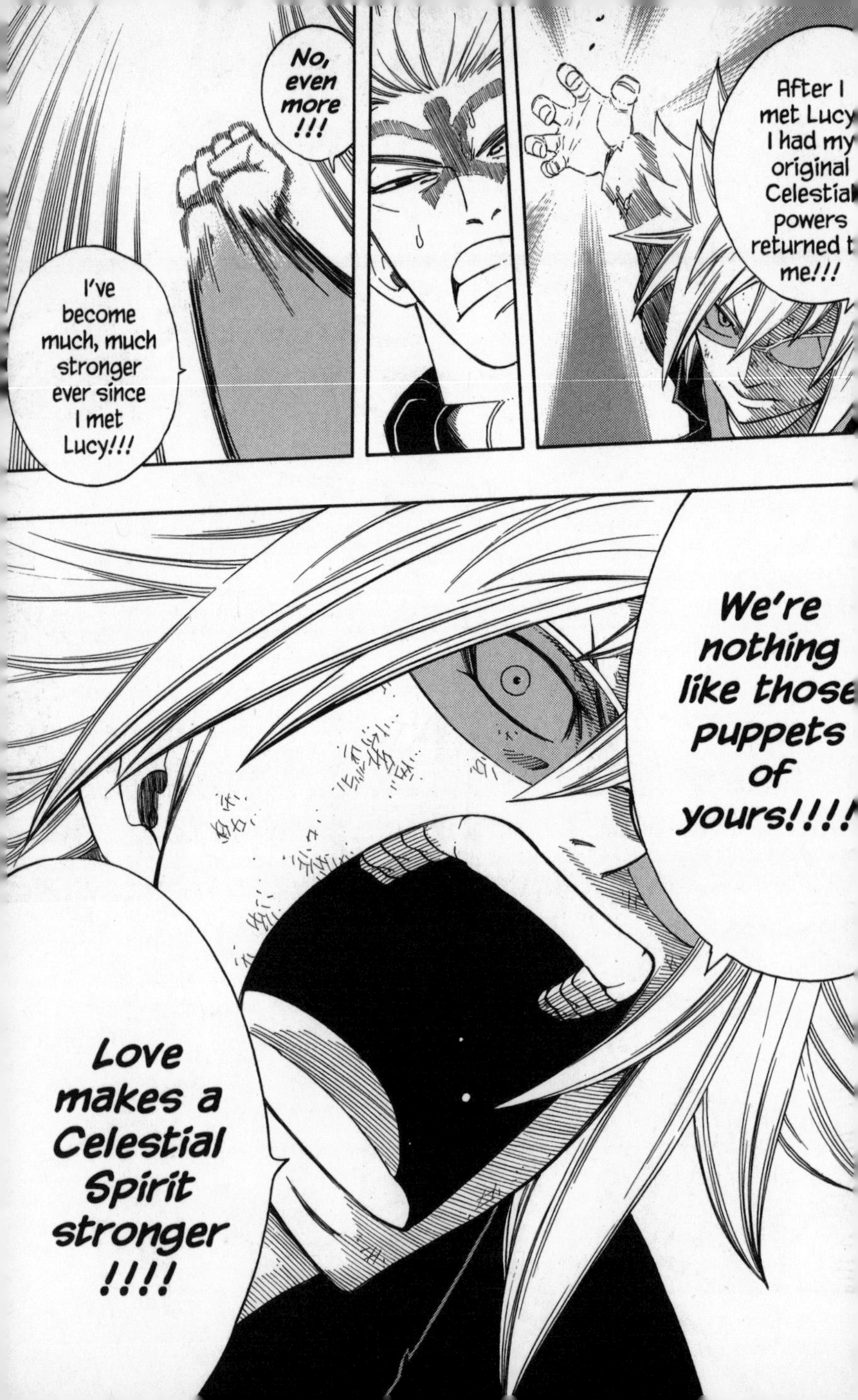
After I met Lucy I had my original Celestial powers returned t me!!!
No, even more!!!
I've become much, much stronger ever since I met Lucy!!!
We're nothing like those puppets of yours!!!!
Love makes a Celestial Spirit stronger!!!!

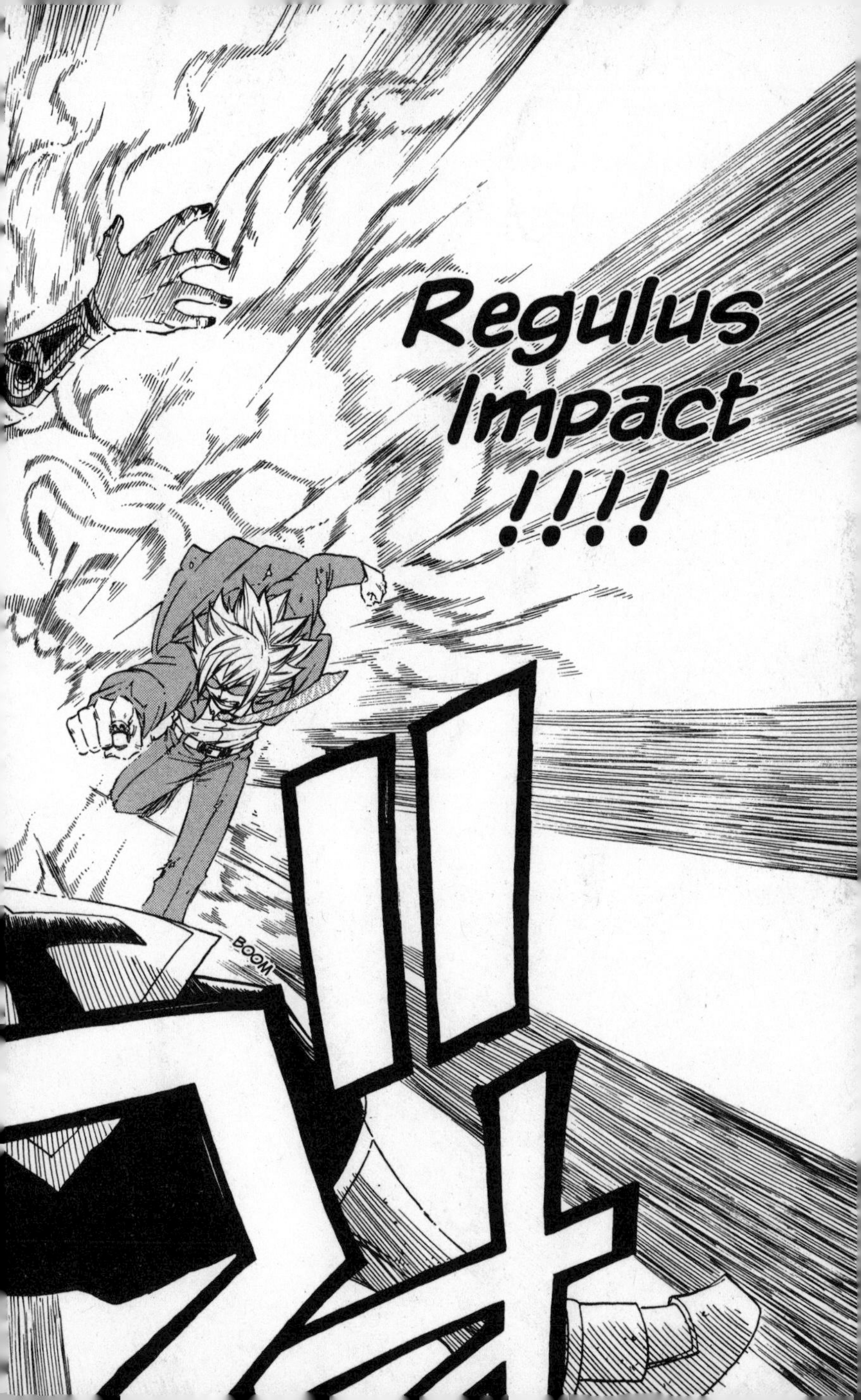

Regulus Impact !!!!
BOOM

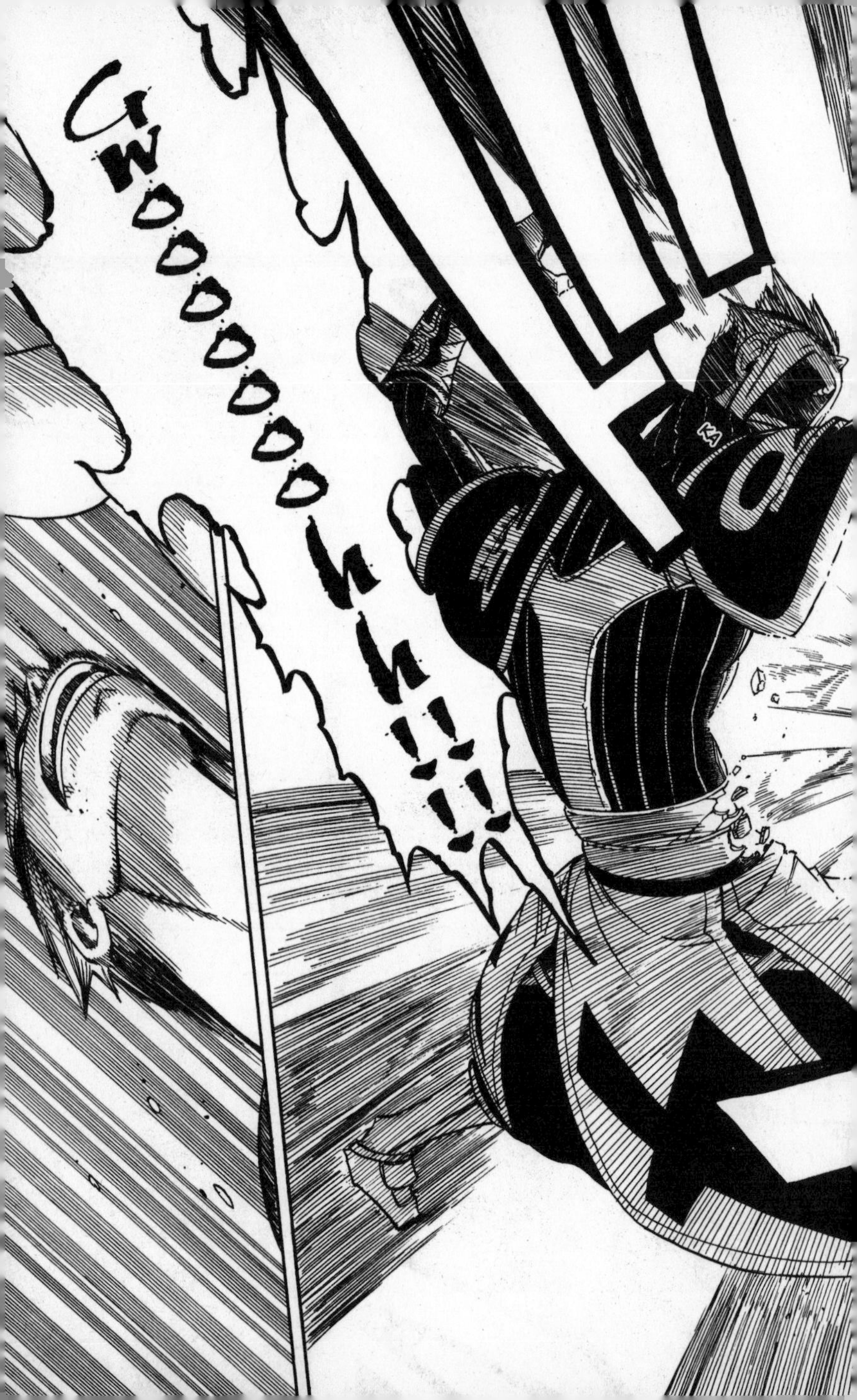
GWOOOOOOOHH!!!

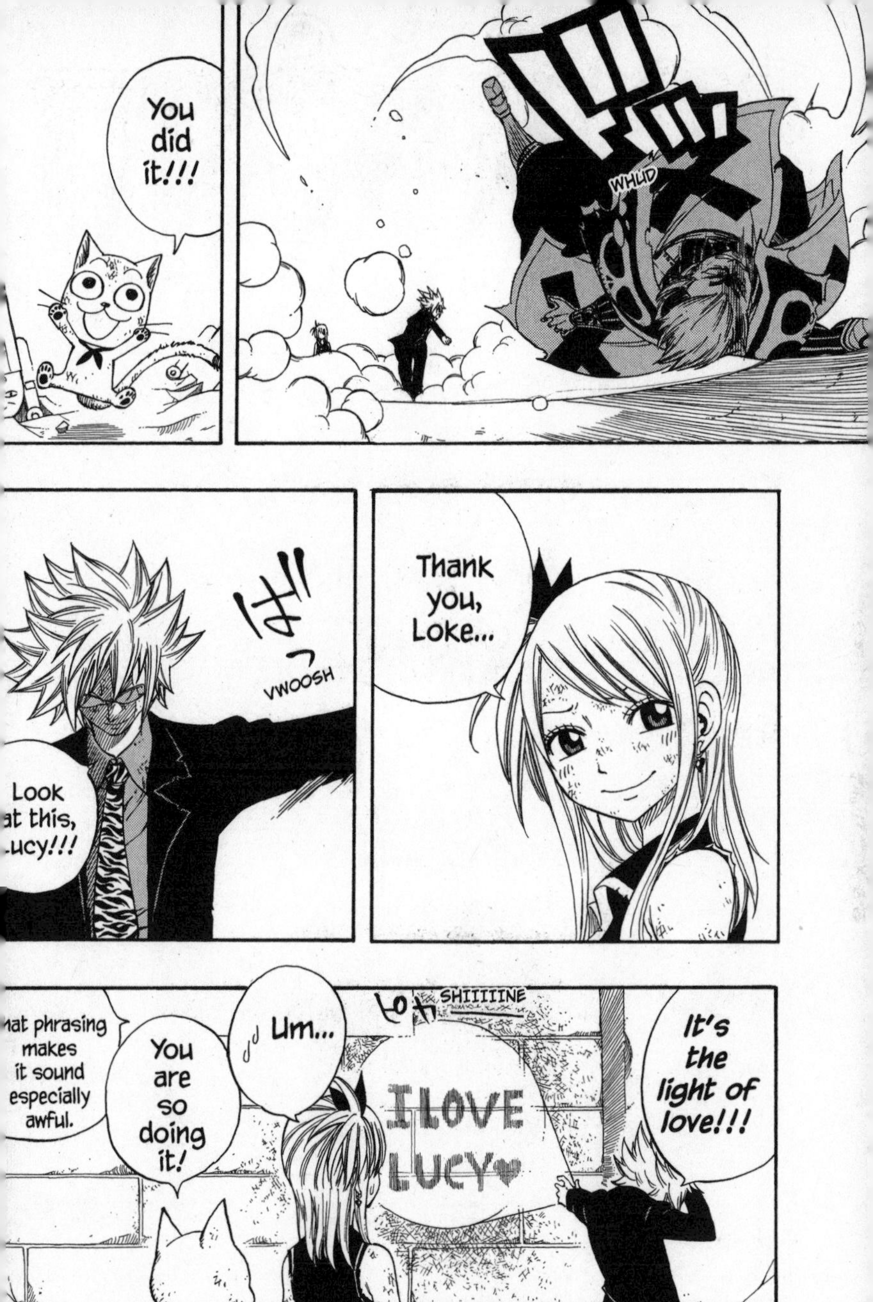
WHUD
You did it!!!
Thank you, Loke...
VWOOSH
Look at this, ucy!!!
It's the light of love!!!
SHIIIIINE
I LOVE LUCY♥
Um...
You are so doing it!
hat phrasing makes it sound especially awful.

FAIRY TAIL

Chapter 116:
Cana vs. Juvia

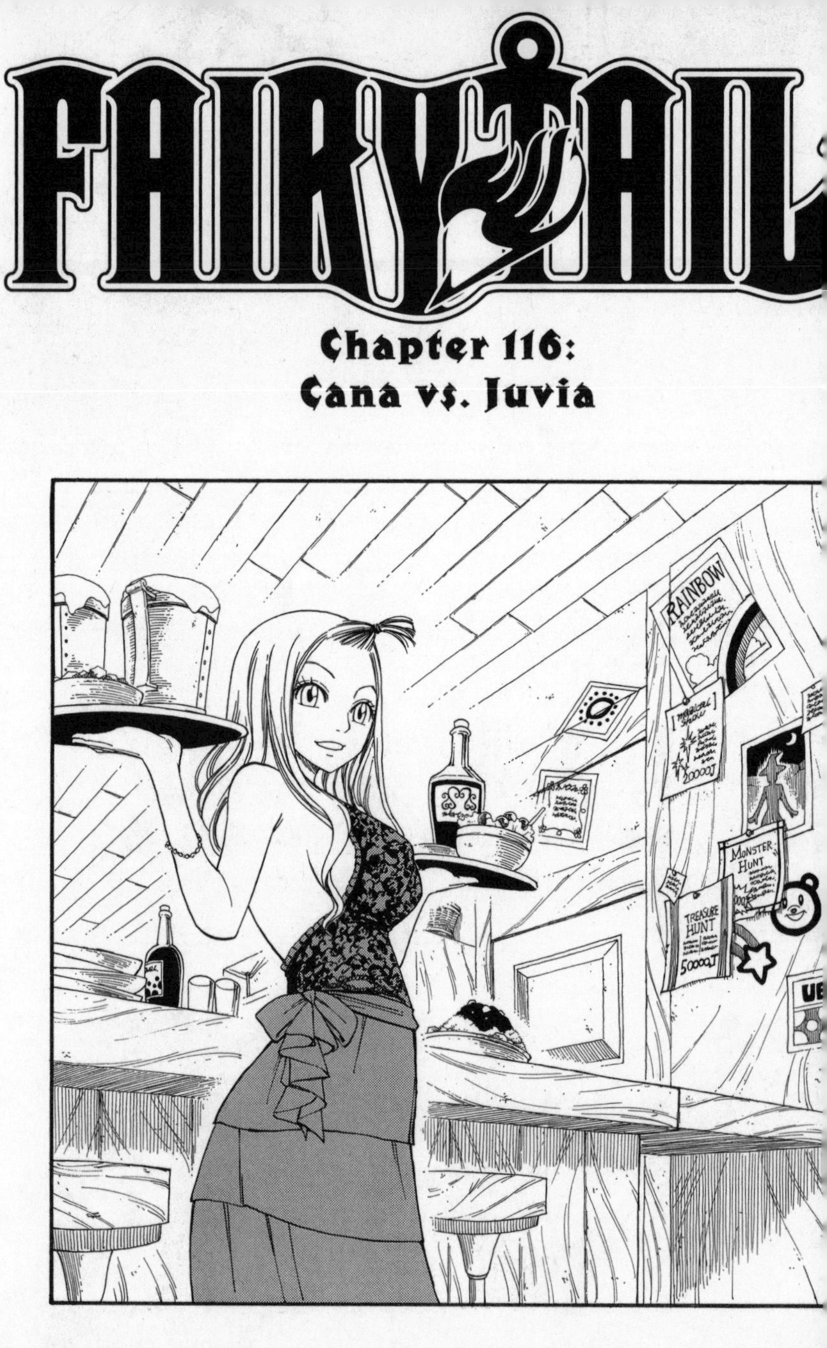
RAINBOW
MAGICAL SHOW
20000J
MONSTER HUNT
TREASURE HUNT
50000J

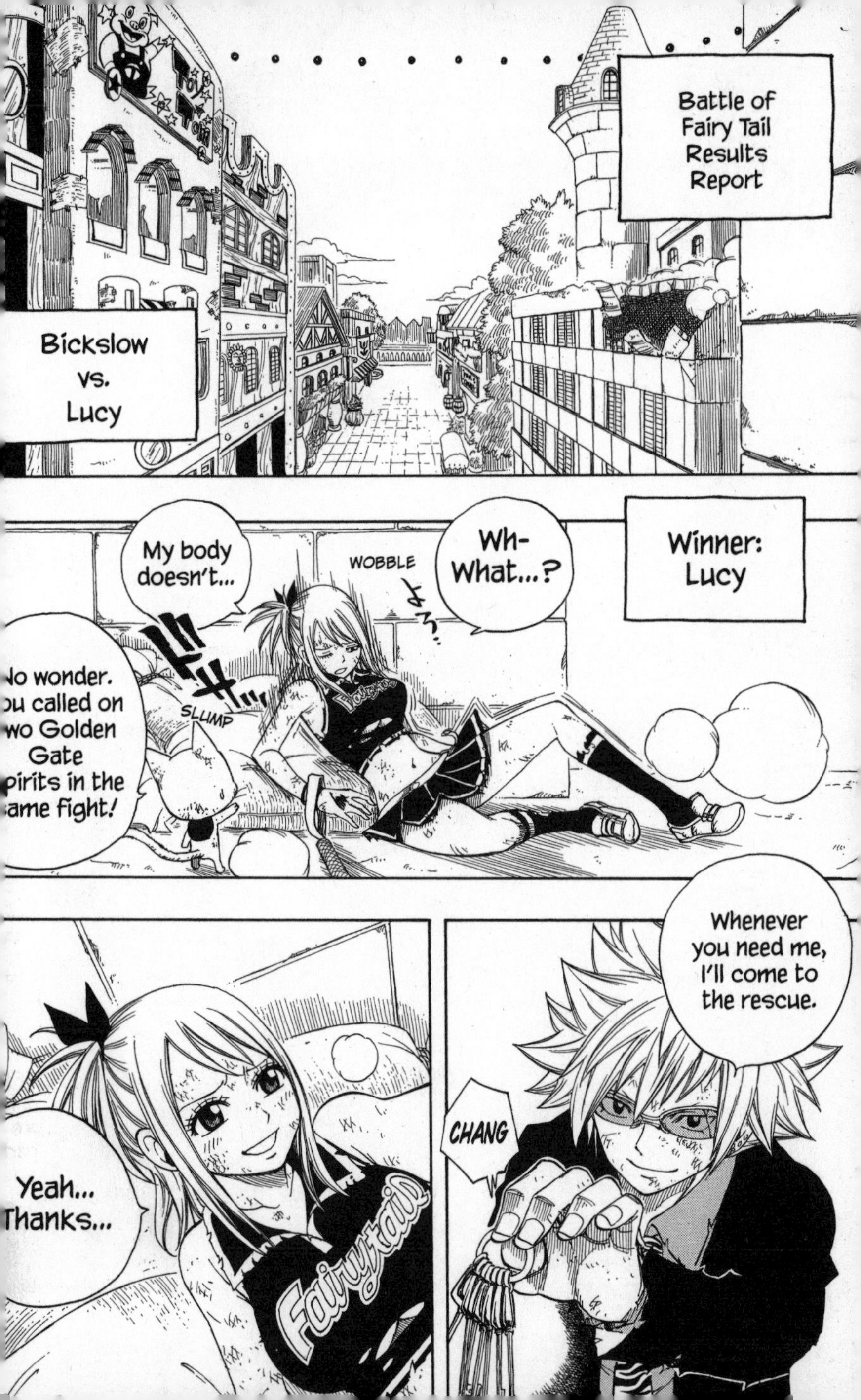
Battle of Fairy Tail Results Report
Bickslow vs. Lucy
Winner: Lucy
Wh- What...?
WOBBLE よろ…
My body doesn't...
SLUMP
lo wonder. ou called on wo Golden Gate pirits in the ame fight!
Whenever you need me, I'll come to the rescue.
CHANG
Yeah... Thanks...

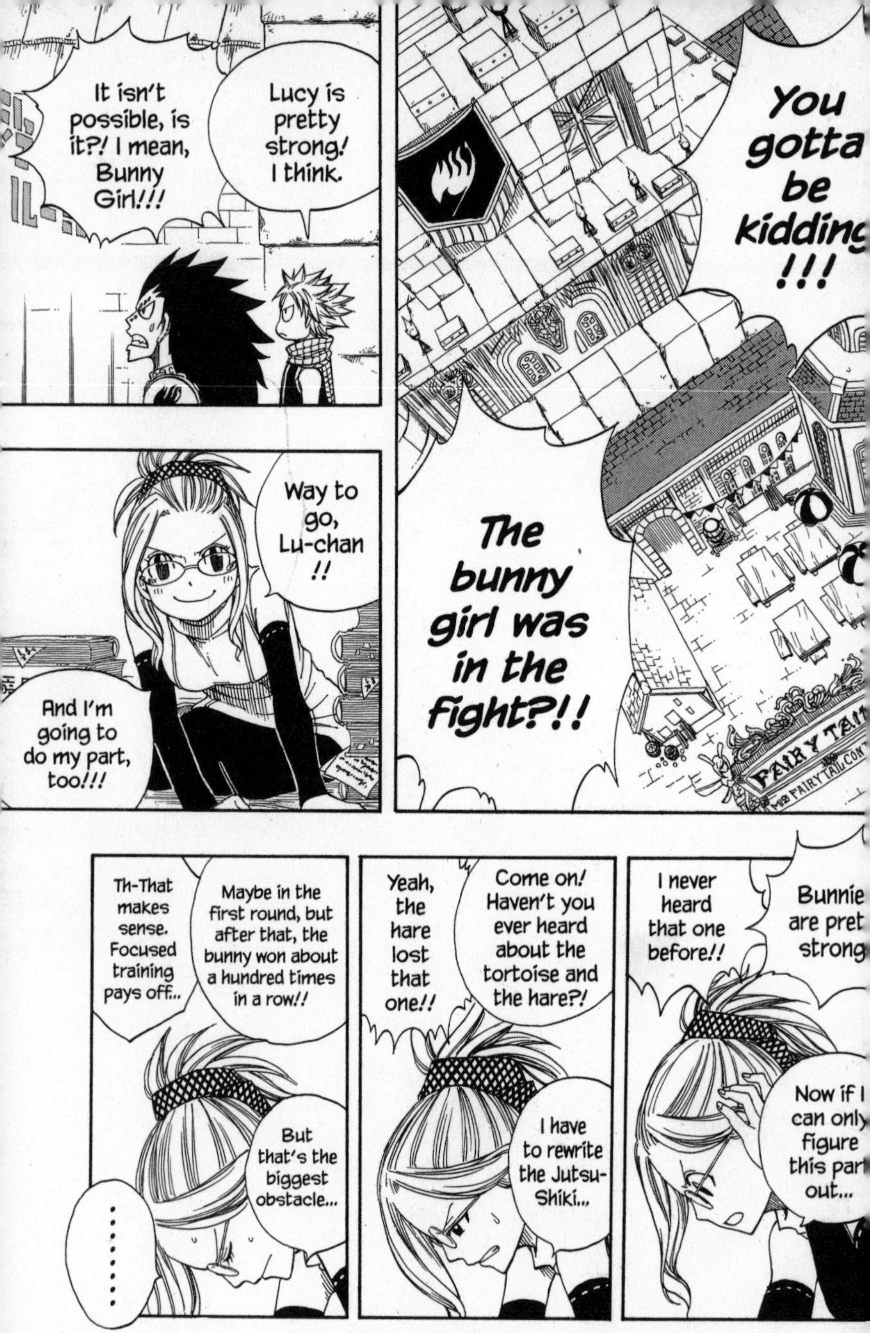
You gotta be kidding!!!
The bunny girl was in the fight?!!
FAIRY TAIL
Lucy is pretty strong! I think.
It isn't possible, is it?! I mean, Bunny Girl!!!
Way to go, Lu-chan!!
And I'm going to do my part, too!!!
Bunnie are pret strong
I never heard that one before!!
Now if I can only figure this par out...
Come on! Haven't you ever heard about the tortoise and the hare?!
Yeah, the hare lost that one!!
I have to rewrite the Jutsu-Shiki...
Maybe in the first round, but after that, the bunny won about a hundred times in a row!!
Th-That makes sense. Focused training pays off...
But that's the biggest obstacle...
....

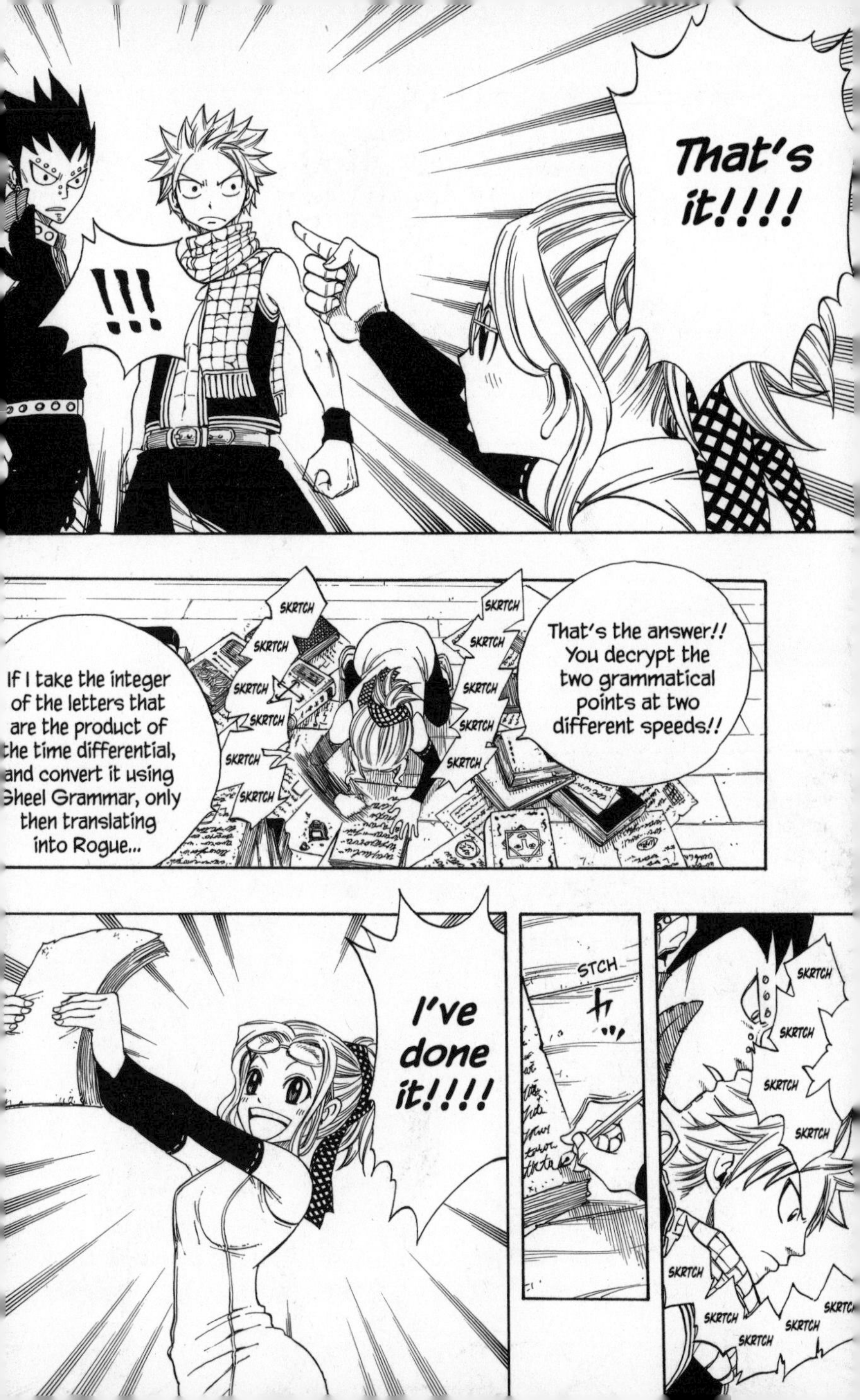
That's it!!!!
!!!
That's the answer!! You decrypt the two grammatical points at two different speeds!!
SKRTCH
SKRTCH
SKRTCH
SKRTCH
SKRTCH
SKRTCH
SKRTCH
SKRTCH
SKRTCH
SKRTCH
SKRTCH
SKRTCH
If I take the integer of the letters that are the product of the time differential, and convert it using Sheel Grammar, only then translating into Rogue...
SKRTCH
SKRTCH
SKRTCH
SKRTCH
SKRTCH
SKRTCH
SKRTCH
SKRTCH
SKRTCH
STCH
I've done it!!!!

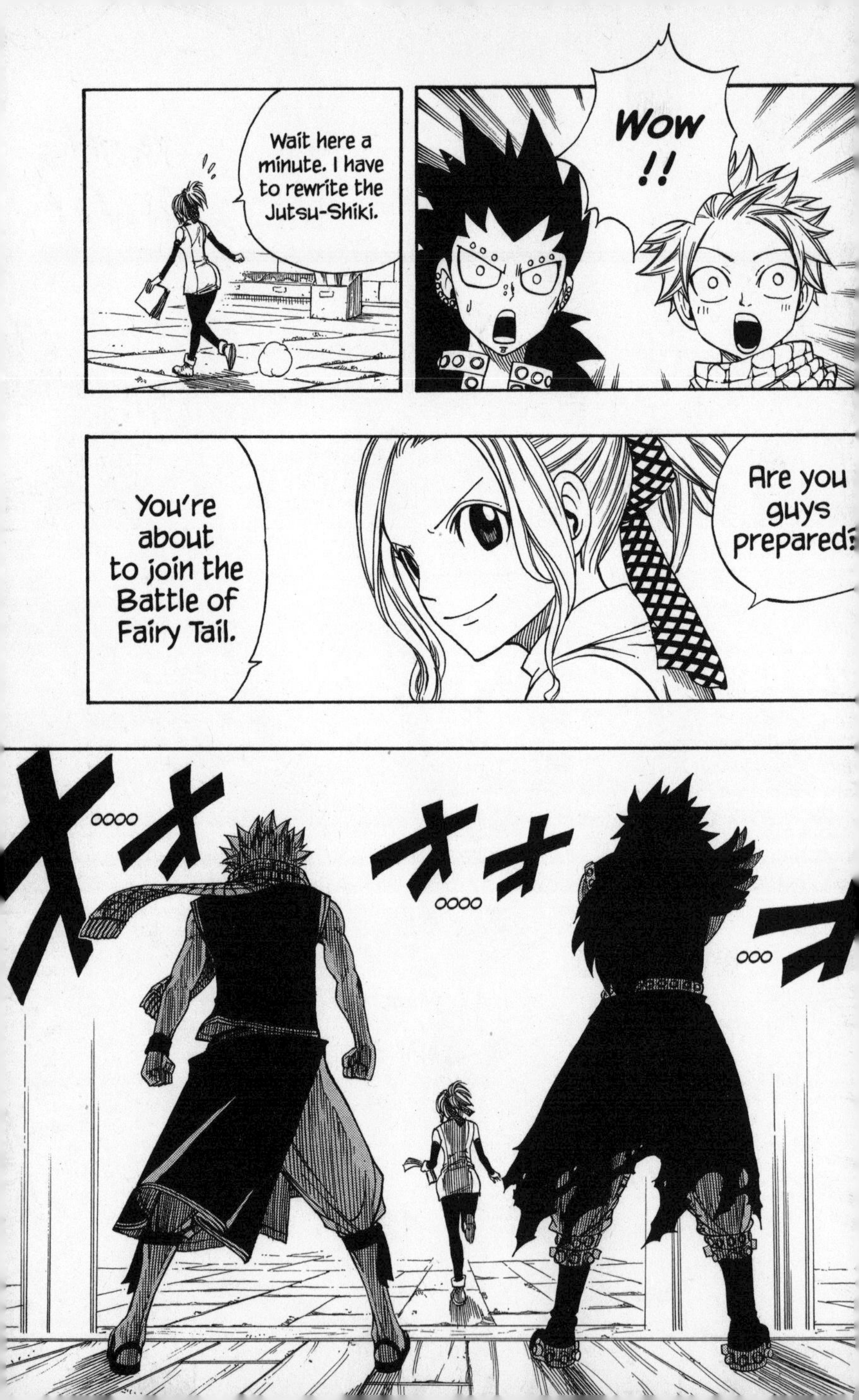
WOW !!
Wait here a minute. I have to rewrite the Jutsu-Shiki.
Are you guys prepared!?
You're about to join the Battle of Fairy Tail.
ooo
oooo
oooo

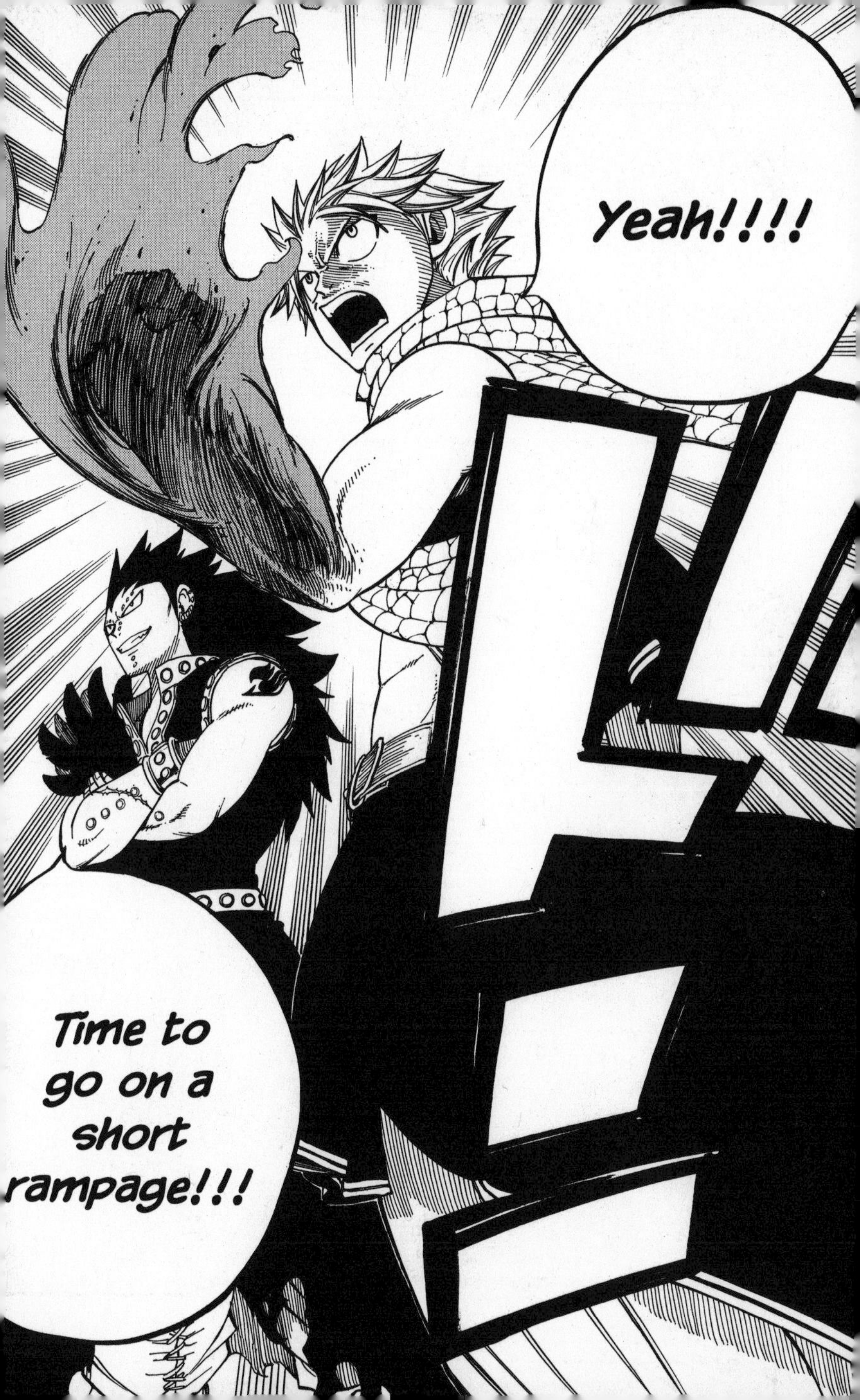
Yeah!!!!
Time to go on a short rampage!!!

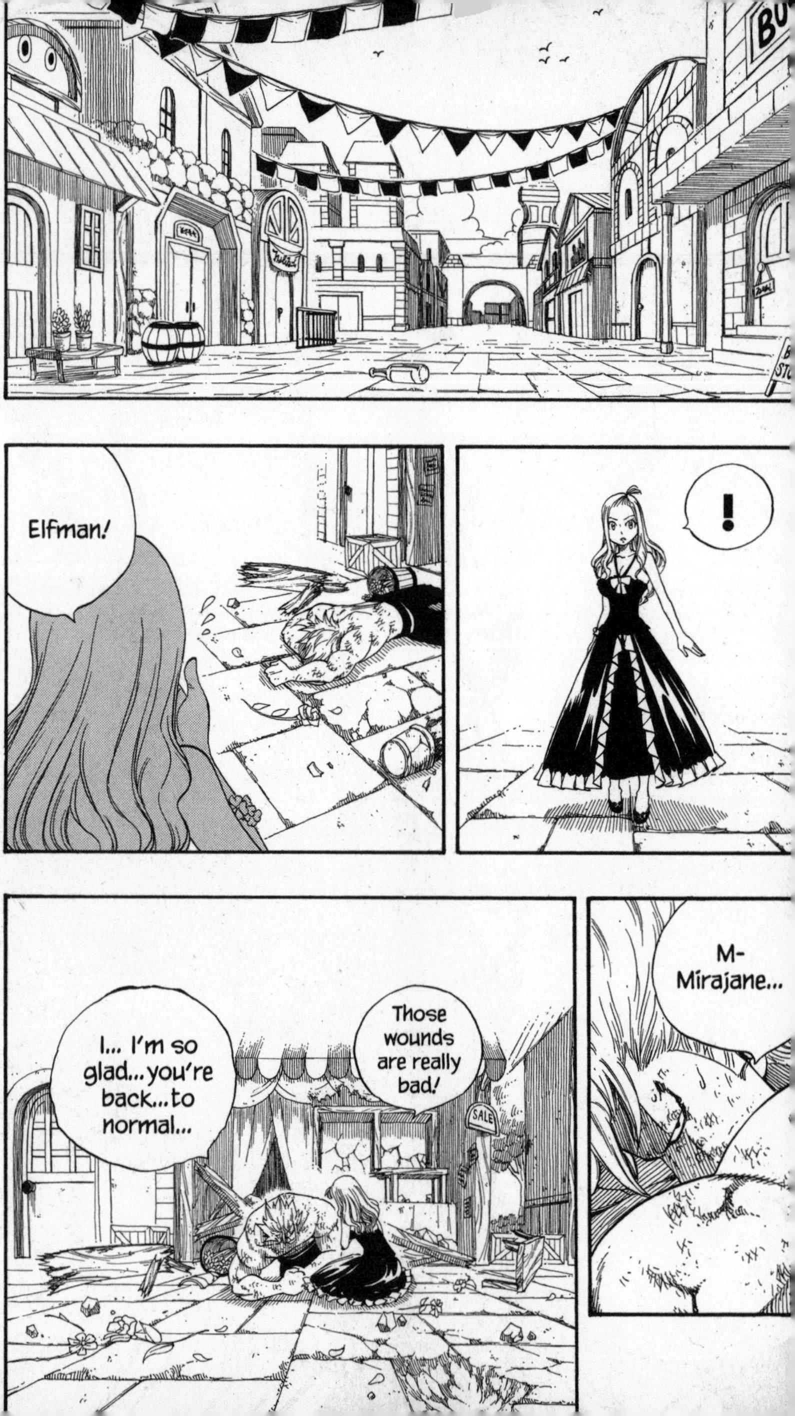
!
Elfman!
M- Mirajane...
Those wounds are really bad!
I... I'm so glad...you're back...to normal...
SALE

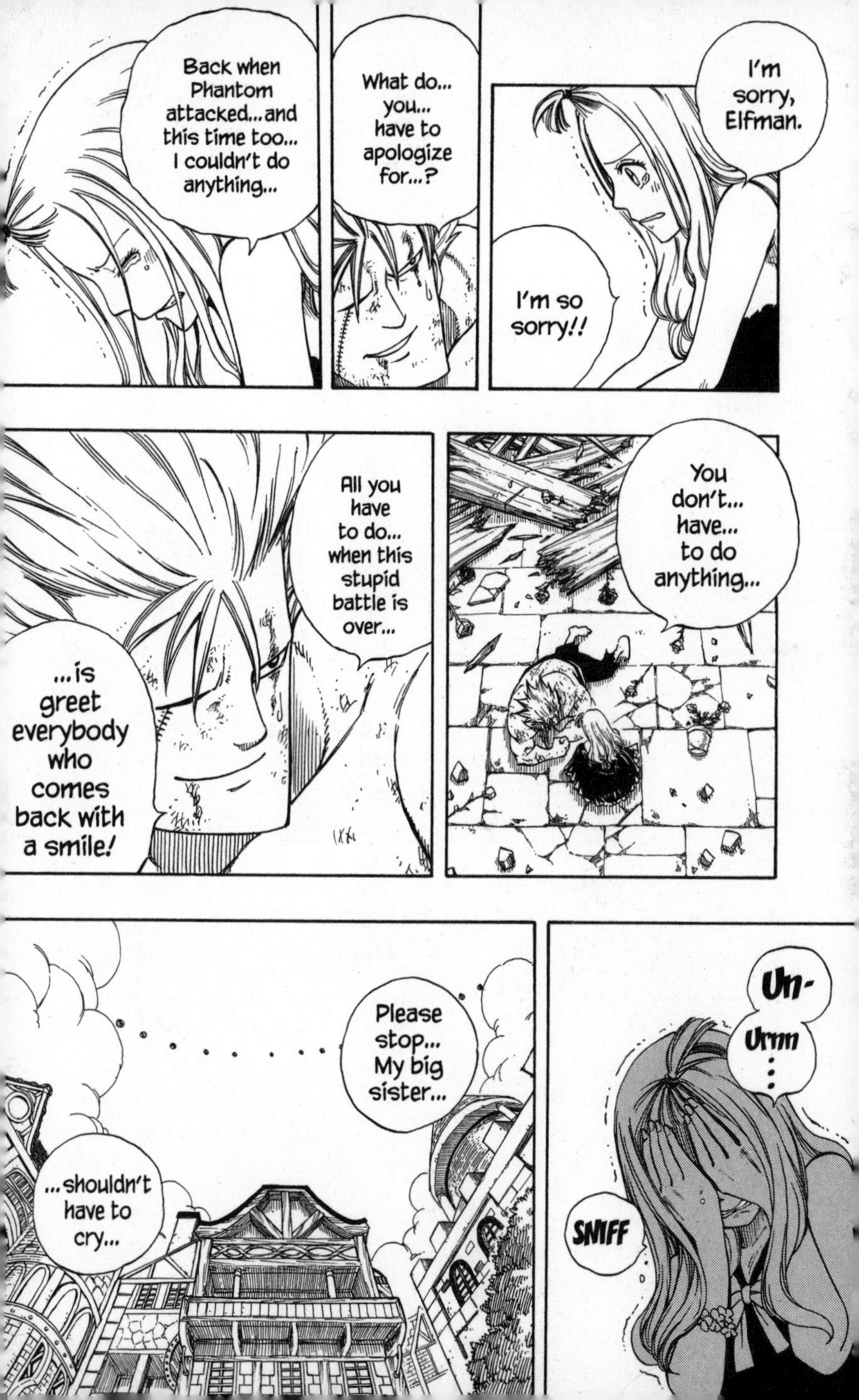
I'm sorry, Elfman.
I'm so sorry!!
What do... you... have to apologize for...?
Back when Phantom attacked...and this time too... I couldn't do anything...
You don't... have... to do anything...
All you have to do... when this stupid battle is over...
...is greet everybody who comes back with a smile!
Un-Urnn...
SNIFF
Please stop... My big sister...
...shouldn't have to cry...

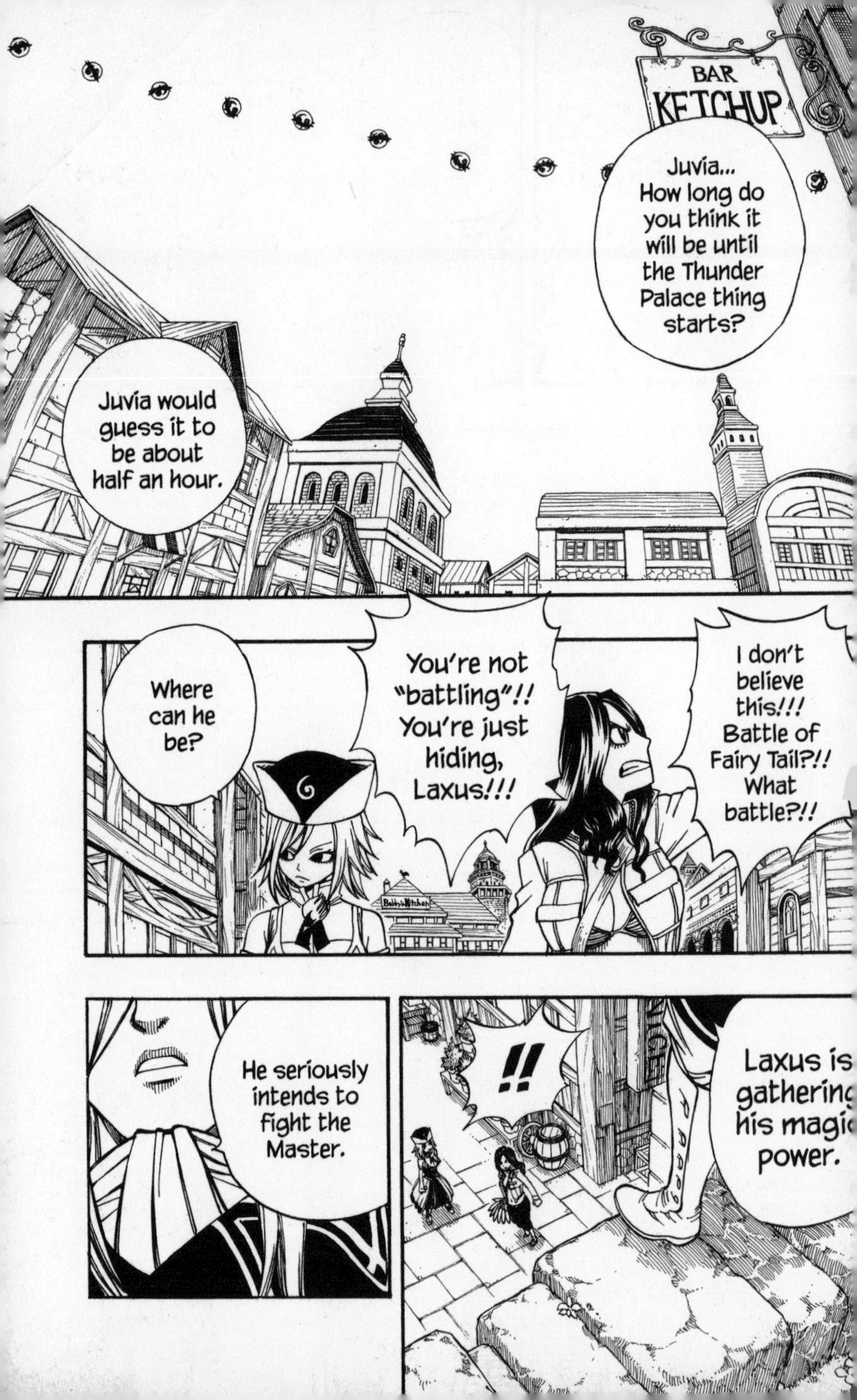
BAR KETCHUP
Juvia... How long do you think it will be until the Thunder Palace thing starts?
Juvia would guess it to be about half an hour.
I don't believe this!!! Battle of Fairy Tail?!! What battle?!!
You're not "battling"!! You're just hiding, Laxus!!!
Where can he be?
Laxus is gatherin his magi power.
!!
He seriously intends to fight the Master.

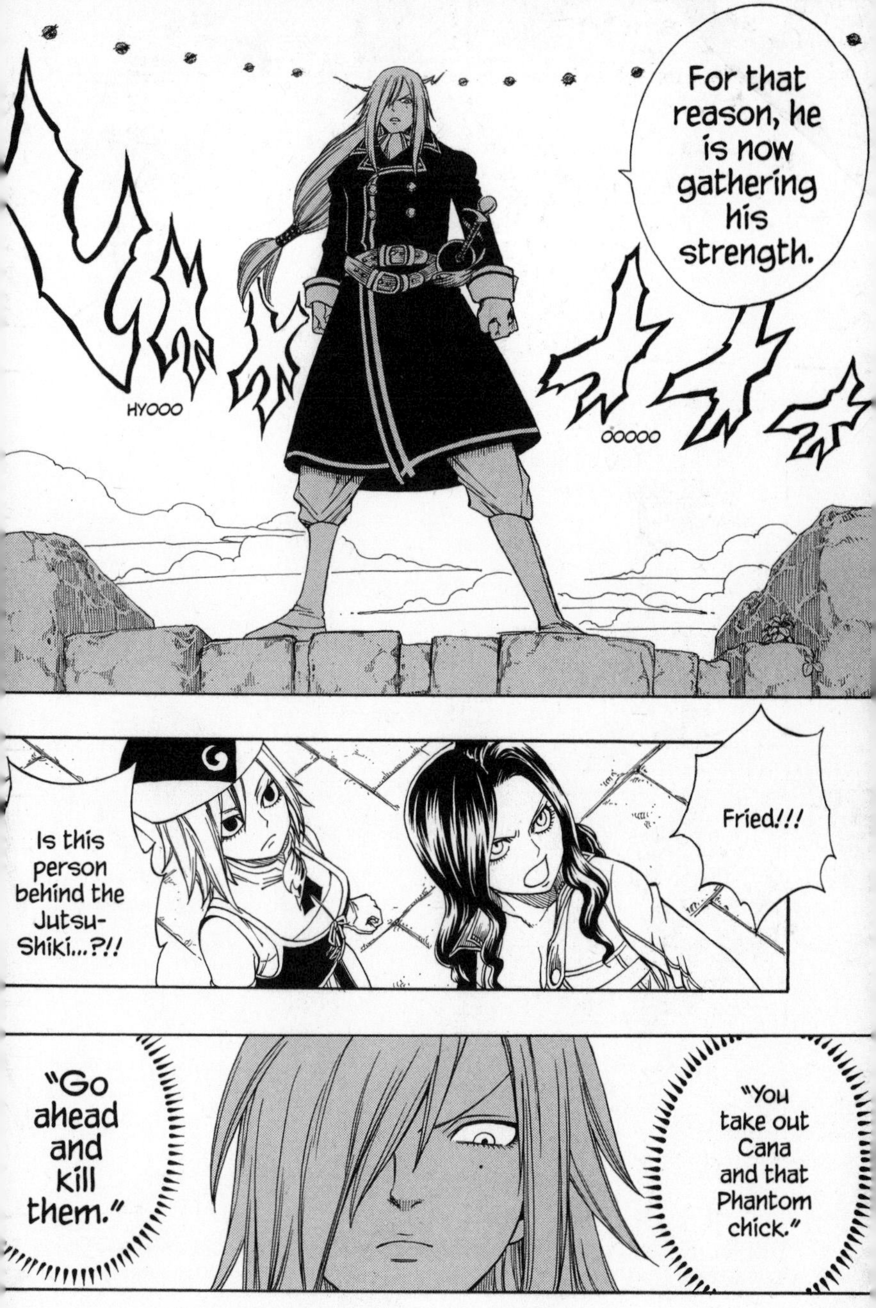
For that reason, he is now gathering his strength.
HYOOO
OOOOO
Fried!!!
Is this person behind the Jutsu-Shiki...?!!
"You take out Cana and that Phantom chick."
"Go ahead and kill them."

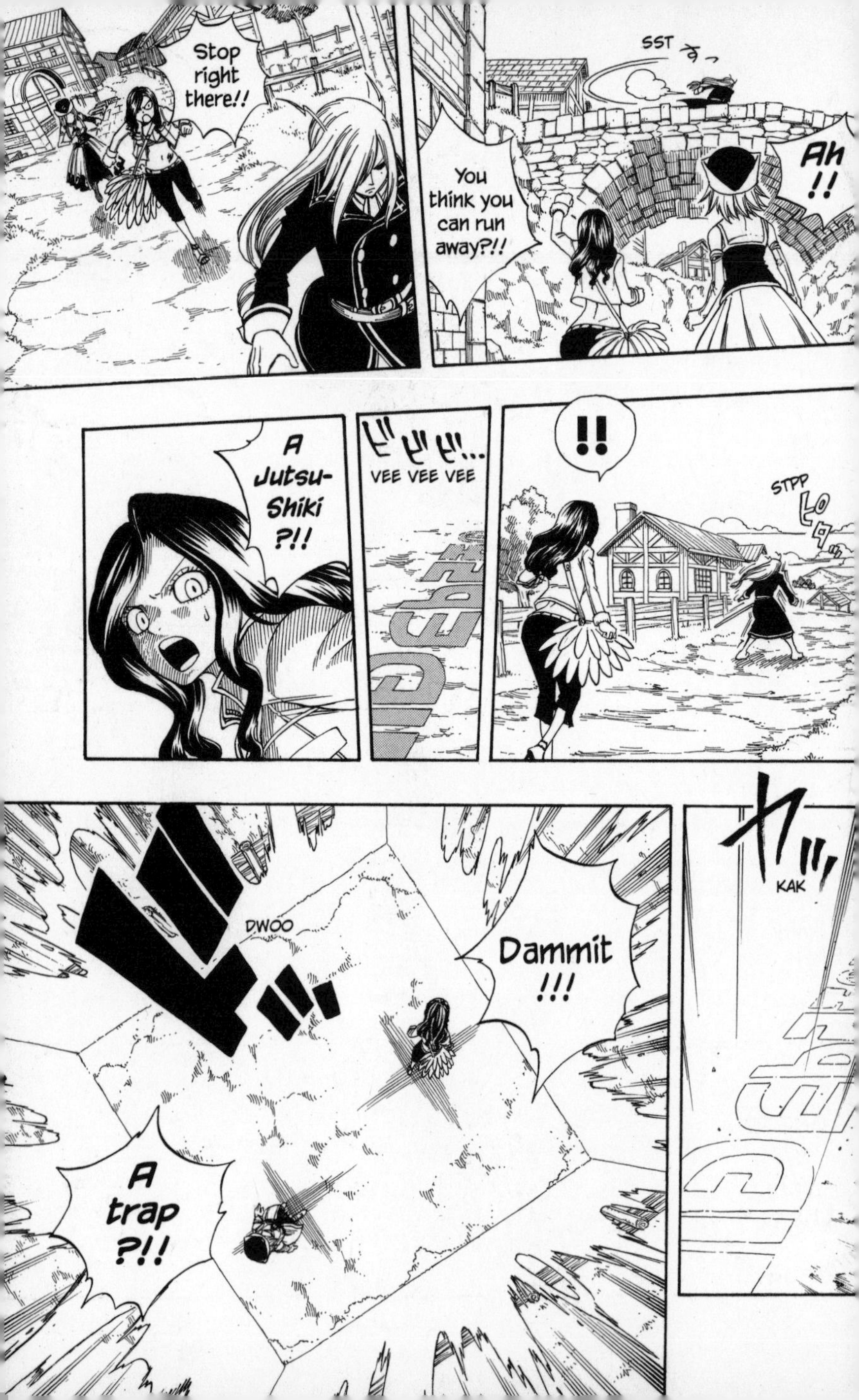

SST すっ
Ah!!
You think you can run away?!!
Stop right there!!
!!
STPP ピタッ
ビビビ...
VEE VEE VEE
A Jutsu-Shiki?!!
ガッ
KAK
Dammit!!!
DWOO
A trap?!!

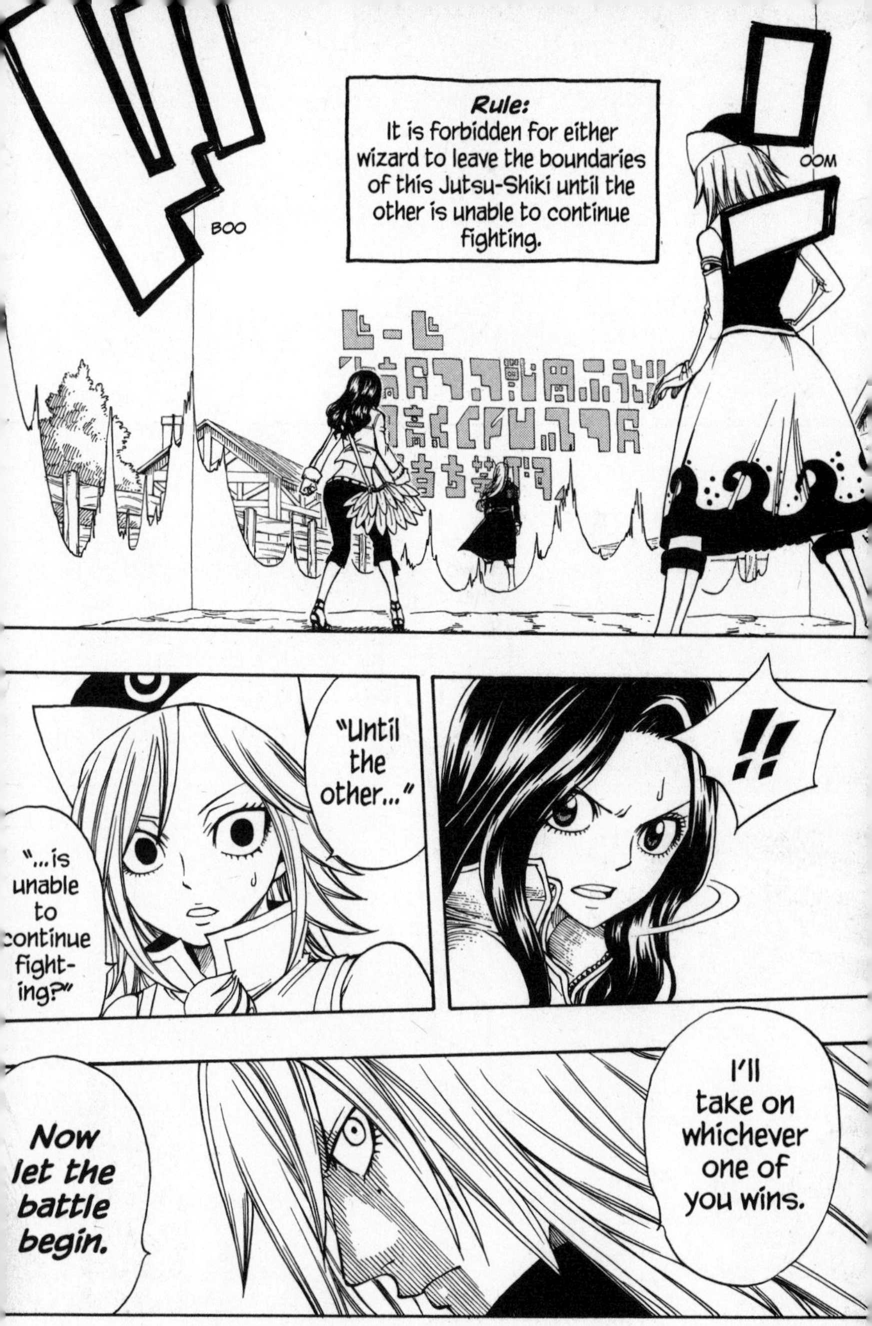
Rule:
It is forbidden for either wizard to leave the boundaries of this Jutsu-Shiki until the other is unable to continue fighting.
BOO
OOM
!!
"Until the other..."
"...is unable to continue fight-ing?"
I'll take on whichever one of you wins.
Now let the battle begin.

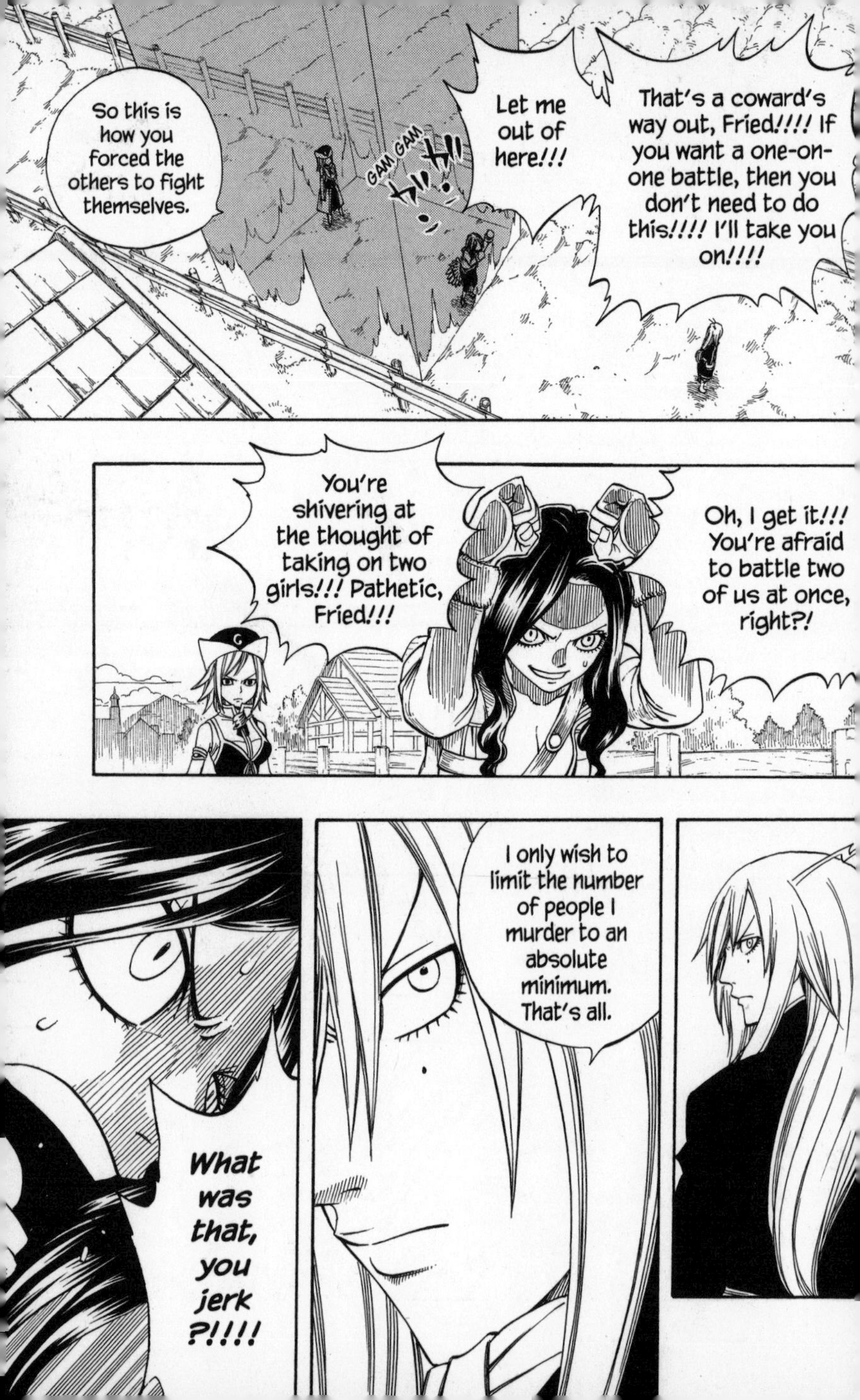

That's a coward's way out, Fried!!!! If you want a one-on-one battle, then you don't need to do this!!!! I'll take you on!!!!
Let me out of here!!!
GAM GAM
So this is how you forced the others to fight themselves.
Oh, I get it!!! You're afraid to battle two of us at once, right?!
You're shivering at the thought of taking on two girls!!! Pathetic, Fried!!!
I only wish to limit the number of people I murder to an absolute minimum. That's all.
What was that, you jerk?!!!!

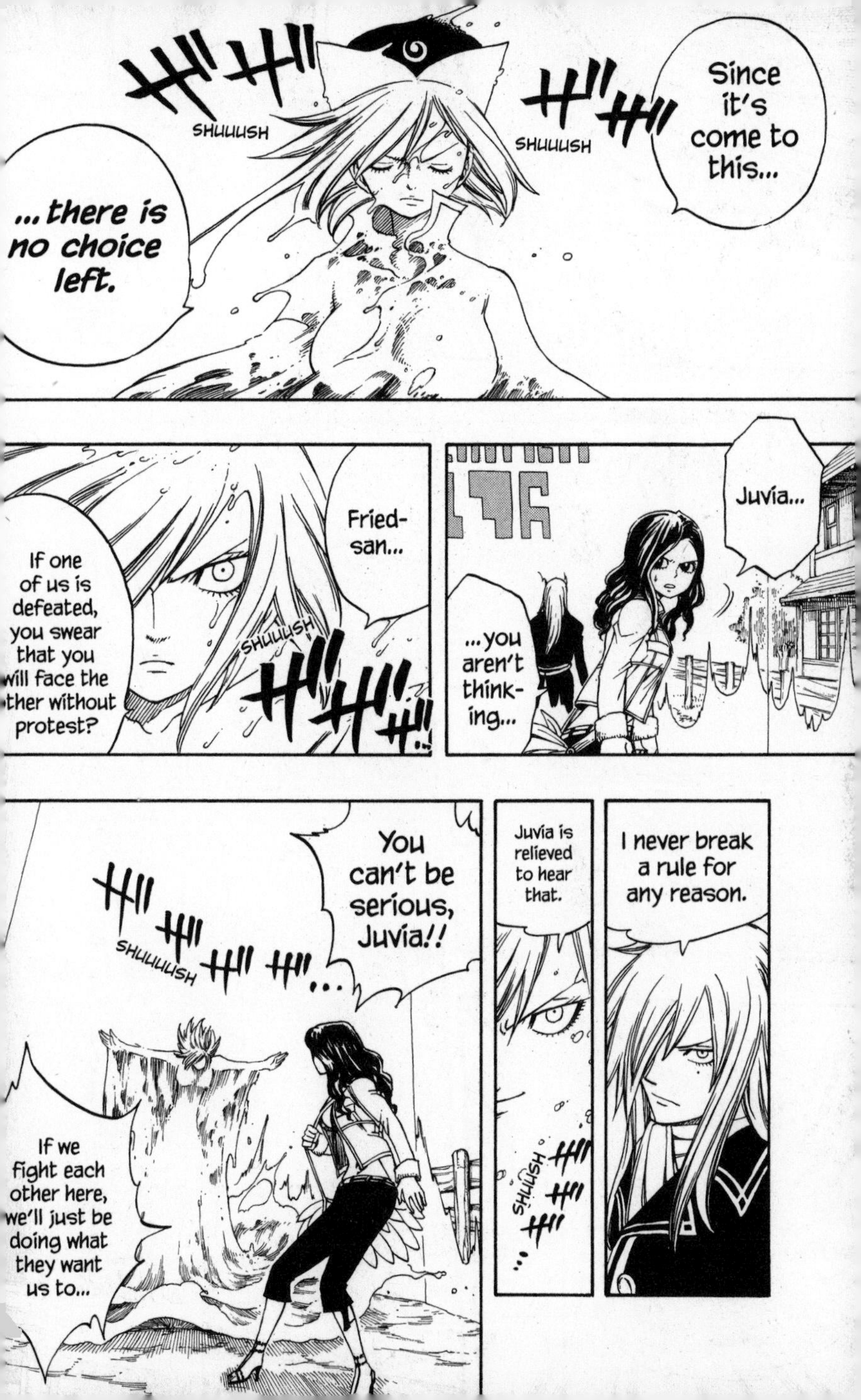

SHUUUSH
SHUUUSH
Since it's come to this...
...there is no choice left.
Juvia...
...you aren't thinking...
Fried-san...
SHUUUSH
If one of us is defeated, you swear that you will face the ther without protest?
I never break a rule for any reason.
Juvia is relieved to hear that.
SHUUSH
You can't be serious, Juvia!!
SHUUUUSH
If we fight each other here, we'll just be doing what they want us to...

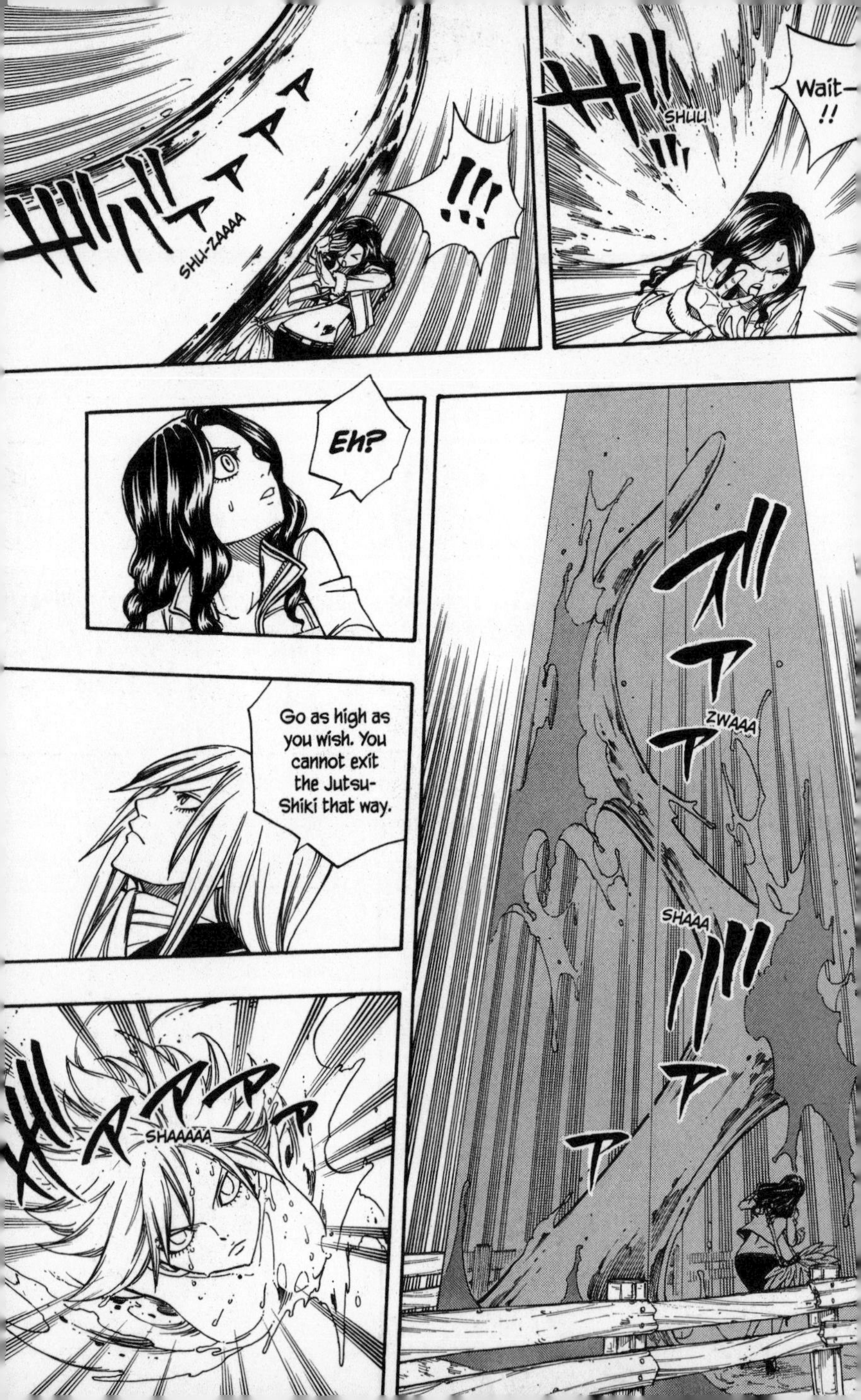
Wait-!!
SHUU
!!!
SHU-ZAAAA
ZWAAA
SHAAA
Eh?
Go as high as you wish. You cannot exit the Jutsu-Shiki that way.
SHAAAAA

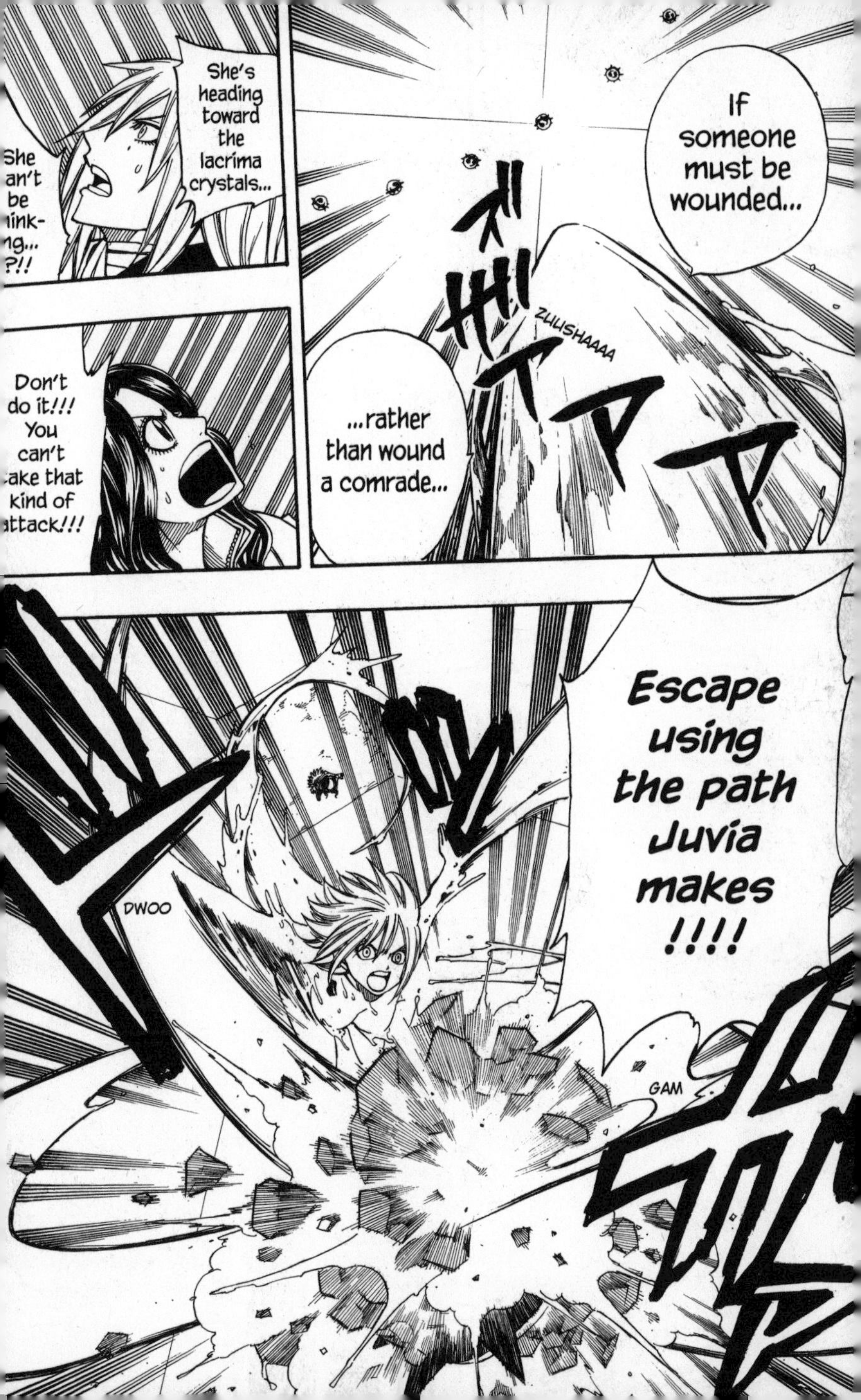

If someone must be wounded...
ZUUSHAAAA
...rather than wound a comrade...
She's heading toward the lacrima crystals...
She an't be ink- ng... ?!!
Don't do it!!! You can't ake that kind of attack!!!
Escape using the path Juvia makes!!!!
GAM
DWOO

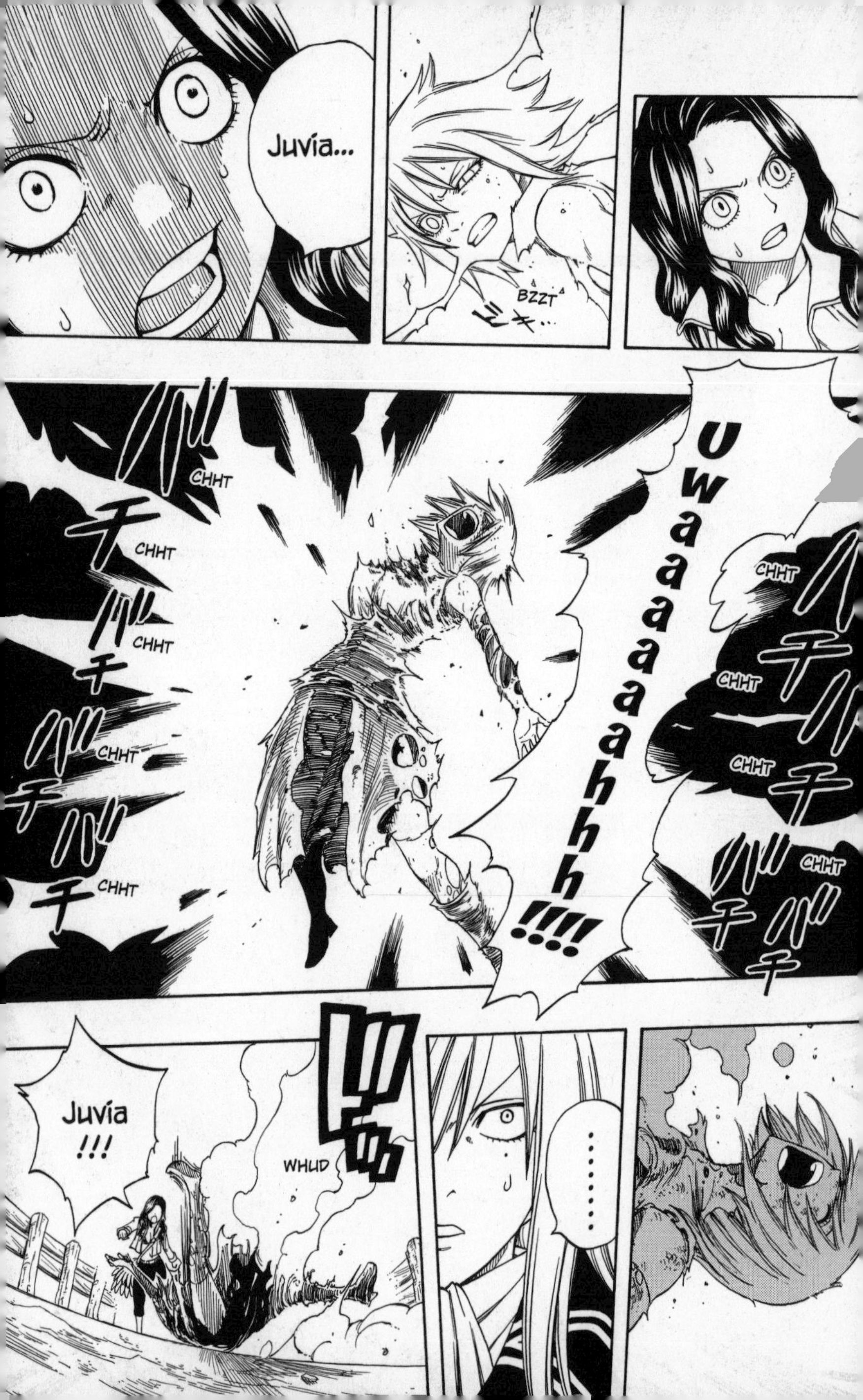
BZZT
Juvia...
CHHT
CHHT
CHHT
Uwaaaaaaaahhh!!!!
CHHT
CHHT
CHHT
CHHT
CHHT
......
WHUD
Juvia !!!

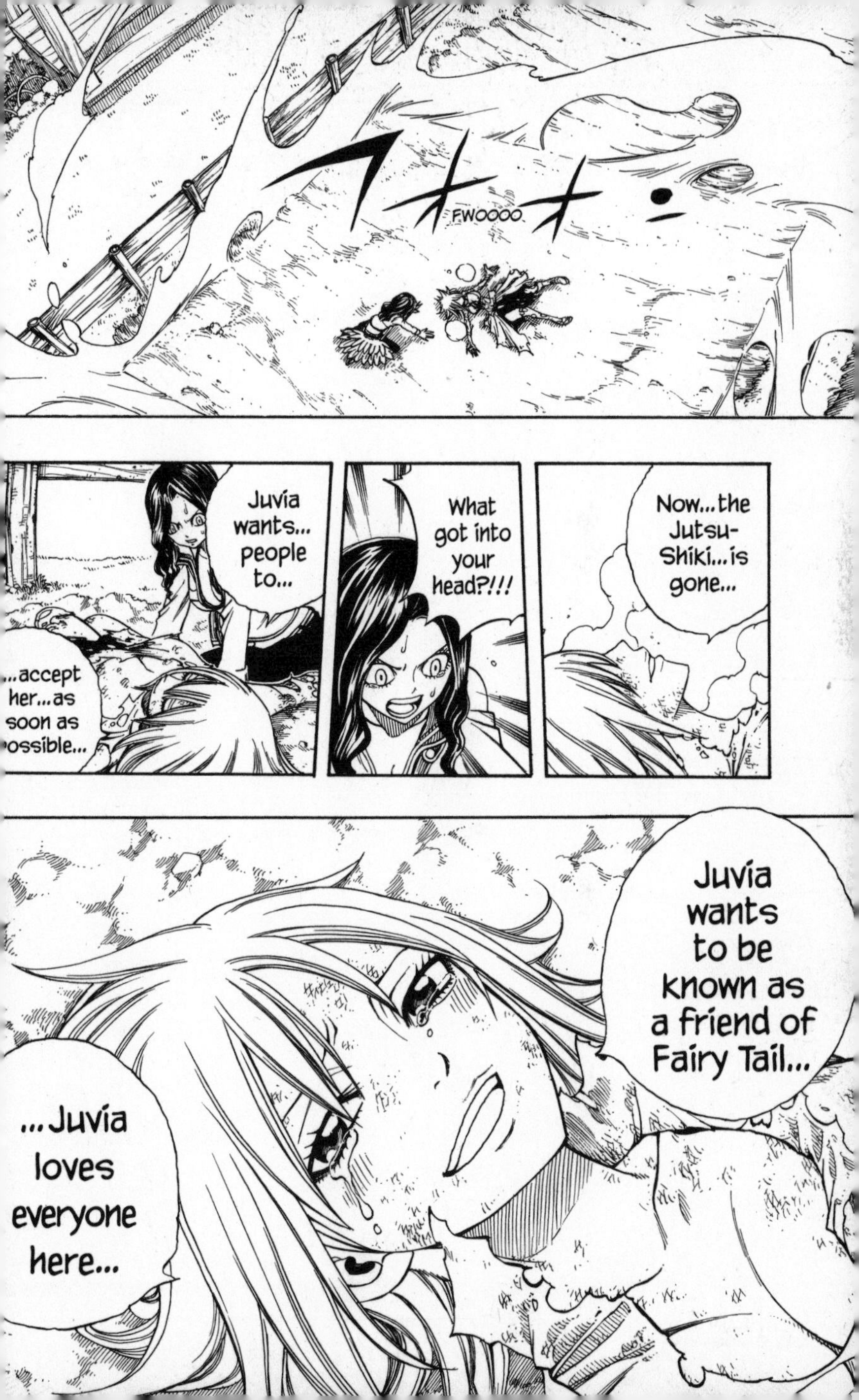
FWOOOO
Now...the Jutsu-Shiki...is gone...
What got into your head?!!!
Juvia wants... people to...
...accept her...as soon as ossible...
Juvia wants to be known as a friend of Fairy Tail...
...Juvia loves everyone here...

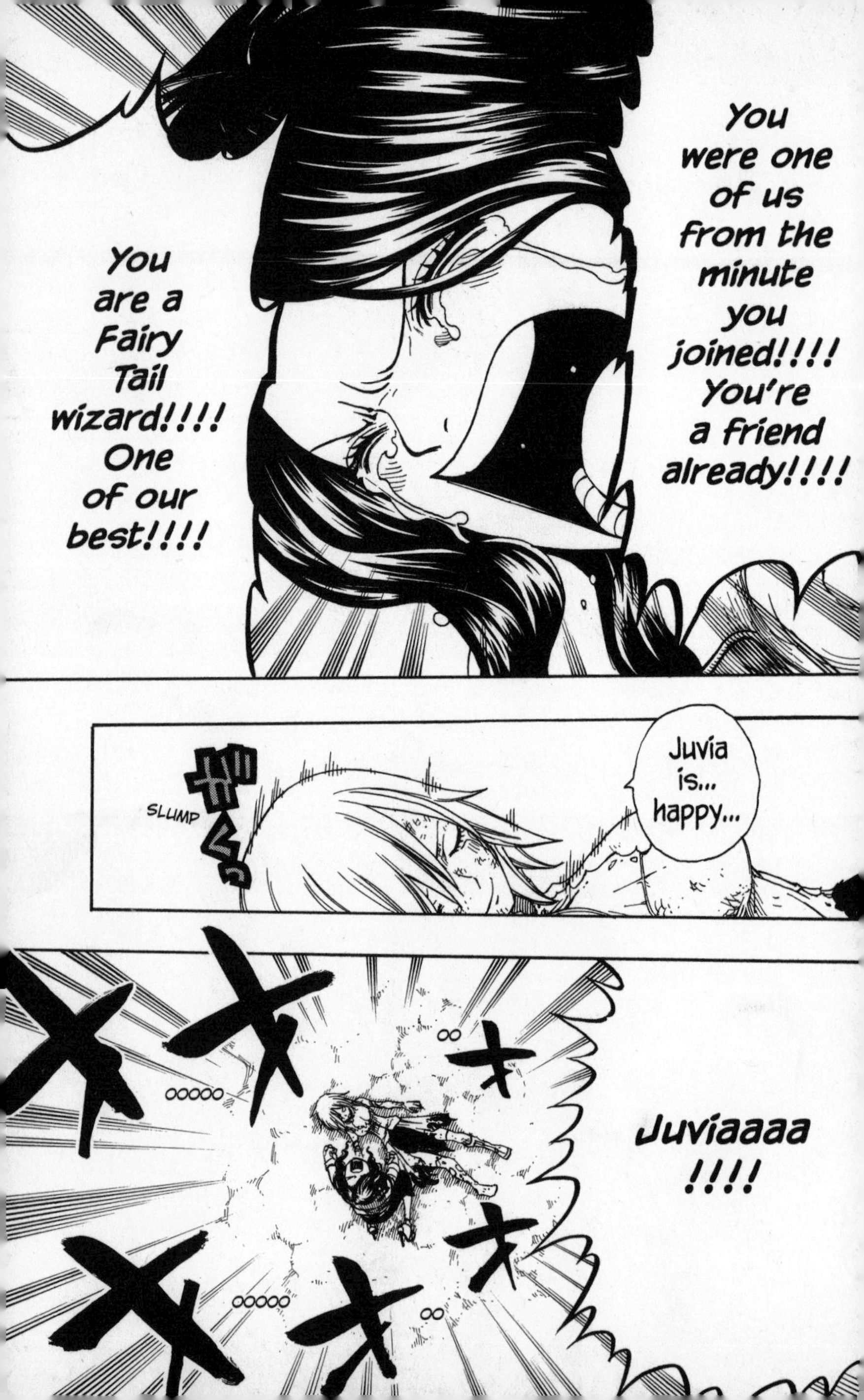
You were one of us from the minute you joined!!!! You're a friend already!!!!
You are a Fairy Tail wizard!!!! One of our best!!!!
Juvia is... happy...
SLUMP
Juviaaaa !!!!
ooooo
ooooo

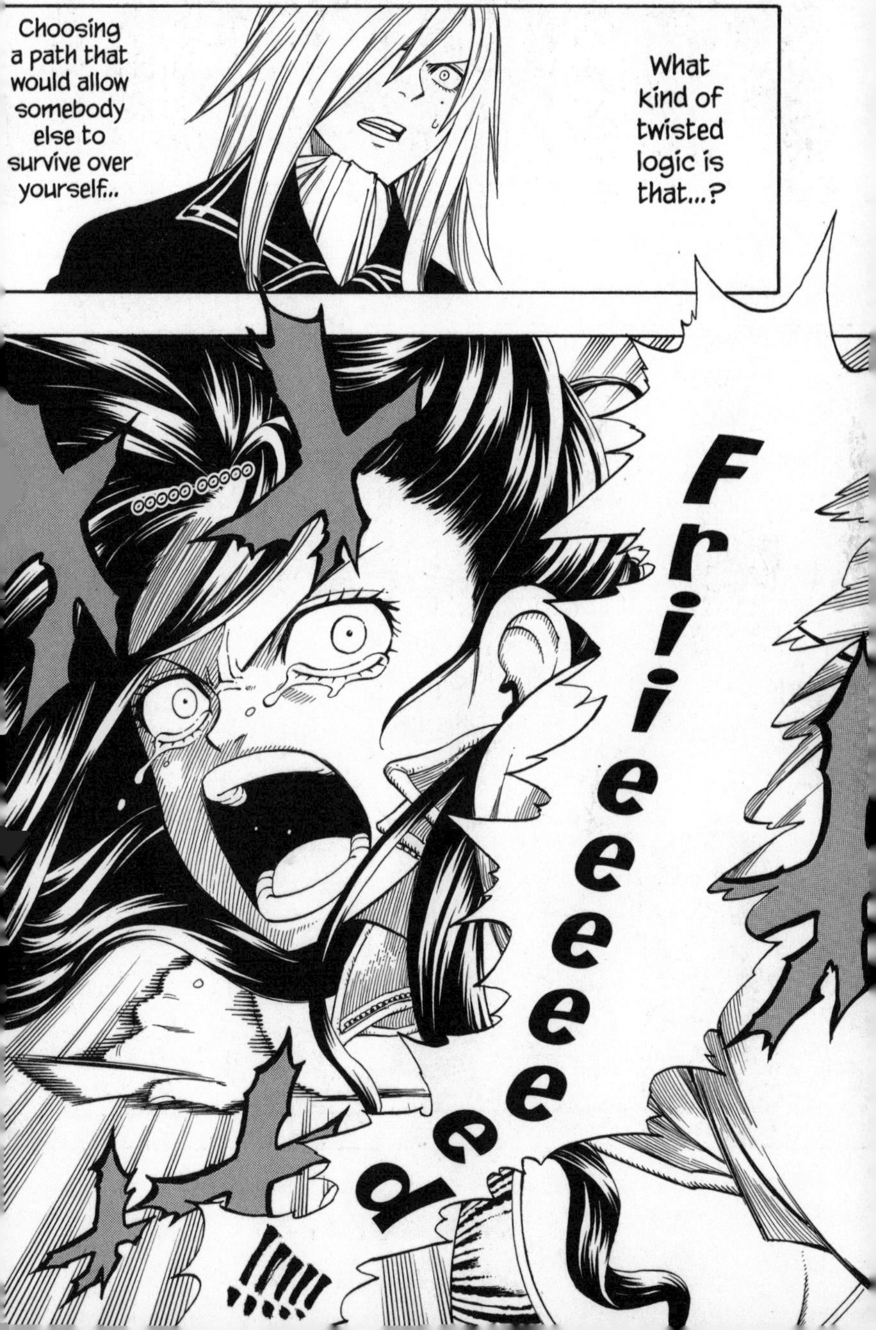
What kind of twisted logic is that...?
Choosing a path that would allow somebody else to survive over yourself...
Friiieeeeeeed
!!!!!!

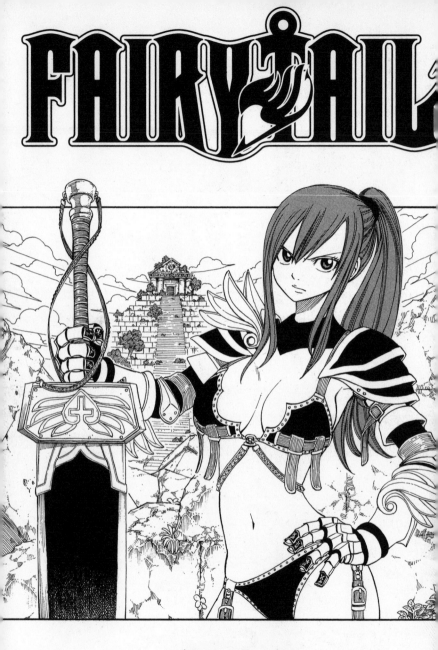

FAIRY TAIL

Chapter 117:
Satan's Halo

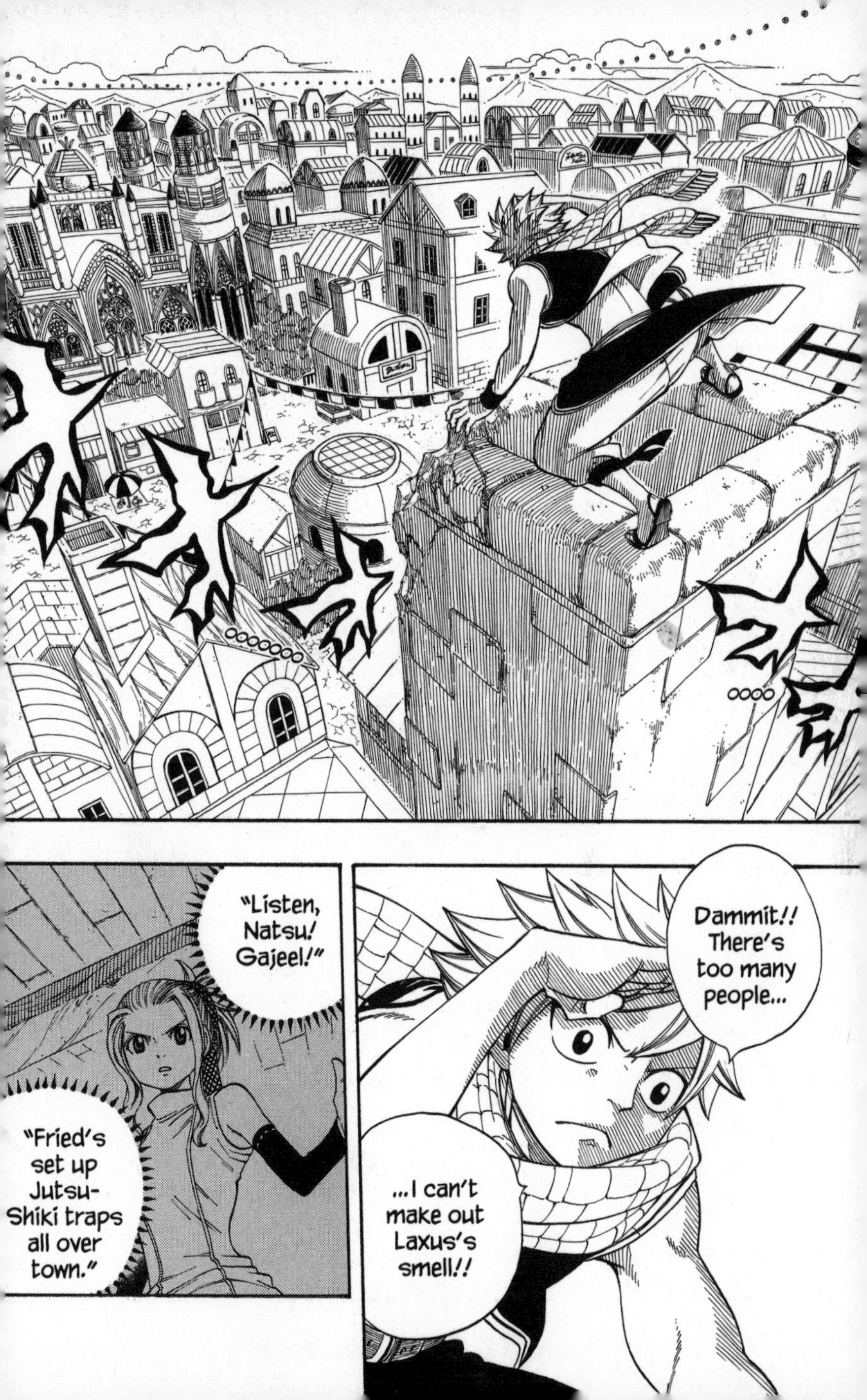
Dammit!! There's too many people...
...I can't make out Laxus's smell!!
"Listen, Natsu! Gajeel!"
"Fried's set up Jutsu-Shiki traps all over town."

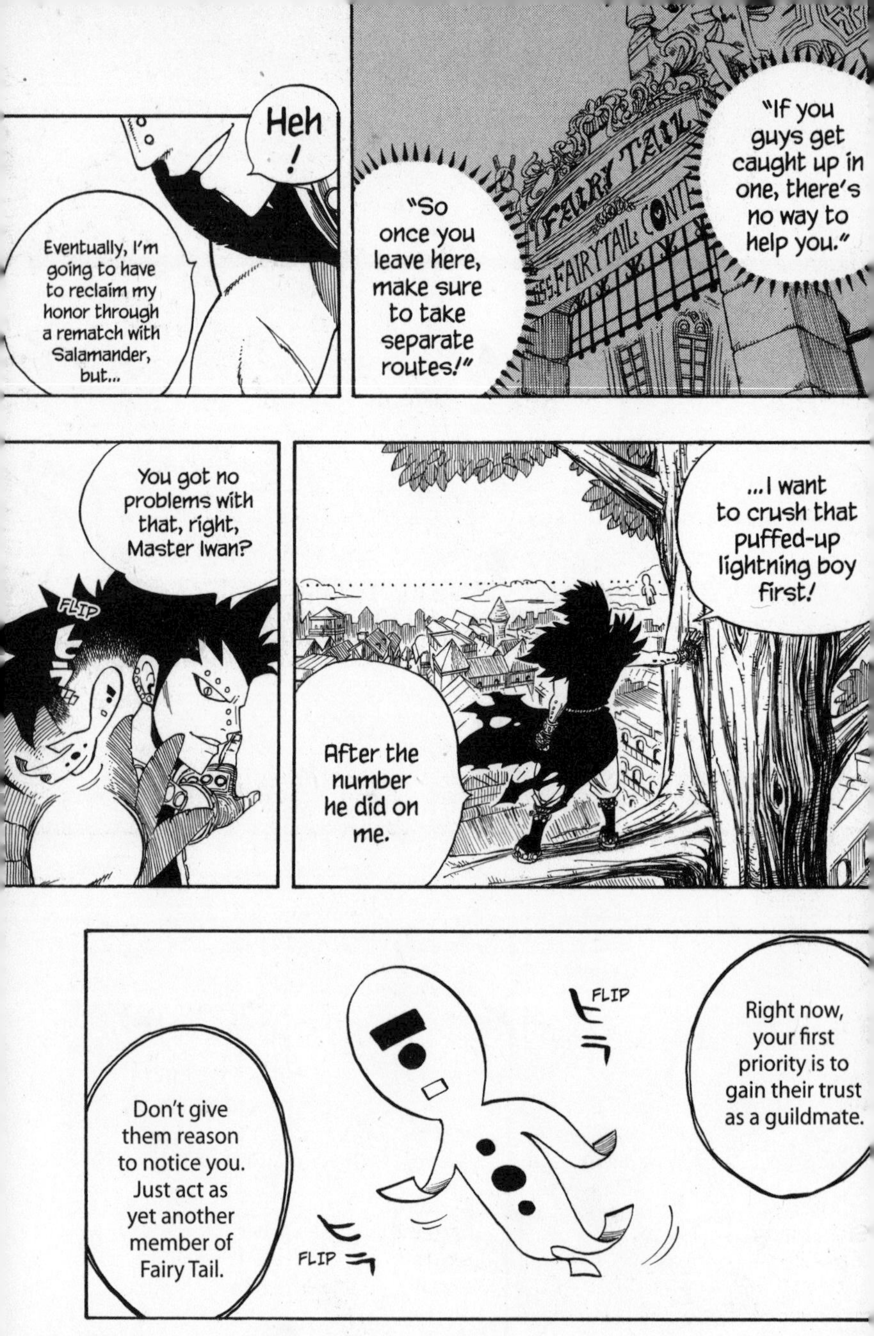
"If you guys get caught up in one, there's no way to help you."
"So once you leave here, make sure to take separate routes!"
FAIRY TAIL
FAIRYTAIL CONTE
Heh!
Eventually, I'm going to have to reclaim my honor through a rematch with Salamander, but...
...I want to crush that puffed-up lightning boy first!
After the number he did on me.
FLIP
You got no problems with that, right, Master Iwan?
Right now, your first priority is to gain their trust as a guildmate.
FLIP
FLIP
Don't give them reason to notice you. Just act as yet another member of Fairy Tail.

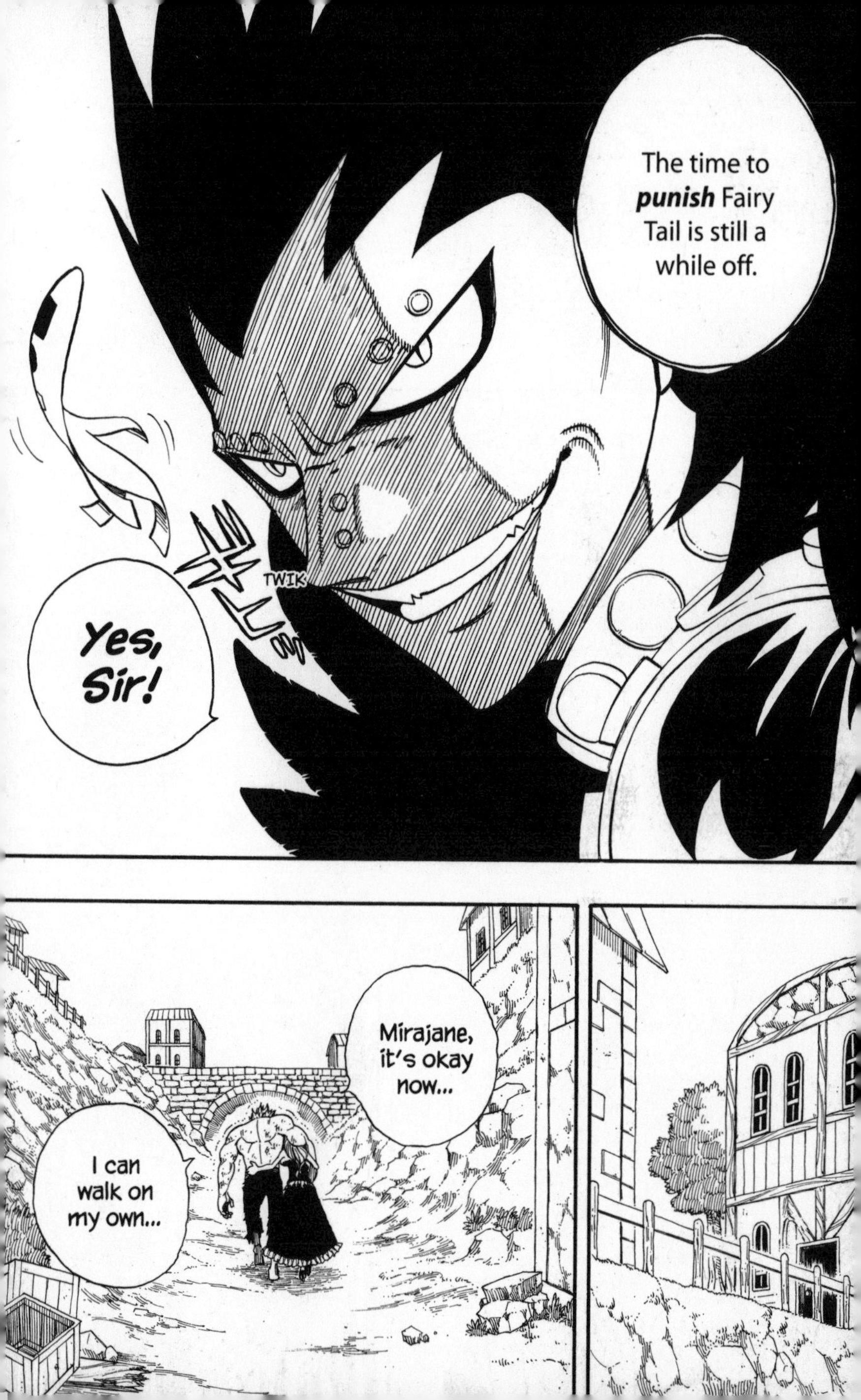
The time to ***punish*** Fairy Tail is still a while off.
Yes, Sir!
TWIK
Mirajane, it's okay now...
I can walk on my own...

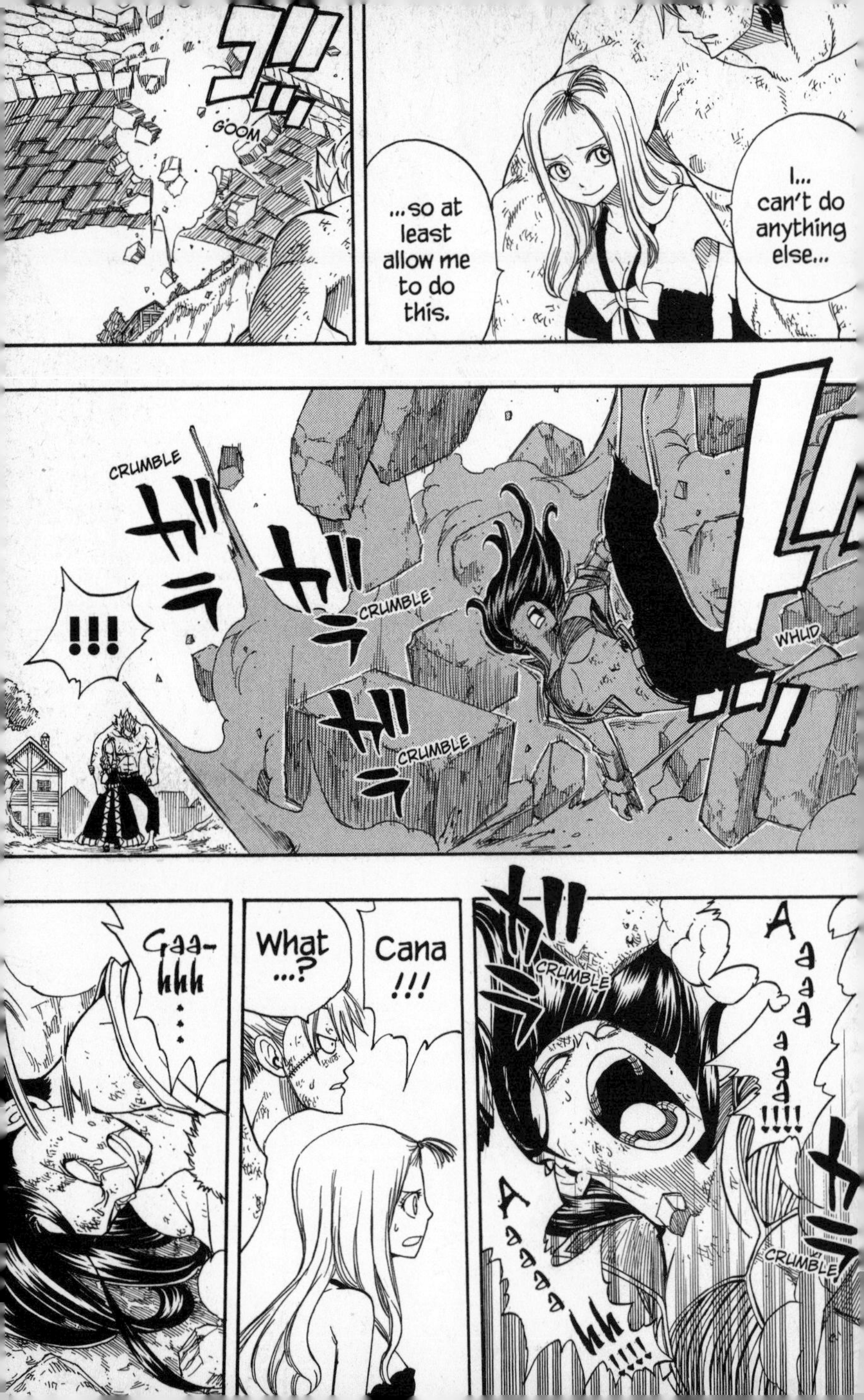
I... can't do anything else...
...so at least allow me to do this.
GOOM
WHUD
CRUMBLE
CRUMBLE
CRUMBLE
!!!
Aaaaaaaaa!!!!!
CRUMBLE
CRUMBLE
Aaaaaaahh!!!!
Cana!!!
What...?
Gaa-hhh...

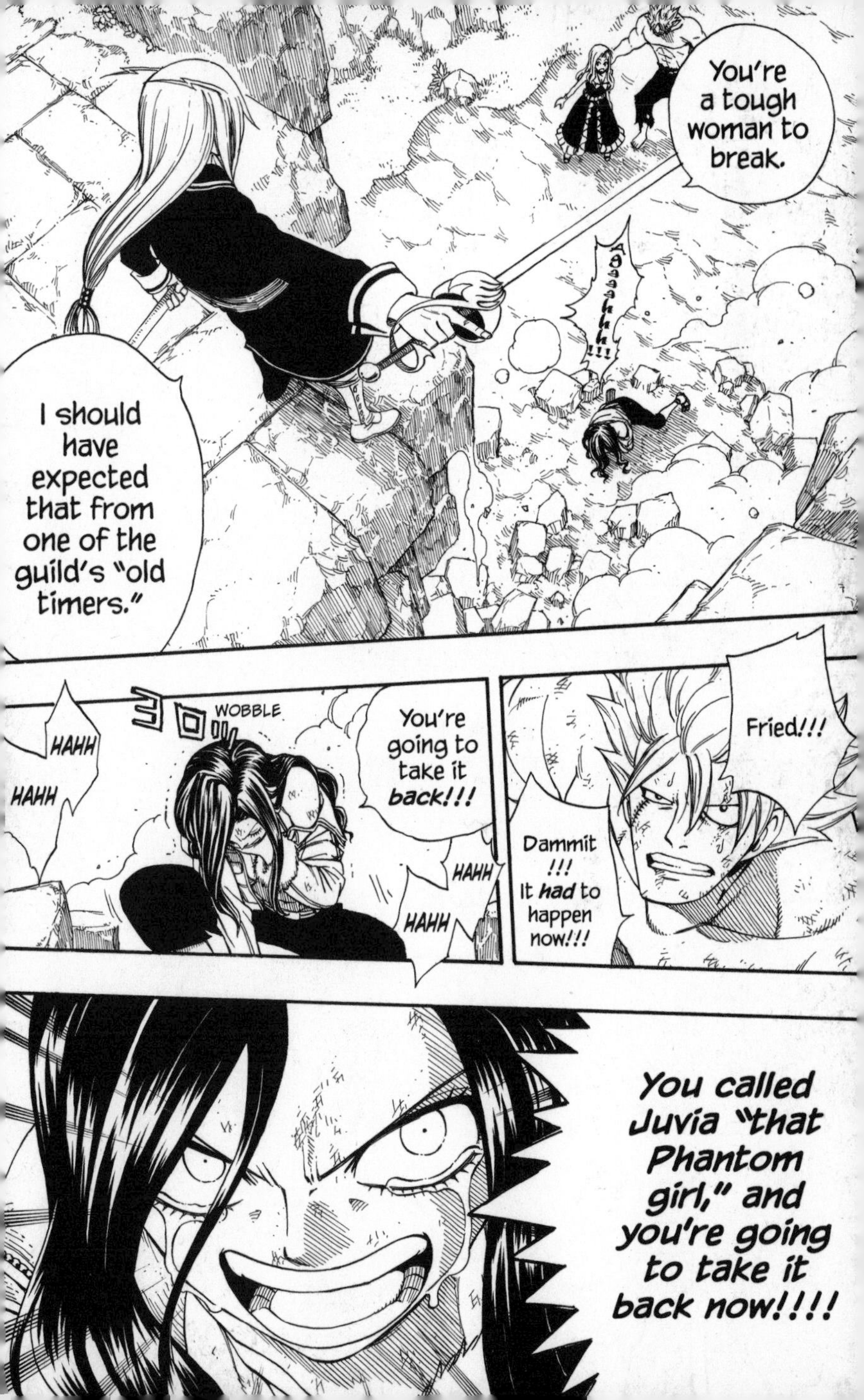
You're a tough woman to break.
Aaaaaahhh!!!
I should have expected that from one of the guild's "old timers."
Fried!!!
Dammit!!! It *had* to happen now!!!
You're going to take it *back!!!*
WOBBLE
HAHH
HAHH
HAHH
HAHH
You called Juvia "that Phantom girl," and you're going to take it back now!!!!

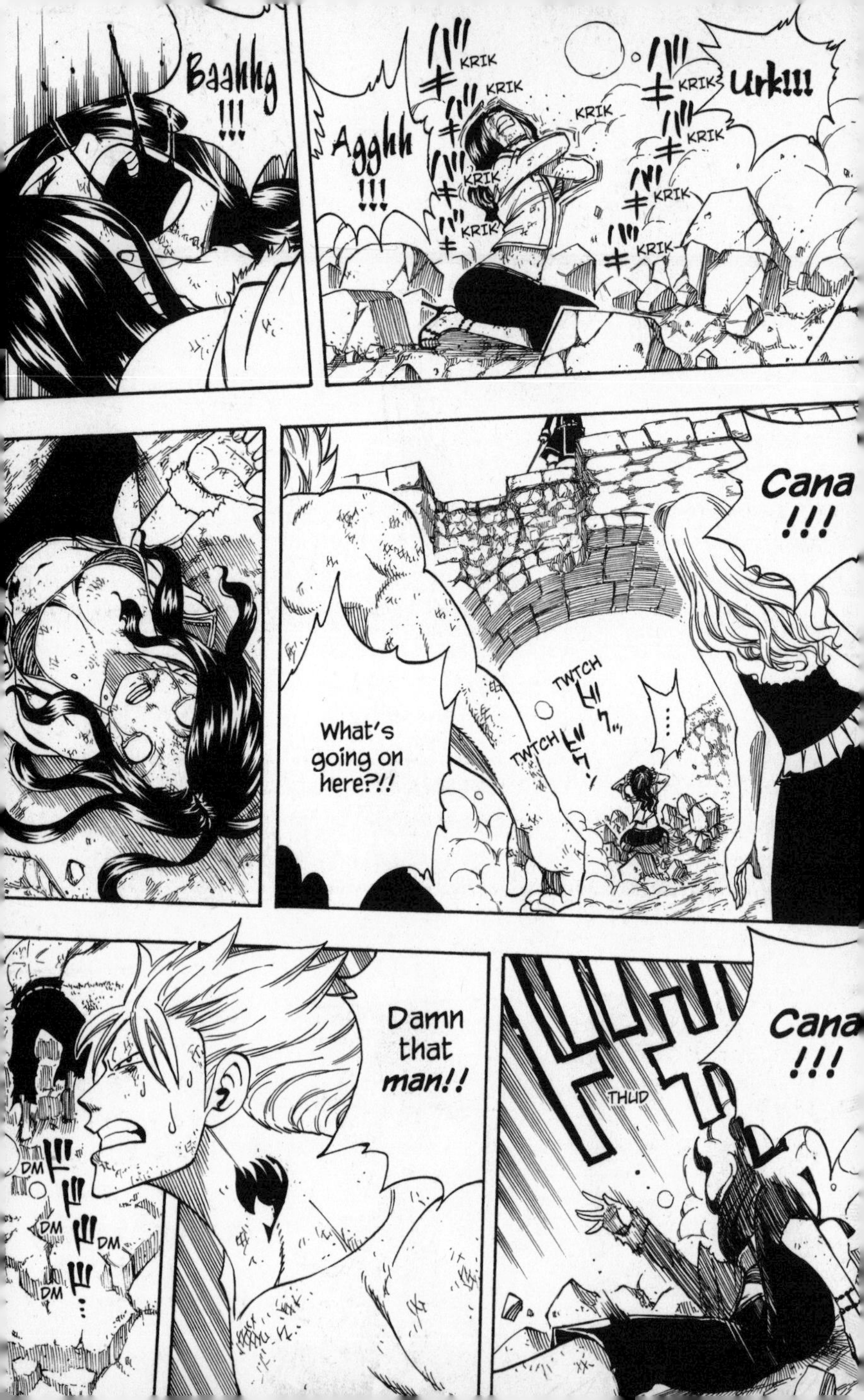
Urk!!!
KRIK
KRIK
KRIK
KRIK
KRIK
KRIK
KRIK
KRIK
Agghh!!!
Baahhg!!!
Cana!!!
...
TWTCH
TWTCH
What's going on here?!!
Cana!!!
THUD
Damn that man!!
DM
DM
DM
DM

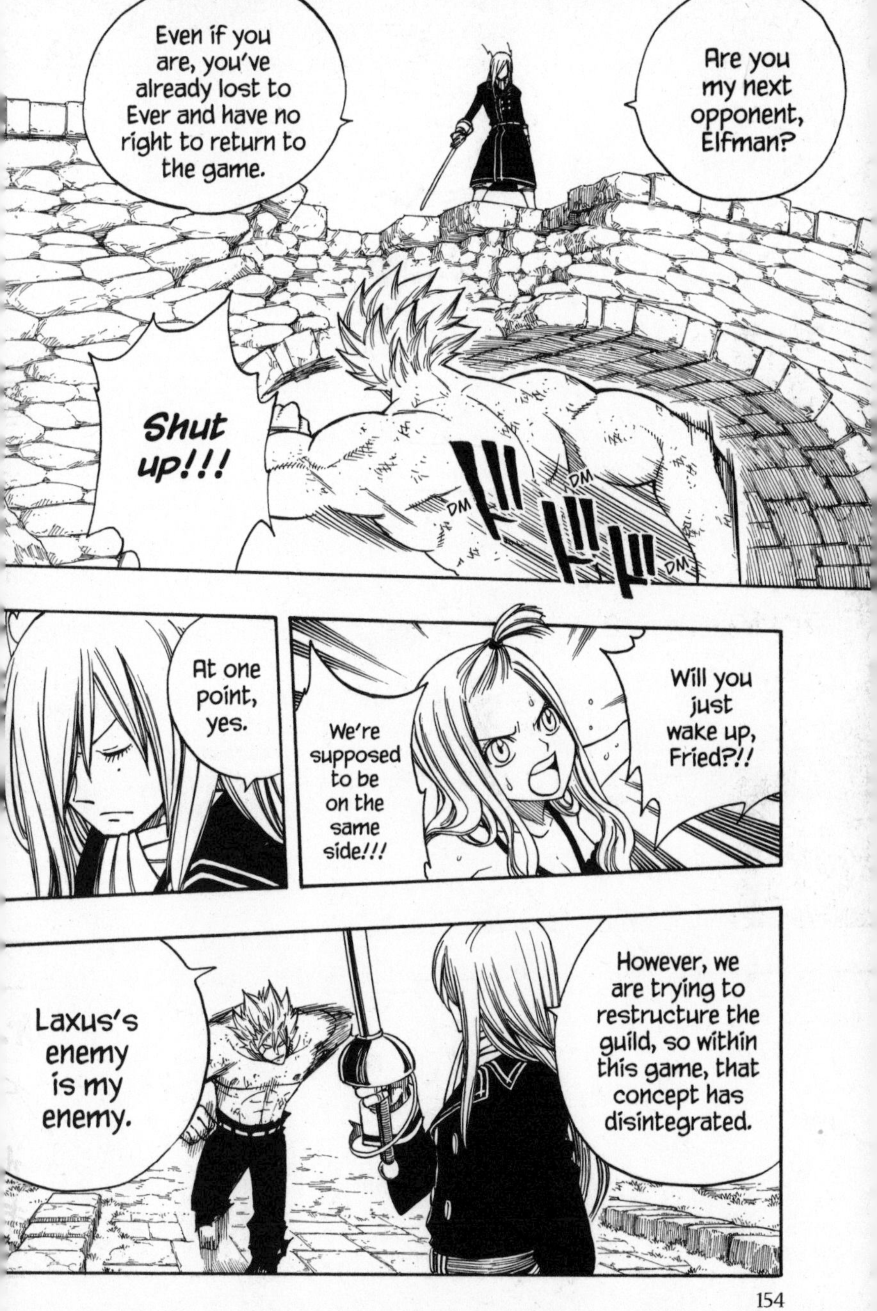
Are you my next opponent, Elfman?
Even if you are, you've already lost to Ever and have no right to return to the game.
Shut up!!!
DM
DM
DM
Will you just wake up, Fried?!!
We're supposed to be on the same side!!!
At one point, yes.
However, we are trying to restructure the guild, so within this game, that concept has disintegrated.
Laxus's enemy is my enemy.

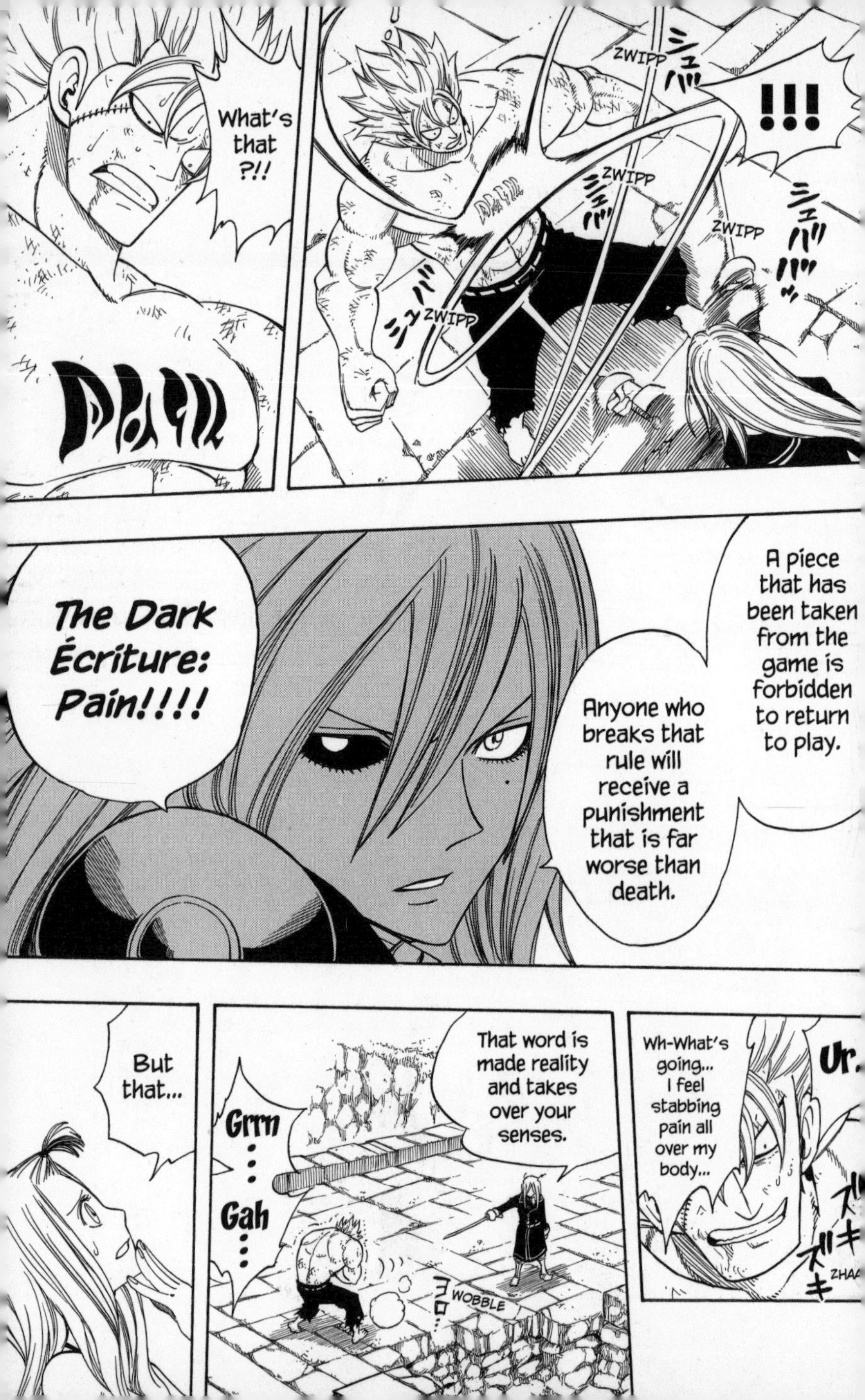

ZWIPP
!!!
ZWIPP
ZWIPP
ZWIPP
What's that ?!!
A piece that has been taken from the game is forbidden to return to play.
Anyone who breaks that rule will receive a punishment that is far worse than death.
The Dark Écriture: Pain!!!!
Ur.
Wh-What's going... I feel stabbing pain all over my body...
That word is made reality and takes over your senses.
Grrn...
Gah...
WOBBLE
But that...

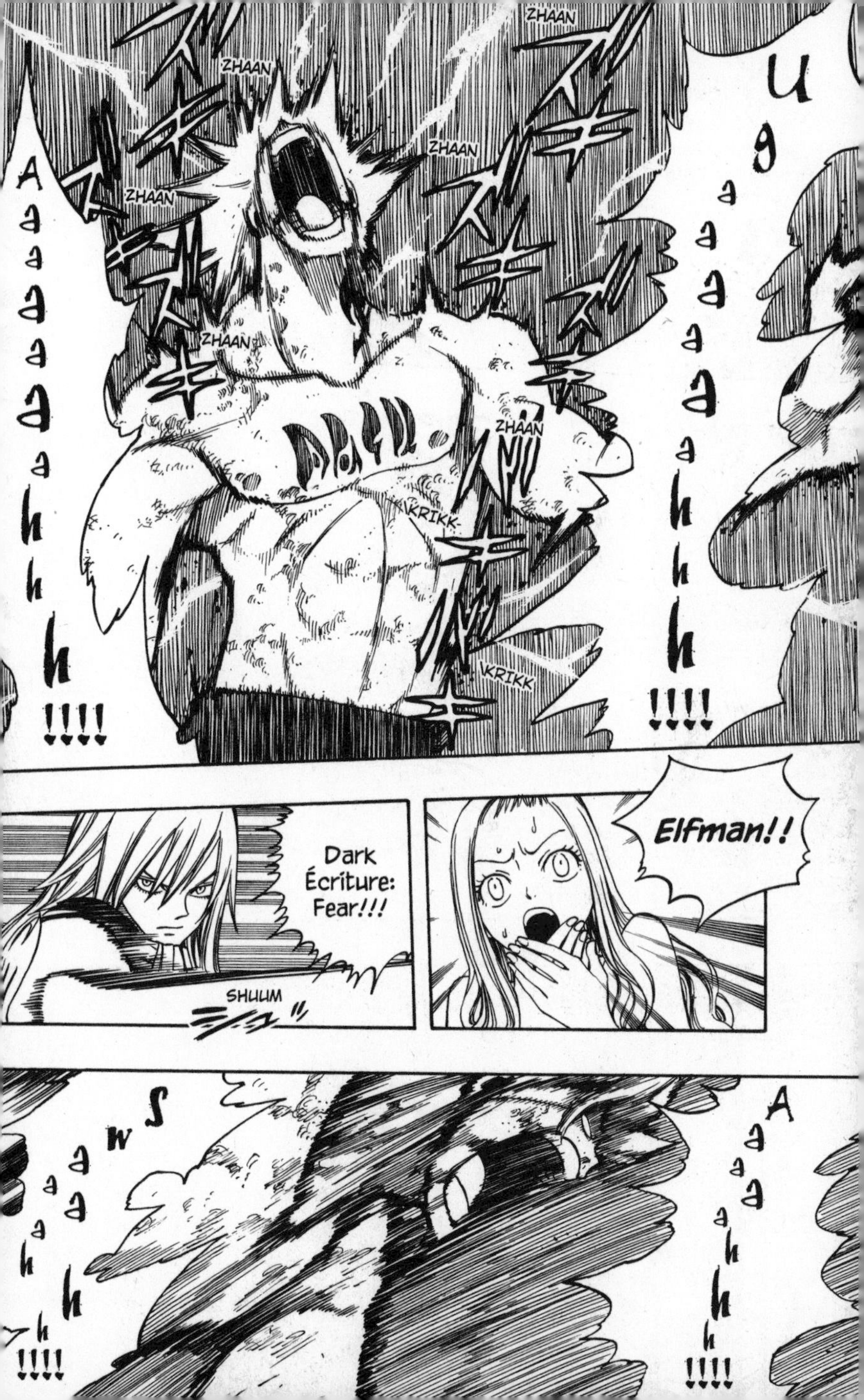

Ugaaaaaahhhh!!!!
ZHAAN
ZHAAN
ZHAAN
ZHAAN
ZHAAN
ZHAAN
KRIKK
KRIKK
Aaaaaaaaahhh!!!!
Elfman!!
Dark Écriture: Fear!!!
SHUUM
Aaaaaahhhh!!!!
Swaaaahhhh!!!!

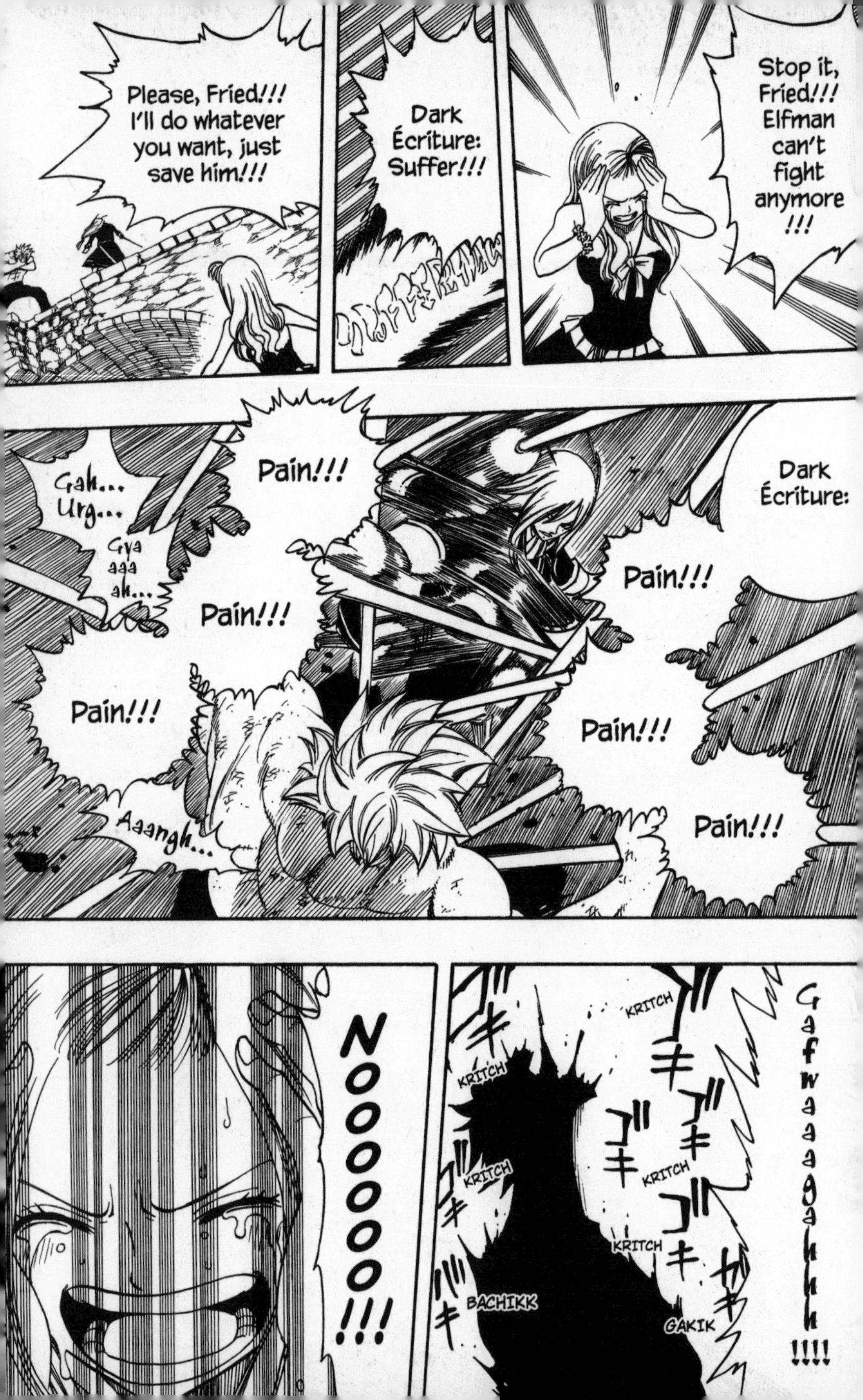
Stop it, Fried!!! Elfman can't fight anymore!!!
Dark Écriture: Suffer!!!
Please, Fried!!! I'll do whatever you want, just save him!!!
Dark Écriture:
Pain!!!
Pain!!!
Pain!!!
Pain!!!
Pain!!!
Gah... Urg...
Gya aaa ah...
Pain!!!
Aaangh...
Gafwaaaaaghhh!!!!
KRITCH
KRITCH
KRITCH
KRITCH
KRITCH
GAKIK
BACHIKK
NOOOOOOO!!!

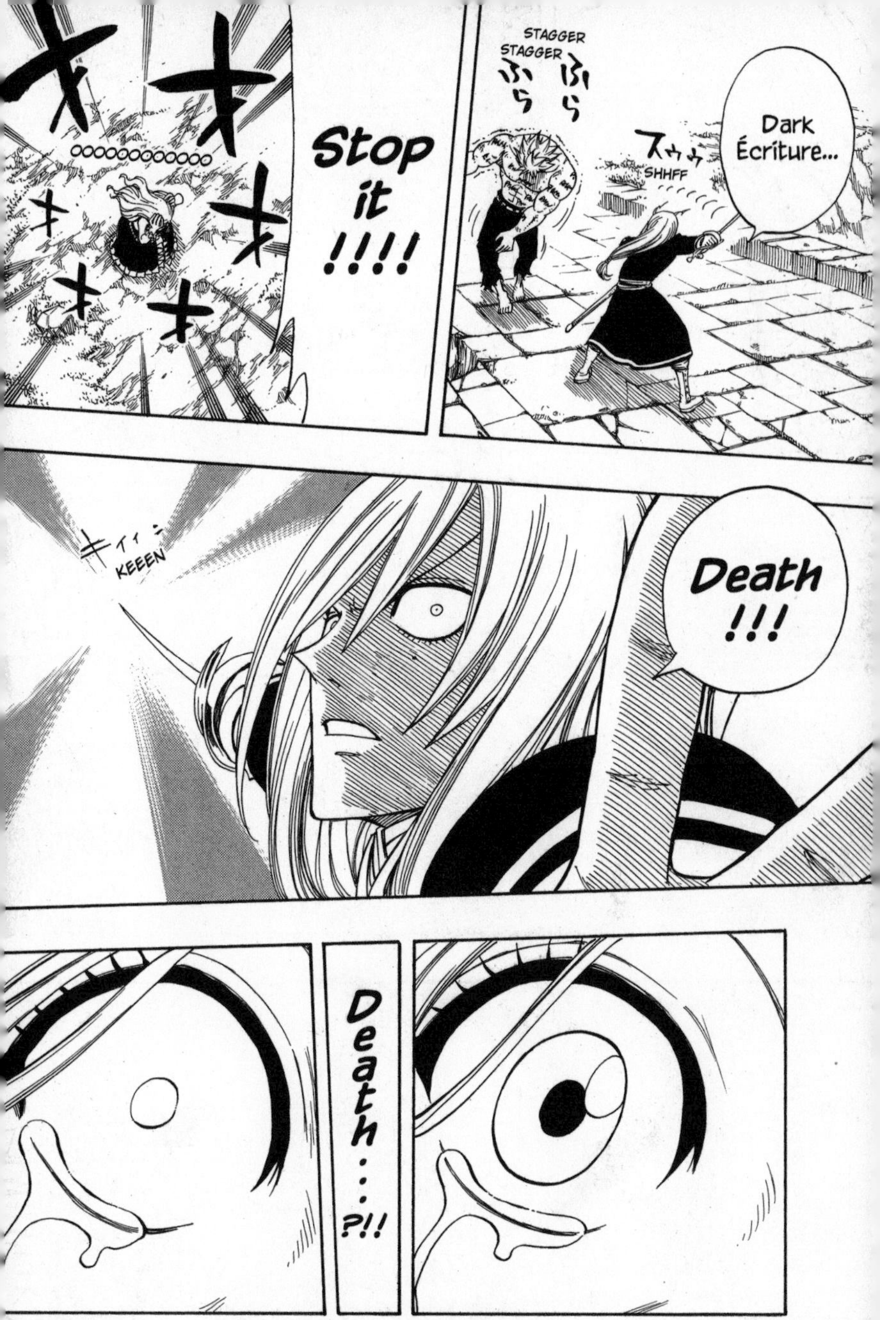
STAGGER
STAGGER
SHHFF
Dark Écriture...
Stop it !!!!
OOOOOOOOOOOO
Death !!!
KEEEN
Death...?!!

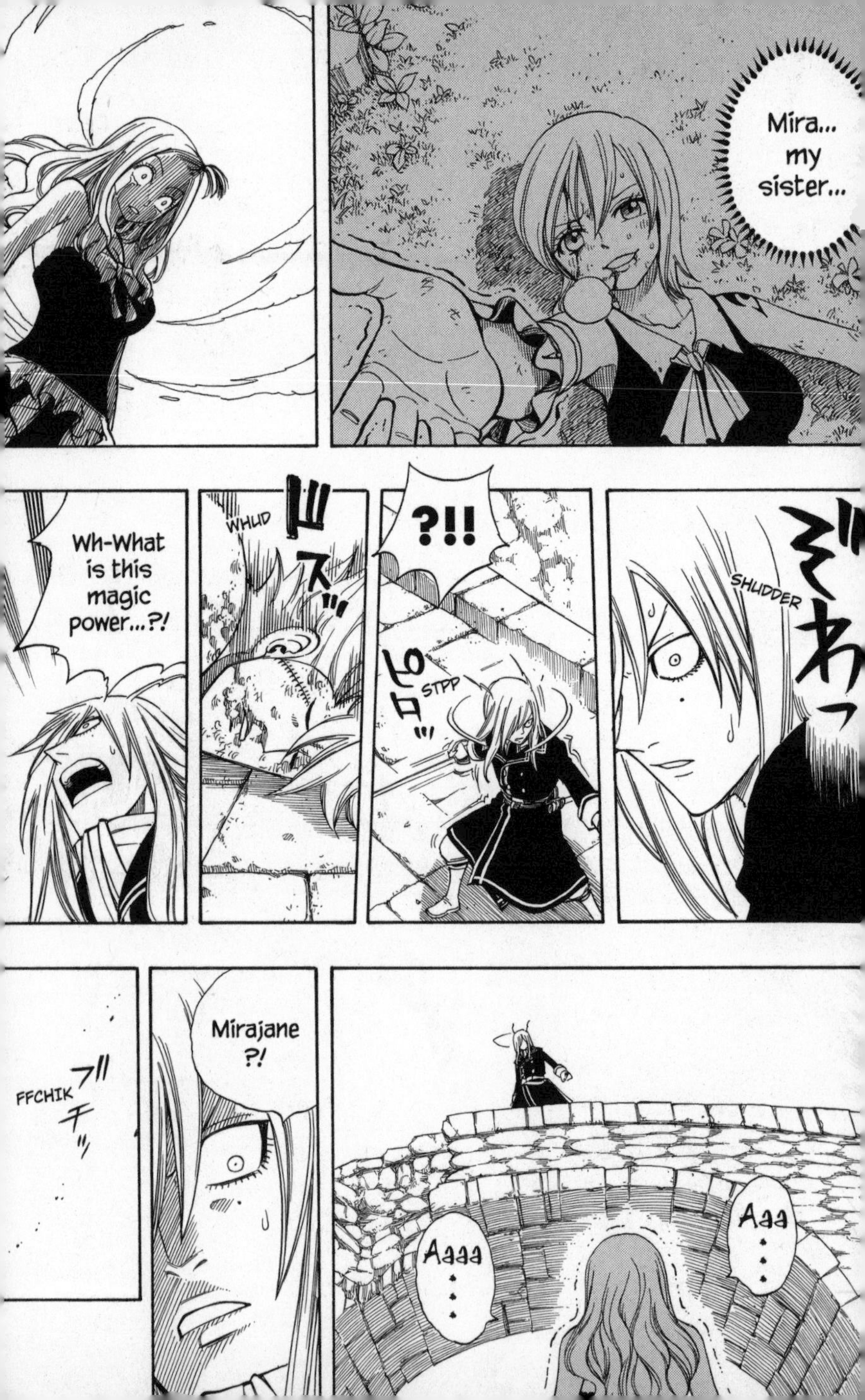

Mira... my sister...
SHUDDER
?!!
STPP
WHUD
Wh-What is this magic power...?!
Aaa...
Aaaa...
Mirajane ?!
FFCHIK

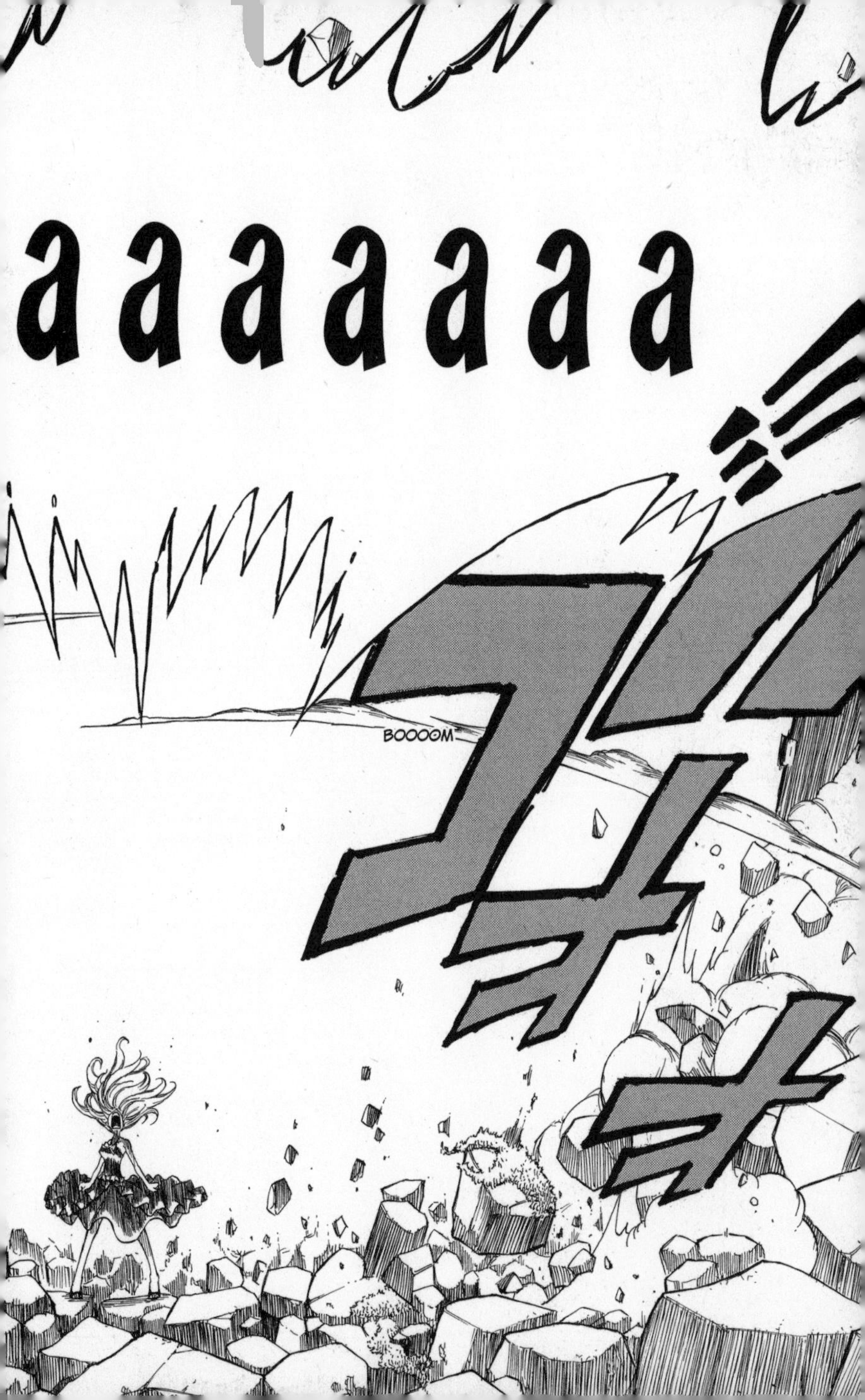
aaaaaaa
BOOOOM

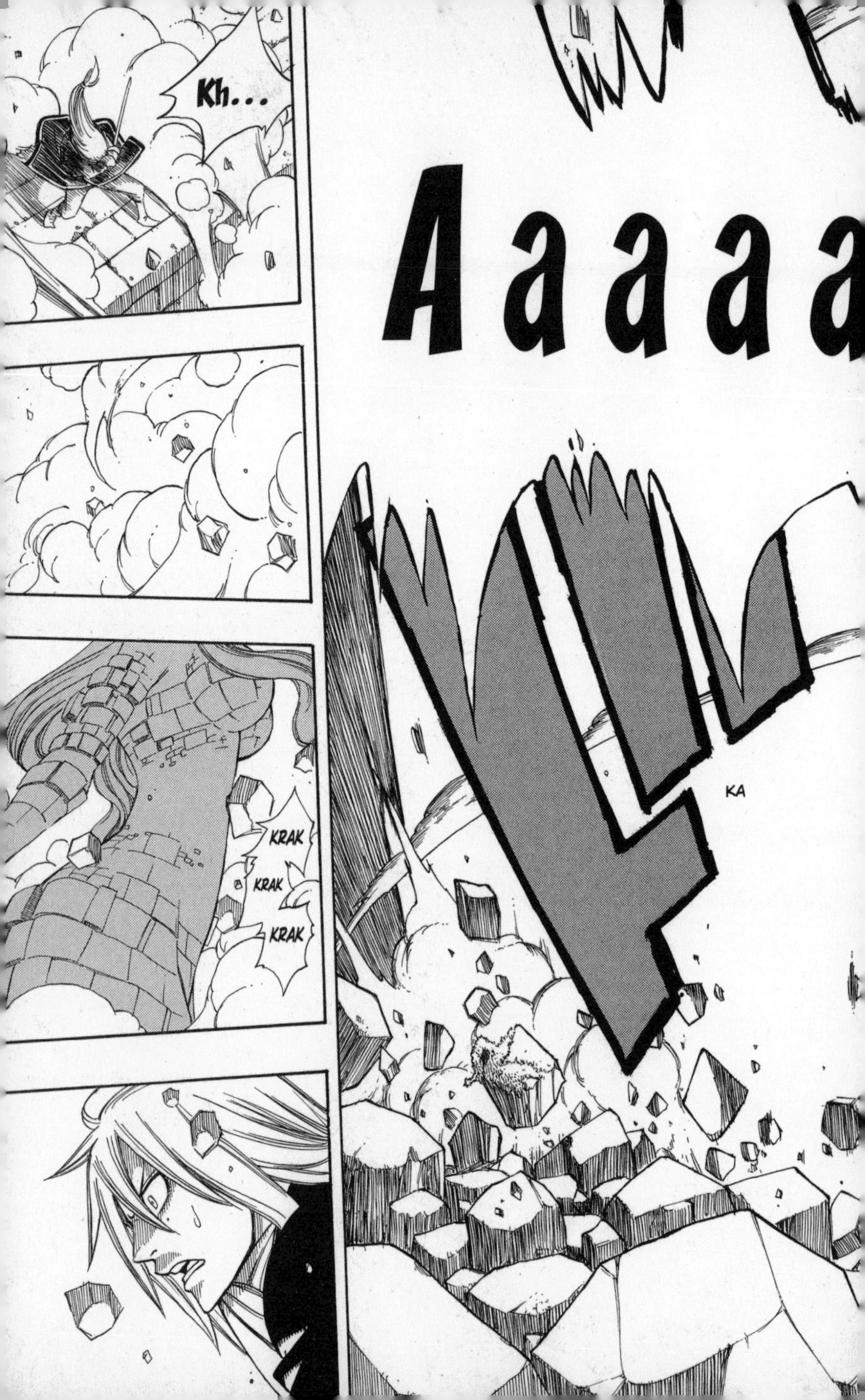
Aaaaa
KA
Kh...
KRAK
KRAK
KRAK

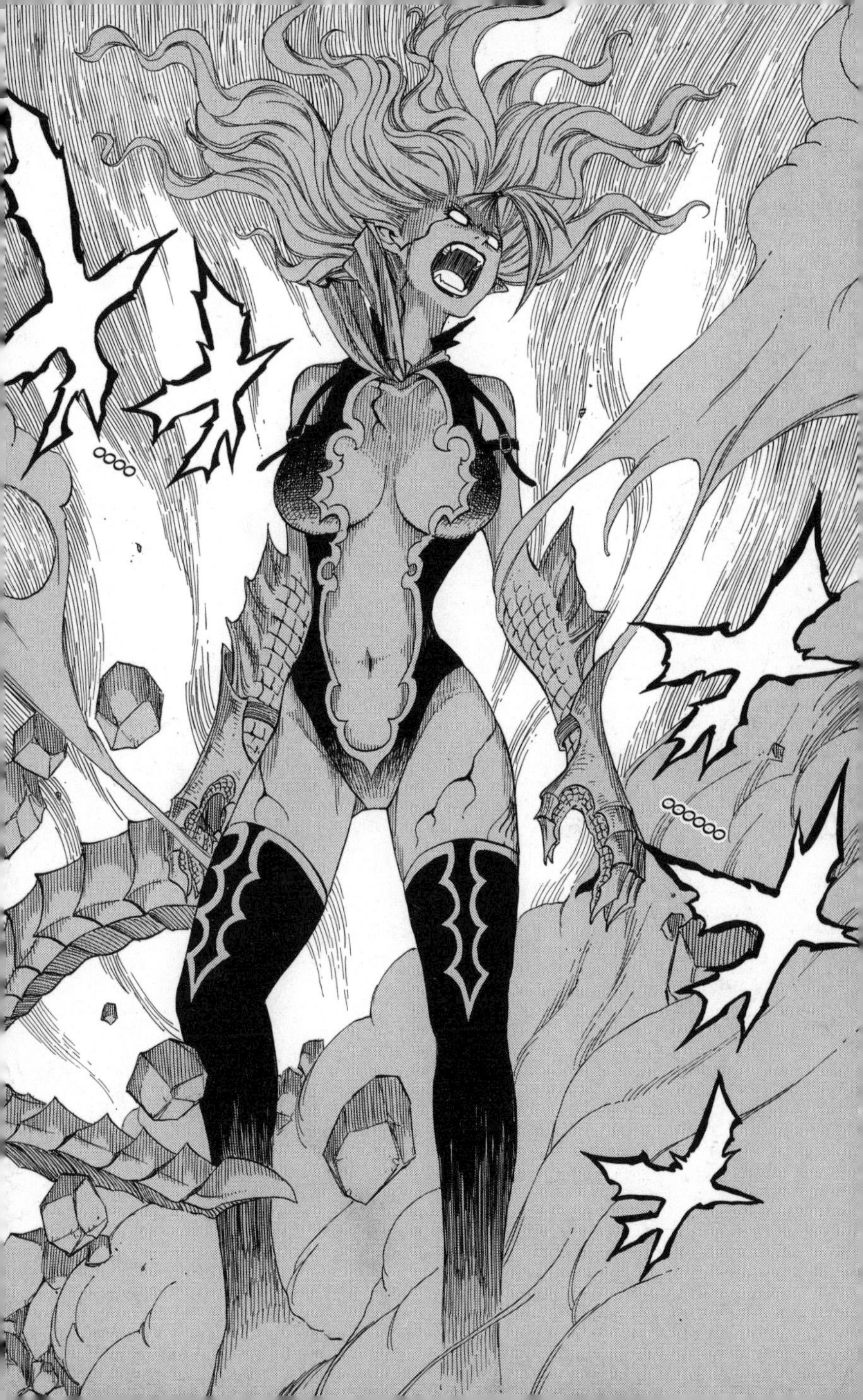

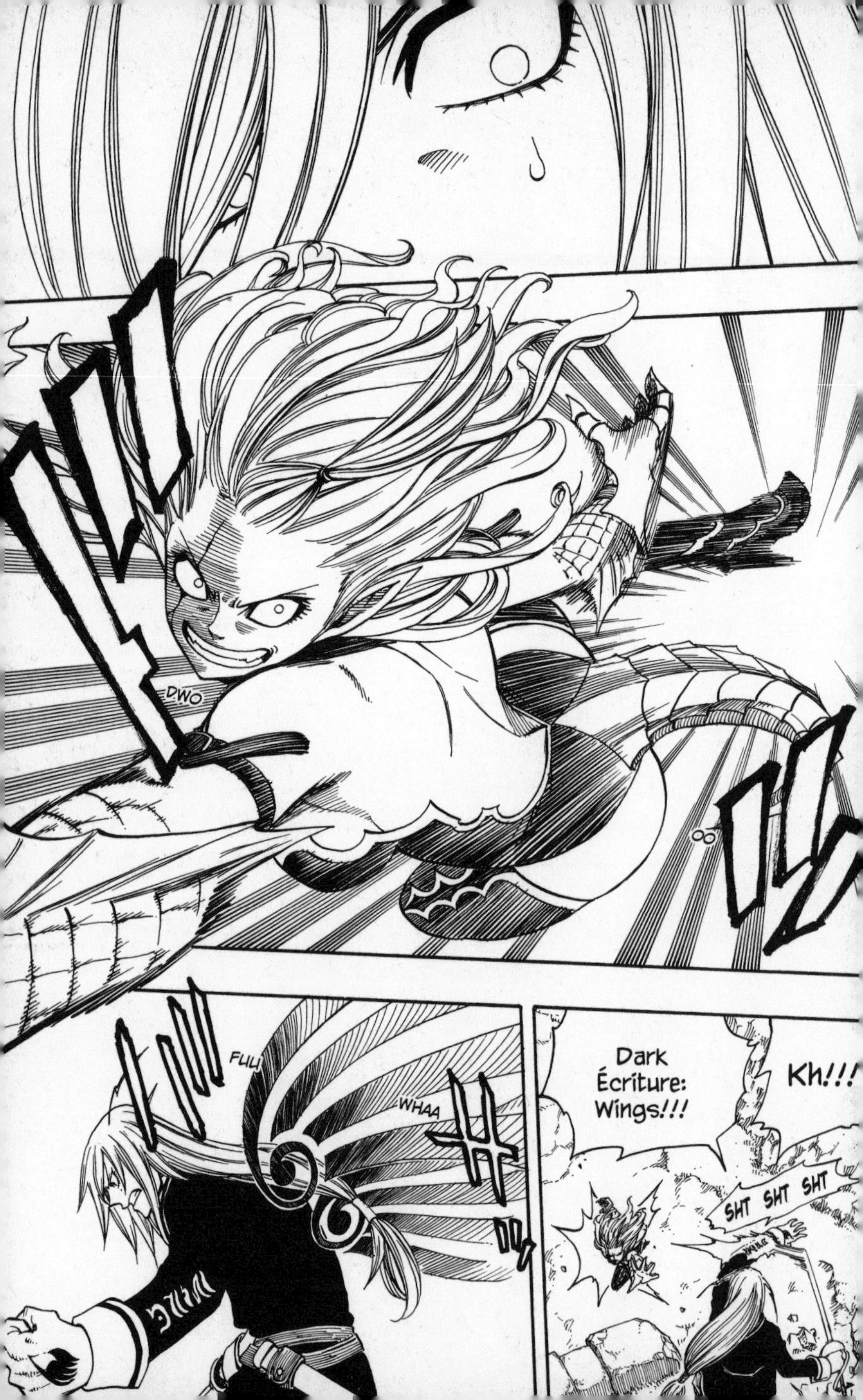
DWO
Dark Écriture: Wings!!!
Kh!!!
SHT SHT SHT
WHAA
FUU

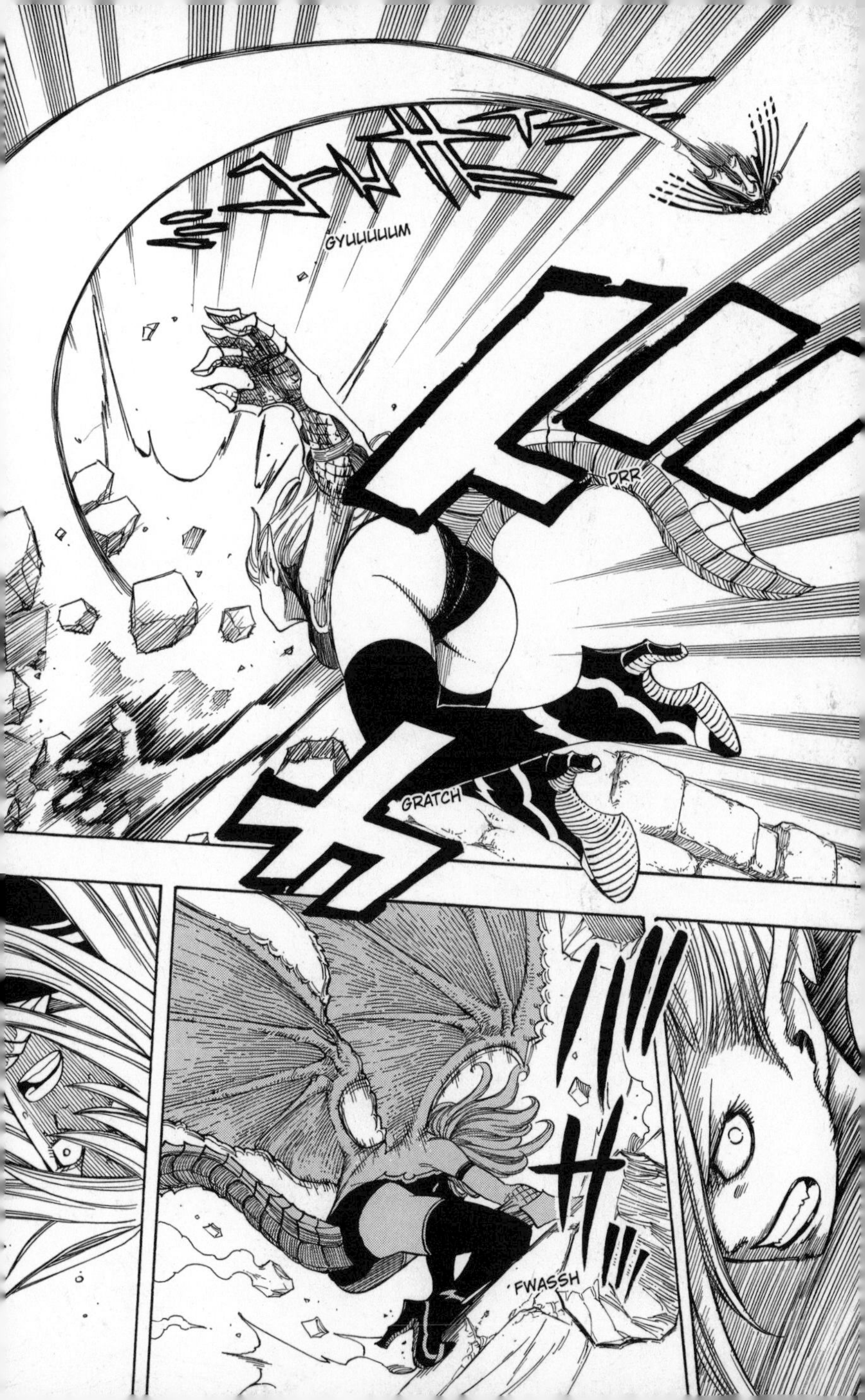
GYUUUUUM
DRR
GRATCH
FWASSH

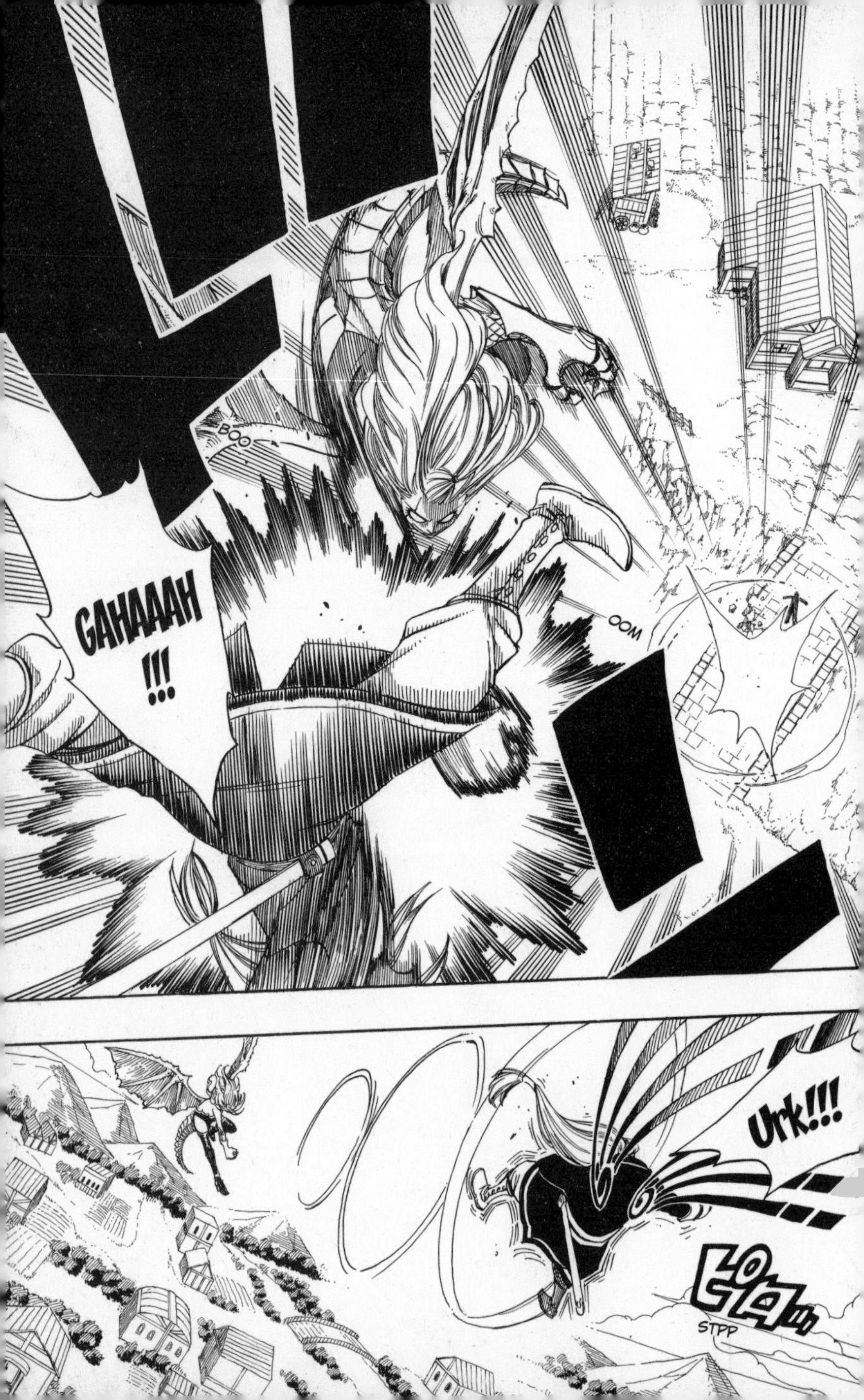
BOO
OOM
GAHAAAH!!!
Urk!!!
STPP

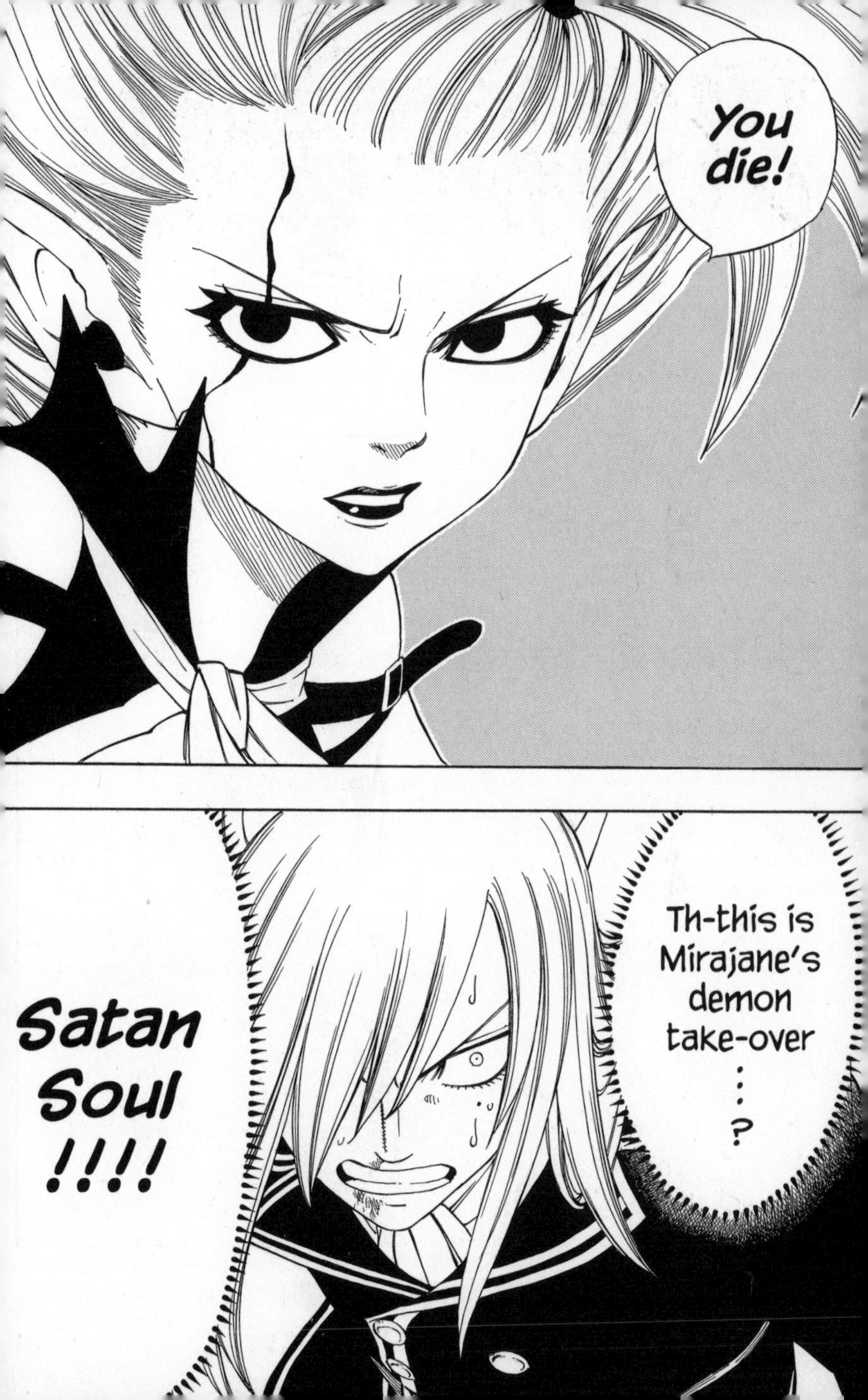
You die!
Th-this is Mirajane's demon take-over ...?
Satan Soul !!!!

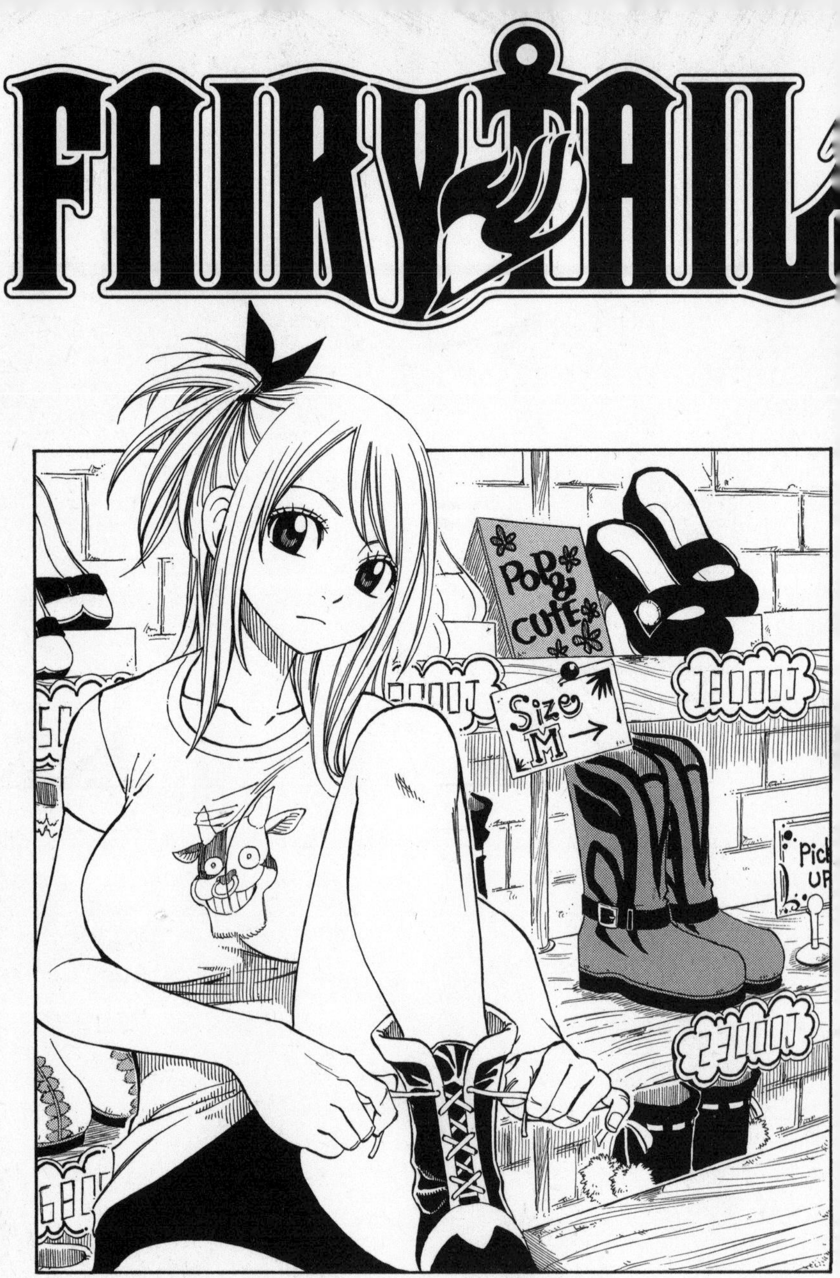
Pop & Cute
Size M →
Pick UP

Chapter 118: Gentle Words

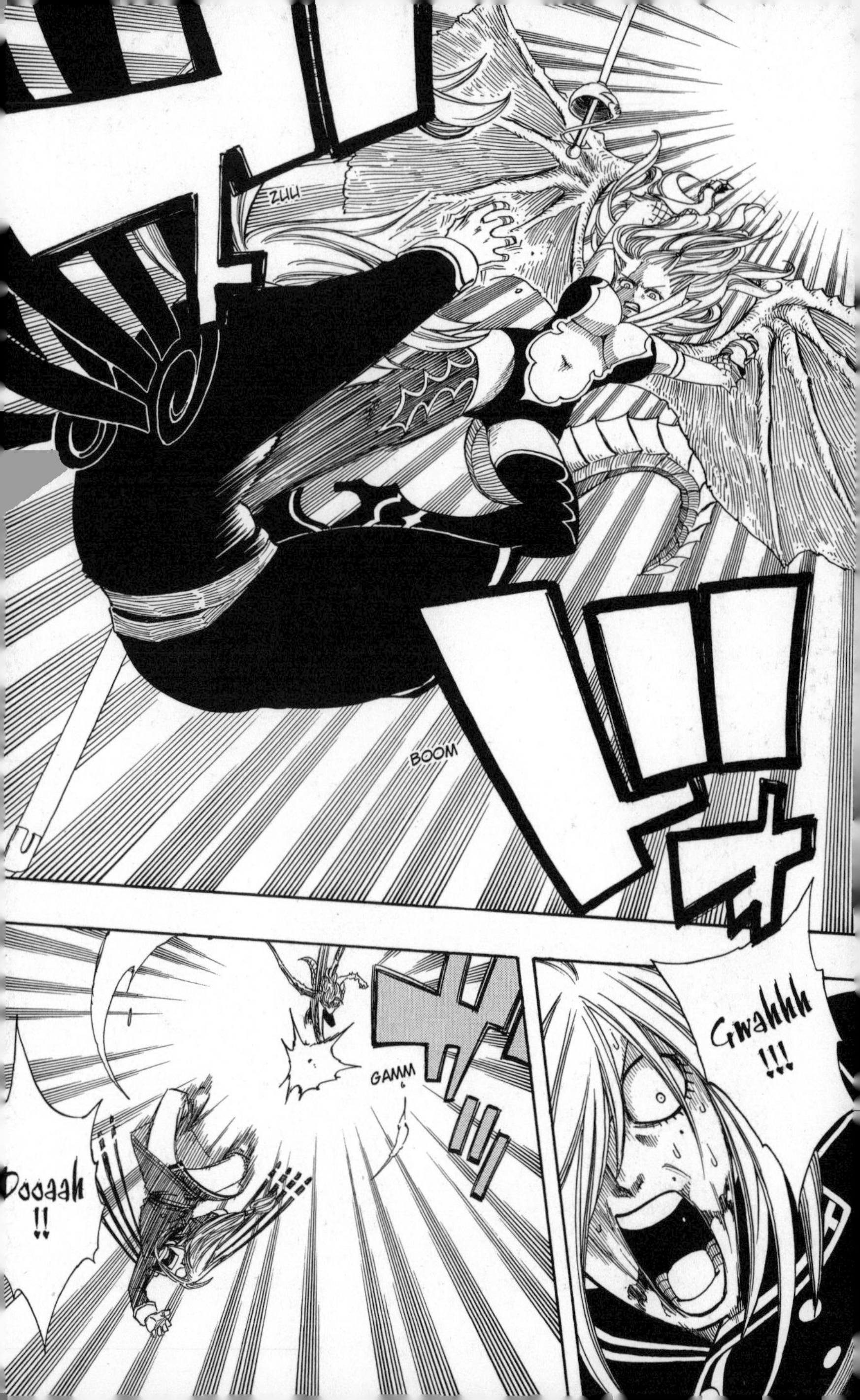
ZUU
BOOM
Gwahhh !!!
GAMM
Dooaah !!

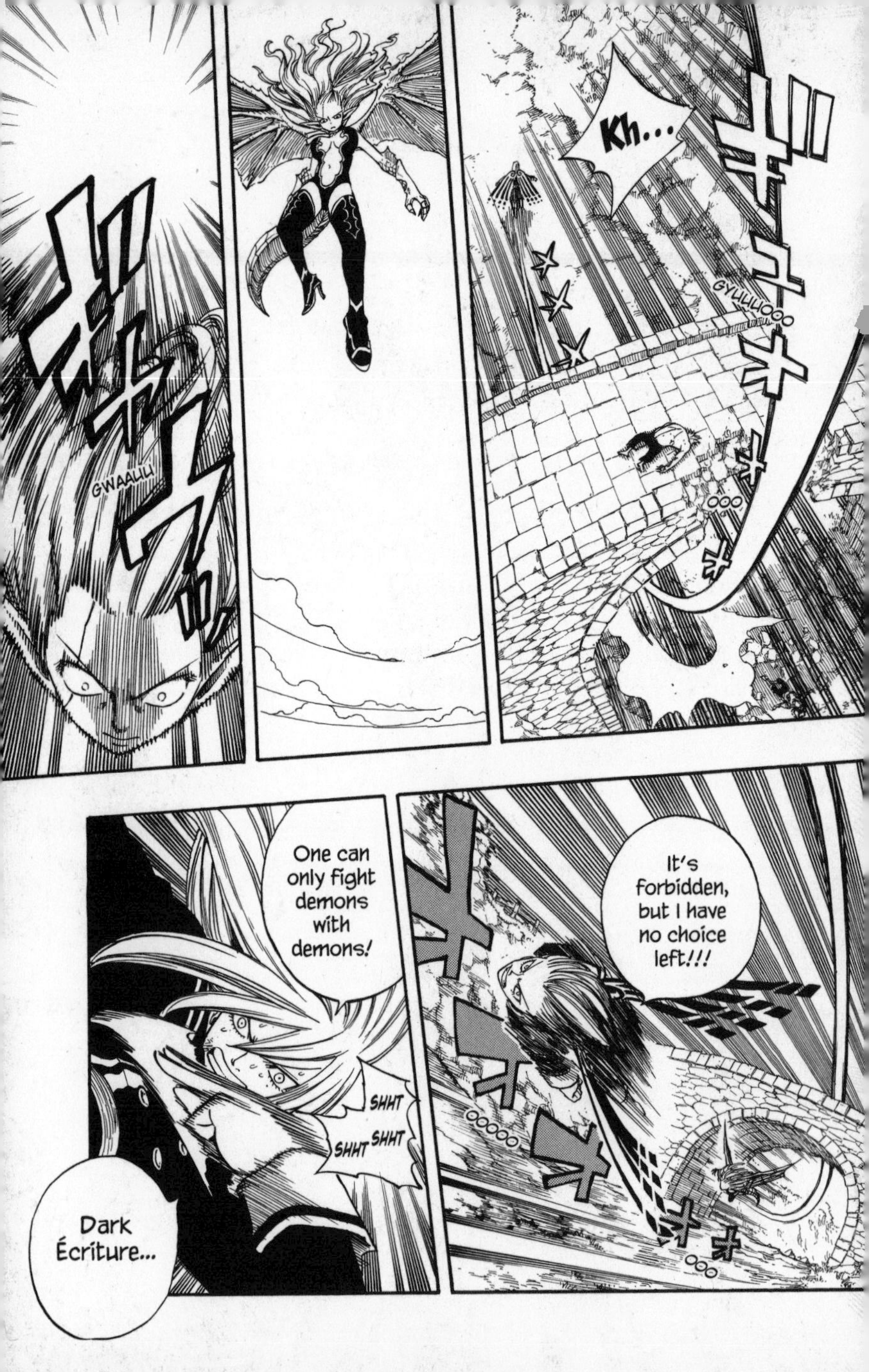
Kh...
GYULLLOOO
OOO
GWAALLL
It's forbidden, but I have no choice left!!!
OOOOO
OOO
One can only fight demons with demons!
SHHT
SHHT
SHHT
Dark Écriture...

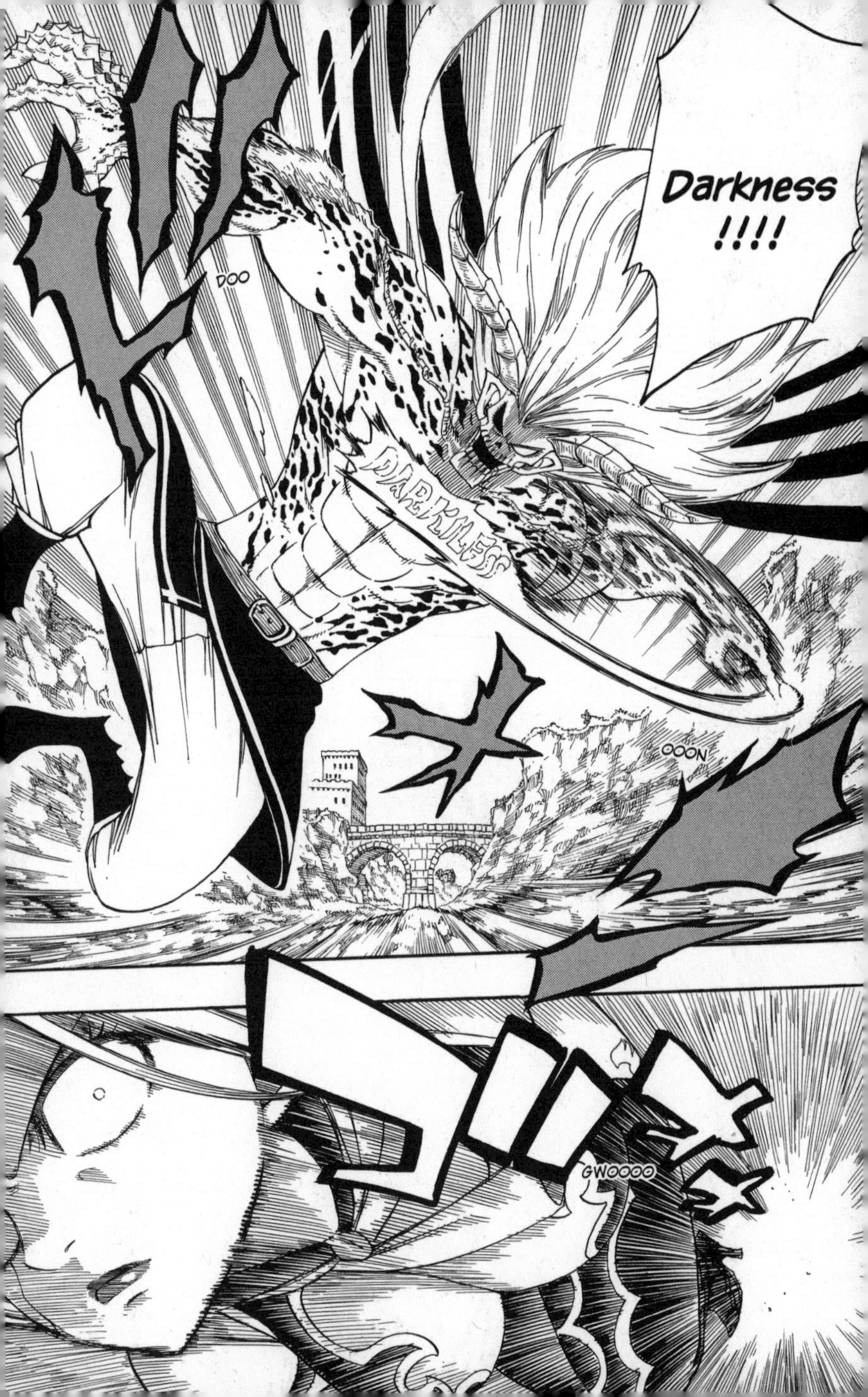
Darkness !!!!
DOO
OOON
GWOOOO

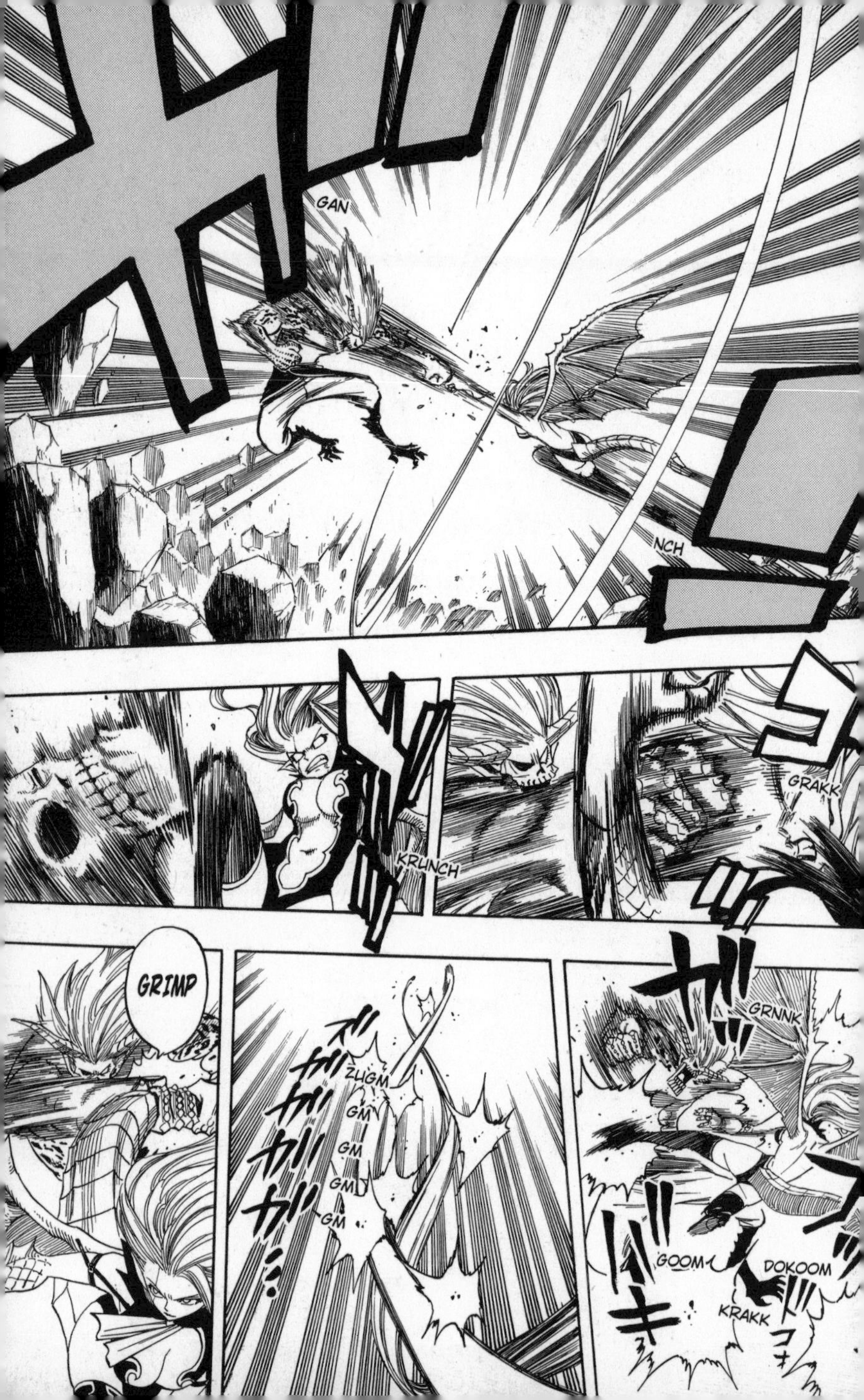
GAN
NCH
GRAKK
KRUNCH
GRNNK
DOKOOM
GOOM
KRAKK
ZUGM
GM
GM
GM
GM
GRIMP

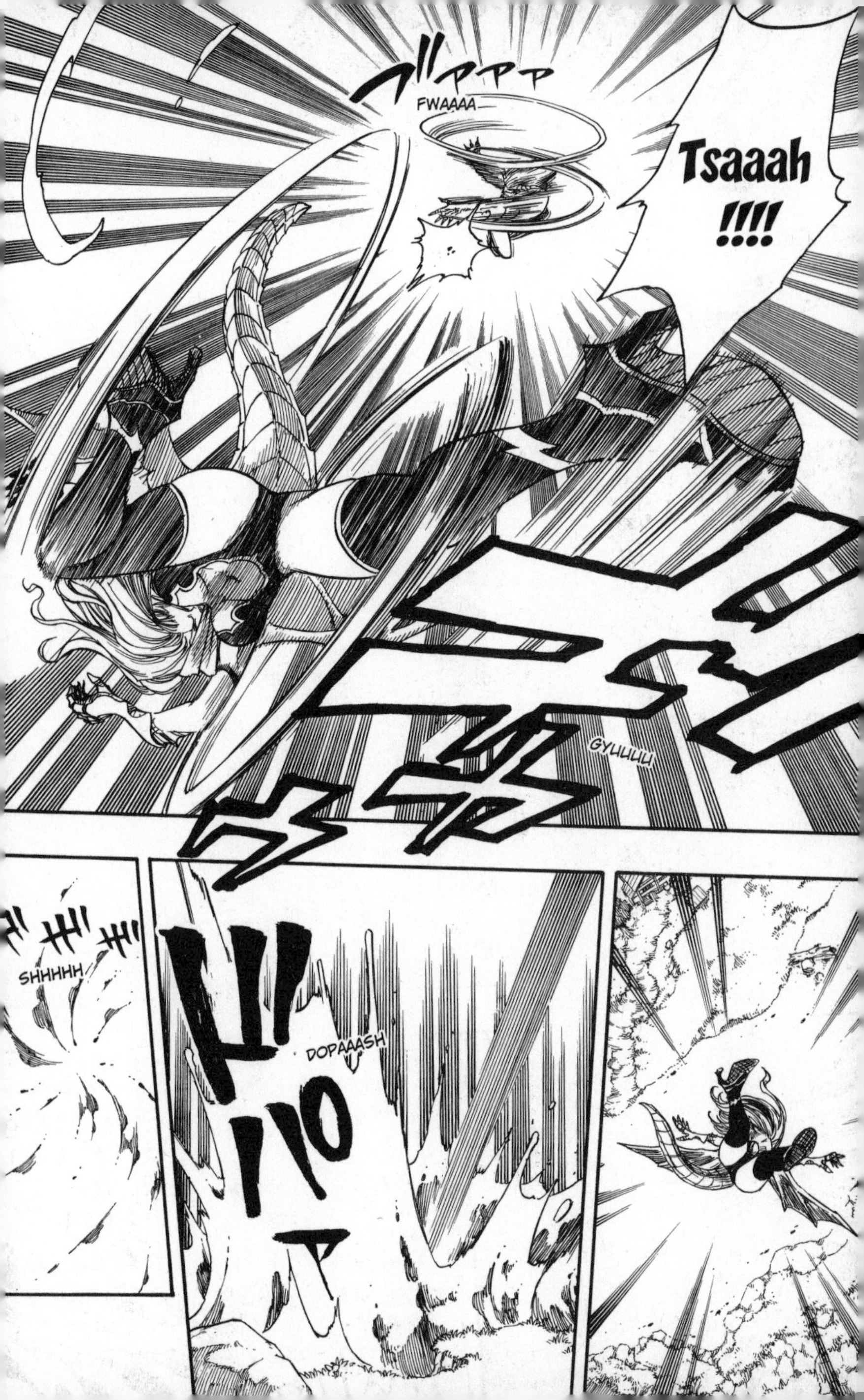
Tsaaah !!!!
FWAAAA
GYUUUU
DOPAAASH
SHHHHH

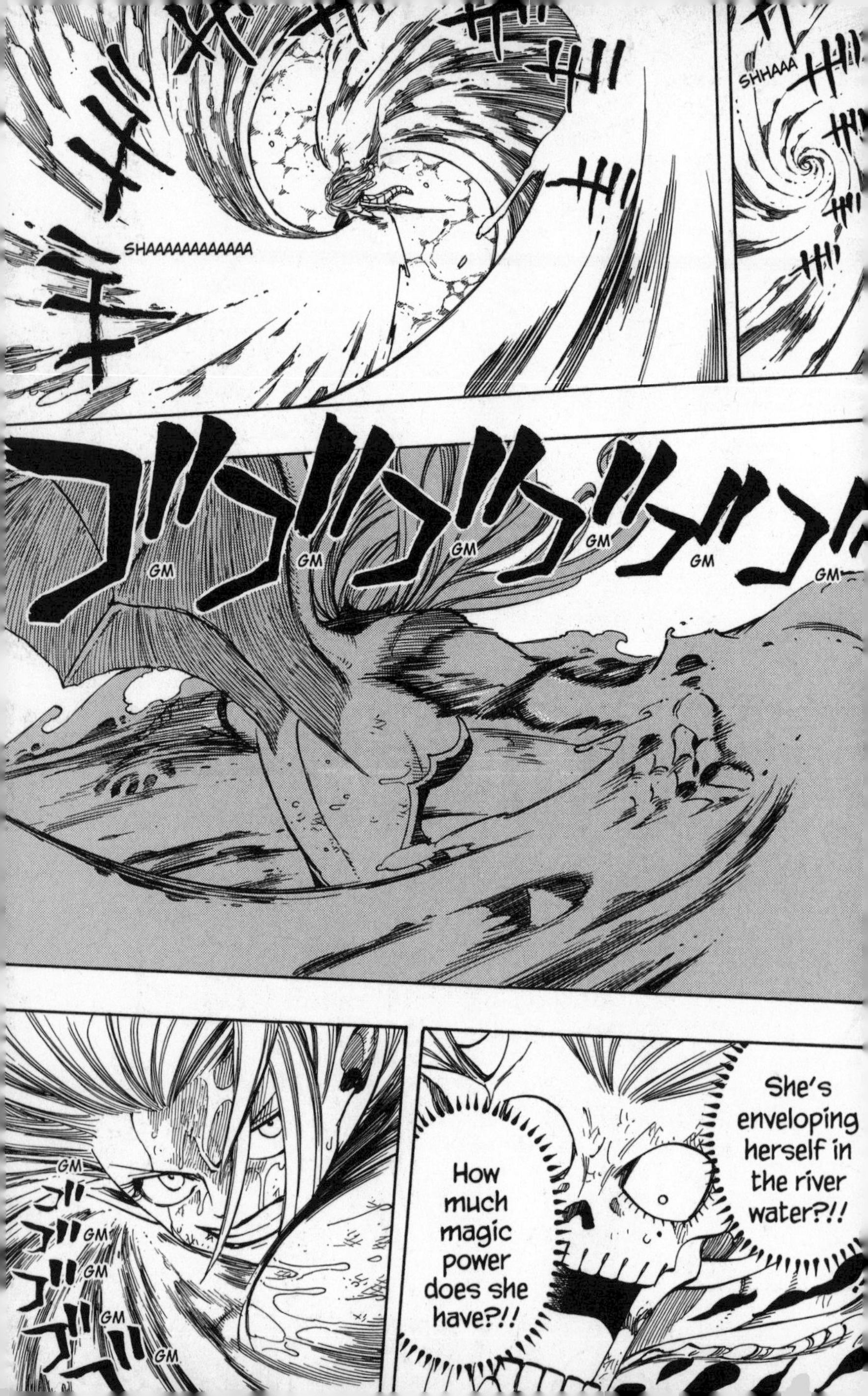
SHHAAA
SHAAAAAAAAAAAA
GM
GM
GM
GM
GM
GM
She's enveloping herself in the river water?!!
How much magic power does she have?!!
GM
GM
GM
GM
GM

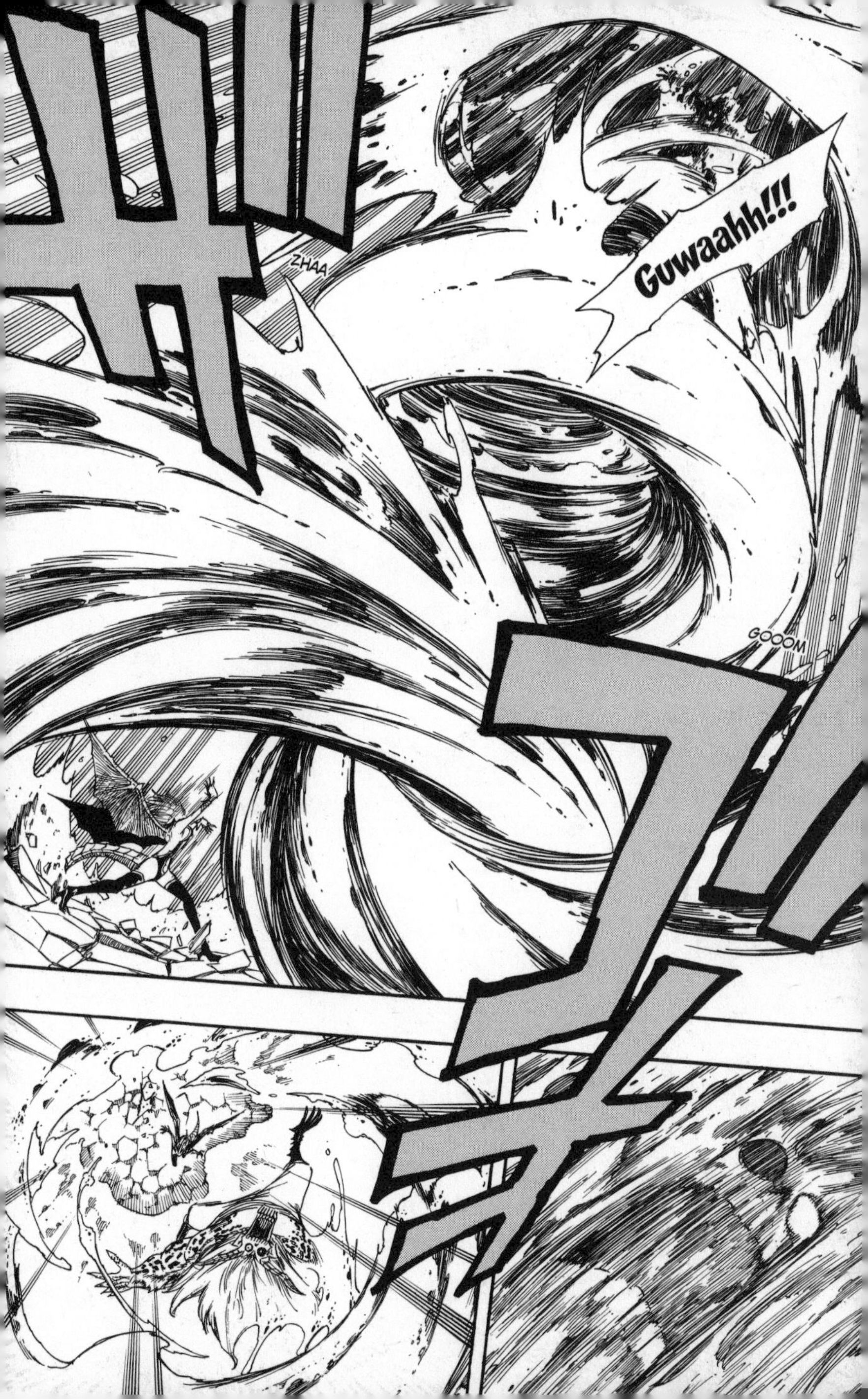
Guwaahh!!!
ZHAA
GOOOM

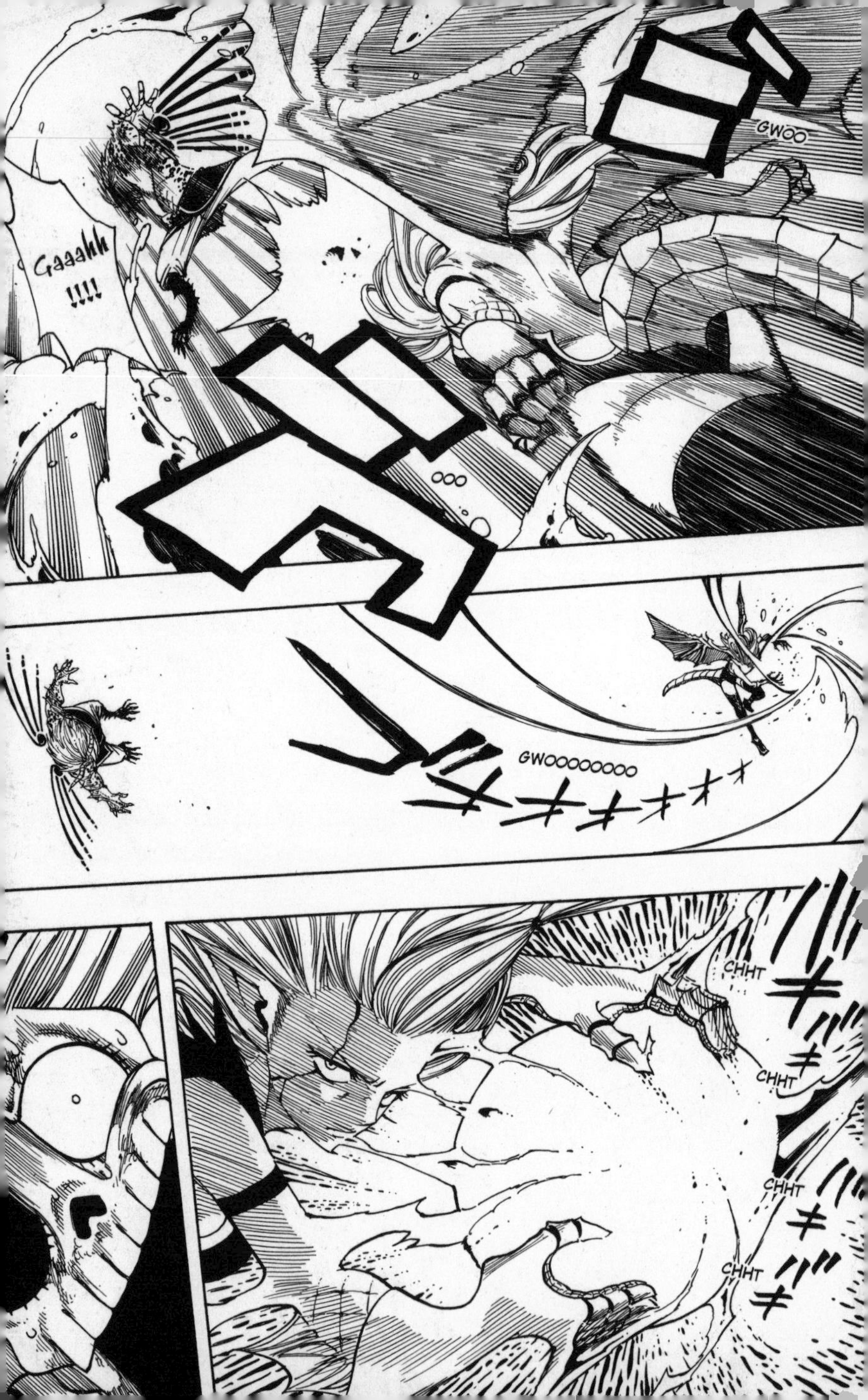
GWOO
Gaaahh !!!!
GWOOOOOOOOO
CHHT
CHHT
CHHT
CHHT

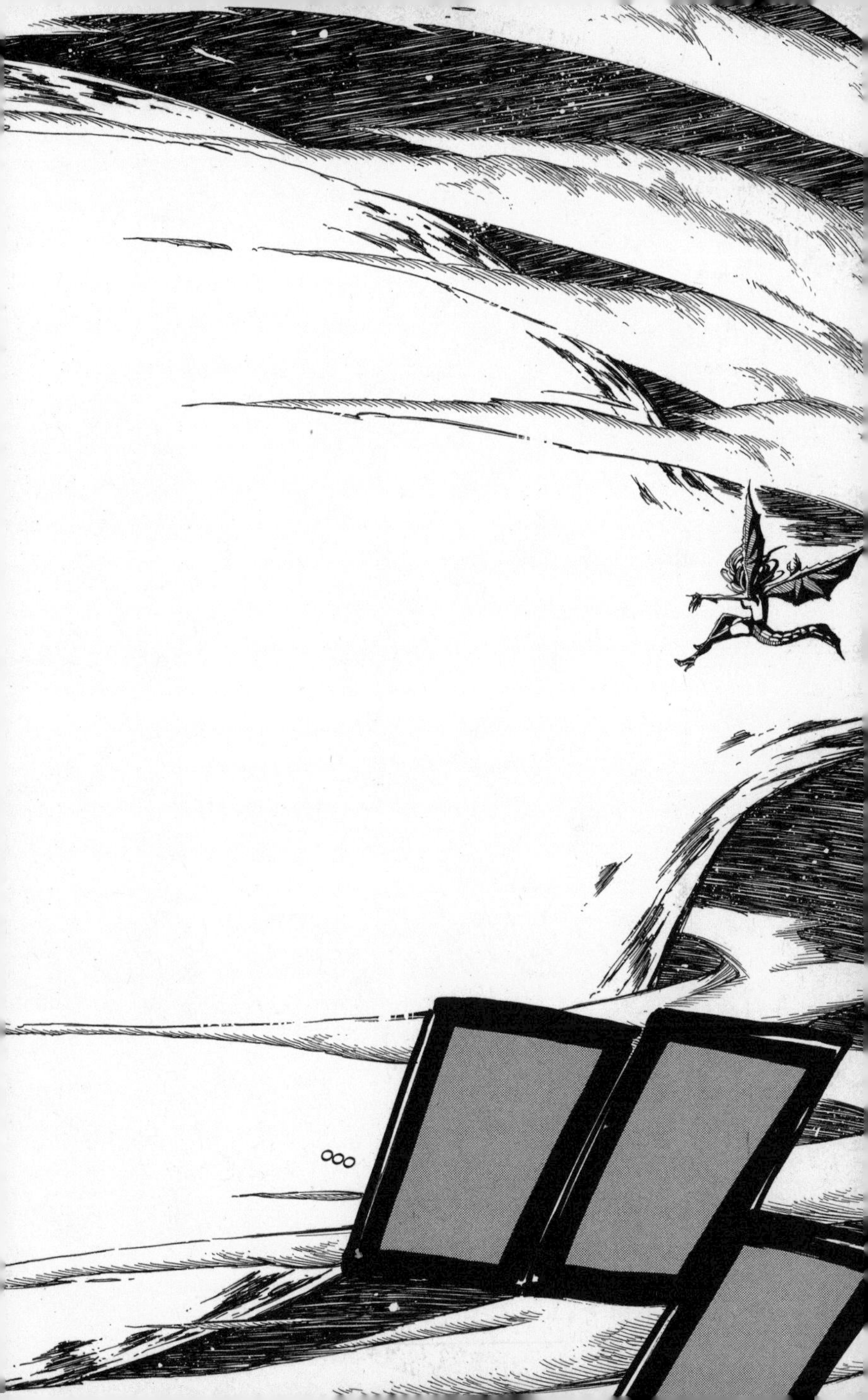
ooo

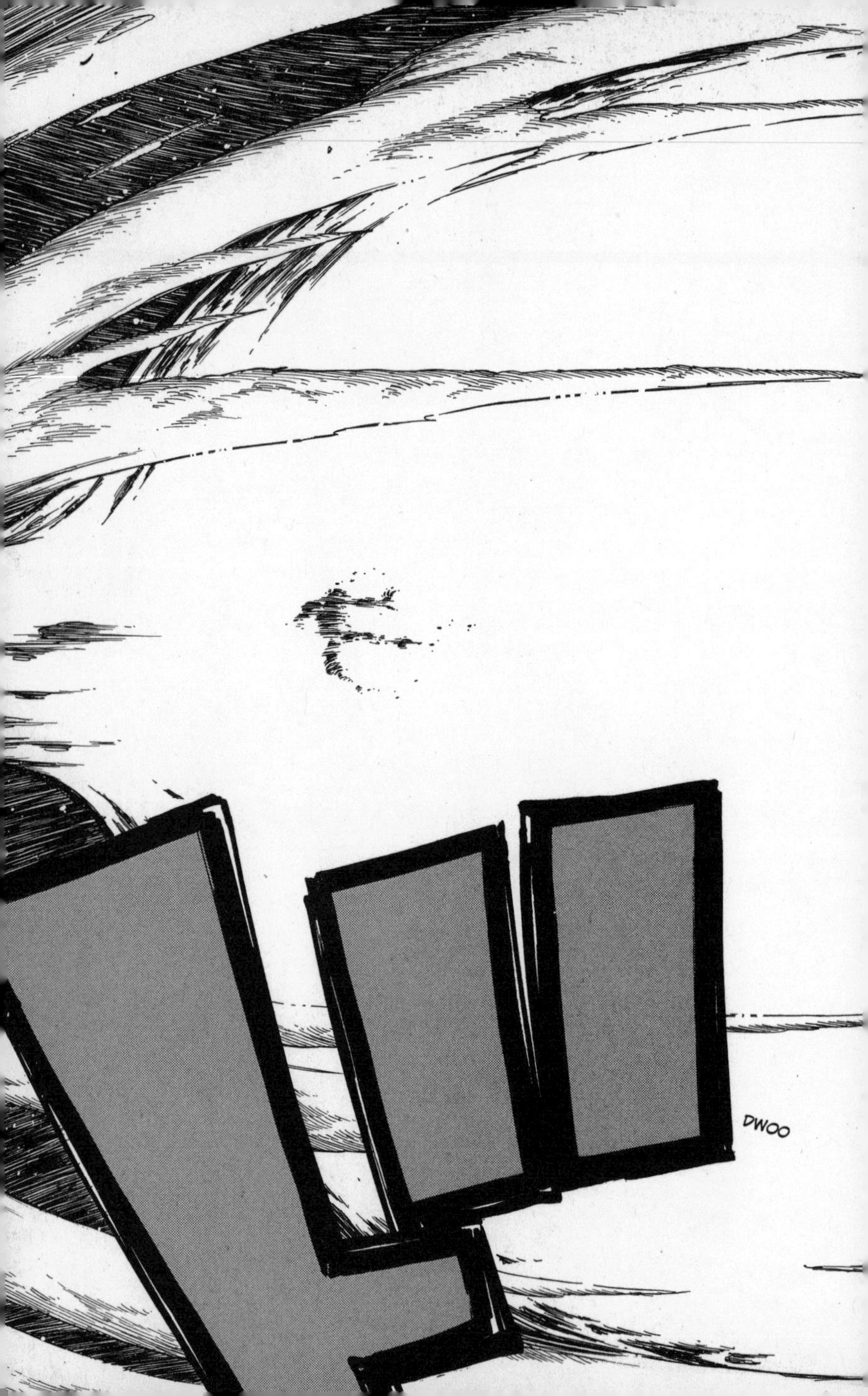
DWOO

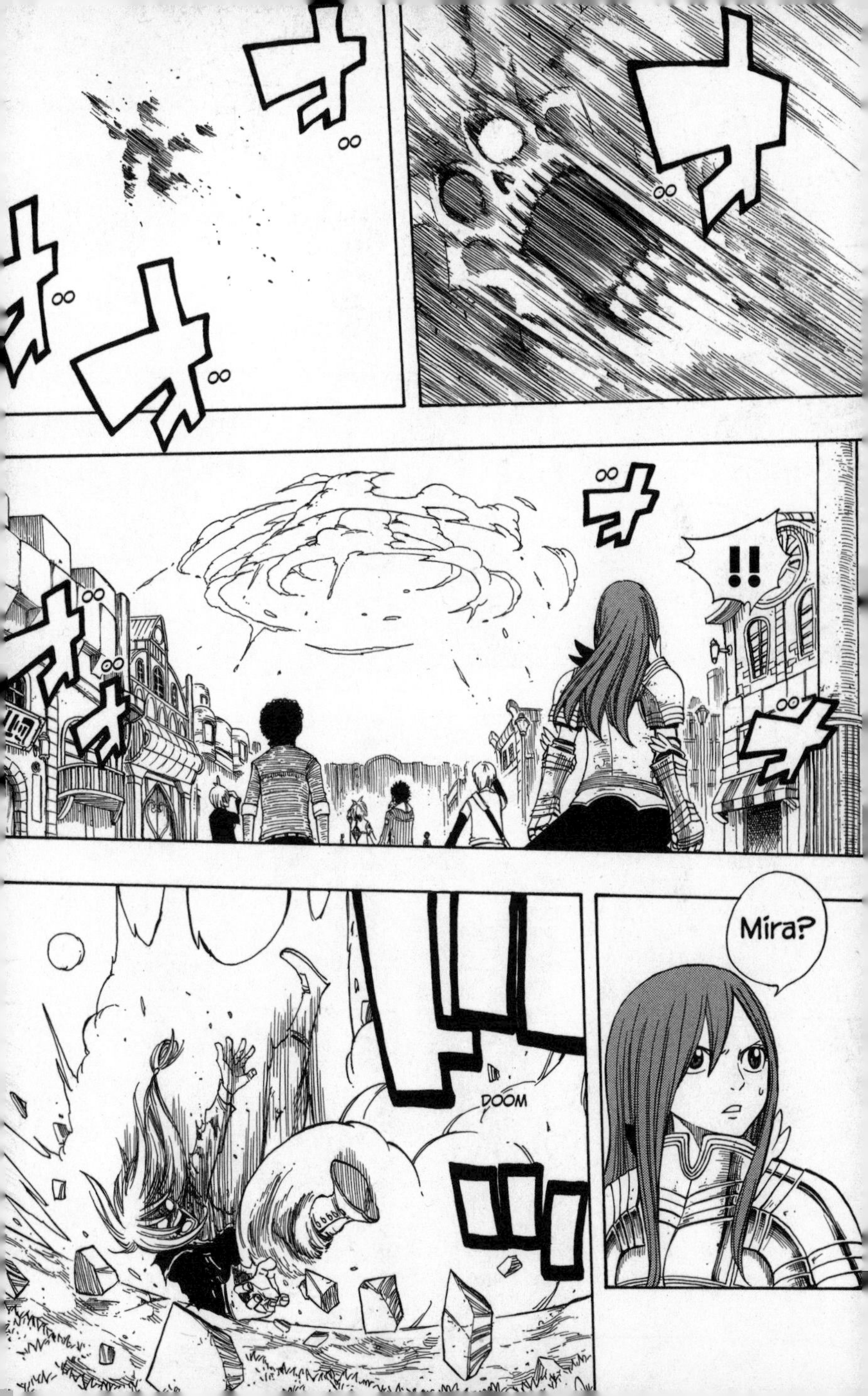
!!
DOOM
Mira?

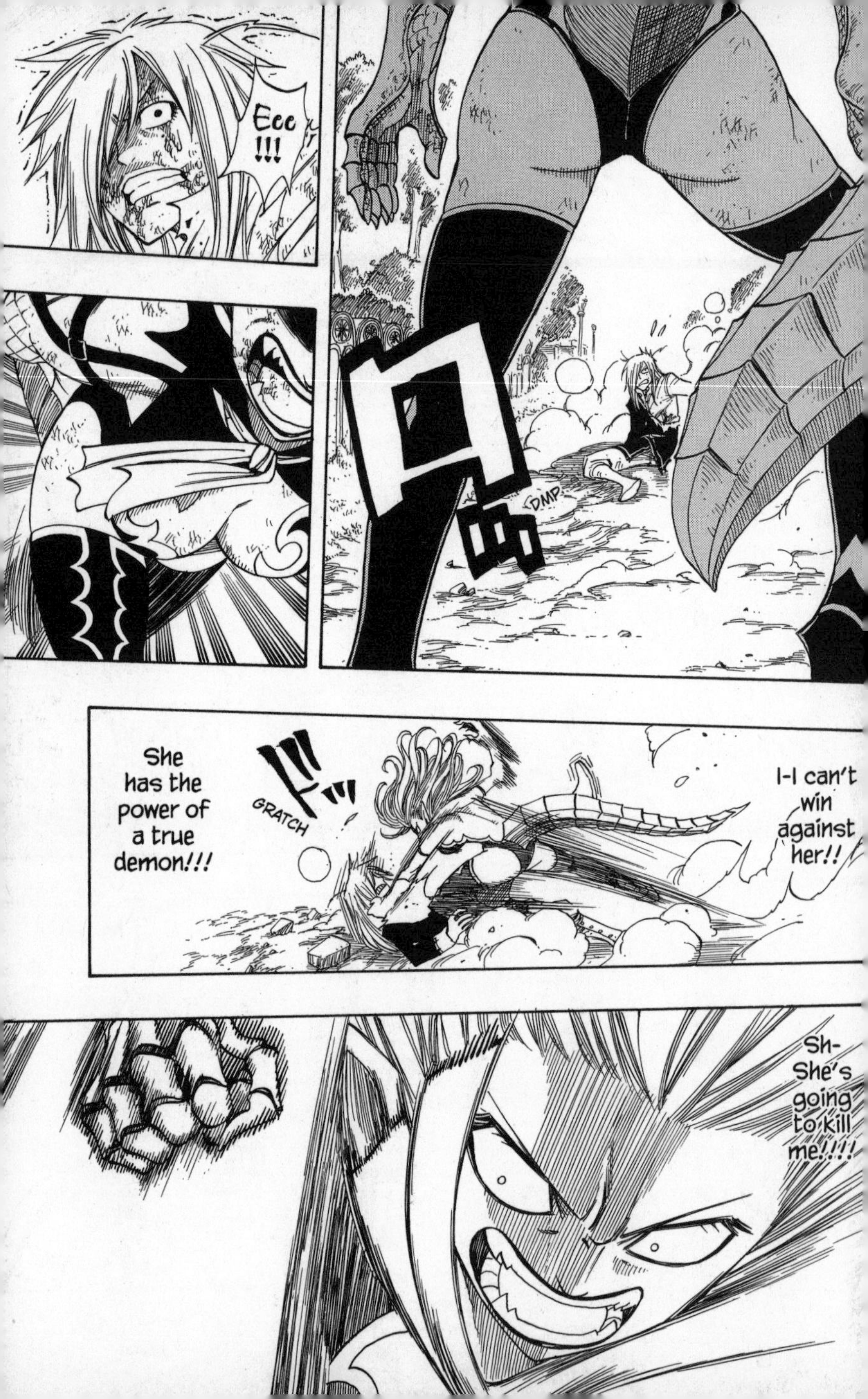
DMP
Eee !!!
I-I can't win against her!!
GRATCH
She has the power of a true demon!!!
Sh- She's going to kill me!!!!

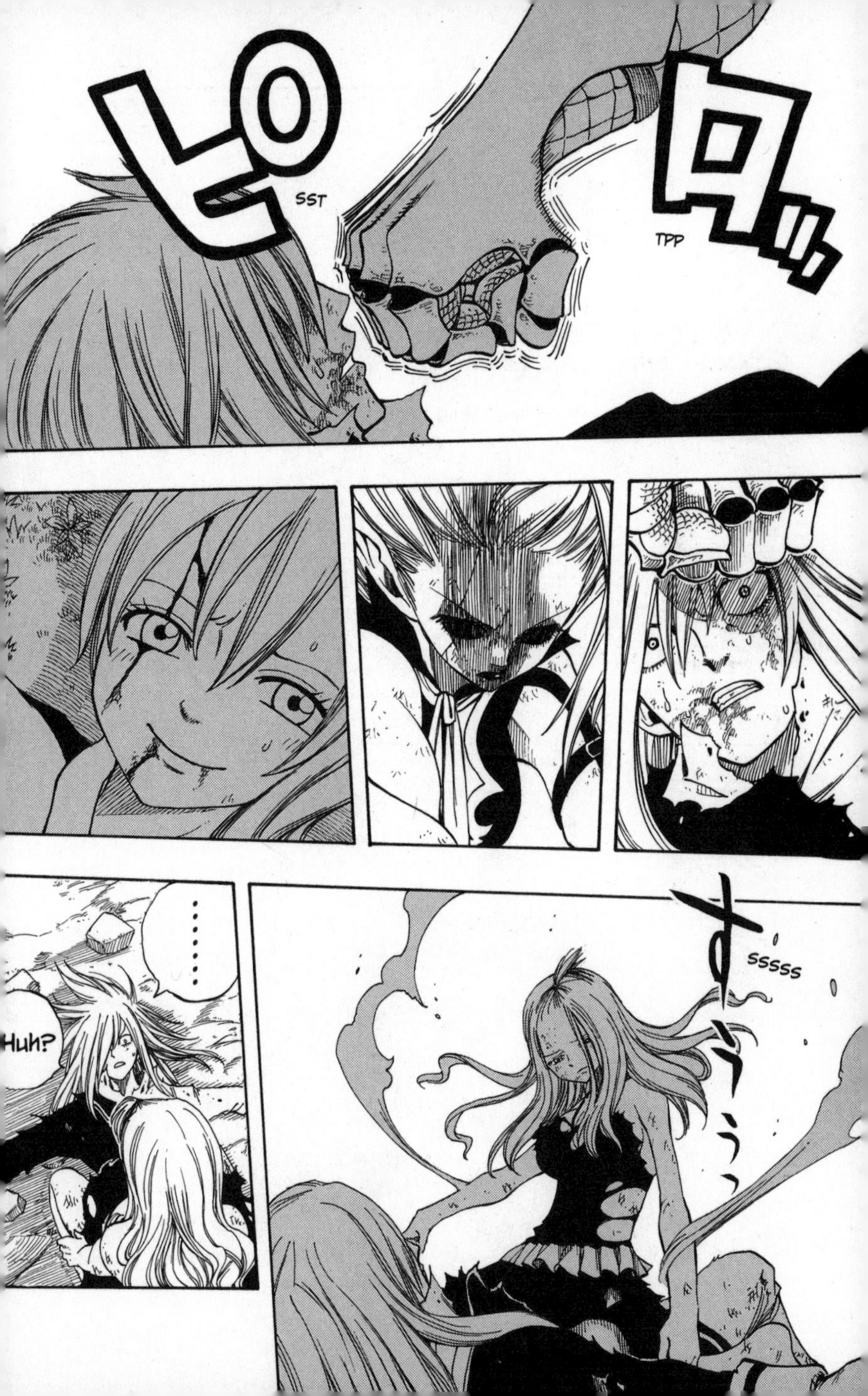
SST
TPP
SSSSS
......
Huh?

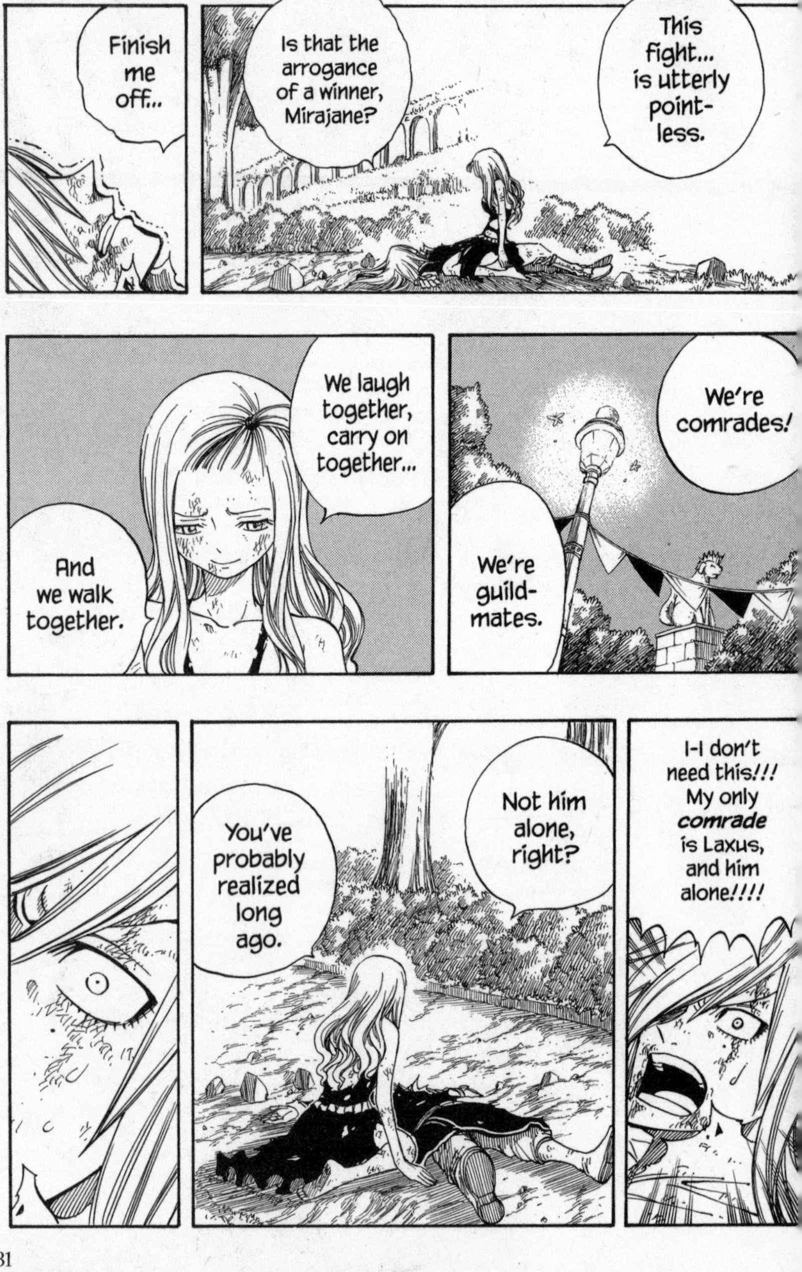
This fight... is utterly pointless.
Is that the arrogance of a winner, Mirajane?
Finish me off...
We're comrades!
We're guildmates.
We laugh together, carry on together...
And we walk together.
I-I don't need this!!! My only *comrade* is Laxus, and him alone!!!!
Not him alone, right?
You've probably realized long ago.

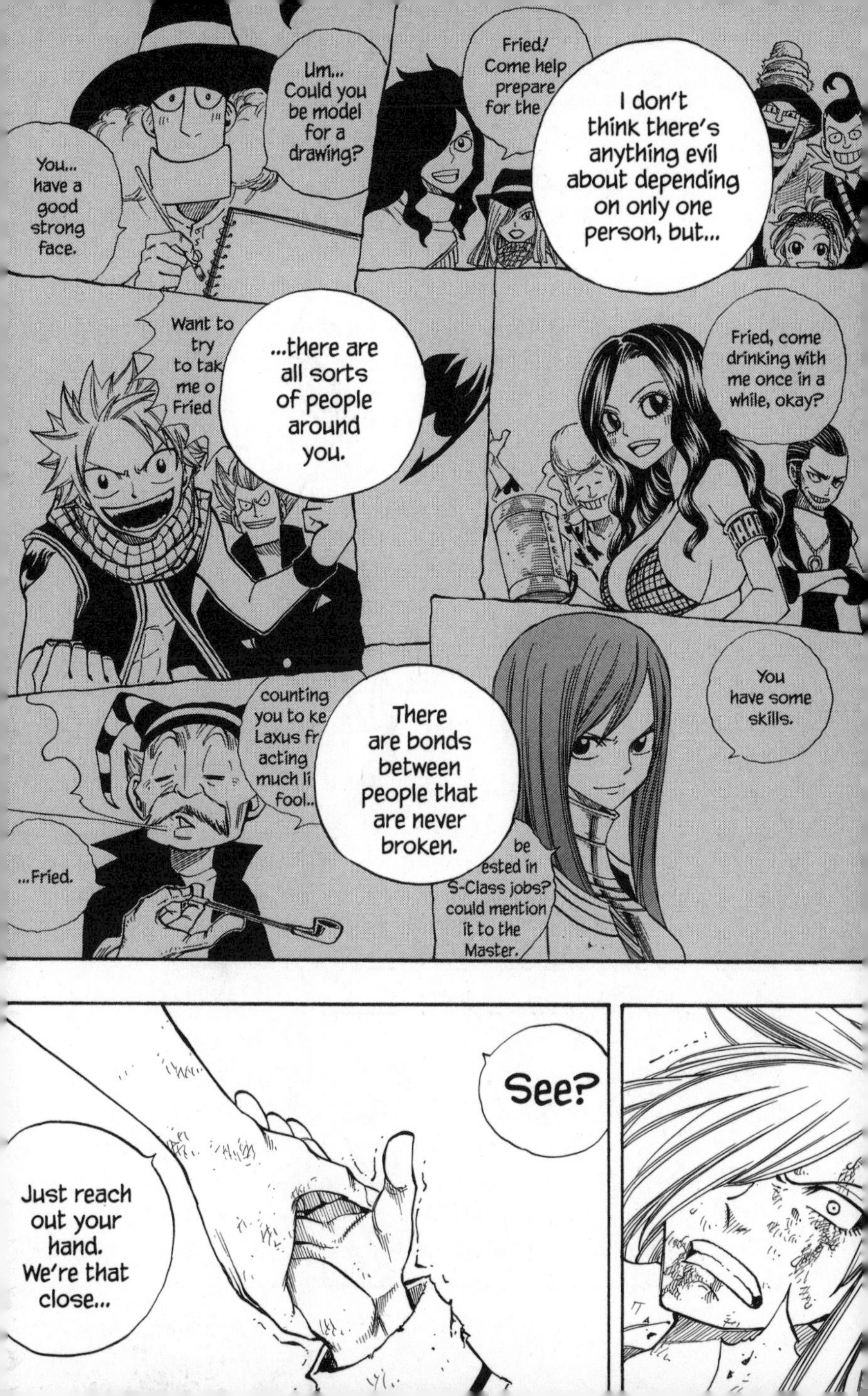

Fried! Come help prepare for the
I don't think there's anything evil about depending on only one person, but...
Um... Could you be model for a drawing?
You... have a good strong face.
Fried, come drinking with me once in a while, okay?
...there are all sorts of people around you.
Want to try to tak me o Fried
You have some skills.
be ested in S-Class jobs? could mention it to the Master.
There are bonds between people that are never broken.
counting you to ke Laxus fr acting much li fool..
...Fried.
See?
Just reach out your hand. We're that close...

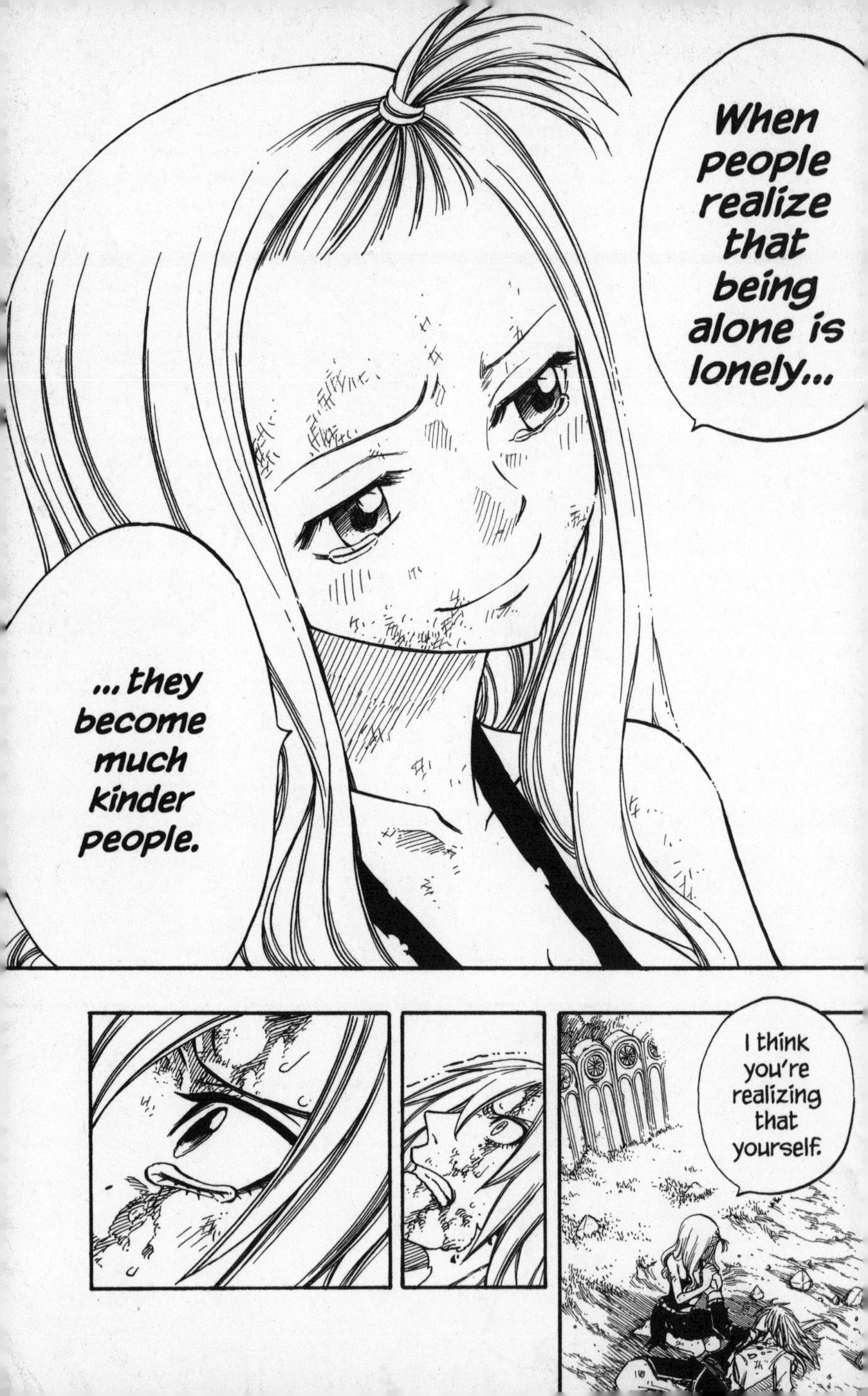
When people realize that being alone is lonely...
...they become much kinder people.
I think you're realizing that yourself.

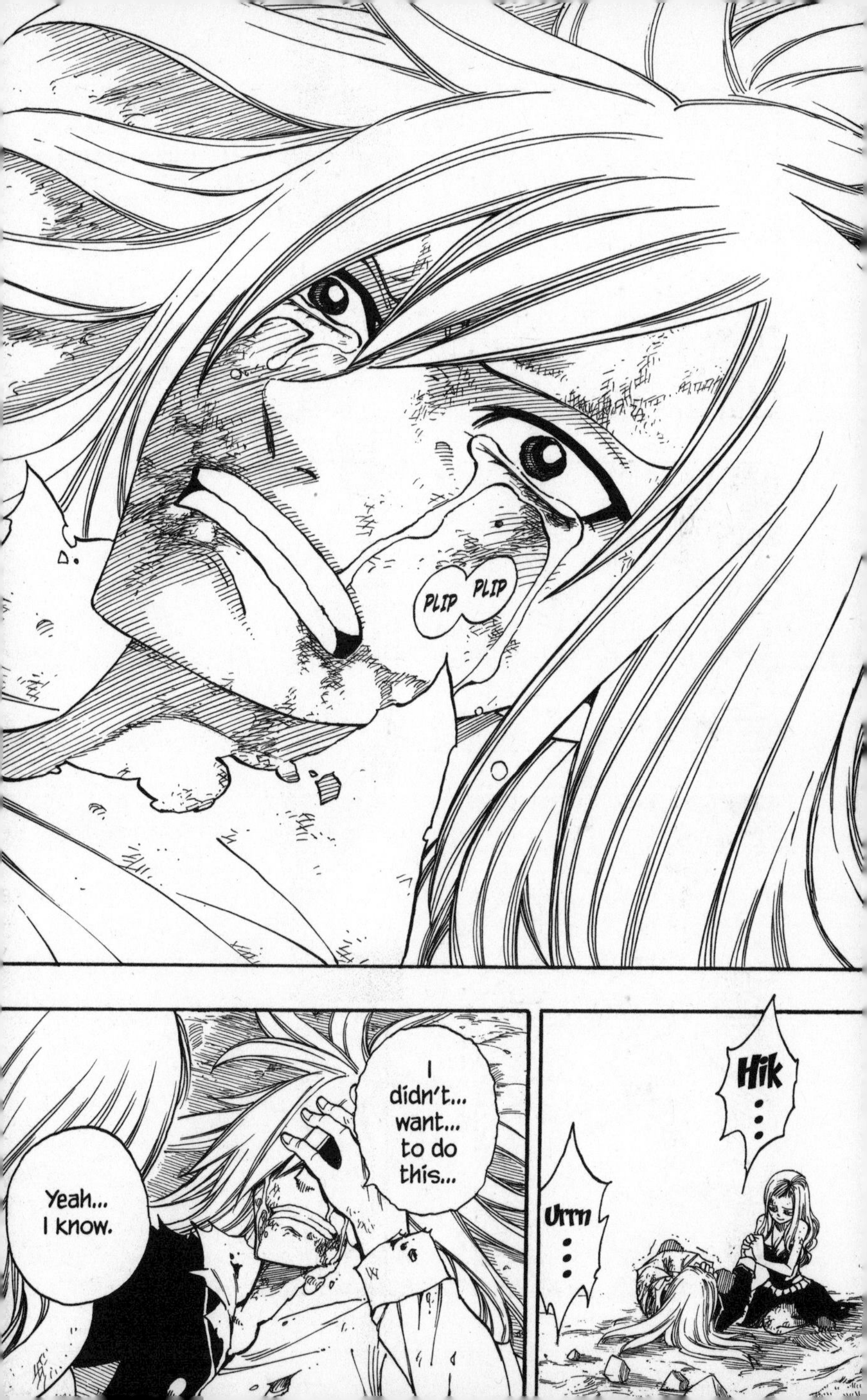
PLIP PLIP
Hik...
Urrn...
I didn't... want... to do this...
Yeah... I know.

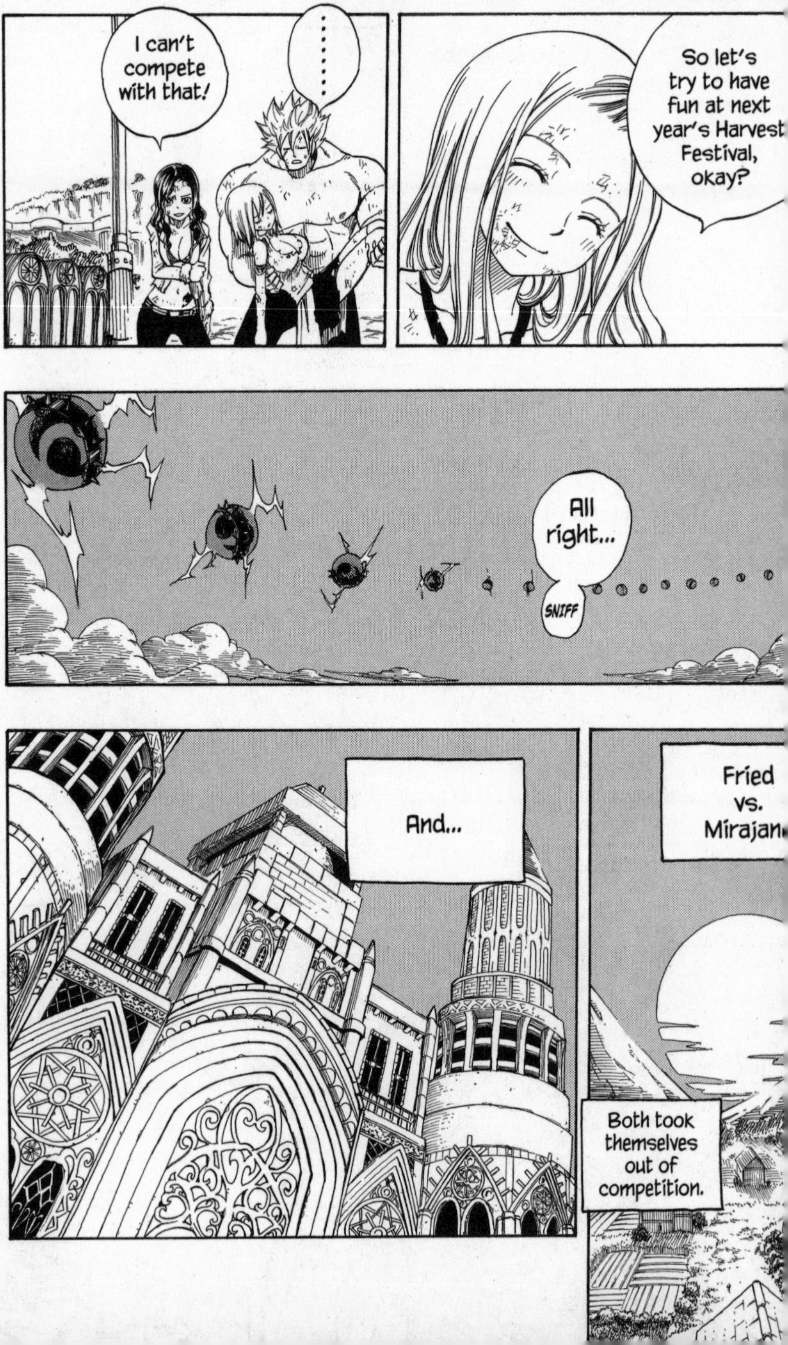
So let's try to have fun at next year's Harvest Festival, okay?
......
I can't compete with that!
All right...
SNIFF
Fried vs. Mirajan
Both took themselves out of competition.
And...

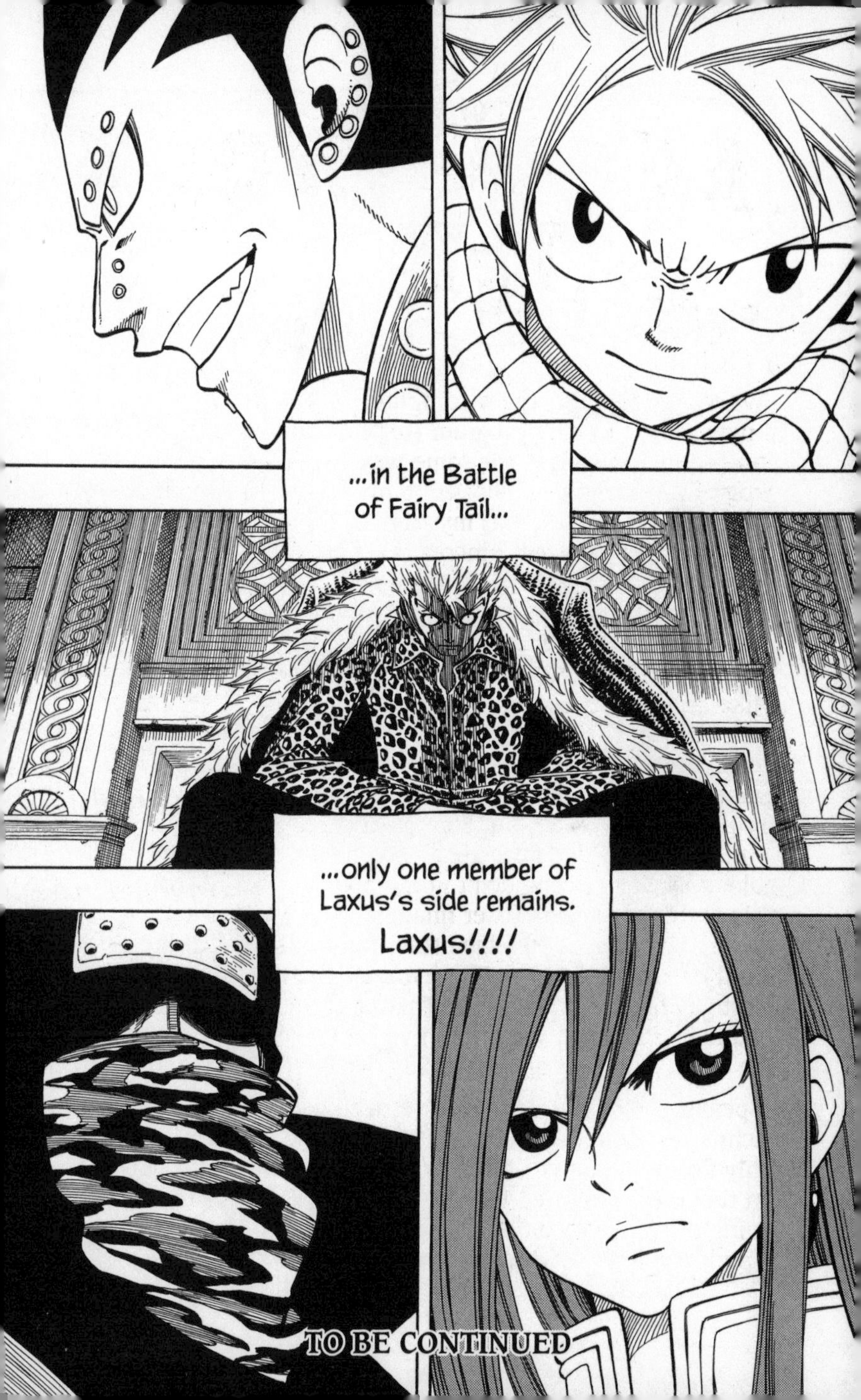
...in the Battle of Fairy Tail...
...only one member of Laxus's side remains.
Laxus!!!!
TO BE CONTINUED

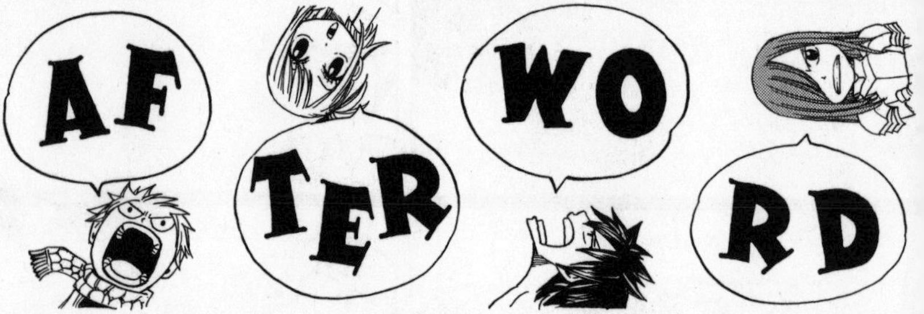
AF
TER
WO
RD

When I updated to a new computer, it was fate that I should buy a new paint software program (for coloring my images). But I can't seem to use it in the same way that I was able to use my old program. Just now, as I finish up my pages, I'm about to go back to coloring training. And as my trial and error approach continues, the time I spend at work increases... And this just repeats and repeats. Up to volume 13, I was using the watercolor tool in Painter 6 to color my images, but with Painter X, the watercolor program is just slightly different, and it's making me lose my bearings. I don't want to draw images that scream, "Yes, this is computer graphics!" I like a hand-painted touch, and that's why I chose the Painter series software in the first place. But I'm the kind of guy who doesn't really "get" machines (although I love to play computer games). And so, after doing all sorts of experiments, I decided to try a different tool within Painter X. The cover for this volume (14) is the first time I've ever used a tool other than "watercolor" to color an image. If you don't notice much of a difference between this and the previous cover images, then it was a success, but... What do you think? On the other hand, it's kind of fun trying my hand at something new. There are all sorts of things that I have to learn, and that's a problem. "This isn't the best way to do colors... and neither is this..." It's like I've returned to my rookie days in the way I spend all day practicing. But it's fun, so I don't mind.

Speaking of "fun," recently I've been trying out some digital techniques on my black & white pages too. Right now, it's really only for laying down screentones (those things that make for gray on the page). I figured I didn't use all that much tone anyway, so doing it this way would be faster, right? But I've found that seeing it suddenly laid down digitally is really fun! That's the main thing!!

Continued from the left-hand page.

Mira: Etherion is a fusion of countless types of magical power, so I think he'd be out of luck.

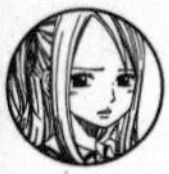

Lucy: By the way, what are those guys doing now-a-days?

Mira: You can get a hint on Volume 13, page 104.

I think Jutsu-Shiki magic is too powerful. Doesn't it have any weaknesses?

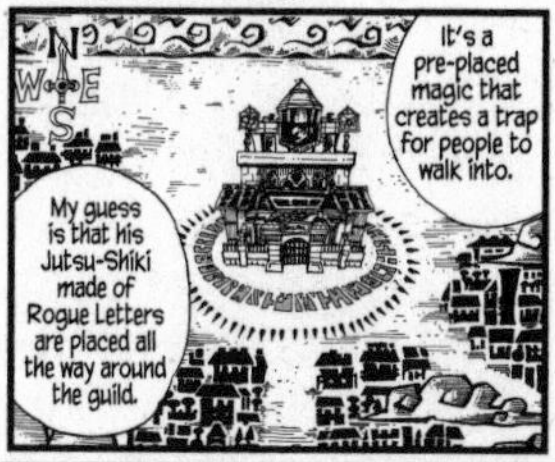
It's a pre-placed magic that creates a trap for people to walk into.
My guess is that his Jutsu-Shiki made of Rogue Letters are placed all the way around the guild.

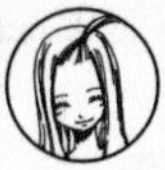

Mira: Yes, it's very powerful magic, but it has an unexpectedly large number of weaknesses.

Lucy: Are you sure? I think it's very unfair! The person who makes the rules wins!

Mira: But writing the letters takes a lot of time. I may be repeating the Master a bit, but... Yes, it's the strongest magic for setting traps, but if you're suddenly attacked, you have no time for writing, right?

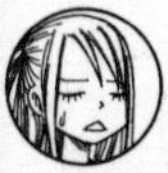

Mira: He wrote words on his enemies, and words on himself. His magic was really powerful!

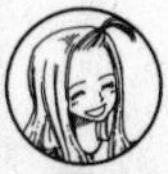

Mira: And that's why I had no choice but to use Satan Soul.

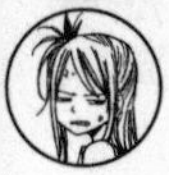

Mira: The final question for this time is...

What days of the week can you call Loke?

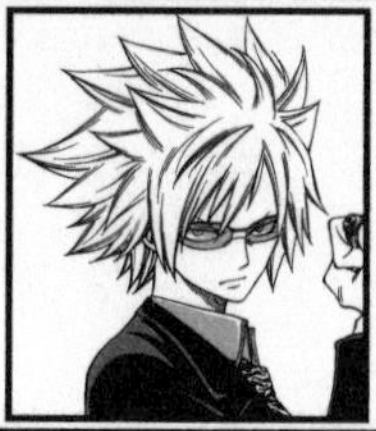

Lucy: My contract with him is that he can be called any time, more or less.

Mira: That's amazing!! Most of the strongest Celestial Sprits have strict limits on the day or time they can be called!

Lucy: Yeah, but with him...every now and again, he comes out on his own.

Mira: I imagine that would be awful if you were, say, in the bathtub.

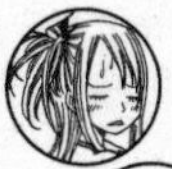

Lucy: That happened once.

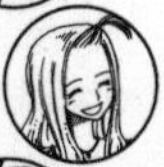

Mira: Poor Loke would get dripping wet!

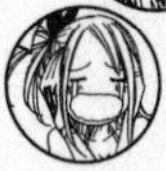

Lucy: You meant "awful" for ***him?!!***

Mira: I see him every so often at the guild. He sure has a lot of freedom.

Lucy: Eh? That's the first I've heard about that!!

Mira: A little while ago. He and Cana went out on a job together.

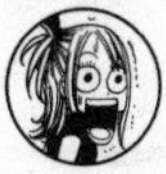

Lucy: Wh-What's that supposed to mean?!!

Mira: Aw, don't be jealous!

Lucy: Th-That isn't what I mean!! It's just if he does that...then what's the point of a contract at all?! That's too much freedom!!!

Mira: And that's all we have time for today! Moun•tain•li•on•poooon!!!

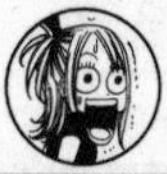

Lucy: Wait, that's my line!! But before that... Hey, Loke!! What's going on?! I don't even have his key!!

Emergency-Request

Fairy Tail Mysteries Explain

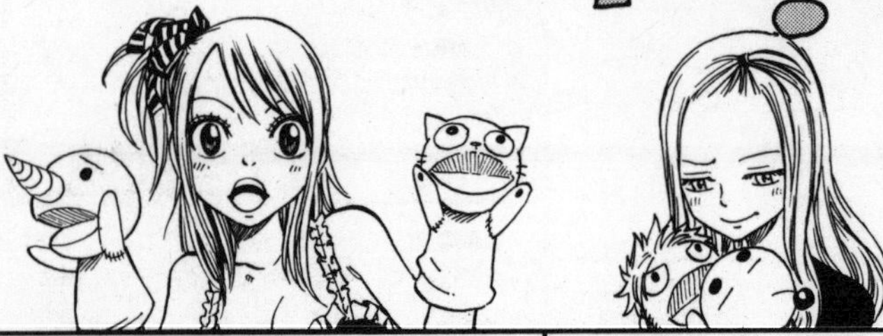

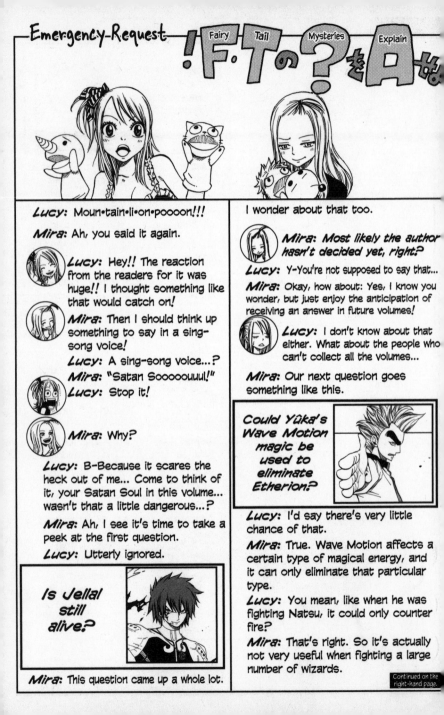

***Lucy*:** Moun•tain•li•on•poooon!!!

***Mira*:** Ah, you said it again.

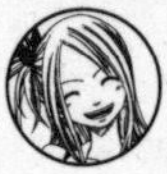

***Lucy*:** Hey!! The reaction from the readers for it was huge!! I thought something like that would catch on!

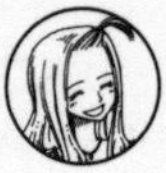

***Mira*:** Then I should think up something to say in a sing-song voice!

***Lucy*:** A sing-song voice...?

***Mira*:** "Satan Soooooouuul!"

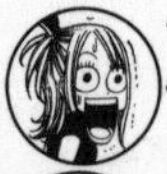

***Lucy*:** Stop it!

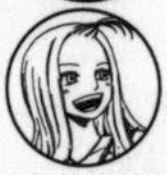

***Mira*:** Why?

***Lucy*:** B-Because it scares the heck out of me... Come to think of it, your Satan Soul in this volume... wasn't that a little dangerous...?

***Mira*:** Ah, I see it's time to take a peek at the first question.

***Lucy*:** Utterly ignored.

Is Jellal still alive?

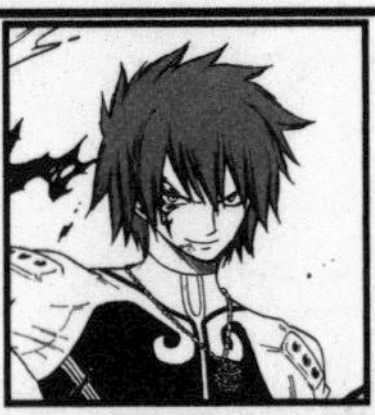

***Mira*:** This question came up a whole lot. I wonder about that too.

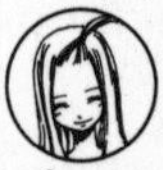

***Mira*: Most likely the author hasn't decided yet, right?**

***Lucy*:** Y-You're not supposed to say that...

***Mira*:** Okay, how about: Yes, I know you wonder, but just enjoy the anticipation of receiving an answer in future volumes!

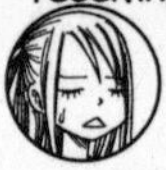

***Lucy*:** I don't know about that either. What about the people who can't collect all the volumes...

***Mira*:** Our next question goes something like this.

Could Yûka's Wave Motion magic be used to eliminate Etherion?

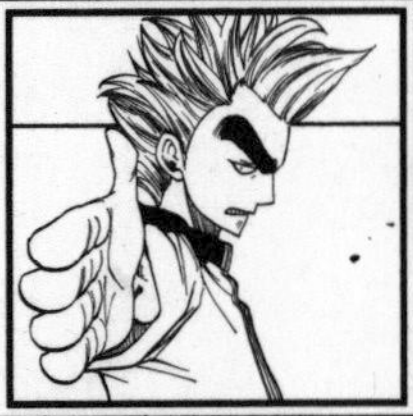

***Lucy*:** I'd say there's very little chance of that.

***Mira*:** True. Wave Motion affects a certain type of magical energy, and it can only eliminate that particular type.

***Lucy*:** You mean, like when he was fighting Natsu, it could only counter fire?

***Mira*:** That's right. So it's actually not very useful when fighting a large number of wizards.

Continued on the right-hand page.

TAIL d'ART

The *Fairy Tail* Guild d'Art is an explosion of fan art! Please send in your black-and-white art on large postcard stock!! Those chosen to be published will get a signed mini poster! ♪ Make sure you write your real name and address on the back of your postcard!

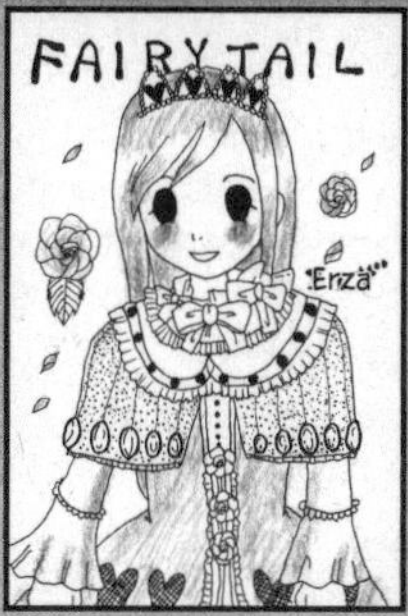
FAIRY TAIL
"Erza"

▼A princess-like Erza. What was up with that Goth-loli look of hers?

Nagano Prefecture, Airu

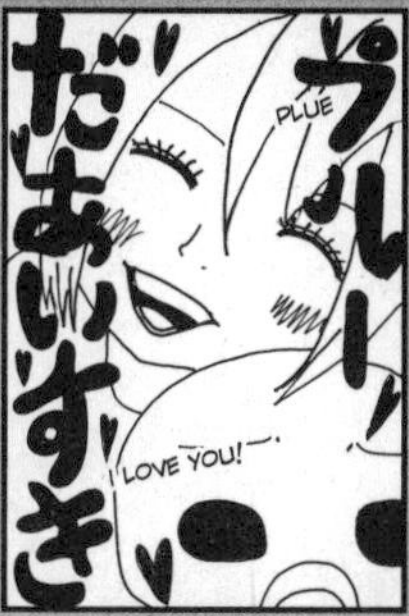
プルーだぁいすき
PLUE
I LOVE YOU!

▼Hmm... A picture that looks like it's taunting me... But... I love Plue too!!

Yûka Sato

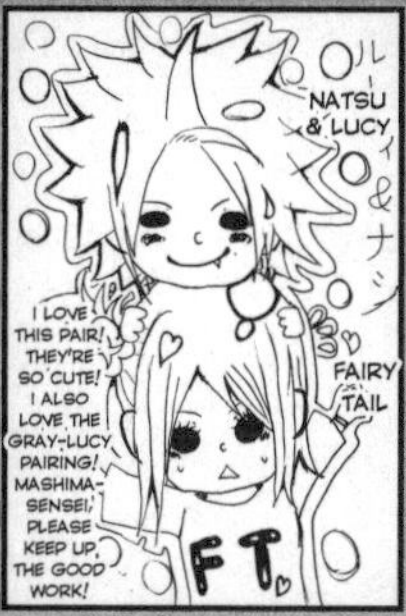
NATSU & LUCY
I LOVE THIS PAIR! THEY'RE SO CUTE! I ALSO LOVE THE GRAY-LUCY PAIRING! MASHIMA-SENSEI, PLEASE KEEP UP THE GOOD WORK!
FAIRY TAIL
FT

▼A really cute Natsu and Lucy. Like a keyholder.

Yamagata Prefecture, Haruka Itagaki

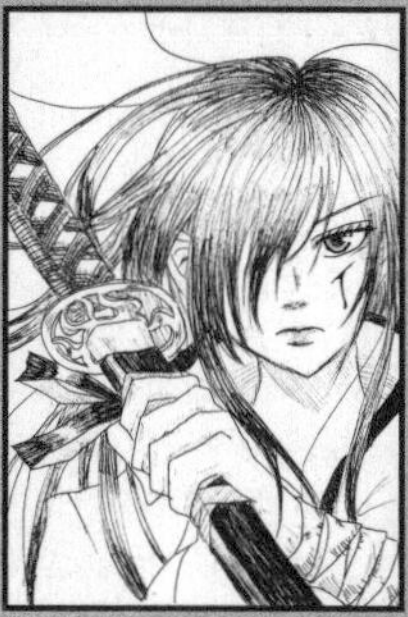

▼A samurai-style Erza. She really looks good in that kind of style!

Hiroshima Prefecture, Clover

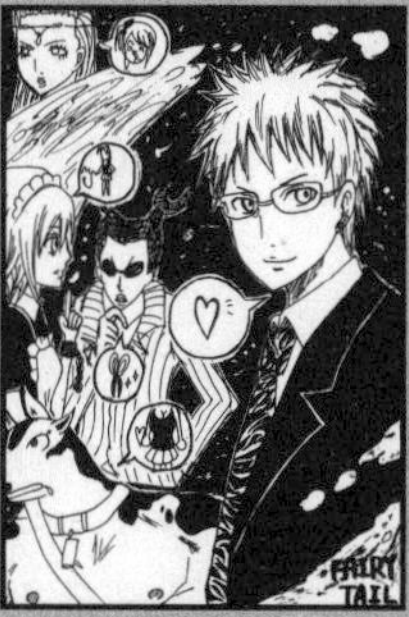
FAIRY TAIL

▼A mass gathering of Celestial Spirits! Everybody has a different view of Lucy, and that makes this fun!

Shizuoka Prefecture, Aruto

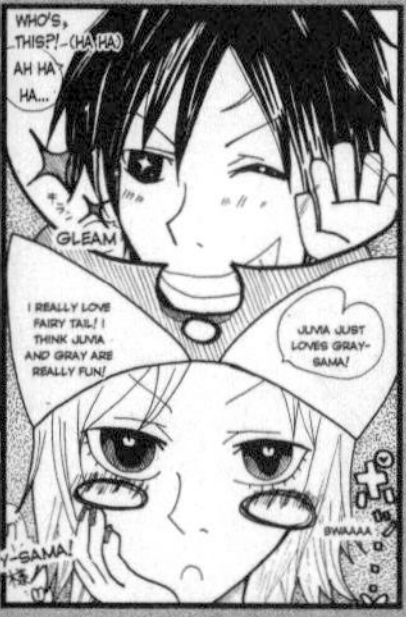
WHO'S THIS?!-(HA HA) AH HA HA...
GLEAM
I REALLY LOVE FAIRY TAIL! I THINK JUVIA AND GRAY ARE REALLY FUN!
JUVIA JUST LOVES GRAY-SAMA!
SWAAAA
Y-SAMA!

▼Juvia is so cute! ♥ Her popularity has really soared!

Wakayama Prefecture, Ayana

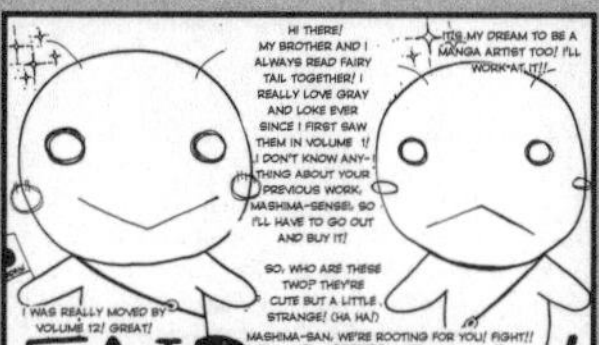
IT'S MY DREAM TO BE A MANGA ARTIST TOO! I'LL WORK AT IT!
HI THERE! MY BROTHER AND I ALWAYS READ FAIRY TAIL TOGETHER! I REALLY LOVE GRAY AND LOKE EVER SINCE I FIRST SAW THEM IN VOLUME 1! I DON'T KNOW ANYTHING ABOUT YOUR PREVIOUS WORK, MASHIMA-SENSEI, SO I'LL HAVE TO GO OUT AND BUY IT!
SO, WHO ARE THESE TWO? THEY'RE CUTE BUT A LITTLE STRANGE! (HA HA)
MASHIMA-SAN, WE'RE ROOTING FOR YOU! FIGHT!!
I WAS REALLY MOVED BY VOLUME 12! GREAT!
FAIRY TAIL!

▼Who are these two people (two things?) supposed to be? And there are too many questions in your accompanying letter! They'll be answered soon in the manga (probably)!

Wakayama Prefecture, Tatsû

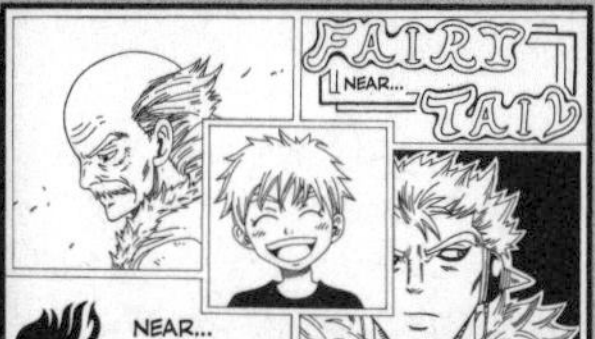
FAIRY TAIL
NEAR...
NEAR...
...YET FAR AWAY.

▼Laxus and the Master. How will their relationship play out?

Tochigi Prefecture, Reiji Katsuki

Send to Send to Hiro Mashima, Kodansha Comics
451 Park Ave. South, 7th Floor New York, NY 10016

FAIRY GUILD

▼ Nice! I like how everybody is reflected in soap bubbles!

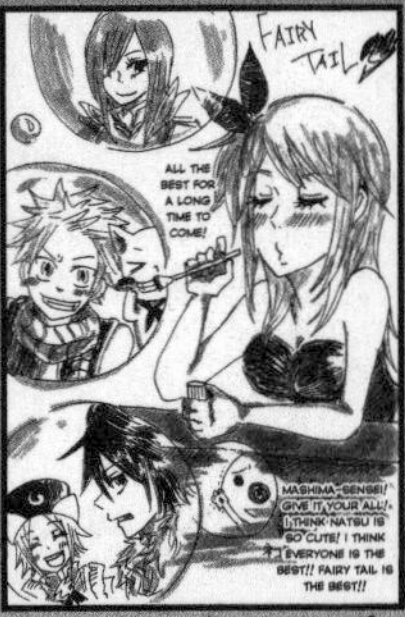
FAIRY TAIL
ALL THE BEST FOR A LONG TIME TO COME!
MASHIMA-SENSEI! GIVE IT YOUR ALL! I THINK NATSU IS SO CUTE! I THINK EVERYONE IS THE BEST!! FAIRY TAIL IS THE BEST!!

Chiba Prefecture, Yû

▼ The birth of a new couple! But I don't think it can happen! (Ha ha!)

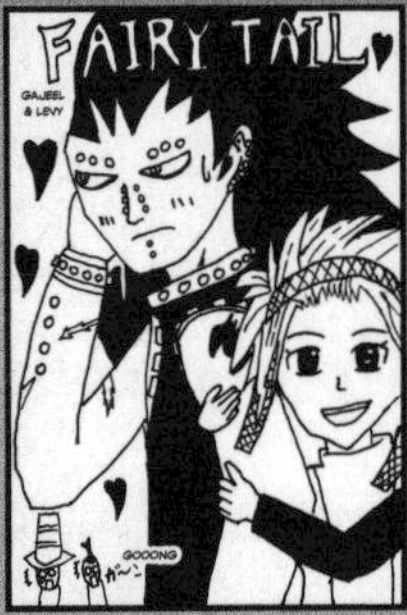
FAIRY TAIL
GAJEEL & LEVY
GOOONG

Nagano Prefecture, Shôya Kobayashi

Rejection Corner

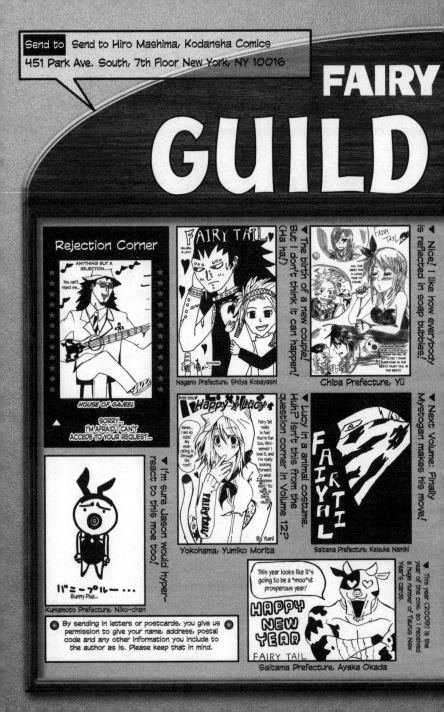

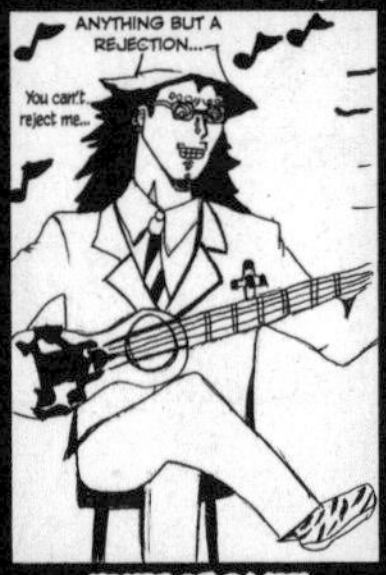
ANYTHING BUT A REJECTION...
You can't reject me...

HOUSE OF GAJEEL

▲ SORRY... I'M AFRAID I CAN'T ACCEDE TO YOUR REQUEST...

▼ Next Volume: Finally Mystogan makes his move!

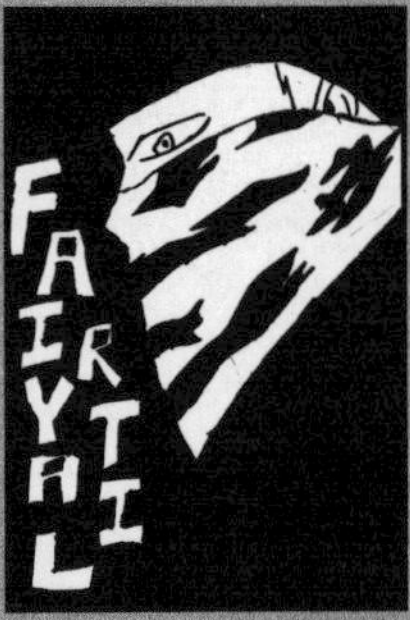
FAIRY TAIL

Saitama Prefecture, Keisuke Namiki

▼ Lucy in a animal costume. Huh? Isn't this from the question corner in Volume 12?

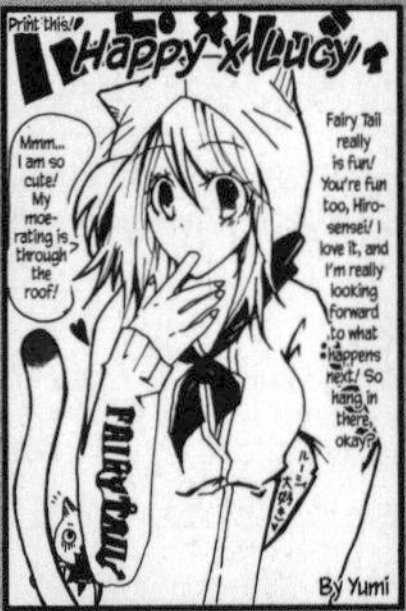
Print this!
Happy x Lucy
Mmm... I am so cute! My moe-rating is through the roof!
Fairy Tail really is fun! You're fun too, Hiro-sensei! I love it, and I'm really looking forward to what happens next! So hang in there, okay?
FAIRY TAIL
By Yumi

Yokohama, Yumiko Morita

▼ I'm sure Jason would hyper-react to this moe too!

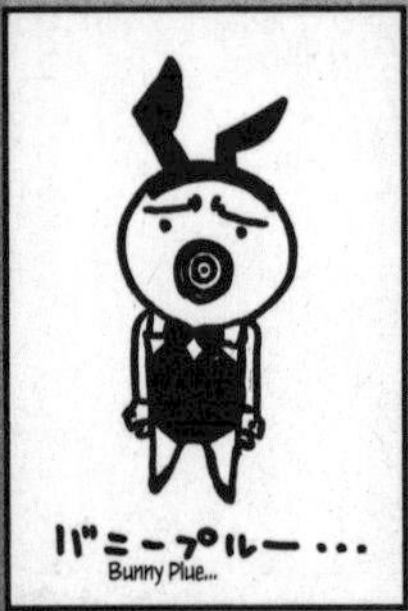
バニープルー…
Bunny Plue...

Kumamoto Prefecture, Niko-chan

▼ This year (2009) is the year of the cow, so I received a huge number of Taurus New Year's cards.

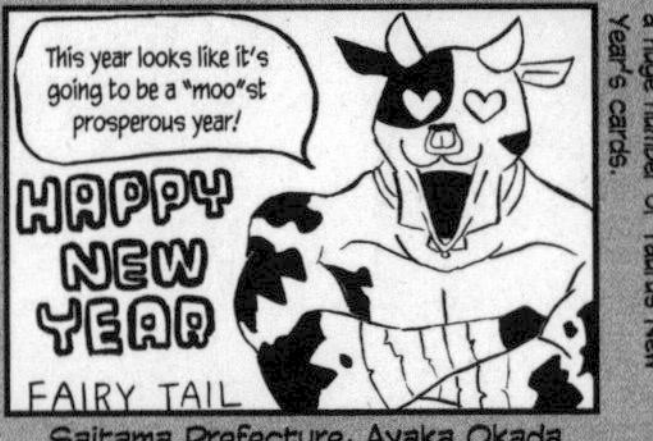
This year looks like it's going to be a "moo"st prosperous year!
HAPPY NEW YEAR
FAIRY TAIL

Saitama Prefecture, Ayaka Okada

By sending in letters or postcards, you give us permission to give your name, address, postal code and any other information you include to the author as is. Please keep that in mind.

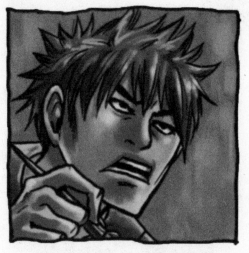

From Hiro Mashima

My first thought was to make the "Battle of Fairy Tail" into a tournament-style story. At least, that's what I thought until I mentioned it to my editor and the look in his eyes said,

"I knew that was coming!!!"

So, I did it in the style you see now instead. I really get into tournament manga… But I know that somebody will accuse me of swiping it from some other manga, right? And say,

"I knew that was coming!!!"

But I really get worked up by that kind of thing…
You know, it's one of those, "I want to do it, but I don't want to do it" dilemmas.

Translation Notes

Japanese is a tricky language for most Westerners, and translation is often more art than science. For your edification and reading pleasure, here are notes on some of the places where we could have gone in a different direction in our translation of the work, or where a Japanese cultural reference is used.

Names

Hiro Mashima has graciously agreed to provide official English spellings for just about all of the characters in Fairy Tail. Because this version of Fairy Tail is the first publication of most of these spellings, there will inevitably be differences between these spellings and some of the fan interpretations that may have spread throughout the web or in other fan circles. Rest assured that what is contained in this book are the spellings that Mashima-sensei wanted for *Fairy Tail*.

Wizard

In the original Japanese version of Fairy Tail, there are occasional images where the word "Wizard" is found. This translation has taken that as it's inspiration, and translated the word *madôshi* as wizard. But *madôshi's* meaning is similar to certain Japanese words that have been borrowed into the English language such as judo (the soft way) and kendo (the way of the sword). *Madô* is the way of magic, and *madôshi* are those who follow the way of magic. So although the word "wizard" is used, the Japanese would think less of traditional western wizards such as Merlin or Gandalf, and more of martial artists.

"That's our Tono," page 3

The Japanese phrase, sasuga (subject), is usually translated as, "I'd expect no less from (subject)," or "That's our (subject) for you." Although these phrases aren't completely unknown in English, they aren't used nearly as often as the Japanese use the sasuga, so they become easy to identify when one reads translations of Japanese entertainment. The phrase is said when the subject does something typical of either the subject's personality or typically impressive if one is at the subject's position/skill level. For example, Sherlock Holmes solving an extremely difficult murder case would garner the comment, "Sasuga meitantei!" or "Just what one would expect from a famous detective!"

Beeehh, page 13

Sticking one's tongue out at a rival/opponent means pretty much the same thing in Japan as it does in the west. However, the Japanese have taken this childish gesture of defiance and expanded on it with a few additions. The sound effect used, "beeehh," is not an onomatopoeia such as one might find "Pbbbt" being used to approximate a raspberry sound. When sticking out one's tongue, many Japanese people actually say, "Beh!" or the more prevalent "Akanbe!" which can be loosely translated as, "You did something you shouldn't!" Another addition to the gesture is pulling down the skin just beneath one eye to reveal the red portion under one's lower eyelid.

Demon-Princess, page 23

Oni (here translated as "demon") are one of the traditional "bad guys" of Japanese folklore. Like ogres of Western fairy tales, the oni tend to be big, strong, stupid, violent, and rove in bands to wreak wanton destruction. Other common features are skin that is bright red, blue or green; horns (two on ether side of the top of the head, or one on the top-back of the head); wooden hammers or spiked clubs; and rough-hewn, tiger-striped loin cloths or other such clothes.

Public baths, page 94

Although having an *ofuro* bathtub in every home and apartment is becoming far more commonplace in Japan, there are still quite a few old apartments (and even some houses) that are not equipped with places to shower or bathe. This need is filled by large public bathhouses that can be found in most residential districts in Japan. One usually brings one's own bath paraphernalia such as a towel, soap, etc., and is allowed to enter into the gender-segregated changing and washing rooms for a nominal fee. After undressing and placing one's clothes in a locker, one enters the bath area, sits before a water spigot, and does one's washing and shampooing first. After one has completely rinsed, the person then can go relax in one of the big tubs for a hot-water soak. The "plip-plooop" sound effect is a translation of the standard public-bath sound effect found in all sorts of manga. It is the sound of condensed water from the ceiling or overhead pipes falling back into the steaming bath water.

Onsen Mark, page 94

The mark of a partial oval with three wavy lines rising above it is the Japanese symbol for an *onsen* hot spring bath. Natural *onsen* hot springs are a sought-after commodity, and if the water is fit for bathing, those locations can become popular resort locations. Although actual *onsen* hot-springs baths are usually found only around volcanically active areas, the mark has also come to indicate public baths of any kind.

You are so doing it!, page 126

The Japanese word Happy used in this instance is *dekiteiru*, a word that means that the two people have become a confirmed couple, but it usually carries connotations that the couple has become "intimate." In the repeat of the joke on page 126, in Japanese, Happy trilled the final "r" sound, making the notion sound even more salacious than when Happy said it the first time. However, it is somewhat out of character for Happy to trill his "r" sounds since that is a habit of street punks and yakuza gang members.

Écriture, page 155

Écriture is French for "writing."

Honorifics Explained

Throughout the Kodansha Comics books, you will find Japanese honorifics left intact in the translations. For those not familiar with how the Japanese use honorifics and, more important, how they differ from American honorifics, we present this brief overview.

Politeness has always been a critical facet of Japanese culture. Ever since the feudal era, when Japan was a highly stratified society, use of honorifics—which can be defined as polite speech that indicates relationship or status—has played an essential role in the Japanese language. When addressing someone in Japanese, an honorific usually takes the form of a suffix attached to one's name (example: "Asuna-san"), is used as a title at the end of one's name, or appears in place of the name itself (example: "Negi-sensei," or simply "Sensei!").

Honorifics can be expressions of respect or endearment. In the context of manga and anime, honorifics give insight into the nature of the relationship between characters. Many English translations leave out these important honorifics and therefore distort the feel of the original Japanese. Because Japanese honorifics contain nuances that English honorifics lack, it is our policy at Kodansha Comics not to translate them. Here, instead, is a guide to some of the honorifics you may encounter in Kodansha Comics manga.

-san: This is the most common honorific and is equivalent to Mr., Miss, Ms., or Mrs. It is the all-purpose honorific and can be used in any situation where politeness is required.

-sama: This is one level higher than "-san" and is used to confer great respect.

-dono: This comes from the word "tono," which means "lord." It is an even higher level than "-sama" and confers utmost respect.

-kun: This suffix is used at the end of boys' names to express familiarity or endearment. It is also sometimes used by men among friends, or when addressing someone younger or of a lower station.

-chan: This is used to express endearment, mostly toward girls. It is also used for little boys, pets, and even among lovers. It gives a sense of childish cuteness.

Bozu: This is an informal way to refer to a boy, similar to the English terms "kid" and "squirt."

**Sempai/
Senpai:** This title suggests that the addressee is one's senior in a group or organization. It is most often used in a school setting, where underclassmen refer to their upperclassmen as "sempai." It can also be used in the workplace, such as when a newer employee addresses an employee who has seniority in the company.

Kohai: This is the opposite of "sempai" and is used toward underclassmen in school or newcomers in the workplace. It connotes that the addressee is of a lower station.

Sensei: Literally meaning "one who has come before," this title is used for teachers, doctors, or masters of any profession or art.

-[blank]: This is usually forgotten in these lists, but it is perhaps the most significant difference between Japanese and English. The lack of honorific means that the speaker has permission to address the person in a very intimate way. Usually, only family, spouses, or very close friends have this kind of permission. Known as *yobisute*, it can be gratifying when someone who has earned the intimacy starts to call one by one's name without an honorific. But when that intimacy hasn't been earned, it can be very insulting.

Preview of Fairy Tail, volume 15

We're pleased to present you a preview from volume 15, now available from Kodansha Comics. Please check our Web site (www.kodanshacomics.com) for more information on Fairy Tail and our other great series!

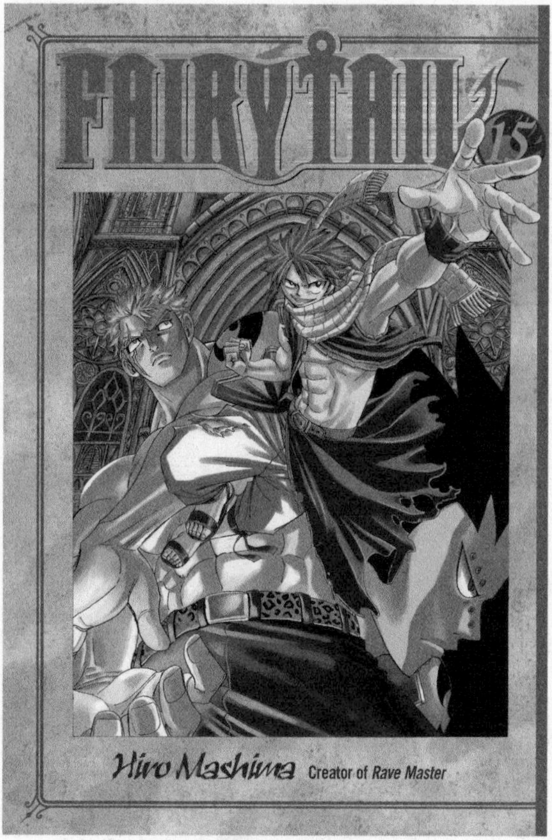
FAIRY TAIL
15
Hiro Mashima Creator of Rave Master

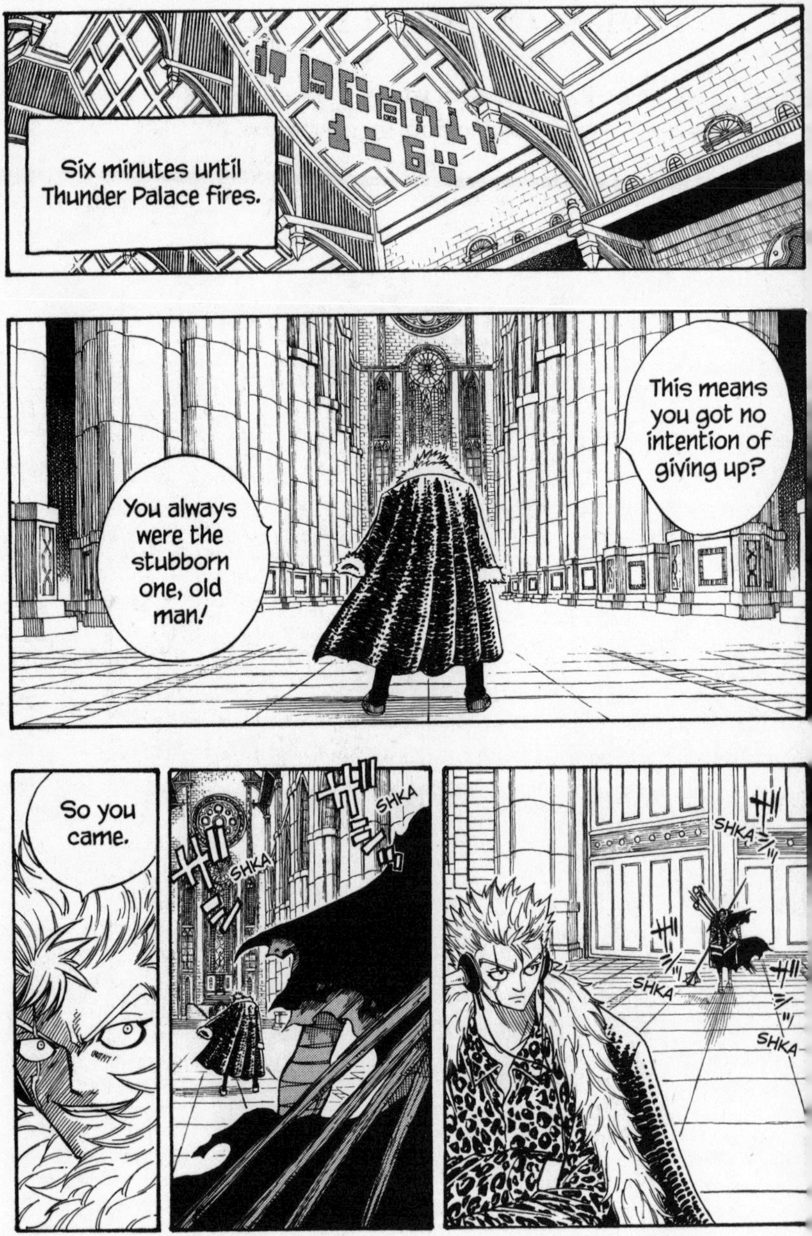
Six minutes until Thunder Palace fires.
This means you got no intention of giving up?
You always were the stubborn one, old man!
SHKA
SHKA
SHKA
SHKA
SHKA
So you came.

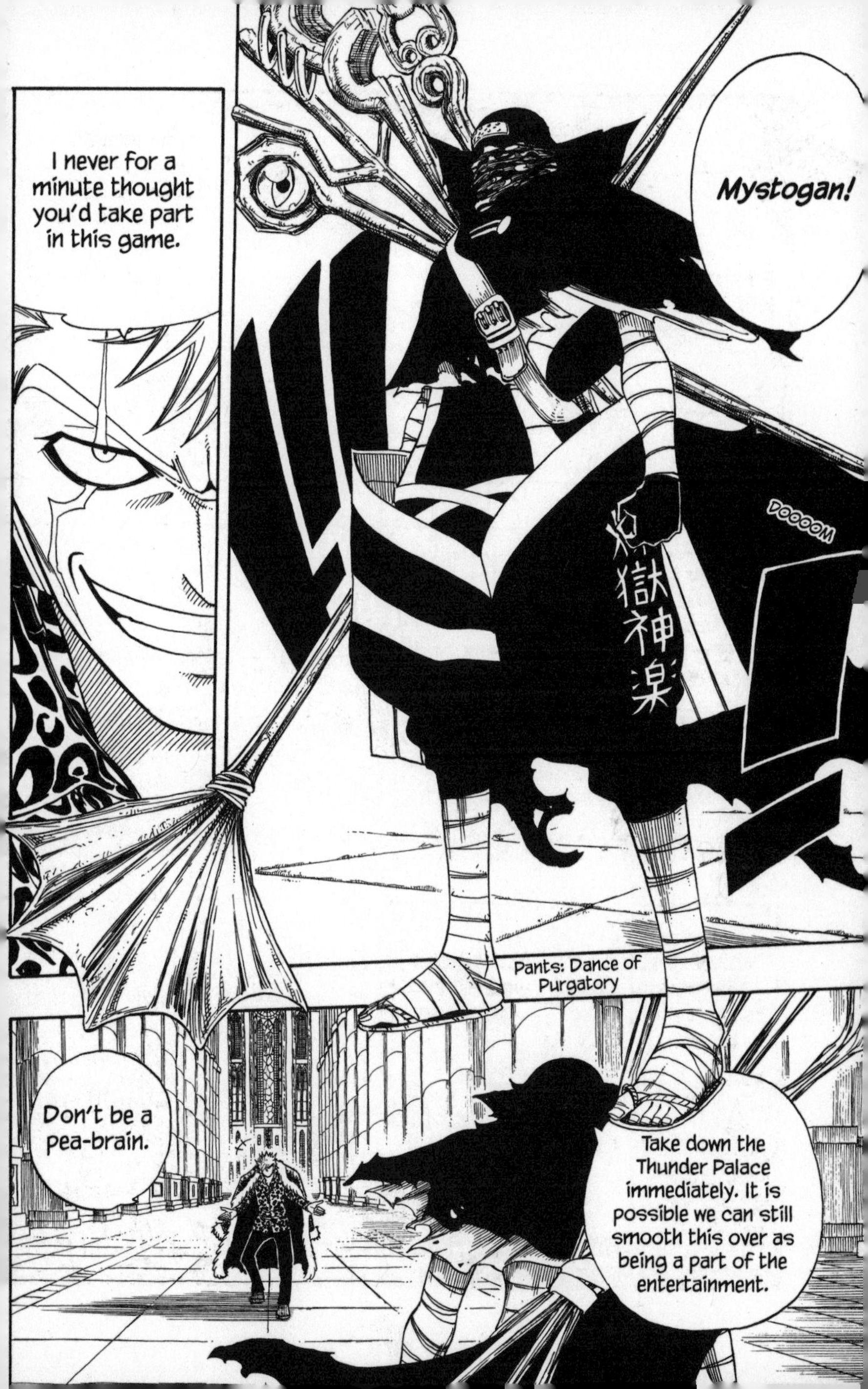

Mystogan!
DOOOOM
Pants: Dance of Purgatory
I never for a minute thought you'd take part in this game.
Don't be a pea-brain.
Take down the Thunder Palace immediately. It is possible we can still smooth this over as being a part of the entertainment.

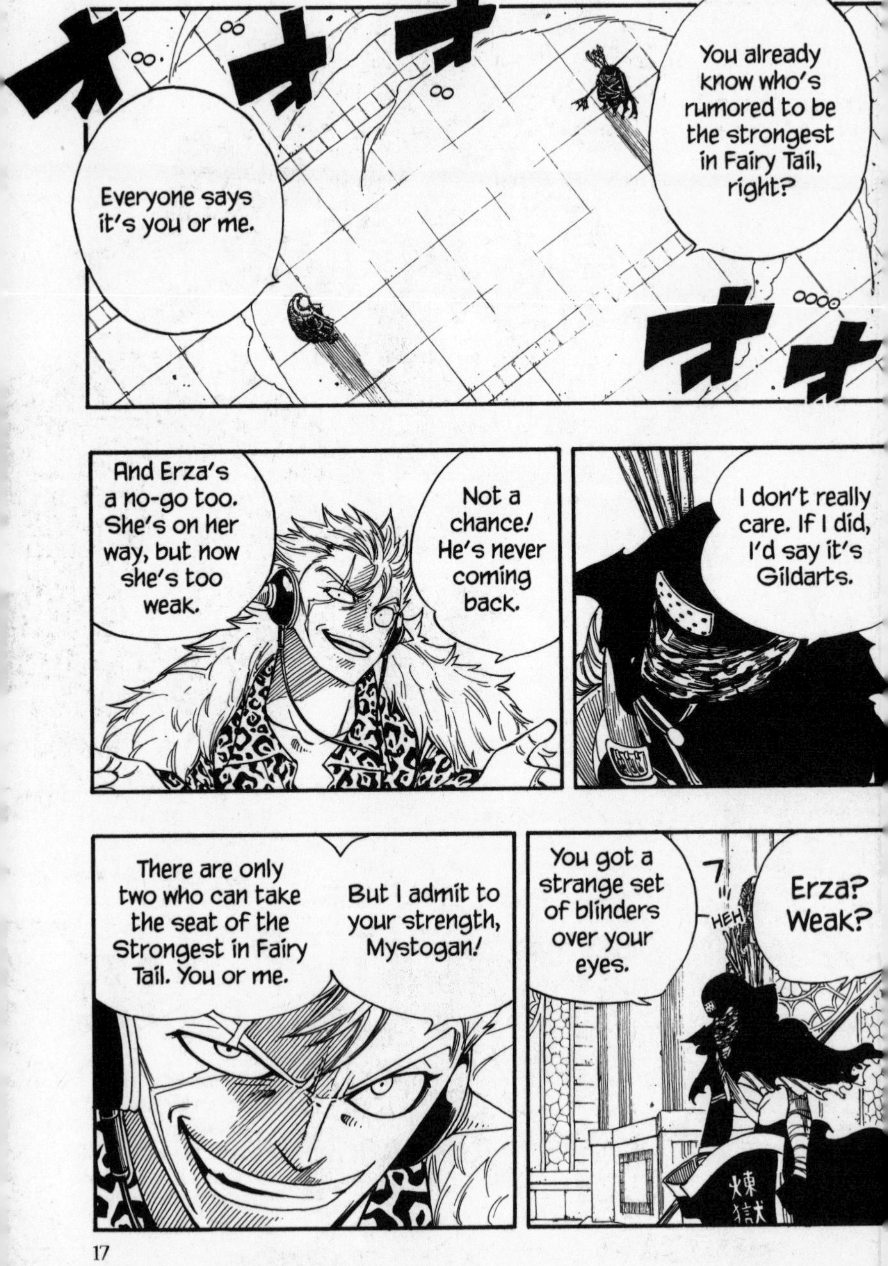
You already know who's rumored to be the strongest in Fairy Tail, right?
Everyone says it's you or me.
オオオ
オオ
I don't really care. If I did, I'd say it's Gildarts.
Not a chance! He's never coming back.
And Erza's a no-go too. She's on her way, but now she's too weak.
Erza? Weak?
HEH
You got a strange set of blinders over your eyes.
煉獄
But I admit to your strength, Mystogan!
There are only two who can take the seat of the Strongest in Fairy Tail. You or me.

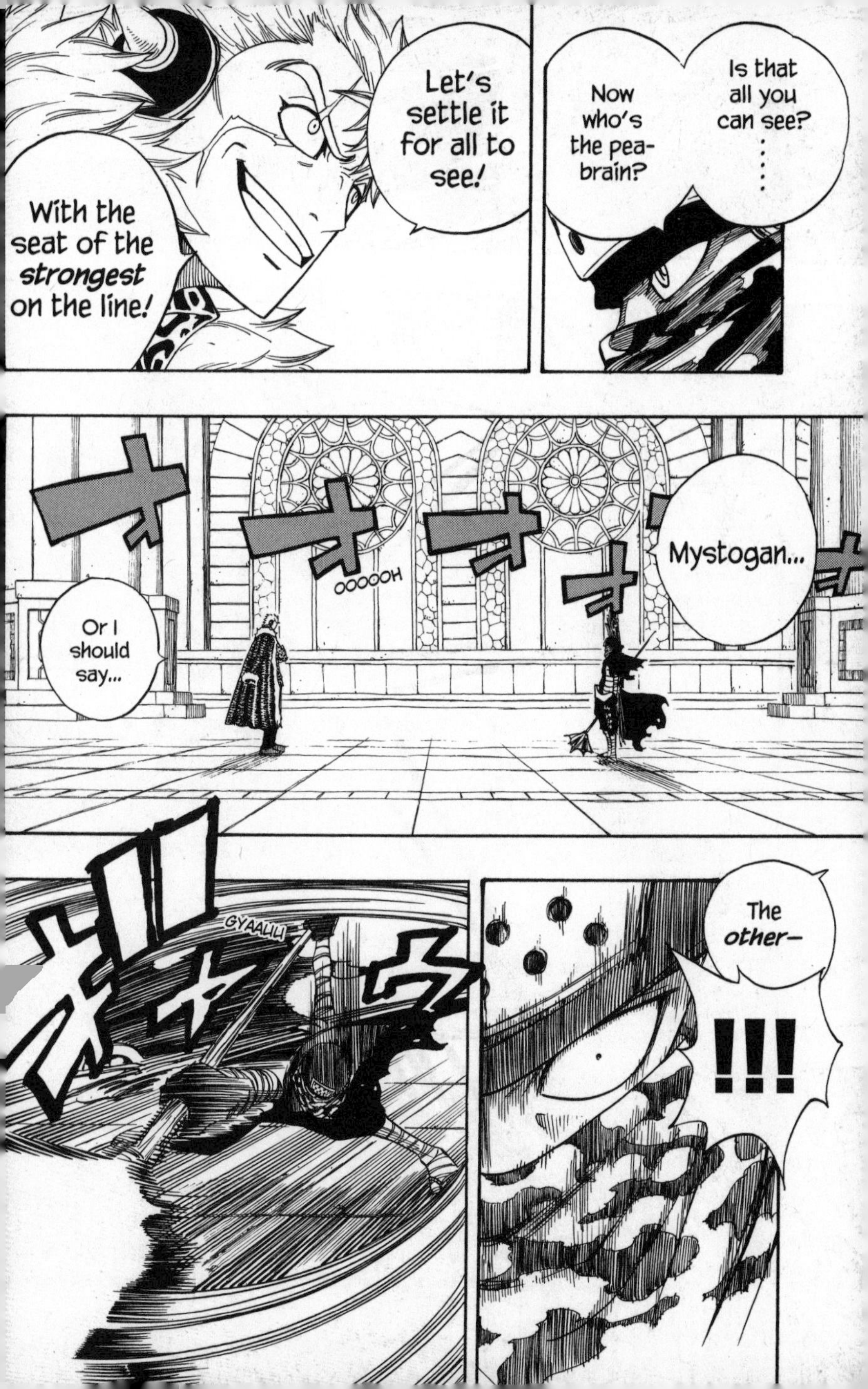
Is that all you can see? .....
Now who's the pea-brain?
Let's settle it for all to see!
With the seat of the *strongest* on the line!
Mystogan...
OOOOOH
Or I should say...
The *other–*
!!!
GYAALILI

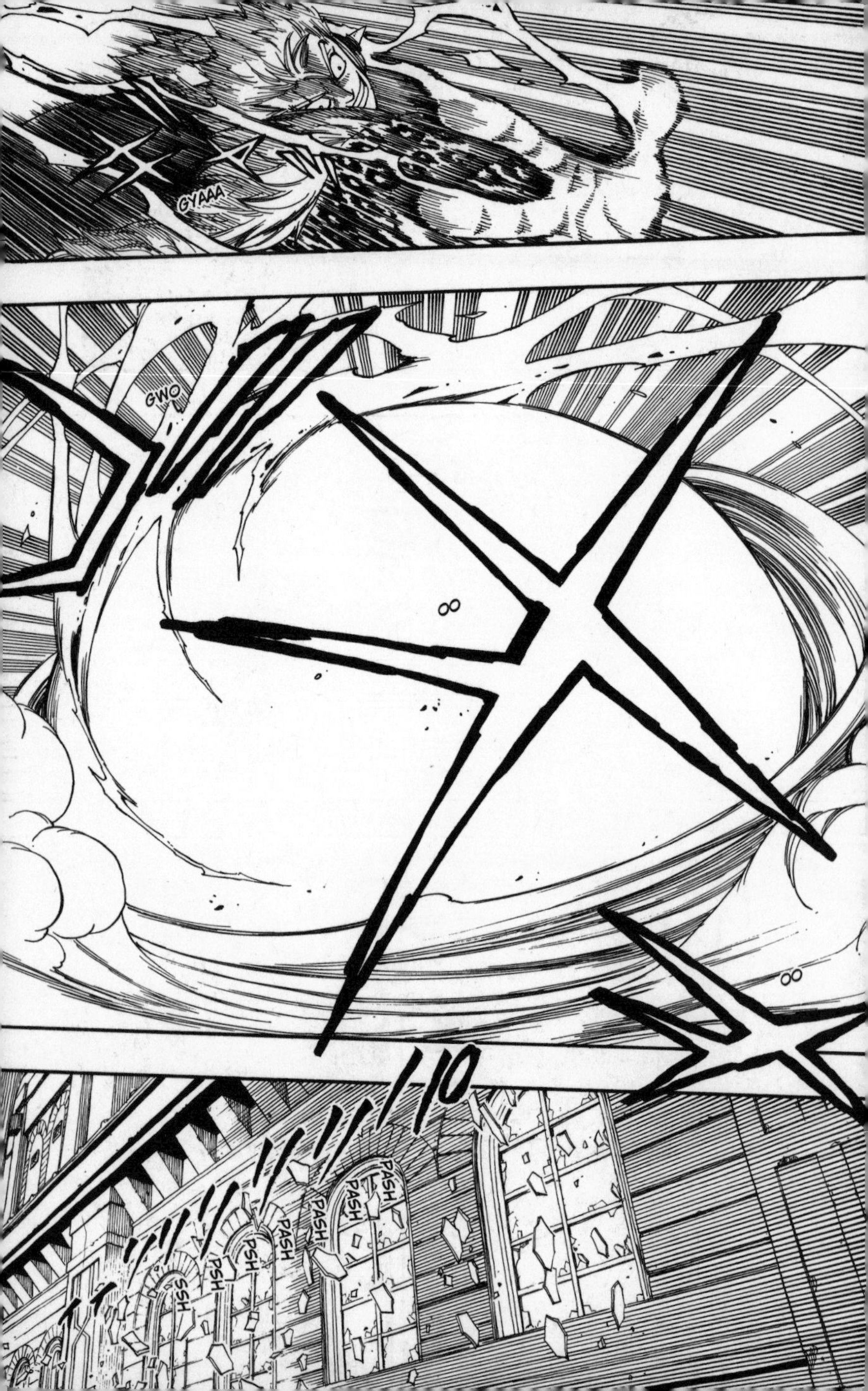
GYAAA
GWO
PASH
PASH
PASH
PASH
PSH
PSH
SSH

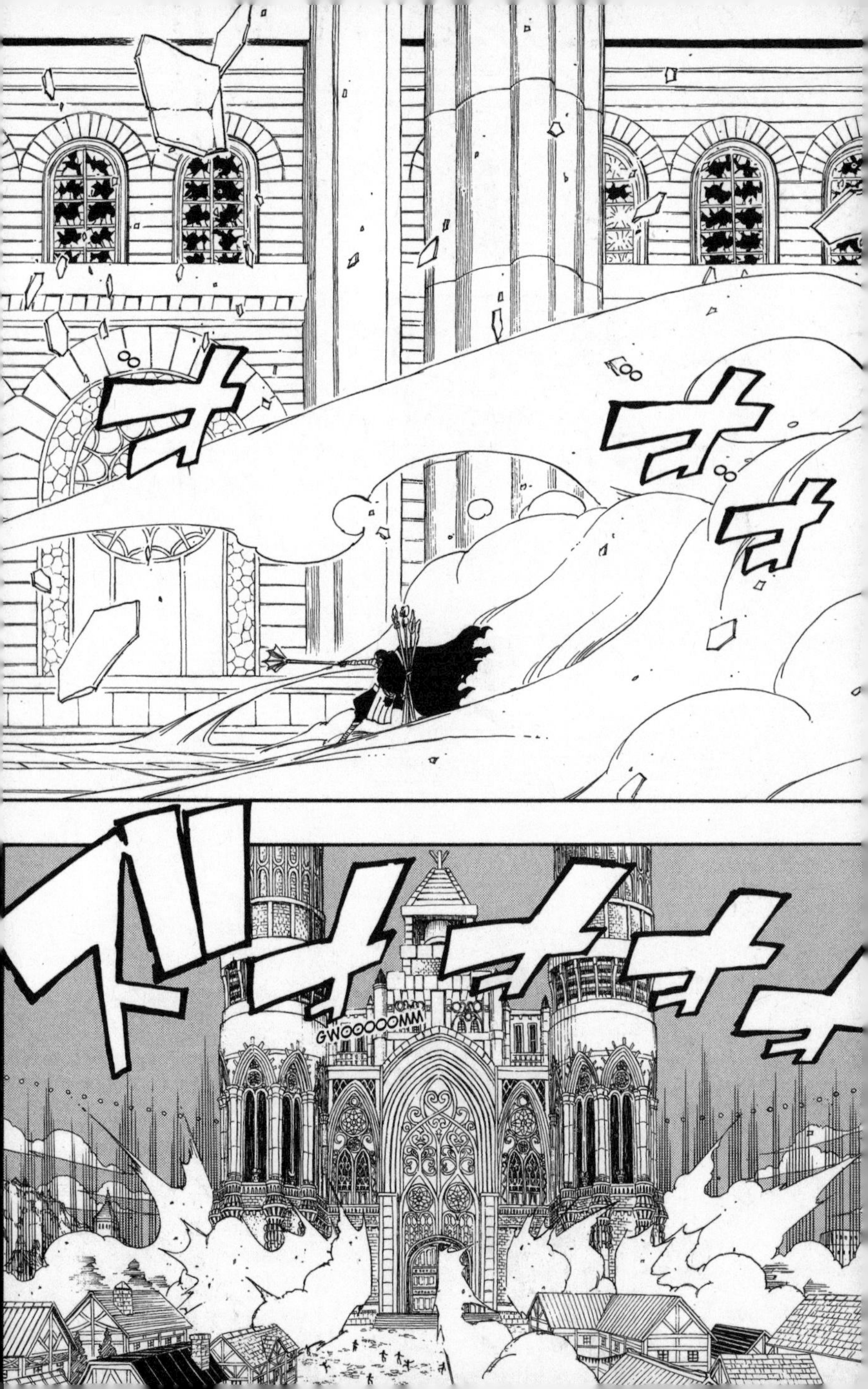
GWOOOOOMM

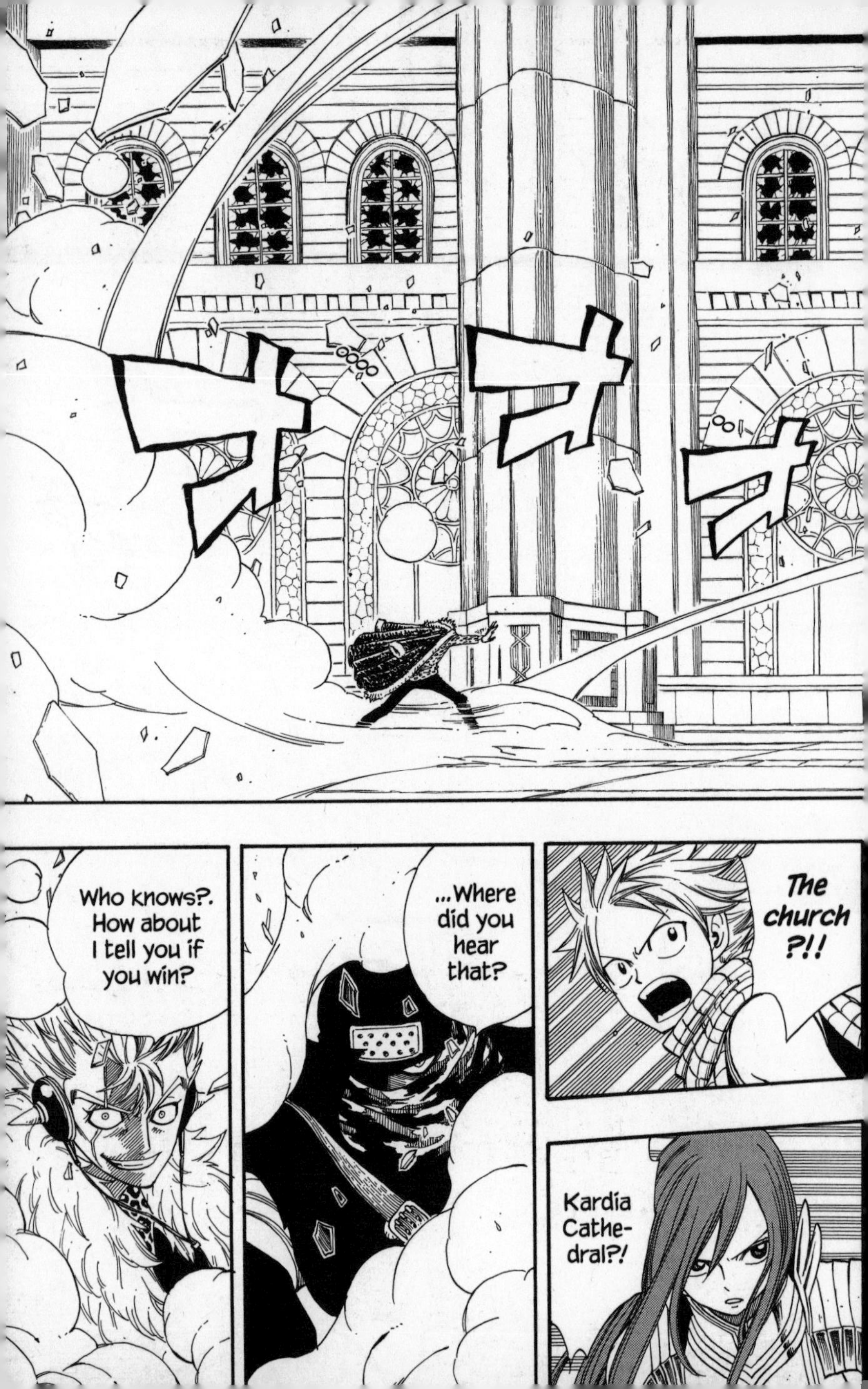
オオオ
The church?!!
Kardia Cathe-dral?!
...Where did you hear that?
Who knows?. How about I tell you if you win?

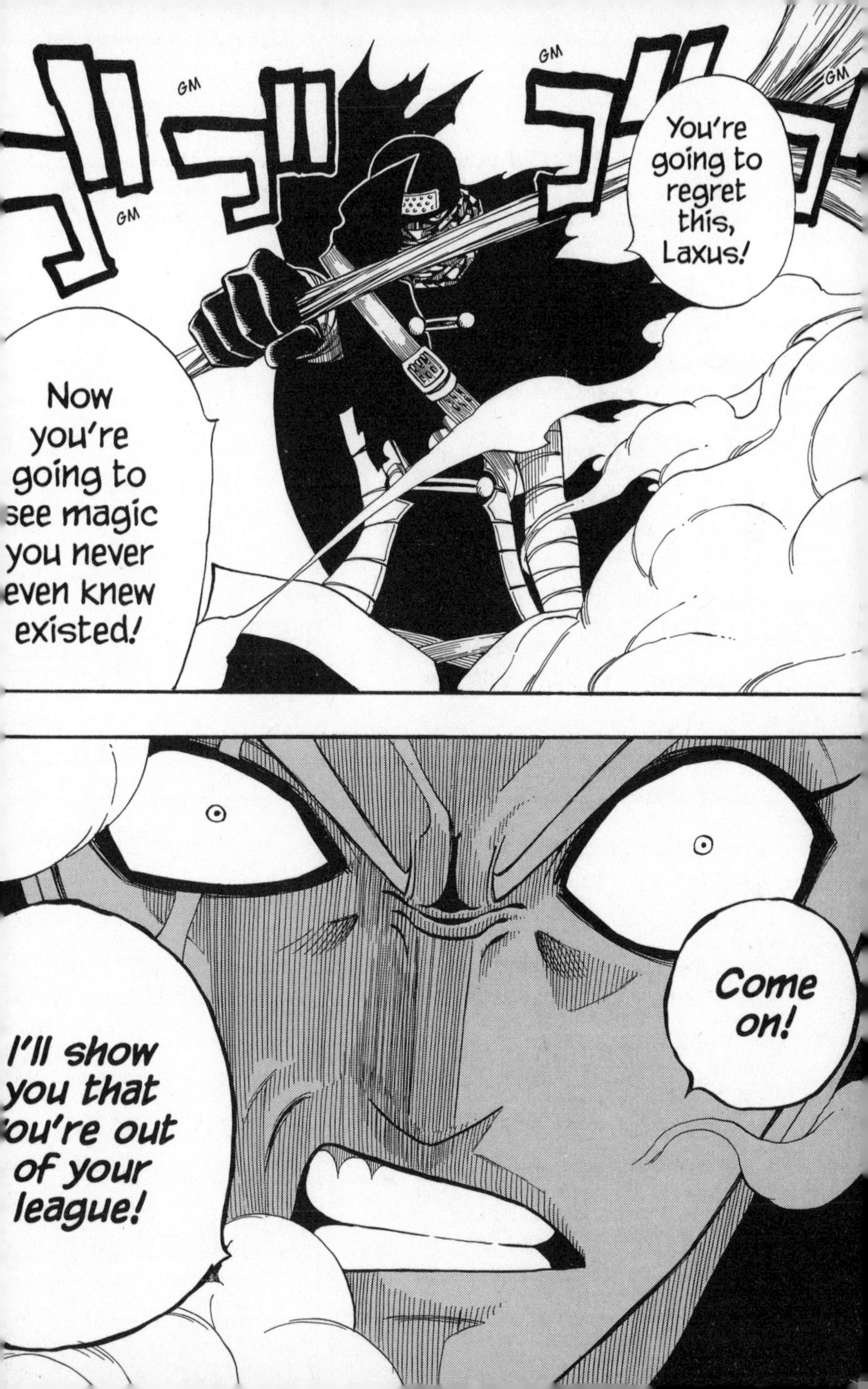
GM
GM
GM
GM
You're going to regret this, Laxus!
Now you're going to see magic you never even knew existed!
Come on!
I'll show you that 'ou're out of your league!

Fairy Tail volume 14 is a work of fiction. Names, characters, places, and incidents are the products of the author's imagination or are used fictitiously. Any resemblance to actual events, locales, or persons, living or dead, is entirely coincidental.

A Kodansha Comics Trade Paperback Original.

Fairy Tail volume 14 copyright © 2009 Hiro Mashima
English translation copyright © 2011 Hiro Mashima

All rights reserved.

Published in the United States by Kodansha Comics, an imprint of Kodansha USA Publishing, LLC., New York.

Publication rights for this English edition arranged through Kodansha Ltd., Tokyo.

First published in Japan in 2009 by Kodansha Ltd., Tokyo.

ISBN 978-1-935-42933-3

Printed in the United States of America.

www.kodanshacomics.com

9   8   7   6   5

Translator/Adapter: William Flanagan
Lettering: North Market Street Graphics

TOMARE!

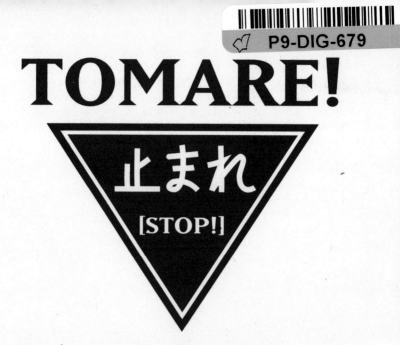

止まれ

[STOP!]

You're going the wrong way!

Manga is a completely different type of reading experience.

To start at the *beginning*, go to the *end*!

That's right! Authentic manga is read the traditional Japanese way—from right to left, exactly the *opposite* of how American books are read. It's easy to follow: Just go to the other end of the book and read each page—and each panel—from right side to left side, starting at the top right. Now you're experiencing manga as it was meant to be!